Assessing and Guiding Young Children's Development and Learning

Fourth Edition

Oralie McAfee

Metropolitan State College of Denver

Deborah J. Leong

Metropolitan State College of Denver

PEARSON

Boston   New York   San Francisco
Mexico City   Montreal   Toronto   London   Madrid   Munich   Paris
Hong Kong   Singapore   Tokyo   Cape Town   Sydney

This book is lovingly dedicated to
John, Rob, and our families

Series Editor: Kelly Villella Canton
Series Editorial Assistant: Angela Pickard
Marketing Manager: Krista Clark
Production Editor: Annette Joseph
Editorial Production Service: Omegatype Typography, Inc.
Composition Buyer: Linda Cox
Manufacturing Buyer: Linda Morris
Electronic Composition: Omegatype Typography, Inc.
Cover Administrator: Kristina Mose-Libon

For related titles and support materials, visit our online catalog at www.ablongman.com.

Between the time website information is gathered and then published, it is not unusual for
some sites to have closed. Also, the transcription of URLs can result in typographical errors.
The publisher would appreciate notification where these errors occur so that they may be
corrected in subsequent editions.

Library of Congress Cataloging-in-Publication Data

McAfee, Oralie.
    Assessing and guiding young children's development and learning / Oralie McAfee,
Deborah J. Leong.
        p.   cm.
    Includes bibliographical references and index.
    ISBN 0-205-49718-7 (paperback)
    1. Early childhood education—United States.   2. School children—Rating of—United
States.   3. Educational tests and measurements—United States.   4. Classroom
management—United States.   I. Leong, Deborah.   II. Title.

    LB1139.25.M4   2007
    372.21—dc22

                                                                        2006041656

Photo Credits: pp. 1, 11, 32, 75, 99, 142, 180, and 198: Morey Kitzman/Metropolitan State
College of Denver; pp. 50, 124, and 159: William Harvey Jr.

Printed in the United States of America

10 9 8 7 6 5 4 3   10 09 08

Contents

Part II   Assessing and Teaching

Chapter 3   Why, What, and When to Assess   32

Chapter 4   Documenting: Collecting Information   50

Chapter 5   Documenting: Recording Information   75

Chapter 6   Compiling and Summarizing Information   99

Chapter 7   Interpreting Assessment Information   124

Chapter 8   Using Assessment Information   142

Chapter 9   Organizing for Assessment   159

Part III   **The Classroom and Beyond**

Chapter 10   Standardized Tests: What Early Childhood
Teachers Should Know   180

Chapter 11   Communicating and Collaborating Using
          Assessment Processes and Results   198

x   **Contents**

Preface

Authentic assessment, done in the familiar context of the classroom, is at the heart of teaching and learning in the early childhood classroom. Only through knowing children's current knowledge and understandings, their skills, interests, and dispositions, can we develop a curriculum that builds on their strengths and provides experiences that support their continued development and learning. The purpose of this book is to demonstrate how to do authentic classroom-based assessment, and then how to interpret and use the information to plan curriculum that is responsive to and supportive of children's learning. The fourth edition of *Assessing and Guiding Young Children's Development and Learning* has been revised and updated to reflect the rapidly developing concepts of appropriate assessment, expected educational outcomes, and the way young children develop and learn.

Underlying Themes

The underlying themes that have guided us are congruent with national trends in early childhood education and in assessment at all levels.

Assessment as Classroom-Based and Authentic

The book's focus is classroom assessment—ways of finding out about and keeping track of children's development and learning that are an authentic part of ongoing classroom life and typical activities of children. We explain and describe how to do this in nontechnical language. These assessment procedures can be used by people working with young children in varied early childhood settings. Standardized testing is treated from the perspective of the classroom teacher.

Assessment as a "Work in Progress"

The text presents assessment as a growing, developing aspect of teaching and learning. The extensive section on portfolios reflects their popularity with teachers, children, and parents. Sections on standards, benchmarks, and rubrics define and show how these concepts relate to assessment. Guides and examples show how teachers can be sensitive to linguistic, social, cultural, and individual diversity. We describe teachers' roles and responsibilities in assessment related to inclusive education. The legal framework relating to assessment is outlined. Current best thinking is incorporated throughout.

Assessment as a Process

Assessment is treated as a flexible, practical process. The process begins with the "why, what, and when" of assessment; progresses through data collection and recording; and then shows how to compile, interpret, and use the results. Numerous examples from different developmental and curriculum areas show how each step is carried out with young children.

Assessment as a Professional Activity

Assessment is treated as a highly professional activity, not something done casually, haphazardly, or simply because it is required. The book is designed to help teachers improve "the conceptual and procedural foundations for assessment" (Hiebert & Calfee, 1989, p. 50). There are suggestions for improving the reliability and validity of alternative assessment, for meeting ethical and legal responsibilities, and for communicating with others about assessment results. Most important, we emphasize the teacher's professional responsibility to interpret and use assessment results to help children learn. The concepts and procedures that are presented are grounded in sound conceptual and scientific bases. They meet the guidelines for appropriate classroom assessment outlined by the National Association for the Education of Young Children and the National Association of Early Childhood Specialists in State Departments of Education (NAEYC & NAECS/SDE, 2003).

We recognize that learning how to assess children and use that information to guide classroom decision making is not easy. It requires learning new concepts and making fine distinctions, such as between collecting information and recording it. It implies conscious control over the way you interact with children, so you can ask questions and present tasks that elicit thoughtful responses.

Philosophical Orientation

Although the assessment procedures presented can be used with any approach to early childhood education, the examples reflect the authors' convictions about young children's growth. We see development and learning as an integrated process that fuses the universal yet variable process of human development with an individual child's personal encounter with the social and cultural world. We see adults and other children as active participants in that development and learning—responding, modeling, guiding, assisting, and scaffolding in developmentally appropriate ways. We see learning "processes" and "products" as equally important as children develop and learn in a supportive, responsive environment.

Organization

Topics and chapters are organized to provide readers maximum flexibility in meeting their own learning needs. Chapters can be read in order: Part I (Chapters 1 and 2) prepares teachers to approach assessment professionally; Part II (Chapters 3 through 9) takes teachers through the steps in the assessment process; Part III (Chapters 10 and 11) takes assessment beyond the classroom—to what an early childhood teacher needs to know about standardized testing in today's society; and how to communicate and collaborate with parents, other professionals, and the larger community. Each part and chapter can also stand alone so that readers may select topics to meet their own needs.

Features

Mandated Assessment

The reality of mandated assessment and increased expectations in early childhood is recognized.

Legal, Ethical, and Professional Responsibilities

The legal, ethical, and professional context of assessment of young children is summarized, with emphasis on teachers' responsibilities.

Standardized Testing

A chapter on standardized testing distills this lengthy topic into what early childhood teachers need to know to fulfill their roles and responsibilities in today's society.

Assessment and Analysis Guides

Easy-reference assessment and analysis guides in Appendix A present development and learning accomplishments and continua for major child development and curriculum areas. These are ready for readers to use as references for interpreting assessment and for curriculum planning in response to assessment.

Red Flags

Appendix B lists developmental "red flags" that alert teachers to patterns of behavior that signal the need for a closer look.

Reflection, Study, and Discussion Prompts

Personal reflection prompts bring the teacher as a person into the concepts under consideration. Study and discussion prompts promote complex thinking about the application of assessment concepts and principles in early childhood classrooms.

Summaries and Suggested Readings

Summaries highlight important points in each chapter; suggested readings related to the subject of that chapter show readers where to find additional information.

A Sourcebook for Teachers

The book recognizes that when students become teachers they need information they can refer to. The book functions as a sourcebook as well as a text. Teachers can refer to the developmental continua; red flags; recording forms; and the many guides for assessment, analysis, and planning.

Glossary

The glossary defines currently used assessment and curriculum terminology in clear, nontechnical language.

Examples and Applications

Numerous charts, figures, forms, and illustrations make clear what is being discussed and link the topics to the real world of children and schools. Many forms are ready to copy, adapt, and use. There are examples from published instruments and teachers' classroom data collections. Examples of children's work from the range of early childhood show how assessment is carried out at all these ages.

New to This Edition

- Expanded section on the concepts essential to teachers' understanding of their role in standardized testing and in the administration of other standardized instruments.
- Updated and enlarged sections throughout the text on standards, benchmarks, and rubrics as educational outcomes, including literacy, mathematics, and science.
- New section on developmental accomplishments and current curriculum standards in literacy, math, and science that reflects new research and practice. Assessment to document progress on standards has become a major role of the early childhood educator.
- New section on standardized tests and other published instruments typically used in current early childhood classrooms that will help teachers use these tests and the test results appropriately.
- Enlarged section on the essential understandings of the legal framework of assessment.

This book is grounded in our own teaching and learning experiences. These include teaching young children and working with parents from all socioeconomic levels and diverse cultures. We expanded that teaching and learning to preservice and inservice early childhood personnel in a variety of settings, helping them learn about assessment and curriculum and how to create classrooms that are responsive to children. The examples and illustrations are "real," although names and places are fictitious. To avoid the problems presented by the lack of a gender-neutral pronoun for *child* and *teacher,* we use *he* and *she* alternately, because children and teachers come in both genders. To recognize the diverse structures of families, we use the terms parents, families, and guardians interchangeably.

Acknowledgments

Our work has been enriched by the young children, college students, and practicing teachers we have taught and learned from; our colleagues throughout the country who have shared their insights with us; and preschool and primary teachers, administrators, and agency personnel in the Denver metropolitan area and throughout Colorado who let us share assessment practices in the real world.

We appreciate the many individuals and agencies that lent support and encouragement in the preparation and publication of the previous editions of this book. Metropolitan State College of Denver has supported our work in many ways.

For the fourth edition, we would like to thank MSCD President Stephen Jordan, Provost Joan Foster, Extended Campus staff Carol Svendson and Susan Call, and our colleagues in the Department of Psychology. We would also like to thank

Elena Bodrova for her help in thinking through the issues regarding assessment and standards, and our colleagues Ellen Frede, Jacqueline Jones, Peg Griffin, M. Susan Burns, Ed Greene, Kathleen Roskos, Barbara Goodson, Carolyn Lazar, Jean Lazar, Deborah Rowe, Steve Barnett, and Carol Copple. Thanks also to Ruth Hensen, Amy Hornbeck, Danielle Erickson, Carolyn Erhart, and the teachers and administrators in the Tools of the Mind Curriculum Research Project for practical insights into the dual roles of classroom teacher and assessor; and to Marilyn Jerde, Adams 12 Five Star Schools, Thornton, Colorado; and Judy Edwards, Jefferson County (Colorado) Head Start.

The National Institute for Early Education Research (NIEER) partially funded our recent work on assessment. Thanks to Jeff Peierls at the Peierls Foundation for his continued support.

Special thanks go to Jeremy Leitz, Leslie and Brian Fauver, and Andrew and Emily McAfee for letting us see the world as they see it.

In addition to our colleagues who reviewed the manuscript and made helpful suggestions for the previous editions of this book, we wish to thank the reviewers for the fourth edition: Sabrina Brinson, University of Memphis; Heidi Malloy, Metropolitan State University; Lillian Phenice, Michigan State University; and Debbie Stoll, Cameron University.

About the Authors

Oralie McAfee is professor emerita of early childhood education at Metropolitan State College of Denver. She is the author of books, research papers, articles, curriculum and teacher-training materials, and other publications related to working with young children and their families in the classroom and home, and has presented on these topics throughout the United States. She has done research on assessment practices and needs in Head Start and in selected state-funded prekindergarten programs. She is author (with Deborah J. Leong and Elena Bodrova) of *Basics of Assessment: A Primer for Early Childhood Educators* (National Association for the Education of Young Children, 2004).

Deborah J. Leong is a professor of psychology at Metropolitan State College of Denver and director of the Tools of the Mind Curriculum Research Project, a Vygotskian-based early childhood teacher-training program. She is also a research fellow at the National Institute for Early Education Research (NIEER) working on a computerized Pre-K state standards database and a database of preschool assessment instruments with Elena Bodrova. She is co-author with Dr. McAfee and Dr. Bodrova of *Basics of Assessment* (National Association for the Education of Young Children, 2004). Dr. Leong is also co-author with Dr. Bodrova of *Tools of the Mind: The Vygotskian Approach to Early Childhood Education* (Merrill/Prentice Hall, 1996) and four educational videos (Davidson Films). She has written many articles on assessment, play, early literacy, and the development of self-regulation in young children.

CHAPTER 1

Assessment in Early Childhood: A Work in Progress

Early childhood teachers in classrooms throughout the United States study and assess children's development and learning. They observe children at work and play, and record information about what they observe. They collect and analyze samples of children's work, and set up portfolios to display children's competence. They ask children to explain and describe their thinking processes. They may administer teacher-made or published tests, or evaluate each child's general progress as required by a school or program. They may give tests that focus on diagnosing children's strengths and needs in mathematics or literacy. They document children's learning through checklists, rubrics, narratives, photographs, recordings, and other means.

Teachers assist in identifying children who may need special services because of a disability. They work with families to get the family's understanding of their child's development, and with other teachers and specialists to share information and knowledge. They may evaluate their classrooms and the experiences they offer children using a locally developed or published scale. They compile and study the information they have obtained and seek to understand what it means for a child or for a group of children.

All these activities, and more, are part of assessment. Not every school or center will require or expect that teachers do each of these things. What teachers are expected to do will vary depending on the age and grade levels of the children, sponsoring agency (public or private school, specialized prekindergarten), and the requirements placed on the school or center. Regardless of the setting, good early childhood education includes appropriate assessment of children's development and learning.

Assessment Vocabulary

The term *assessment* refers to almost any form of measurement and appraisal of what children know and can do, including tests, observations, interviews, reports from knowledgeable sources, and other means. The term is frequently used to refer to one appraisal or one measure, or to avoid the negative connotations of words such as test, testing, or evaluation. For example, a test or inventory of basic skills might become an assessment of basic skills. One systematic observation of a child's ability to interact with other children might be called an assessment. Some sources use *test* or *measurement* as synonyms for assessment (No Child Left Behind, 2002; Popham, 2005).

Assessment is also used in a specific way, to mean "the process of gathering information about children from several forms of evidence, then organizing and interpreting that information" (McAfee, Leong, & Bodrova, 2004, p. 3). In this usage, assessment involves several sources of information gathered at different times and in different situations, then recorded, integrated, and interpreted by people sensitive to children's learning (Airasian, 2001; Mendelson & Atlas, 1973).

This book focuses on classroom assessment of children—how to gather and document the information teachers need to identify the strengths, needs, and progress of the children in their classrooms so they can plan to help those children learn. However, teachers frequently do other types of assessment: assist in developmental screening, give standardized tests of different types, fill out official reports on each child's progress, and inventory and report on their own classroom environment and practices. The book includes information to help teachers fulfill these other assessment responsibilities.

The terms connected with different approaches to classroom assessment can be confusing. Measurement experts make fine distinctions among terms that are often used interchangeably by others. *Alternative assessment* refers to almost any type of assessment other than standardized tests and similar developmental inventories and achievement tests. Sometimes such alternative assessment is referred to as *informal assessment,* as opposed to formal assessment using standardized and other published instruments. *Performance assessment* refers to a specific type of assessment in which children demonstrate a skill or create a product that shows their learning (Stiggins, 1995). If motor coordination is being measured, the child performs an appropriate action. If writing is under consideration, the child writes. The term *authentic assessment* applies to assessment as part of children's ongoing life and learning in the classroom, playground, hallway, lunchroom, and other typical school and center settings. In authentic assessment, tasks are as close as possible to "bona fide practical and intellectual challenges" (Finn, 1991, p. 10). For instance, instead of underlining a picture or "bubbling in" a circle as evidence they can match, sort, and classify pictures of objects, children actually match, sort, and classify objects or information in school projects. Instead of counting dots or pictures on a page, children count to solve a classroom or individual problem.

Formative assessment or evaluation refers to gathering information that is then used to shape and improve—to help in the formation of—an instructional program. Most classroom assessment is done for formative purposes. The information is used to plan intentional instruction to help children learn. *Summative assessment* or evaluation is done at the end of a period of time, such as a school year or the end of a research project, to determine the effectiveness of a program. Grades are sometimes considered a summative evaluation of what children learned.

Assessment, however it is done, should be aligned with the program's curriculum—what is taught and what children are expected to learn. Curriculum-based assessment implies that children are assessed on what is taught. Curriculum-embedded assessment suggests assessment that is integrated with teaching and learning experiences, in contrast to tests that require children to perform on-demand. These and other vocabulary terms related to assessment are defined in the glossary and explained further in the text.

Expectations of Teachers

Professional organizations, policymakers, parents, the general public, administrators, specialists, and other educators have high expectations of teachers as assessors of children's learning.

Professional Organizations

Leaders of organizations focusing on the care, development, and education of children expect teachers to be competent in assessment as an integral part of teaching. In addition to a general statement about appropriate assessment (see Figure 1.1), the National Association for the Education of Young Children specifies that people preparing to teach young children should (1) understand the "goals, benefits, and uses of assessment"; (2) know about and use "observation, documentation, and other appropriate assessment tools and approaches"; (3) understand and practice "practical assessment"; and (4) know about "assessment partnerships with families and other professionals" (NAEYC, 2001).

A 1990 statement issued jointly by the National Education Association, the National Council on Measurement in Education, and the American Federation of Teachers identified seven standards for teacher competence in educational assessment. Teachers should be skilled in the following areas:

1. Choosing assessment methods appropriate for instructional decisions
2. Developing assessment methods appropriate for instructional decisions
3. Administering, scoring, and interpreting the results of both externally produced and teacher-produced assessment methods

Figure 1.1   Position on Assessment in Early Childhood Education of the National Association for the Education of Young Children and the National Association of Early Childhood Educators in State Departments of Education
••

The National Association for the Education of Young Children (NAEYC) and the National Association of Early Childhood Specialists in State Departments of Education (NAECS/SDE) . . . take the position that policymakers, the early childhood profession, and other stakeholders in young children's lives, have a shared responsibility to: . . . Make ethical, appropriate, valid, and reliable assessment a central part of all early childhood programs. To assess young children's strengths, progress, and needs, use assessment methods that are developmentally appropriate, culturally and linguistically responsive, tied to children's daily activities, supported by professional development, inclusive of families, and connected to specific, beneficial purposes: (1) making sound decisions about teaching and learning, (2) identifying significant concerns that may require focused intervention for individual children, and (3) helping programs improve their educational and developmental interventions.

NAEYC & NAECS/SDE, 2003, p. 2.

4. Using assessment results when making decisions about individual students, planning teaching, developing curriculum, and school improvement
5. Developing valid pupil grading procedures which use pupil assessments
6. Communicating assessment results to students, parents, other lay audiences, and other educators
7. Recognizing unethical, illegal, and otherwise inappropriate assessment methods and uses of assessment information (*Standards for Teacher Competence in Educational Assessment of Students*, pp. 3–5)

Additional guidance for teachers is found in the Student Evaluation Standards developed by the Joint Committee on Standards for Educational Evaluation, a committee supported by sixteen respected national education organizations. The twenty-eight standards provide a framework for assessing children's learning in ways that are fair, useful, feasible, and accurate. They are grouped into four broad categories relating to "propriety," "utility," "feasibility," and "accuracy" (Figure 1.2). Propriety standards set forth the rights of individuals affected by evaluation, and discuss student and parent rights and access to information. Utility standards focus on the need for student evaluations to be clear, informative, timely, and influential. Feasibility standards address practical matters involved in evaluating students, such as time and classroom constraints. Accuracy standards aim to increase the soundness of an evaluation.

As an example, one of the standards under propriety (properness or fairness) specifies that "Evaluations of students should provide information that identifies both strengths and weaknesses, so that strengths can be built upon and problem areas addressed" (Joint Committee on Standards for Educational Evaluation, p. 1). An expanded summary of the student evaluation standards can be downloaded at http://ec.wmich.edu/jointcomm/ses/All_Summary.htm.

Parents, Policy Makers, and the General Public

Federal, state, and local policy makers, parents, and the general public hold schools and teachers responsible for children's school-related achievement.

Figure 1.2   Summary of the Categories of the Student Evaluation Standards

....

Proprietary Standards	The propriety standards help to ensure that student evaluations will be conducted legally, ethically, and with due regard for the well-being of the students being evaluated and other people affected by the evaluation results. [Seven standards]
Utility Standards	The utility standards help to ensure that student evaluations are useful. Useful student evaluations are informative, timely, and influential. [Seven standards]
Feasibility Standards	The feasibility standards help to ensure that student evaluations can be implemented as planned. Feasible evaluations are practical, diplomatic, and adequately supported. [Three standards]
Accuracy Standards	The accuracy standards help to ensure that a student evaluation will produce sound information about a student's learning and performance. Sound information leads to valid interpretations, justifiable conclusions, and appropriate follow-up. [Eight standards]

Joint Committee on Standards for Educational Evaluation, 2003

Under the general term accountability, educators are expected to report their procedures and results. Large-scale accountability reports, such as those required by federal and state laws and regulations and by many large school districts, depend heavily on standardized test scores. Even when accountability tests are not given to children before third grade, as is recommended by most professional organizations, assessment practices with younger children are likely to be influenced. School personnel are sensitive to expectations that children do well on accountability tests. Teachers may be expected to administer tests or compile other results to track children's progress. In many states, programs use information that teachers gather through observation, work sampling, interviews, and other types of assessment more appropriate to young children than tests. Assessment results are expected to be available, and are often highly publicized as they are reported to parents and to the general public (Popham, 2005). Teachers are expected to understand and explain assessment results to people who may have no background in educational assessment.

Other Professionals

Other professionals expect teachers to understand and contribute assessment information about children's development and learning to staff meetings and conferences, and to any data the school is required to supply. For example, teachers must have well-documented information ready to present if they intend to make a contribution to a team that assesses and makes recommendations about children with special needs. They must be able to provide specific examples if they ask a specialist for help or seek guidance from fellow teachers. The short notes that teachers often make as reminders to themselves may not be sufficient for people unfamiliar with the task, context, or child (Valencia, Hiebert,

& Afflerbach, 1994). Teachers are also expected to understand assessment terms that others use.

Many families relocate frequently. Teachers need to understand and use any assessment information children bring with them, and to send with departing children information that will help their next teacher plan appropriately for that child. As children go from prekindergarten to kindergarten to first and second grade, their records should help the receiving teacher know that child's strengths and needs.

Factors Contributing to Current Practices in Assessment

Political, demographic, social, and educational trends contribute to current practices in assessment. These trends include

- Mandated testing and assessment
- The diversity of children and families
- Concepts about children's development and learning
- Limitations and inadequacies of standardized testing

Mandated Testing and Assessment

The development of educational standards by professional organizations and states was accompanied by mandated assessment of children's progress toward those standards. Every state in the United States has developed standards for K–12 education and mandates assessment, usually testing, at designated grade levels to determine if children meet those standards (Meisels, 2000). Federal testing and reporting requirements, such as in the No Child Left Behind Act and the National Reporting System for Head Start (see Chapter 2) influence state and local requirements and expectations. Although most states have no mandated assessments before the end of third grade, some school districts begin testing in kindergarten. Early childhood teachers, whether in preschool or primary, feel the increased pressure and implied threat of such high-profile, high-stakes accountability testing. Children are retained in grade or recommended for summer school based on the outcomes of tests. The test scores of schools, school districts, and different population groups are publicized and compared. Federal-, state-, and district-required testing is almost universally dreaded by teachers and children, and is regarded as misguided and inappropriate by assessment specialists. It is praised by policy makers who regard testing for accountability as central to improving education.

The Diversity of Children and Families

Children in early childhood programs mirror the diversity of the larger society. They are diverse in almost every way: race, ethnicity, culture, and language used in the home; household income and family structure; educational level attained by parents; urban, suburban, or rural home setting; and how often they move from place to place. Continued immigration from countries around the world and differing birth rates among groups indicate that diversity will increase over time (Capps, Passel, Perez-Lopez, & Fix, 2003; Hodgkinson, 2003). Assessment that yields a true picture of what children from diverse backgrounds know and can do is essential (Bowman, 1992).

Linguistic differences present a special challenge. Early childhood classrooms across the United States have children whose home language is not English. As English language learners they are learning to comprehend, speak, read, and write a new language. In one example of this diversity, Minnesota has made its Early Childhood Screening brochure available in Arabic, Cambodian, English, Hmong, Laotian, Oromo, Russian, Serbo-Croatian, Somali, Spanish, and Vietnamese (NAECS/SDE Minnesota State Summary, 2003).

The type and number of planned educational experiences children have had varies. Some children entering kindergarten or first grade may have been in group child care since infancy. For others, kindergarten or first grade may be their first experience in a group. Some children will have attended every "enrichment" experience available—swimming classes, soccer teams, science workshops, and music lessons. Others will have had none of these experiences.

Inclusion of children with special needs increases the diversity in early childhood classrooms. As a group, "young children with special needs are . . . tremendously diverse" (Wolery, Strain, & Bailey, 1992, p. 95). Assessing their strengths and needs requires flexible assessment practices that include a child's functioning in everyday life (Alper, 2001).

Diversity among families and children in the United States is increasing, not decreasing, as is its influence on assessment practices.

Concepts about Children's Development and Learning

Children are expected to learn more at an earlier age than in years past. Every state now has a document or documents that specify what that state expects children to learn in kindergarten through high school—its *standards,* or *essential learnings.* Every state that funds prekindergarten programs has specified what children are expected to learn in those programs—its *early learning standards.* Head Start, the federal early childhood program for low-income children, has Child Outcome Statements that identify expected outcomes for children.

Several important research syntheses summarize knowledge about young children's learning and urge greater attention to cognitive and skill development, particularly in language, literacy, and mathematics (Bowman, Donovan, & Burns, 2001; Shonkoff & Phillips, 2000; Snow, Burns, & Griffin, 1998). National and state policy makers emphasize an early focus on academic skills related to school readiness and school success (White House, 2002). For example, research on preventing reading difficulties identifies specific skills and knowledge that help young children learn to read: phonological awareness, concepts of print, vocabulary, and letter and letter sound knowledge. These are expected outcomes of early learning and part of the curriculum in many kindergarten and prekindergarten programs.

There is also more information about *how* young children learn. Children actively construct knowledge within a social context that affects what and how they learn. They do not acquire knowledge and skills all on their own, automatically developing more complex skills, ideas, and understandings as they mature. Nor do they simply learn what is taught and "reinforced"—the behaviorist psychology that once dominated learning theories. Learning and teaching are complex enterprises in which children, adults, the things children work and play with, language interactions, and all aspects of the child's life—in and out of school—interact to influence that learning (Bodrova & Leong, 1996). Children don't simply learn more and more discrete facts and skills. Rather, they try to organize information, develop theories, see relationships, and "develop their own cognitive maps of the interconnections among facts and concepts" (Shepard, 1989, p. 5).

Assessment practices should mirror the active learning processes implied in this complex, dynamic, and holistic view of child development and learning (Shepard, 2000).

Limitations and Inadequacies of Standardized Testing

Standardized tests are the focus of much of the criticism of testing and assessment. Standardized tests are administered, scored, and interpreted in a standard manner. They include developmental inventories, prekindergarten developmental screening tests, reading tests and inventories, academic readiness tests, diagnostic tools for special needs, group aptitude and achievement tests, and tests in almost any developmental or curriculum domain. They are usually developed, published, and distributed by commercial publishers. Criticisms of these commercial tests include the power given to them by political and educational policy makers and by society, the overuse and misuse of tests and test results, and problems with the quality of the tests. For example, items may be poorly constructed, ambiguous, and open to several interpretations, only one of which is "right" (Kamii, 1990). Scoring, analyzing, and reporting the results of these large-scale tests is subject to error. Other concerns are the tests' unsuitability for a diverse and young population, and the undue influence of tests and testing on what is taught. Because states and some school districts have developed or adopted standardized tests, almost all children and teachers are affected in some way. Chapter 10 elaborates on these concerns, and outlines what early childhood teachers need to know about standardized tests and testing: how such tests are constructed and scored; and how to evaluate them, prepare young children to take them, and explain the resulting scores to others. Chapter 10 also helps early childhood educators understand what standardized testing can and cannot do, its appropriate uses, and their responsibilities relating to it.

Professional Responsibility
....

Teachers carry out assessment responsibilities concurrently with their other teaching responsibilities. Demands on their time and expertise can become great. It takes time and effort to develop the knowledge and skill to assess well, to integrate sound assessment practices into instruction, and to use those results to help children learn. When testing and assessment for other purposes are also part of teachers' responsibilities, assessment may seem burdensome. However, there is no easy way to make mandated accountability testing and assessment vanish, even when their sometimes adverse effects are recognized. Educators have to balance the public's need to know the outcomes of educational programs with a teacher's need for different information to guide classroom decisions.

Likewise, there are no easy testing or assessment techniques to tell teachers all they need to know to make good instructional decisions; there are, however, many ways to increase the amount and quality of information we have about children. Regular use of classroom assessment to guide decision making may help teachers and parents regain faith in their own educational judgment and wisdom and in their ability to sensitively appraise, understand, and assist in the development of young children (Eisner, 1995). "More than new forms of assessment, what is needed is a refusal to accept bondage to any single technology . . . [but to thoughtfully select] different kinds and mixes of assessments for different purposes" (Haney & Madaus, 1989, p. 687).

The purpose of this book is to help teachers learn about those "different kinds and mixes" of appraisals. Our hope is that teachers will then take the initiative to integrate assessment and instruction into a coherent, responsive curriculum that enhances and supports children's development and learning.

Summary

Teachers in schools and centers throughout the United States assess children's development and learning in a wide variety of ways and use that information for different purposes. An assessment vocabulary has been developed to describe and distinguish these different approaches to assessment. The focus in this book is on authentic classroom assessment: finding out what children know and can do and their attitudes, interests, and approaches to learning, in order to guide and assist children's growth, development, and learning—not simply to grade, rank, sort, or group children.

Teachers are expected to be competent in assessment. Professional organizations have set high standards for assessment literacy and professional practice. The general public and policy makers expect teachers to be accountable in their work with children, and to provide information needed for large-scale assessment, as well as that designed for classroom use. Communicating with other professionals requires that teachers be able to document and explain assessment results.

Factors contributing to current practices in assessment include mandated testing and assessment; the diversity of children and families served by early childhood education; concepts about children's development and learning; and the limitations and inadequacies of standardized testing.

Teachers have a professional responsibility to know about and thoughtfully select assessment strategies appropriate to the young children and families they are working with, then to use that information to guide and support the youngsters' development and learning.

For Personal Reflection

1. Reflect on your concept of "teachers and teaching." In what ways is it congruent with the expectations of "teachers as assessors of children's learning and development" as described in the section Expectations of Teachers? In what ways is it incongruent? What are the implications for you at this point in time?

2. You have just accepted a teaching position in the first grade in Lakeshore School District, your first choice. In meetings before school you find that the school board has adopted a policy requiring summer school for children who do not pass the new proficiency exams given at the end of the school year. What are your personal reactions?

For Further Study and Discussion
....

1. Demographic, social, educational, and political forces influence assessment practices. In what ways are these forces influencing assessment in education in your community? Substantiate your conclusions with current evidence from newspapers, radio or television news, school newsletters, or personal experience.

2. Interview a kindergarten teacher about kindergarten entrance policies. Are any formal or informal tests used to determine children's readiness? If so, what are they? What other considerations go into determining "readiness"? In what ways do these policies conform to or deviate from current research and recommendations regarding school entrance and retention?

3. Explore the diversity of the young children in your state, town, or community. If you need to, visit some classrooms. Explain the implications of your findings for assessment.

4. A study of teachers' assessment practices showed that the assessment's primary purpose was "judging students' achievement for assigning grades" (Stiggins & Conklin, 1992, p. 47). Discuss this finding, relating it to current thinking about the purposes of assessment.

Suggested Readings
....

Airasian, P. W. (2000). *Assessment in the classroom: A concise approach* (2nd ed.). Boston: McGraw-Hill.

Bodrova, E., & Leong, D. J. (1996). *Tools of the mind: The Vygotskian approach to early childhood education.* Englewood Cliffs, NJ: Merrill.

Bredekamp, S., & Rosegrant, T. (Eds.). (1992). *Reaching potentials: Appropriate curriculum and assessment for young children* (Vol. 1). Washington, DC: National Association for the Education of Young Children.

Bredekamp, S., & Rosegrant, T. (Eds.). (1995). *Reaching potentials: Appropriate curriculum and assessment for young children* (Vol. 2). Washington, DC: National Association for the Education of Young Children.

Herman, J. L., Aschbacher, P. R., & Winters, L. (1992). *A practical guide to alternative assessment.* Alexandria, VA: Association for Supervision and Curriculum Development.

Kamii, C. (Ed.). (1990). *Achievement testing in the early grades: The games grown-ups play.* Washington, DC: National Association for the Education of Young Children.

National Association for the Education of Young Children & National Association of Early Childhood Specialists in State Departments of Education. (2003). *Early childhood curriculum, assessment, and program evaluation.* Washington, DC: Author. Position statement available at www.NAEYC.org.

Shepard, L. A., Kagan, S. L., & Wurtz, E. (Eds.). (1998). *Principles and recommendations for early childhood assessments.* Washington, DC: National Educational Goals Panel.

CHAPTER 2

Legal, Ethical, and Professional Responsibilities in Assessment

"**F**airness, the rights of all concerned, and professional ethical behavior must undergird all student assessment activities, from the initial planning for and gathering of information to the interpretation, use, and communication of the results" (American Federation of Teachers et al., 1990, p. 5). To do this, teachers must know what "professional ethical behavior" in assessment means, and develop the habits and dispositions to act accordingly.

Teachers collect and record important, sensitive information about children. Decisions and recommendations based in part on that information can influence children's opportunities to learn and are thus considered "high stakes." A recommendation for inclusion in a program for gifted or talented learners; for special help for a learning-disabled youngster; or for a kindergartner to be retained, promoted, or required to attend summer school relates to that child's opportunity to learn and must be made with the greatest of care. Even decisions about instructional methods and goals have an impact on children's opportunities to learn. For example, overemphasis on drill and practice may deprive children of opportunities to apply knowledge to practical problems. Reports to parents and other school personnel must be fair and factual. To fulfill their legal, ethical, and professional responsibility in assessment, teachers

- Know federal and state laws that mandate assessment
- Protect child and family rights as established by law and court ruling
- Are sensitive to individual, social, and cultural differences
- Are fair and impartial
- Collect trustworthy information
- Use assessment information in appropriate ways
- Know and abide by school and center policies

This chapter is long and weighty because the topic is weighty. It reflects the importance of educational assessment in schools and society.

Know Federal and State Laws That Mandate Assessment

No Child Left Behind

The 2002 reauthorization of the Elementary and Secondary Education Act (ESEA), popularly known as "No Child Left Behind" (NCLB), mandates nationwide, test-based accountability for schools receiving federal money (2002). The major provisions of this law that influence assessment in early childhood education are listed below.

1. In order to receive continued Title I federal funding, all states, schools, and school districts must comply with the federal regulations.
2. All public school students in grades three through eight are to be tested in reading and mathematics every year.
3. All schools must make "adequate yearly progress" (AYP) toward the goal of 100 percent proficiency in reading and mathematics.
4. Each state develops its own tests and determines its own definition of "proficient" on the test.
5. Progress on the selected tests must be shown for all students, and all student subgroups, including children who are disabled, economically disadvantaged, limited-English-proficient, and from each major racial and ethnic group.
6. Data are made public.

Even though testing does not begin until third grade, early childhood teachers and administrators are likely to feel pressure to make sure all children reach the stated goal of every child reading by the end of third grade.

The specifics of how NCLB are applied in each state are negotiated between the state and the U.S. Department of Education. Readers can expect to see modifications in the regulations and in how those regulations are interpreted in each state as those negotiations proceed.

Head Start and Other Federally Funded Prekindergarten Programs

In 2003 the federally funded Head Start program for low-income children began a testing and reporting initiative known as the National Reporting System. Each 4-year-old child in Head Start is tested in the autumn and spring. The individually administered standardized test focuses on general knowledge, vocabulary, and identification of letters and numerals. Test results are used for accountability purposes. Other federally funded programs use different procedures.

State Laws and Regulations

States have varying approaches to accountability. Many have developed their own tests aligned with their state standards and objectives. Some use existing standardized achievement tests.

State requirements for assessment of children in state-funded prekindergarten programs also vary. Some states have no state-funded prekindergarten programs. Some states require rigorous monitoring of early childhood programs (such as adult–child ratio, floor space, equipment, and activities offered) but no assessment of children. Other states require reporting of child progress but leave the nature of that reporting up to local programs. Some states require that all programs receiving state funds use a certain instrument and process (such as the Work Sampling System) so that results from all programs can be put together (aggregated) and analyzed.

Protect Child and Family Rights

Classroom practices and instructional decisions may seem far afield from the courtroom and legal processes, but they are not. Legal issues relating to assessment and its use revolve around three rights of individuals: equal protection under the law, due process, and privacy (Sandoval & Irvin, 1990). Laws and court interpretations change, but basic principles and rights and their implications for teachers, schools, and programs do not.

The Right to Equal Protection under the Law

Equal protection under the law means that in actions by the government, including school personnel, "an individual should enjoy the same rights and receive the same benefits or burdens as all other citizens," unless there is a valid reason why the person should not (Sandoval & Irvin, 1990, p. 86). Information that is used to assign a child to a specific treatment, such as special education, must be justified and valid. If one group disproportionately receives or doesn't receive benefits, there is a possibility that the equal protection principle is not being upheld.

Most of the court decisions relating to equal protection have to do with the placement of ethnic minority children in special education or in lower academic "tracks" on the basis of tests and other measures. Laws prohibit the use of discriminatory tests and mandate measures that are valid for the proposed use. States must have policies and procedures to prevent overidentification and misidentification of children with disabilities. School districts that overidentify minority students must implement prereferral strategies to reduce the number of students inappropriately referred to special education (*Diana* v. *California State Board of Education et al.,* 1970; Mercer, 1972; P.L. (Public Law) 94-142 [the Education for All Handicapped Children Act of 1975]; P.L. 101-576, P.L. 105-17, and P.L. 108-466 [the Individuals with Disabilities Education Acts of 1990, 1997, and 2004]).

Assessments must be provided and administered in the language and form most likely to yield accurate information on what the child knows and can do academically, developmentally, and functionally (IDEA, 2004).

The Right to Due Process

Due process means that people have "the right to protest and be heard prior to any action taken" with respect to them (Sandoval & Irvin, 1990, p. 86). They have a right to a hearing before any action and cannot have their rights and privileges as citizens arbitrarily, unreasonably, or capriciously removed. Two major laws spell out the responsibilities of educational institutions to parents and children relating to due process: P.L. 94-142, the Education for All Handicapped Children Act, and P.L. 93-380, the Family Educational Rights and Privacy Act of 1974. Together, they require that parents or guardians of young children be notified of their rights in advance of any major decisions or procedures. Parents or guardians have the right to submit evidence; to have appropriate legal representation; to cross-examine witnesses; to examine all school records and challenge those they do not agree with; and to receive an independent psychological evaluation provided by the state. Screening of a student by a teacher or specialist to determine appropriate instructional strategies is not sufficient evaluation for special education and related services (IDEA, 2004). Schools and centers have worked to meet these requirements in staff and family conferences—"staffings"—where all concerned with a major decision about a child confer to consider evidence and options.

Parents of children who attend a school that receives federal assistance may see all information in the official files, including portfolios and other assessment documentation, notes on behavioral problems, family background items, attendance and health records, class rank, test scores, grade averages, psychological reports, and all other records except personal notes made by staff members solely for their own use.

The Right to Privacy

The right to privacy involves an individual's right to choose "whether, when, and how behaviors, attitudes, beliefs, and opinions are to be shared with others" (Sandoval & Irvin, 1990, p. 87). The same laws that provide for due process require that parents give permission before any testing or release of information to someone other than the parent or the educational institution. Parents must give written consent before school officials release records to unauthorized persons or institutions. Schools must keep a written record of who has seen or requested to see a child's records (P.L. 93-380, the Family Educational Rights and Privacy Act of 1974).

In addition, there are ethical constraints. When you work with children all day, it is easy to carry incidents, frustrations, or interesting observations into a teachers' lounge, nearby restaurant, or social gathering. Don't. Share information about children only with people who have a need and a right to know. Never make potentially damaging oral or written remarks. Keep written notes, checklists, or other records—even those that are in progress—in a place where they are not readily accessible to adults or other children who might casually read them. Place private information in the appropriate file, and discuss it only on a professional basis. Teachers are in a position of trust. In this privileged role, they know many things about children and families that may never appear on paper, much less arise in casual conversation. Teach ethical behavior related to confidentiality of information to any classroom assistants or volunteers.

Keep sensitive information about family background or children's problems in confidential files. Children's portfolios that consist primarily of work products are usually all right in open folders in the classroom. However, if you share classroom space with other community groups, find a lockable cabinet in which to store the folders. Keep portfolios that contain information usually considered private, such as performance results or summary reports, confidential. Children's journals present a special case. Although they are done as part of classroom work, they sometimes contain children's feelings, concerns, and problems, including ones from home. Make a distinction between journals that simply report on a child's project or class work and those that may be more personal. Young children can seldom make a distinction between what is private and what is to be shared with other children and teachers. Teachers may have to screen student's work.

Notes, full or partly completed checklists, rating scales, or other forms should be placed in a file folder or drawer or slipped to the bottom of the stack on a clipboard, away from casual reading by anyone.

Major Legislation

Legal responsibilities relating to assessing and planning educational services for young children are contained in several federal laws providing for children with special needs. They build on basic civil rights accorded to all citizens.

P.L. 94-142 (1975) established national educational policy for children with disabilities from ages 3 to 21. The Education for all Handicapped Children Act specified appropriate safeguards for testing and measurement, and formalized use of the Individualized Education Program (IEP).

P.L. 99-457 (1986) effectively mandated the provisions of P.L. 94-142 for children with disabilities ages 3 through 5 and provided incentives for serving younger children. The law required an Individualized Family Service Program (IFSP) for families of infants and toddlers.

P.L. 101-576 (1990) renamed the Education for All Handicapped Children Act (P.L. 94-142) as the Individuals with Disabilities Education Act (IDEA) and reauthorized its basic provisions.

P.L. 101-336 (1990), the Americans with Disabilities Act, requires equal access and reasonable accommodation for individuals with disabilities, including equal access to enrollment in early childhood facilities (Wolery & Wilbers, 1994).

Together, these laws, their amendments, and regulations establish that

- Measures used to identify, classify, and place children in special needs programs must be nondiscriminatory. They must be used for the purpose for which they are intended and administered by qualified individuals. Assessment practices must be free from bias.
- Parents must have appropriate prior notification and give informed consent before administration of any measures for classification, planning, and placement.
- Parents may request an evaluation or reevaluation of their child and an independent evaluation.

- Parents may have children assessed in the language children know best.
- Parents may review their child's records, obtain copies, challenge questionable information, and have it withdrawn.
- Young children with disabilities, preschool through primary, are entitled to free appropriate public education.
- Parents can question and challenge actions related to their child's education taken by a school.
- Young children with disabilities must have an IEP prepared by a team that includes a general educator, special educator, someone knowledgeable about assessment and the implications of assessment results for classroom practices, parents, and other involved persons. Parents have a right to be involved in children's assessment and educational plans (Alper, 2001; ERIC Clearinghouse on Disabilities and Gifted Education, 1994).

Related to assessment, the Individuals with Disabilities Education Acts of 1997 and 2004 expand and further specify previous guidance.

- A variety of culturally and linguistically fair assessment tools and strategies should be used. No single procedure can be the sole criterion.
- Assessment tools and strategies should provide information that directly assists in determining the educational needs of the child academically, developmentally, and functionally.
- Information from all sources must be documented and carefully considered. This includes (1) evaluation information provided by the parent, (2) current classroom-based assessments and observations, and (3) observation by teachers and related service providers.
- The educational team is responsible not only for developing the IEP but also for evaluation, delivery of instruction, and monitoring student progress.

The statutes also address the inclusion of all children with disabilities in general state- and districtwide assessment programs, specifying that accommodations must be made for children who need such consideration (Alper, 2001; CEC, 2005). Alternate assessments must be aligned with the individual state's academic content and achievement standards.

Be Sensitive to Individual Differences

Assessment will reveal many individual differences among children. Acknowledging and trying to provide for differences has been a concern of educators since the 1920s, when the testing movement revealed great disparity among children's achievements in the typical classroom (Gage & Berliner, 1998). Three types of individual difference are of particular concern to early childhood educators: children with special needs, children and families "at risk," and children who need challenge. Inclusive education is a way of acknowledging the many things children have in common, as well as their individual differences.

Children with Special Needs

Probably no area of child assessment has received more attention and criticism than the process of identifying children with special needs—disabilities or developmental delays. Research and theory on identifying and educating these youngsters is expanding. Terminology changes in response. Many children with special needs do not fit any categories, or fit several. Children who have severe hearing or vision impairment or severe neurological, orthopedic, muscular, or multiple handicaps are usually identified and diagnosed before they enter the classroom setting. Less obvious needs, such as learning disabilities, speech and language problems, emotional disturbance, attention deficit disorders, or mild mental retardation may first be detected by a classroom teacher. The developmental "red flags" in Appendix B will alert you to possible need for referral.

Even as teachers are sensitive to possible problems, they must be careful not to overidentify. Many school "problems" are perfectly normal behavior for children of a given age, developmental level, or cultural group (Armstrong, 1995; Gage & Berliner, 1998). For example, young children are unlikely to pay attention to something that is not interesting (McAfee, 1985). Children's abilities to listen and attend are influenced by the time of day, number and type of distractions, their interest in the activity, and other variables. Inappropriate educational programming or classroom guidance may result in child behavior that is distracting or disruptive, or in failure to learn. For instance, active young children who are asked to sit and work at tasks beyond their developmental level may seek unacceptable outlets. Children who need to manipulate, arrange, rearrange, and solve problems with objects may fail to learn if the same task is presented with symbols only.

Developmentally and individually appropriate programs lessen unrealistic expectations of young children and allow identification of children who truly have special needs. To do this, use the recommended assessment process: describe and document the child's behavior using multiple sources, methods, and settings; compare it with developmental expectations and with other children; talk with parents; study, discuss, and interpret the information, including any information on the classroom environment that might contribute. Then decide whether the situation is something that you can handle or if consultation with a specialist is required. If there is any doubt, always consult. Most schools, centers, and agencies have multiple safeguards to ensure that children's and families' rights are protected, including clinical evaluations to check out any referrals. Evaluations that lead to placement in special programs are considered "high stakes," and teachers work with many other people in making those recommendations.

Children at Risk

Early identification and intervention with children and families "at risk" is increasing, as educators and policy makers realize that kindergarten or first grade may be too late for many children. The first of the major educational goals of the National Governors' Association is that every child should enter first grade ready to learn and able to benefit from an appropriate education (National Governors' Association, 1990). Further definition of this goal calls for attention to physical well-being and motor development, social and emotional development, approaches toward learning, language development, and cognition and general knowledge as factors that make a difference between being ready to learn and being at risk. How does this relate to assessment? First, selection of children and families to be in programs for children at risk calls for sensitive, multiple validations of need. Second, assessment of children's status and progress as a guide to educational programming is imperative. Third, teachers in such programs need to be vigilant for indicators that call for evaluation and possible intervention by a specialist. Even the best screening will miss many children who may need a closer look, just as it may wrongly identify children who actually have no problems of any kind. Children with subtle, intermittent, or inconsistent problems may be missed (Patterson & Wright, 1990). In addition, problems may develop after screening. Teachers must always be alert for signals to "look again" (see Appendix B).

Children Who Need Challenge

Young children may need special challenge for many reasons: the richness and variety of their educational and family experiences; early learning of basic skills; precocious development in a particular area; generally advanced development; being older than other children in the group; or being creative, gifted, talented, or of "high potential." Classroom assessment can identify children who need challenge, the areas in which they need it, and some guidance for appropriate activities to nurture their interests and abilities. Not all children who need challenge are gifted or talented, but teachers should be as alert to these children's needs as to those who have difficulty.

As with any other assessment of young children, the potential for error is great. It is easy to mistake rapid learning, early maturation, or special training for true giftedness. Teachers are likely to confuse conformity, neatness, and good behavior with giftedness (Gage & Berliner, 1998). Giftedness and talent take many forms, but early childhood schools frequently recognize only intellectual prowess—being "smart." Parental pressures to have children in gifted programs can have negative effects on the child. Designating a youngster as gifted, talented, or of high potential should be done with all legal and ethical safeguards.

Inclusive Education

"Inclusive education" implies the inclusion of youngsters with special needs as fully as possible in all aspects of education and community life. In an ideal situation, teachers receive the specialized help they need to assess special needs and implement appropriate curricula. This does not always happen, and teachers may find themselves taking much responsibility for assessment and educational programming. Even when specialized help is available, teachers need accurate descriptions and adequate documentation to participate in development and educational decisions with other specialists. At one time, children with special needs were usually taken out of the regular classroom and placed in self-contained "special ed" classrooms. Once such children had been identified, the regular teacher's responsibility ended. Now, all children are included in the regular classroom as much as possible. Likewise, many schools that once provided programs for developmentally advanced children—whether called gifted, talented, or high potential—are no longer doing so, and teachers have responsibility for identifying those children and developing programming to match their capabilities.

Be Sensitive to Linguistic, Social, and Cultural Differences

Young children in the United States come from diverse backgrounds. They vary in race and ethnicity; culture and degree of acculturation; language dominance and fluency; family income and educational level; rural, urban, suburban, inner-city, or rural–isolated home location; family structure and values; and prior school experience. So do their teachers. And regardless of whether they recognize it, both bring those differences to the classroom assessment process. Teachers, families, and children are often unaware of cultural differences that may influence children's performance (Gonzales-Mena, 1997; Phillips, 1983; West, 1992). In a fast-changing cultural setting such as the United States, acculturation occurs at varying speeds, and our knowledge of the powerful and subtle ways home, community, and culture influence children's development is incomplete.

Fair, continuous, authentic assessment of all children is essential if early childhood schools and centers are "to help children become educated no matter what their social, economic, or cultural background" (Committee for Economic Development, 1991, p. 5). Within that overall task are special challenges and concerns that stem from sociocultural and individual differences. To differences in "racial and cultural heritage, language, health, family situation, and preparation for schooling" (Committee for Economic Development, 1991, p. 8) could be added gender, place of residence, economic resources, educational level of parents or guardians, genetic inheritance, and the many other influences that shape human development and make each person unique.

Standardized tests are criticized for lack of sensitivity to sociocultural influences on children's learning. Classroom assessment holds the promise of being more sensitive. This will not happen automatically, or even easily. In practice, the challenge of developing equitable assessment processes for children from diverse backgrounds may be the classroom teacher's. Efforts to devise "culture-fair" or "culture-free" means of measuring children's development, achievement, and learning potential have not lived up to expectations (Cronbach, 1990). Teachers must acknowledge and understand the influence that sociocultural background has on classroom assessment, ranging from such a simple thing as whether the child is used to answering "testlike" questions to deep-seated family attitudes—supportive, nonsupportive, or indifferent—toward anything connected with educational institutions. For example, some families may help their children in anything connected with schooling, coaching them on how to behave and respond. Others may not know how to help children bridge that gap.

Teachers, too, are products of a particular sociocultural background, often with little conscious knowledge of why they have certain values, expectations, or ways of acting. When they interact with people who speak languages or dialects other than theirs, or act in different ways, they may have a tendency to judge those people's behavior by their own standards. Understanding their own sociocultural values will help teachers become more sensitive to sociocultural differences in children and families (Frank, 1999).

Local sources offer the best guidance about cultural, language, and other differences in a given community. Families, a family coordinator, a school–home liaison, cultural guide, or language specialist, if available, should have local and current information that will increase understanding. Schools, centers, and human resource agencies often distribute printed information or conduct workshops on significant differences likely to be found wtihin cultural groups in a particular area. Economic, language, ethnic, or cultural groups are not monolithic in their attitudes and practices (Suro, 1992), and generalizations may or may not apply to particular individuals, families, or communities.

> People have individual values, personal inclinations, and behavior styles that
> determine how they will act. Any statement about culture is a generalization

and doesn't tell you how an individual in that culture will act. You can see trends, themes, and probabilities, . . . but be careful about generalizing that information to individuals. (Gonzalez-Mena, 1997, p. 98)

It is easy to equate sociocultural differences with skin color, ethnic origin, name, or economic status, but reality is not that simple. Many families have mixed ethnic, racial, and religious backgrounds through marriage, adoption, and other circumstances. Some families have definite preferences and choices about the cultural orientation and education they want their children to have—regardless of family background.

Cultural Differences That May Influence Assessment

Children's backgrounds influence their knowledge, skills, attitudes, vocabulary, and ways of interacting with other people. Knowledge about the ocean or the desert, inner-city or suburban life, street games, families, food, and anything else will be related to the place of that knowledge in a particular culture, and may be quite different from what we expect. Children may have had limited opportunity to learn about things we assume "everyone" knows—sports, television programs, movies, holidays, advertisements, and celebrities.

Rules for expressing opinions, discussing, and taking turns in conversation may differ from one culture to another (Gumperz & Gumperz, 1981). Politeness and respect are communicated in different ways: averting the eyes, looking "straight in the eye"; silence or response; saying or not saying "Yes, ma'am," or "No, sir." Even "thinking seriously" is communicated in different ways. When asked a difficult question, children from one culture may look up, whereas children from another culture may look down. Teachers filter this behavior through the school or their own culture to determine its meaning. Chances are that the child looking up will be assessed as "trying harder" than the child who looks down, unless the teacher is aware of the cultural difference. One culture may emphasize fine motor skills so that children may be advanced in cutting and drawing and behind in jumping, kicking, or running. Another may emphasize large motor development so that children's physical development is far ahead of expectations. Some cultures emphasize independence; some dependence.

Children from one cultural group may have learned ways of responding to questions that put them at a disadvantage in school. One researcher found that African American children's responses were more likely to describe objects and events in relation to themselves or their experience rather than to name the object or event (Lawson, 1986). The expected response in most school settings is the name of the object or event. Studies of Native American communities found that "participant structures"—rules that govern conversations—differ from what is expected in school. Participant structures involve turn-taking and pace in conversations, pauses and silence, and who asks and answers questions. Imagine the miscommunication, even when everyone is speaking English (Gage & Berliner, 1992). Children's interactions with adults—when they are to talk, to whom they are to talk, and what kind of language they are to use—are influenced by their home culture (NAEYC, 2005). All these factors may influence assessment.

The thinking processes and learning styles that children develop and use are closely linked to the sociocultural environment in which they develop, as those processes are nurtured in collaboration with others or in social arrangements of children's activities (Bodrova & Leong, 1996; Rogoff, 1990). Learning processes, such as memory strategies, classification processes, and approaches to problem solving, are not developed solely within the individual, but "are intrinsically related to social and societal values and goals, tools, and institutions" (Rogoff, 1990, p. 61). For example, taxonomic classification—putting things together in abstract categories on the basis of their presumed relationships—is emphasized in school and some cultures. Perceptual categories—how things look the same or different—are emphasized in others (Ceci, 1991). As schools and centers aim to assess and teach complex cognitive processes, as opposed to simpler notions of reading, computation, and recall of facts, the influence of sociocultural differences may be more, not less, important.

Assessment that occurs in school settings is subject to the biases of the school culture. All schools have a "culture," including certain values, rules for interaction and behavior, and expectations (Frank, 1999; Gage & Berliner, 1998). All children must make some adjustments to being away from home. For most youngsters, these adjustments expand their world and the repertoire of behavior and skills they have at their command (Powell, 1989). However, children from some ethnic, cultural, and community backgrounds must make more, often difficult adjustments (Kagan, Moore, & Bredekamp, 1995). They may not be used to following oral directions, performing on demand, or the restrictions of the setting. They may base their answers on social cues rather than on what they "think" or know (Sattler, 2001). These children may need more explicit directions and support.

Implications for Assessment

"Assessment . . . presents a formidable problem for teachers of children outside the economic and cultural mainstream" (Bowman, 1992, p. 136). Little definitive research exists on the way assessment should be done to be sensitive to diversity. Whenever human judgment is involved, the potential for human bias increases. Teachers should take extra care to overcome that possibility. The following guidelines are based on available information, older research that has implications for current practices, strategies particularly suited to working with young children, and personal experience in assessing and teaching young children.

Assume there will be sociocultural influences on children's actions in the classroom. If nothing more, there will be differences among expectations of the home and community, previous schools, and the current setting. Children coming from a preschool that stresses individual choice, initiative, creativity, and much peer verbal interaction may be sized up in initial assessment differently from children who are quiet and wait for direction. These differences may be present across all cultural, social, or economic backgrounds. Assume, also, that there may be lack of congruence among the school culture and the sociocultural settings of the home and community. Competitiveness and cooperation, gender-role differentiation, the importance of schooling in the life of the family or community, the relationship of the child to adults, and many other aspects related to learning and teaching may be involved. If you suspect that cultural, language, or other differences may be operating, check it out. Use this information to understand why children may be having trouble, and then gradually help them learn whatever it is they need to know. However, don't make the mistake of blaming all problems on a child's home background.

Distinguish social, cultural, language, and ethnic differences from deficits or disabilities. The disproportionate representation of minority groups in special education is a national concern. They are overrepresented in special needs programs and underrepresented in gifted and talented programs (Burnette, 1998).

Sometimes sensitivity to cultural differences in assessment and instruction is sufficient safeguard. Other safeguards related specifically to assessment include

- A clear referral system that rules out cultural differences, lack of English language proficiency, or economic disadvantage as contributing factors
- Documentation of prereferral efforts and their results
- Multiple assessment measures and a broad base of student data
- Tests and procedures that are technically acceptable and culturally and linguistically appropriate
- Personnel who can interpret results in a culturally responsive way

Involve parents and the community. These local experts, plus any available language and cultural specialists, can help determine relevant similarities and differences. All too often we focus on perceived differences and overlook the similarities (Jones & Derman-Sparks, 1992; Rogoff, 1990). Similarities may give points of entrance for assessment and instruction.

Use multiple assessment measures and forms in a supportive, familiar context. Use both verbal and nonverbal measures. Set up assessment situations so children can demonstrate their full capabilities. The freedom to do that is one of the big differences between classroom assessment and standardized tests. "Most children in low-income and minority communities have mastered [developmental tasks similar to those expected of all children], but their mastery may be displayed in unfamiliar dress" (Bowman, 1992, p. 134). If one approach is not appropriate, another may be; one provides a check against the other, so that a youngster who is unable to respond in one context or to one method of assessment has some options (Villegas, 1991).

Be prepared to rephrase, restate, or recast a task or expectation in terms familiar and sensible to the youngsters. Change the assessment context to a more familiar one. Assess using children's interests and activities, which should, in turn, be linked to their homes and communities—the sociocultural setting.

Children who are unable or unwilling to respond to structured performance tasks may be able to demonstrate their knowledge in informal "real-life situations." When she was asked to name colors, 4-year-old Leila simply refused to respond. Less than a half-hour later, during informal lunchtime conversation with her teacher, Leila said all the color names correctly, linked with examples and incorporated into functional, real conversation. Which is Leila's true competence level? Assessing in noncontrived "contextualized" situations—informal, comfortable, and familiar—may enable children to perform at higher levels (Cazden, 2001).

Appreciate and accommodate the similarities and differences among children's cultures. Identify and work with these differences in a positive manner. Above all, do not assume a lack of ability or potential based on social, cultural, ethnic, or language differences (Burnette, 1999; Gonzalez-Mena, 1997; NAEYC, 2005).

Be Fair and Impartial

Probably no issues related to assessment are more emotionally and educationally charged than those related to bias and fairness. One of the harshest criticisms of standardized tests is that they may be biased against children who are not of the dominant culture and language or are from families with low income and educational levels. This concern for fairness extends to all assessment procedures. Indeed, informal appraisals that rely on an individual to gather information and determine its meaning increase the potential for bias (Smith, 1990).

Bias usually refers to a test, procedure, result, or use that unfairly discriminates against one group in favor of another. It is a complex concept, not easily simplified, and involves not only tests and assessment procedures but also use of the results (Berk, 1982; Cronbach, 1990; Jones, 1988; Shepard, 1982). The overplacement of young minority group children in special education classes on the basis of test results is a frequently cited example of test bias (Mercer, 1972).

To be fair to all children in our socially, economically, and culturally diverse society, be as objective as possible and ensure the accuracy and trustworthiness of assessment information.

Be as Objective as Possible

To be objective, try to obtain and use facts, information, or data without distortion by personal feelings or prejudice. Lack of objectivity happens when personal experiences or characteristics strongly influence perceptions of events, facts, or behavior. For example, if we believe that boys are "better at" mathematical and mechanical tasks, we may perceive children through those beliefs unless we take great care to look at what individual children know and can do. If we believe that girls are "better at" language and reading, those beliefs may influence our assessment and instruction in many subtle ways.

No one is totally objective. The information we choose to collect is influenced by our personal experience, beliefs, and interests. One teacher observing children at play may focus on their social interactions; another may note the cognitive and language aspects of what they are doing; still another may zero in on their physical development. We may judge children on whether their hair is clean and neatly combed; the appropriateness of their clothing; dialect variations in their speech; the match of their personality and interests to ours; and deeply embedded cultural values—often so much a part of us and so subtle that we do not realize they are there. Although we usually think of prejudging in connection with low-income or minority families, it extends to all children: those with nontraditional family structures; those whose mothers work outside the home; children who are intellectually, socially, or economically privileged; or those who are "different" in any way.

In addition to personal experiences and beliefs that may color what we see and hear, we become accustomed to observing certain things or getting certain results, and thus take them for granted, failing to notice their importance or significance. Or we may assume that other people think, feel, and act as we do (Irwin & Bushnell, 1980).

Objectivity in collecting, recording, understanding, and using information about children can increase the fairness, accuracy, and usefulness of assessment. By no means should personal insights, feelings, and intuition be excluded, but most of us need the discipline of objectivity to achieve impartiality (Bentzen, 2000).

Avoid Categories and Labels. It is easy to place a "halo" on some children and see everything they do in the best possible light. We may consistently interpret the actions of other children less favorably. Others may always be seen as simply average, regardless of their performance (Almy & Genishi, 1979). This lack of objectivity may mask the needs of the "halos" and substantive progress of the others.

Labels—often in current jargon—slip out so easily: "ADHD" (Attention Deficit Hyperactivity Disorder), "Asperger's," "shy," "withdrawn," "acting out," "under-achiever," "gifted," "troublemaker." A label may give the false impression that a real and unchanging characteristic has been identified, and can stick to a child for years regardless of its accuracy. Labels usually have connotations, often negative, that may set up inappropriate expectations about individual children. Concentrate on describing and understanding individual children instead of labeling them (Goodwin & Driscoll, 1980).

Sometimes children have to be diagnosed as being in a certain group to receive appropriate services, but such diagnoses are beyond the authority of the classroom teacher.

Be Objective in Collecting Information.   An objective description focuses on the facts and details of what is occurring with as little interpretation and filtering of information as possible (Boehm & Weinberg, 1997). The observer captures what is seen and heard without analyzing the information. An inference is an interpretation of a child's behavior and may include speculation about the child's possible feelings, intentions, motivations, thinking processes, attitudes, or dispositions. Inferences may also include evaluations and judgments about the significance of a behavior for future development or comparisons of behavior with past actions. Distinguish between the description of what happened and the interpretation or analysis of what happened. Both are important but are different.

Almost everyone has trouble separating facts and details about an experience from inferences based on those facts and details. This skill is essential for responding appropriately to children. Teachers usually interpret the intentions and motivations of a child simultaneously with behavior. Ms. Dupont sees Marcia rush at Julia with her arms raised, yelling. If Ms. Dupont thinks that Marcia is just "pretending to be King Kong" and is not intending to hurt the other children, she will react one way. Her reaction will be different if Ms. Dupont thinks that Marcia intends to hurt Julia. To make assessment objective, a teacher must separate the two (Almy, 1969; Jagger, 1985). Momentarily suspend interpretation and analysis, and concentrate on what is seen and heard: "Marcia rushes at Julia with her arms raised and yells."

Be Objective in Recording Information.   A record should be an objective, accurate recounting of what occurred. Record information in precise terms in the sequence in which it happened (Bentzen, 2000). In some cases, the context or setting is important, including the people involved, where the child is sitting, time of day, and activity. As much as possible, capture what children actually say, rather than paraphrasing it. Sometimes this requires inventing spellings for sounds such as "suspusketti" (spaghetti) or "wainbow" (rainbow).

In initial recording, avoid words that convey emotional tone, feelings, motives, or thinking processes. Such conclusions cannot be directly observed but are inferred from what took place. For instance, record "Tyler paused, looked around the room, then moved the block into place," rather than "Tyler thought about all the things he might want to do with the block, then moved it into place." What Tyler is thinking is an inference. Another person might observe the same behavior and conclude that Tyler was nervous, uncertain, slow, or something else altogether.

Record inferences so they can be identified and distinguished from the factual recounting of what took place. Write the inference in a special place on the record labeled "interpretation," with a different colored pen or on a separate piece of paper attached to the record.

Inferences should be separated from the record of behavior for several reasons. Isolating what was seen or heard from inference decreases recording errors (Cronbach, 1990). Inferences made immediately may or may not prove useful later. For example, a teacher may have a different interpretation of "Megan offers to share the blocks with Josh" after one incident than after several observations over a period of time. Keeping inferences separate allows a teacher to go back and examine the pattern of behavior from a different perspective.

Inferences or conclusions help summarize and interpret information so it can guide future classroom activities. Appropriate inferences are those that evaluate the developmental and learning significance of a behavior or identify a behavior that should be monitored in the future. Examples of acceptable inferences are "Needs more practice"; "Should be monitored"; "Progressing satisfactorily." Avoid inferences that label children: "She's always out to hurt other people" or "Another example of gifted behavior."

Be Objective in Evaluating Classroom Procedures and Instructional Practices. Being objective involves more than objectivity in collecting information about children. Teachers should observe and evaluate not only children, but also how classroom procedures, instructional practices, and teachers influence children's behavior and learning. Not everything can be attributed to child characteristics or learning needs. A child who is "distractible" in a noisy, chaotic classroom may be task oriented in a different setting. In a study of "circle time" in early childhood classrooms, teachers blamed children's restlessness and lack of attention on the children or their poor home background rather than considering whether the circle time was too long, uninteresting, or held in a place with competing activities (McAfee, 1985). A teacher who has worked hard to help a group of children master something may find evidence showing that children still have much to learn difficult to believe. Even more difficult to achieve is the insight that instructional practices may need to be changed.

Ensure the Accuracy and Trustworthiness of Assessment Information

The freedom that teachers have in alternative, informal assessment is accompanied by professional responsibility to make sure the information is accurate, trustworthy, and dependable (Cambourne & Turbill, 1990). Reliability and validity, concepts most often associated with test construction and development, also apply to classroom assessment. Standardized achievement and screening tests meet rigorous standards before they are deemed reliable and valid, and statistical information relating to reliability and validity is published so that potential users can evaluate it. Such rigor is not necessary for information used for ongoing, *continuous assessment* (Shepard, 2000), yet there must be some check on reliability and validity to make sure the results represent what a child can do.

Evaluation of the trustworthiness of assessment information is part of the overall process of assessment and should be done continuously—as information is being collected and recorded, as it is summarized, analyzed, and used to make decisions or reports. It is easy to assume that because you are directly measuring something, the appraisal is valid and reliable. This is not the case. Although there are no statistical tests that apply to informal, in-class assessments, these general guides will increase reliability and validity.

Reliability.   The results of assessment should be reliable, consistent, and dependable. They should be reproducible—you should be able to obtain a similar performance at another time or place. The way information is collected, the assessment situation, the child's mental or physical state, and lucky or unlucky guesses can influence reliability.

The assessment method can cause incorrect answers. Vague or confusing questions and requests yield unreliable results, because they can be interpreted in different ways at different times. Direct and persistent questioning can make children uneasy, resulting in a performance that does not reflect their true abilities. The situation in which the assessment takes place influences reliability. Environmental distractions such as a noisy group discussion in another part of the room, interruptions by other children, or a strange situation can cause unreliable results (Maeroff, 1991). Unexpected events such as a loose hamster, unplanned assembly, or fire drill can affect a child's responses and, therefore, the reliability. How the child is feeling, including mental state, illness, fatigue, lack of interest, anxiety, or a "bad day," also impacts reliability. An argument at home, on the school bus, or on the playground can make appraisal done that day unreliable.

An assessment can also be unreliable if a child's performance is influenced by a number of lucky or unlucky guesses. Check to make sure differences between performances are related to learning and not luck.

Be alert for uncharacteristic behavior or inconsistencies. The information obtained on one occasion should be comparable to information obtained on other occasions and consistent with other information collected at other times from other sources and methods (Sattler, 2001). Ms. Maclaren is measuring social interaction of a group. As she reviews her record of the interaction, she finds that José stayed alone most of the morning. Ms. Maclaren thinks, "This is so unlike José, he is usually right in there making suggestions." Ms. Maclaren concludes that this is not a reliable sample of José's social interaction because it does not capture his normal behavior. On another day, he would probably interact freely. The difference in performance suggests unreliability of the assessment.

To increase reliability, make more than one measurement of the same behavior. If you decide information from an assessment is unreliable, do not use it. If you suspect information may be unreliable, mark it, and have the child repeat the activity or demonstrate the behavior in a different situation. One of the big advantages of informal assessment is that youngsters can have more than one chance to demonstrate their capability.

Validity.   Validity has to do with both the assessment and the interpretations, conclusions, or inferences that can be made based on the information gathered (Cronbach, 1990). Valid assessments appraise what they were designed to; that is, they provide accurate information about the item under consideration. The interpretations or conclusions are also reasonable and fair given the information that has been collected (Gage & Berliner, 1998).

In addition, teachers need to think of validity in terms of what is being assessed (Herman, Aschbacher, & Winters, 1992). Is it significant and important? Is it aligned with curriculum—what children have had or will have an opportunity to learn? Will it be meaningful to you, the child, and others who are concerned with the child's learning and development?

Validity can be increased by (1) having enough samples to cover or adequately represent a behavior; (2) having "balance" in the samples—that is, not overemphasizing one type of information or one context; (3) checking to see if information obtained in different ways converges; and (4) ensuring that the objective of the assessment is being met.

All assessments are samples, because it is physically impossible to assess every possible incidence of a behavior (Sattler, 2001). A valid assessment must have enough samples to be representative of the entire behavior. There are no hard and fast rules about how much information is needed to cover or adequately represent a behavior (Cronbach, 1990). This depends partly on the behavior being assessed. It takes only a few items to yield valid results on a specific behavior such as using a ruler or equal-arm balance. Much information will be necessary to make valid statements about development in a large and complex domain such as cognitive or social development.

To be valid, the representative sample must be balanced (Hopkins, Stanley, & Hopkins, 1990). The assessment should not overemphasize one type of information or oversample one context. An assessment of a child's ability to identify letters should not rely solely on information gathered from written work. To obtain a valid measure of a child's sharing behavior, a teacher must observe the child in several contexts: outdoor play, snack, cooperative learning groups, and others. Evidence from a variety of sources, methods, and contexts measuring the same thing should converge (Cronbach, 1990).

To be valid, assessment must provide evidence about what it is supposed to assess and not something else. Suppose a teacher is interested in the number of roles children will assume during a dramatic play activity. He sets up a bus and invites several children to play. During the assessment, one child makes herself bus driver and insists that all the other children act as the children on the bus. When any of the other children suggest roles other than children, the "bus driver" shouts them down. The total number of roles played in the session is one per child, although different children attempted but were not allowed to change roles. The appraisal is not measuring the number of roles children take but the social interaction when one child dominates the group. The teacher must make another assessment to measure role-taking and role-changing behavior.

One way to check validity is to compare children who do well with those who do not and to identify reasons for those differences. If the reason for the differences is the behavior you are trying to measure, then the assessment is probably valid. If differences are caused by something else, then the assessment is not valid. For example, Ms. Aptos designed an art activity using small seeds glued to paper to measure patterning abilities in children. Comparing the group who produced a pattern with those who did not, she found that there were no differences in the ability to make a pattern with blocks and beans—objects larger than the small seeds she used. But results from the seed project were similar to those of her appraisal of fine motor skills. Children who did well in the fine motor assessment did this patterning activity well also. This was not a valid assessment of patterning, because fine motor skills were assessed, not the ability to produce patterns.

Do not use invalid data. Repeat the assessment, modifying the way information is gathered for that particular individual or group. If information was not representative or too few indicators were included, assess to obtain the missing data.

Use Assessment Results in Appropriate Ways

Know the Limitations of Each Method of Assessment, and Guard against Overreliance on Any One

Each way of getting and recording information about children has strengths and limitations. Checklists, for example, are a good way to record the presence or absence of knowledge or skills but give little information about the precision and subtlety of children's thinking processes. Interviews, discussions, or children's reflections are needed to tap thinking processes. One type of information complements the other. For important, high stakes decisions, use multiple assessment windows—several sources, methods, and contexts—to get the best information you can (American Educational Research Association, 2000; American Psychological Association et al., 1999; NAEYC/NAECS/SDE, 2003). Results of standardized tests or inventories should be weighed against the outcomes of other types of assessment. Appropriate tests, clinical assessment, or in-depth diagnosis by a specialist can validate or cast doubt on the results of informal appraisals. Human behavior is complex, and our instruments for assessing it are relatively crude. Assessment results are estimates, at best. Teachers must regard them as tentative, subject to error, and subject to revision on the basis of additional information.

Use Assessment Results for the Intended Purposes

Assessment results should be used for "specific, beneficial purposes: (1) making sound decisions about teaching and learning, (2) identifying significant concerns for individual children, and (3) helping programs improve their educational and developmental interventions" (NAEYC/NAECS/SDE, 2003, p. 2). Other purposes include reporting to and communicating with families, other professionals, administrators, funding and regulatory agencies, and citizen groups, and helping to know and understand the children with which we work. Inappropriate uses include delaying children's entrance to school; retaining children in grade; recommending children for special programs without proper safeguards; or placing them in rigid, unvarying groups or "tracks."

Know and Abide by State, School District, and Center Policies

Follow state, school district, and center policies about assessment, record keeping, and reporting. Find out what is in cumulative files, personal files, and health records and who sees the files for what purposes. Determine policies and recommendations about what teachers and children put in classroom portfolios. Secure information on policies and procedures for referral of children for further assessment, including prereferral strategies. Know procedures for documenting and reporting required information about children and families, such as suspected child abuse and neglect.

Determine what information is transferred from one early childhood setting or program to another and how. As primary-school children move to the intermediate grades, what reading and other samples will go with them? These are local decisions and will vary, unlike federal laws and court decisions that have national application.

Summary

As early childhood teachers assume assessment responsibilities, they also assume professional responsibilities specific to assessment. Federal, state, and local requirements for assessment and accountability impact many classrooms. Legal and ethical responsibility relates to giving children equal opportunity to learn. Teachers should know and abide by laws and court rulings pertaining to assessment information and its use; be sensitive to individual, social, and cultural differences; be fair, objective, and impartial; guard the trustworthiness of classroom assessment data and use it in appropriate ways; and abide by school and center policies.

Children and parents have the basic rights of equal protection under the law, due process, and privacy. These are safeguarded by laws and court interpretations that apply to all children, families, and schools. Policies relating to assessment vary but influence how and what teachers assess and how that information is reported. Fairness, impartiality, and objectivity will help teachers avoid discrimination against children because of race, ethnicity, language, culture, gender, economic or educational level—or any other bias. Teachers should be as objective as possible in assessment and be knowledgeable about and sensitive to the ways in which diversity in children and families may influence assessment. Of particular concern in contemporary society are sociocultural differences and individual differences.

Three types of individual difference are of special concern to early childhood educators: children with special needs relating to disabilities and developmental delays, children and families "at risk," and children who need challenge. Inclusive education keeps most of these children together in the classroom and the community whenever possible.

Diversity in preparation for school; in physical, emotional, social, cognitive, and language strengths and needs; in family, community, and economic circumstances must be considered in assessment. Young children at risk of being unable to achieve their full potential may need experiences to help them with physical well-being, emotional maturity, social confidence, language development, and general knowledge. Assessment concerns include selection of children and families to be in such programs, assessment of children's status and progress as a guide to educational programming, and vigilance for indications of the possible need for the help of a specialist.

Teachers must be sensitive to the way children and families from different cultures and backgrounds respond to assessment and make appropriate adjustments or changes. Obtain information from families and communities in culturally sensitive ways.

Teachers work to increase trustworthiness, reliability, and validity of assessment. Reliable information is consistent, reproducible, and dependable. Teachers increase reliability by being aware of the ways in which information is collected, the situation in which assessment takes place, the child's mental and physical state, and the effect of guessing can influence reliability. They are alert for uncharacteristic behavior and inconsistencies and make more than one measurement of items they assess.

Valid assessments appraise what they were designed to and result in reasonable interpretations or conclusions. Teachers can increase the validity of classroom assessment by having enough samples to represent what they are assessing, having "balance" in the samples, checking to see if information obtained in different ways converges, and making sure they assess what they intend to.

Legal and ethical responsibilities demand that teachers know the limitations of each type of observation and measurement, guard against overreliance on any one method, and use the results only for appropriate purposes.

For Personal Reflection

1. Objectivity is essential in assessment, yet no one is totally objective. Reflect on your thoughts, feelings, and attitudes in your interactions with young children. What do you detect that might interfere with your objectivity? What do you detect that could aid your objectivity? Identify some possible reasons for these tendencies.

2. Every culture, including the school culture, has "rules" that govern its members' behavior. We usually learn those rules so well that we notice them only when someone doesn't follow them. Identify the "rules" of a classroom setting with which you are familiar. Which are explicit (stated) and which are implicit (not stated, but assumed)?

For Further Study and Discussion

1. The school you are teaching in plans to use paraprofessional classroom assistants to help observe and make records of children's performance. Identify what classroom assistants and teachers need to know and do to safeguard the ethical and legal responsibilities of the school.

2. Underline the portions of the following observation record that are inferences and not a description of what was actually observed. Justify your decisions.

   Tina and Norm are playing a game of tag outside. Tina accidentally trips Norm. He lashes out at her, pushing her to the ground. Her feelings hurt, Tina begins to cry and runs to the teacher. The teacher is more sympathetic toward Tina than Norm because he is usually a discipline problem in the classroom. She says, "What happened to you, Tina?" Tina replies, "Norm pushed me down and I hurt myself." The teacher takes her hand and walks over to Norm, who by now is quite angry and feeling sorry for himself. "Norm," says the teacher, "did you push Tina down? Why did this happen?" Norm says, "She tripped me first." Tina says, "Well, I didn't mean to." Tina and the teacher realize that there is a misunderstanding. Norm is an aggressive child and always responds aggressively.

3. Mr. Hiller is assessing Matthew's reading comprehension and recall by evaluating an oral book report given in front of the class. Matthew says very little when giving his book report orally to the class. Mr. Hiller suspects that Matthew's anxiety level is very high, so he talks to Matthew informally and confirms his suspicions: Matthew was too nervous to talk! Using the concepts of reliability and validity, discuss how Mr. Hiller should understand this assessment and in what other ways he could check Matthew's reading comprehension and recall.

4. Children who need challenge are sometimes overlooked in the regular classroom. What are some reasons for this? What could you, as a teacher or future teacher, do to respond to those children's assessed strengths and needs?

Suggested Readings

American Educational Research Association. (2000). AERA position statement concerning high-stakes testing in preK–12 education. Washington, DC: Author.

American Psychological Association, American Educational Research Association, & National Council on Measurement in Education. (1999). *Standards for educational and psychological testing.* Washington, DC: Author.

Council for Exceptional Children. (2005). *What's new with the new IDEA? Frequently asked questions and answers.* Arlington, VA: Author.

Epstein, A. S., Schweinhart, L. J., DeBruin-Parecki, A., and Robin, K. B. (2004). Preschool assessment: A guide to developing a balanced approach. *Preschool Policy Matters.* Issue 7/July 2004. National Institute for Early Education Research. Online at www.nieer.org.

Gonzalez-Mena, J. (1997). *Multicultural issues in child care* (2nd ed.). Mountain View, CA: Mayfield Publishing Company.

Kendall, F. (1996). *Diversity in the classroom: New approaches to the education of young children.* New York: Teachers College Press.

Kusimo, P., Ritter, M., Busick, K., Ferguson, C., Trumbull, E., & Solano-Flores, G. (2000). *Making assessment work for everyone: How to build on student strengths.* San Francisco, CA: WestEd.

National Association for the Education of Young Children (NAEYC). (2005). *Screening and Assessment of Young English-Language Learners: Supplement to the NAEYC Position Statement on Early Childhood Curriculum, Assessment, and Program Evaluation.* Washington, DC: Author. Online at www.naeyc.org.

Wolery, M., & Wilbers, J. S. (1994). *Including children with special needs in early childhood programs.* Washington, DC: National Association for the Education of Young Children.

CHAPTER 3

Why, What, and When to Assess

Imagine yourself with a new job in a school or center that emphasizes developmentally appropriate practices for young children, including developmentally appropriate assessment. The case study you spent a semester on in college can't possibly be done with a room full of children. There are many requirements and even more expectations. Where do you start? How do you approach this task without having it detract from teaching? Like many things teachers do, there is no one way or even a "best" way. Teachers put their personal stamp on what and how they assess, how they organize files, and how they use information. However, a systematic way to think about assessment can help organize the process and make it workable.

Assessment Decisions

Decisions have to be made before the process even starts: Why is assessment being done? What will be assessed? When? Deciding how to assess requires decisions about collecting and recording information (see Chapters 4 and 5). Compiling, summarizing, and interpreting information help us understand what it means so we can use it for the intended purposes (see Chapters 6, 7, and 8). To simplify the process, consider assessment as a decision-making task. Figure 3.1 highlights major decisions in the assessment cycle.

A group of teachers, building committees, parent councils, administrators, or funding or regulatory agencies may already have decided some of the why, what, and when to assess. Certain tests or official reports may be required. Within those requirements, teachers exercise much professional judgment. Information required for official purposes is seldom sufficient or even appropriate for classroom instruction purposes.

Figure 3.1   Major Decisions in the Assessment Cycle

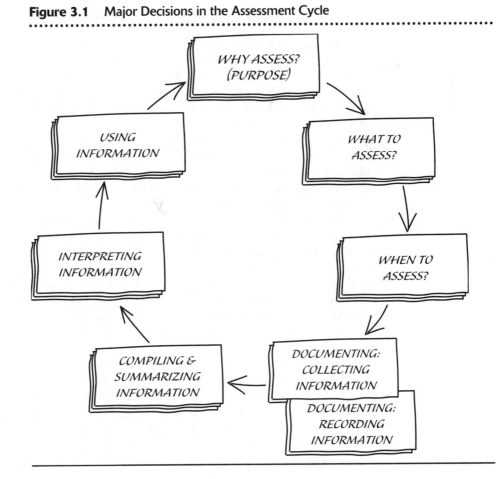

Why Assess?

"The intended use of an assessment—its purpose—determines every other aspect of how the assessment is conducted" (Shepard, Kagan, & Wurtz, 1998, p. 6). We assess to determine individual children's developmental status at a given time and their progress and change over time. *Status* refers to children's current condition or situation with respect to any particular aspect of growth, development, or learning. What do they know? What are they able to do? What are their feelings, interests, attitudes, and dispositions as well as their physical health and well-being? Status is concerned with "where children are" in their development. This basic information is then used for other purposes:

1. To monitor children's development and learning
2. To guide classroom planning and decision making
3. To identify children who might benefit from special help
4. To report to and communicate with others

These purposes are not entirely separate, of course. Information that guides classroom planning may also be used for reporting to parents; assessment during daily activities may reveal concerns about individual children that other measures miss. Let's look at each of these purposes separately.

To Monitor Children's Development and Learning

Teachers can't assume that any given child or group fits their expectations of children that age. All 4-year-olds or 6-year-olds are not the same weight and height, nor do they all know and do the same things. Diversity of every kind, such as language, culture, prior experiences, social skills, and basic temperament, is to be expected. We assess to determine a child's and a group's strengths and needs at a given point in time.

Teachers also monitor and keep track of children's progress and change over time. They do this to (1) provide evidence of learning to themselves, parents and children, (2) guard against the assumption that because "we've worked on that" the children have learned it, and (3) make needed changes in response to what children have or have not learned.

Because teachers and aides work daily with children, they may not realize how much children are developing and learning. Progress often comes gradually, in small increments. Only when a child's or group's performance is compared with what they did on the same task a month or several months ago is progress evident. Such evidence of progress motivates adults and children alike. Most teachers are elated when a child who has been having trouble with something "gets it." They are delighted when the experiences they have planned and implemented result in desired outcomes—and are motivated to continue. Hearing about or seeing examples of what they have learned motivates and reinforces children. Parents should receive regular reports on children's progress.

Assess to guard against the assumption that if children are given an opportunity to learn—whether through experiences, materials, explicit instruction, or simply general support and expectation—they will automatically grow, develop, and progress. All teachers are inclined to think that if something is "taught," learners will "learn." This can't be assumed, either with a preschooler trying to learn how to enter and become a part of a play group or with a primary youngster trying to master regrouping in addition and subtraction. Periodically, a focused look and comparison with earlier information is needed.

To Guide Classroom Planning and Decision Making

Assessment information "is essential for planning and implementing developmentally appropriate programs" (Bredekamp, 1987, p. 4). Assessment "in the service of instruction" helps decide where and how to begin, how long to work on a given goal or objective, when to review, and when to make changes to help children learn. Initial assessment and periodic assessment of progress, placed against program goals and expectations, can help teachers make long- and short-range plans. Assessment also helps teachers in day-to-day classroom planning, because what children do one day prompts changes in plans for the ensuing days. If a new art activity captures the children's interest and leaves them wanting more, a teacher has definite guidance in shifting tomorrow's or the next day's plans to take advantage of that interest.

Teachers use information gained from ongoing, continuous assessment "to understand specific children and to gain information on which to base immediate decisions on how to direct, guide, teach, or respond" (Phinney, 1982, p. 16). Teachers seek to understand children's thinking and learning processes, not only what they know and can do. During interactive teaching and instructional conversations, teachers adjust what they say and do to recognize children's current level of understanding and try out words and strategies to increase that understanding. As children respond, teachers revise and modify approaches in a continuing interplay. They use assessment information to help them choose materials and strategies, select one activity and reject another, allocate more or less time to a given portion of the day, decide what to do about the continuing squabbles in work groups, and decide how to rearrange learning centers to increase interest. Effective, developmentally appropriate programs depend on some kind of assessment.

To Identify Children Who Might Benefit from Special Help

Assessment is used to identify children who may need special help. Teachers may be involved in screening, prereferral strategies, or other processes to identify children who might need an in-depth assessment to see if they could benefit from specialized services. Teachers may also identify children who need special help in the classroom. Some may need more challenge; others may be falling behind and need more help in class.

Systematic assessment also keeps teachers from "losing" individual children. In any group of children, certain ones get lots of adult attention. Some demand it by their spirited behavior; others get it because they are so cooperative or responsive or because they have great need. Others may get lost along the way unless teachers take care to know them and meet their needs.

To Report to and Communicate with Others

Funding and regulatory bodies often specify what information is reported and the way in which it is obtained. For example, they may require that a specific published assessment tool be used at a given time during the year. Information from these official accountability assessments may be used to detect and strengthen weaknesses in programs, plan professional development activities, compare with other schools or programs, or to analyze costs and benefits. Assessment information also guides teachers in their conferences with families and with other professionals, such as speech and hearing specialists, nurses, or developmental specialists.

What to Assess?

Human development is so complex that teachers cannot assess everything of interest. They must focus, select, and sample (Stiggins & Conklin, 1992). Teachers make decisions about what to assess in four categories: major child growth and development domains; expected outcomes of the program for individual children; children's unique patterns of development, knowledge, attitudes, and interests; and problems or concerns about a child or group.

Major Child Growth and Development Domains

Plan to gather information on major aspects of children's development. These major developmental domains may be called different things: cognitive, affective, and psychomotor; or intellectual, social, emotional, and physical. Some people add language as a separate category. Others add aesthetic, moral, and spiritual development. Schools working with older children may think in terms of curriculum areas or subjects, such as literacy development, physical education, social studies, health and nutrition, and others. Even if a school or center emphasizes one or two developmental areas more than others, children cannot be divided up and part of them set aside. Social/emotional development and behavioral self-regulation are as important to young children's development and academic success as is learning to read (Raver, 2002). A youngster's lack of social skills will plague him in all he does; poor muscle development and motor coordination will hold her back in the classroom as surely as on the playground. If reporting on children's progress in certain areas is not required, the information is useful for classroom planning; it is invaluable in getting a sense of and planning for a child as a whole.

Items to be assessed should include those that centers, teachers, and parents can and are willing to do something about, that are sensitive to appropriate instruction or amelioration, or that aid in understanding the child or the group. Sometimes there is little teachers can do with information except use it for understanding and social guidance. For instance, a very tall or short youngster may encounter difficulty, but nothing the school can do will change the child's height.

Expected Outcomes of the Program for Individual Children

Assessment should focus on the program's expected outcomes for children. These expectations are found in curriculum guides and documents developed by school districts, state departments of education, organizations and agencies that sponsor educational programs (such as Head Start), professional organizations (such as the National Council of Teachers of Mathematics), and commercial publishers. They may be called "standards," "early learning standards," "essential knowledge and skills," "child outcomes framework," "goals and objectives," or something else altogether. Every state has developed expected outcomes or standards for kindergarten through grade 12. Every state that funds prekindergarten programs has developed such standards for prekindergarten.

As with the documents themselves, the expectations for children may be grouped and labeled in different ways. What one document calls a goal, another may call a standard, and another essential skills and processes. What one calls a performance standard, another may call a performance indicator or objective. There is no one correct method of organizing the large body of knowledge and the great number of skills we expect young children to learn.

As teachers, we have to look beyond the specific labels to the intent, which is to specify what children are expected to learn, and how various aspects of that learning relate to each other. The organization of the expectations helps us see how children can meet broad, general expectations, such as "understands basic concepts of scientific inquiry" or "knows basic facts about society and one's role in it" by achieving smaller components of those expectations day-by-day and week-by-week. The following example shows how this organization and specification works, using an example from language and literacy development.

1. Broadest and most general expected outcomes in a given domain of development and learning (standards, goals, essential knowledge, skills).

    Example standard
    - Uses general reading skills and strategies.

2. More specific expected outcomes (benchmarks, objectives).

    Example benchmarks related to the standard "Uses general reading skills and strategies"
    - Understands the differences between letters, numbers, and words.
    - Knows that print in English is read from left to right, top to bottom, and books are read from front to back.
    - Understands the relationship between written words and spoken language.

3. Intermediate levels of expectations as needed, depending on the complexity of the topic and the expected outcomes.

4. Most specific expected outcomes (knowledge/skill statements, instructional objectives, indicators).

    Example indicators related to the benchmark or objective "Understands the differences between letters, numbers, and words"
    - Identifies a word as a unit of print.
    - Knows that letters and numerals are different.
    - Identifies uppercase and lowercase letters in a grouping of letters and numerals.

    This level of expected outcome is specific enough to observe, to develop instruction for, and to assess.

A *benchmark* is a clear, specific description of knowledge or skill that students should acquire by a specific point in their schooling. It is a "grade-appropriate or developmentally-appropriate expression of knowledge or skill that is more broadly stated in the content standard" (Kendall, p. 2). Although there is inconsistency in how standards and benchmarks are stated, some examples will illustrate their nature.

A science standard states that children should know about "the structure of matter." The benchmark reads that by the end of second grade, students

"know that objects can be described in terms of the materials they are made of (clay, cloth, paper, etc.) and their physical properties (color, size, shape, weight, texture, flexibility, etc.)." (American Association for the Advancement of Science [AAAS], 1993, p. 76)

A physical education standard is that children should achieve and maintain a health-enhancing level of physical fitness. Kindergarten benchmarks state the expectation that children at that level should be able to

- Sustain moderate to vigorous activity for short periods of time.
- Identify the physiological signs of moderate physical activity, such as heavy breathing and fast heart beat. (National Association for Sport and Physical Education, 1995)

There may be several knowledge and skill statements under each benchmark specifying the expectations in greater detail. These are specific enough that teachers should be able to develop assessment strategies to determine what children know and can do.

Figure 3.2 is one way content standards and benchmarks can be used to organize and specify expected outcomes. This example is from prekindergarten language arts.

Some cautions about benchmarks: Benchmarks that use broad age/grade bands, such as K–2, present significant problems for teachers. If you teach second grade, it is clear what the children are supposed to know by the time the year is over. If you teach kindergarten or first grade, the expected outcome for the children that year is much less clear. There need to be guards against inappropriate expectations for the younger children.

Ideally, standards and benchmarks between age and grade levels, such as kindergarten and first grade, align. Expected outcomes stated in general curriculum frameworks should align with specific curriculum materials such as literacy or mathematics programs. They frequently do not, and teachers have to make the adjustments.

Performance Standards.   Performance standards define the levels of learning that are considered satisfactory and suggest ways of gauging the degree to which content standards have been attained (Kendall, 2001; Lewis, 1995; Ravitch, 1995). Performance standards try to answer the question, "How good is good enough?" Changing expectations about what young children can learn, and at what ages, makes judging performance of young children especially difficult. What was "good enough" at one time or in one setting may not be considered adequate in another. Some child outcome statements include performance standards, such as:

Children will be able to name five (or ten, or all) letters of the alphabet.

Children will count to ten (20 . . . 100).

Adequate performance may also be defined as an acceptable score on a test or inventory, or as a certain level on a scoring rubric.

Rubrics identify different levels and qualities of attainment of each benchmark or standard. The following example states the expectation, "converses ef-

Figure 3.2   Examples of Organization of Expected Child Outcomes by Content Standards and Benchmarks
....

Topic: Phonological Awareness

Language Arts

  Standard 8.   Uses listening and speaking strategies for different purposes

    Level Pre-K [Grade Pre-K]

      Benchmark 15.   Discriminates among the sounds of spoken language

      Knowledge/skill statements

        1. Hears and discriminates the sounds of language in the environment

      Benchmark 16.   Knows rhyming sounds and simple rhymes (e.g., identifies rhymes and rhyming sounds)

      Knowledge/skill statements

        1. Knows what a rhyme is

        2. Recognizes matching sounds and rhymes

      Benchmark 17.   Knows that words are made up of sounds (e.g., that words can begin alike, sound alike)

      Knowledge/skill statements

        1. Knows the beginning and ending sounds of words

        2. Knows that different words can begin with the same sound

      Benchmark 18.   Knows that words are made up of syllables

      Knowledge/skill statements

        1. Knows what a syllable is

        2. Discriminates separate syllables in a word

Source: Reprinted by permission of McREL, © 2004. Kendall, J. K., & Marzano, R. J. (2004). *Content knowledge: A compendium of standards and benchmarks for K–12 education.* www.mcrel.org/standards-benchmarks.

fectively" then describes 4 levels of attainment of that outcome. See Chapters 5 and 7 for examples of more general rubrics and suggestions for using them to judge the quality of a child's performance.

Expectation: Converses effectively in his or her home language, English, or sign language for a variety of purposes relating to real experiences and different audiences.

- During discussions, may listen but doesn't express information.
- During discussions, expresses information that is unrelated to the topic or does not participate at all (e.g., during a discussion about a field trip to the pet store, the child talks about his or her new shoes).
- Describes recent experiences that are sometimes (but not consistently) related to the current topic (e.g., during a discussion about a trip to the pet store, the child tells about a dog that was at the park).
- Describes previous experiences and relates them to new events and/or ideas (e.g., during a discussion about a trip to the pet store, the child shares that she bought her fish . . . at a pet store). (New Jersey Department of Education, 2004)

From the General to the Specific.   If expected outcomes are too general, teachers have to make them more specific in order to assess and teach effectively. For example, references to helping children develop concepts of relative location or space are usually found or implied in most outcome statements. If curriculum guides, frameworks, benchmarks, or suggested assessment tasks do not identify the experience, action, or behavior children will do to show their experience and learning, teachers must. Which of the many concepts of location and space should they learn? Which do they already know, and at what level of understanding? What is involved in understanding and using location and space concepts such as "above/below," "over/under," "left/right," "top/bottom"? What can teachers watch and listen for that will reveal children's understanding and use of these complex spatial concepts?

Developing a specific objective that can be taught and assessed involves breaking down general statements of intent into appropriate objectives, then identifying *indicators* of progress toward, or achievement of, those objectives. Then assessment tasks and activities can be identified or devised. Figure 3.3 shows how a desired outcome, "understands concepts of location and space," can be translated into specific items for assessment and teaching.

One of the advantages of performance assessment is that it is flexible and comprehensive enough to assess progress toward achievement of almost any goal or standard, not only knowledge and skills.

Unique Patterns of Development, Knowledge, Attitudes, and Interests

Children and groups often have their own unique "approaches to learning"— attitudes, values, habits, and learning styles that influence what and how they learn. Approaches to learning include "(1) openness to and curiosity about new tasks and challenges; (2) initiative, task persistence and attentiveness; (3) a tendency for reflection and interpretation; (4) imagination and invention; and (5) cognitive styles" (Kagan, Moore, & Bredekamp, 1995, p. 25). Project Spectrum, based on Howard Gardner's theory of multiple intelligences (1985), deliberately identifies children's "distinctive cognitive and stylistic profiles" in language, mathematics, and mechanical, scientific, spatial, physical, musical, and social abilities (Krechevsky, 1991, p. 43). Knowing these individual approaches to learning enables us to use that uniqueness to help children develop and learn.

Interesting topics, themes, and projects motivate children to learn and to integrate and consolidate their learning. Teachers planning a project or theme should assess "this group's" level of knowledge and interest as well as their attitudes, prior experience, and understanding of the topic. Maybe they already know more about the Pilgrims, dinosaurs, or planets than they ever wanted to.

Assess children's strengths as well as needs. Too often we focus on what children can't do, rather than on the many things they do well.

Problems or Concerns about a Particular Child or Group

Teachers often need information on a problem or concern—about a particular child, a small group, or the total group—to give clues for its solution. "Allie is interested in everything but completes nothing." "What is going on in the dramatic play area? Almost everyone used to participate over the course of a few days.

Figure 3.3   Specification of Items to Assess and Teach, and Indicators of Attainment within a Given Developmental/Curriculum Area

Area of Development/ Curriculum	Cognitive development; language; science (Preschool–Primary)
Relational Concepts	Position/location in space; time; size; weight; quantity; volume of sound; speed; texture; temperature
Specific Focus Concept	Relative location or position in space
Specific Learnings	*Concepts to be developed:* in front of/behind (in back of); beside/next to/between/in the middle; under/over; above/below; front/back; in/out, into/out of, inside/ outside; top/bottom; up/down/upside down; on/off; near/far; first/last; left/right—own body, then projective; others

Ways and levels of knowing:
- Experience
- Experience linked with words (Look, you put this block on the top.)
- Comprehends (place; point to; hand me . . .)
- Recognizes (Is Tran behind you or in front of you?)
- States location (Tell us where you're going to sit.)
- States and uses concepts in new situations
- Uses words and concepts spontaneously and functionally
- Understands relational aspects of position in space
- Understands that position in space is sometimes relative, sometimes not (top of head is always top of head; top of a blank sheet of paper is determined by position)
- Is able to shift perspective and viewpoint physically and mentally
- Understands and states concept of overlapping position (e.g., playground equipment is outside school, but inside fence)

Now Danielle, Monica, and Latasha seem to have taken over." "Jordan talks all the time, but never seems to read or write anything." "I don't like what's happening in our opening class meeting. Instead of thoughtfully planning what they are going to do, the children just say the first thing they think of."

If the problem is clearly an individual one, there is no need to assess the whole class. Focus on the child. However, remember that many things influence what a child does. Often we have to look beyond an individual or group to the physical environment, scheduling, available materials, and other children and adults to find the sources of a problem.

Indications of a developmental "red flag"—is something wrong?—call for gathering more information. Be alert for and document concerns so children who need help can receive it as soon as possible (see Appendix B).

Practical Considerations

Practical considerations influence classroom assessment. These include the number and type of assessments that are required, the balance between recorded and unrecorded information, teaching load, age of children, years of teaching experience, and selection of relevant items to assess. Given the situation in this classroom, this school, this program, what is possible?

Required Assessments.   Teachers have to plan for, and usually administer, any assessments that are required by the school or center. Usually these have to be done during a designated time period, such as during the first or last month of school.

Balance of Recorded and Unrecorded Information.   It is neither possible nor desirable for teachers to record everything. Teachers often assess, then use the information immediately to adjust interactive teaching, shorten or lengthen the time spent in an activity, or guide a child's social interaction.

Other information helps them develop a sense of the child's personality and style over a longer period of time. Much of this is never written, nor is there any need for it to be. However, teachers could keep better track of children's learning if they recorded more. Throughout this book are suggestions for ways to achieve a balance that enhances both assessment and teaching.

Teaching Load.   Class size, adult-to-child ratio, available classroom and clerical assistance, hours per day and week teachers are with children, number of classes a teacher has, number of hours and quality of aide and volunteer assistance, length and placement in the day of planning time, availability of assistance for special needs children, and other factors over which teachers have little control influence the teaching load and the amount and quality of assessment it is possible to do. However, a lighter teaching load does not necessarily mean better assessment. One kindergarten teacher described a comprehensive system of record keeping and explained the reason for it: "I teach two classes of over 25 children each, every day. I have to have good records to keep track of 50-plus children."

Age and Development of Children.   Although teachers always have final responsibility for assessment, children's abilities to record what they have done, select and file their own papers and materials, and self-assess and self-reflect vary with age, development, and prior experience.

Teaching Experience.   A teacher who is still learning how to teach cannot be expected to incorporate systematic assessment into the classroom as easily as one who has taught for several years, has gained confidence and proficiency, and is ready to take on a new challenge.

Expected Outcomes.   If statements of standards, goals, and objectives resemble either idealistic wishes or a shopping list of all possible items, try to determine more realistic expectations. Check with experienced teachers and an administrator. Review reporting instruments—progress letters, report cards, sample portfolios, or other progress reports—to find indications that some objectives are emphasized more than others. They may show items that are not mentioned in objectives, such as the ability to get along with other children, attention span, self-regulation, or work habits. Start with priority expectations: items that are simple, developmentally on target, and related to immediate teaching decisions.

If program objectives are overwhelmingly specific and discrete—perhaps listing all the names of body parts, animals, means of transportation, or nursery rhymes that children might know—try grouping them into logical categories that can be assessed and taught together. Use an integrated curriculum to reach many goals simultaneously. Assess and teach the items to reach broad goals, such as classifying, comparing, seeing relationships, or solving problems.

Representativeness, Significance, and Authenticity of Assessment Items. Select items that are significant and worthwhile in and of themselves or because they stand for a group of other items. For example, many items on readiness inventories bear little relationship to the skills and understandings required in reading. They may or may not be important, but new knowledge and new conceptions of how children learn to read and write have made them obsolete (Snow, Burns, & Griffin, 1998; Sulzby, 1990).

In classroom assessment we can often find out what we need to know directly, rather than through a test or performance task that stands for a whole class of other items. To find out if a child can use classroom tools—crayons, scissors, chalk, paintbrushes, and pencils—assess those skills directly and authentically.

Astute sampling is often appropriate. Children don't have to perform every large muscle task of strength, coordination, and endurance; representative ones may suffice.

When to Assess?

Ideally, a plan for when to do different types of appraisal will be in place before the school year begins. The plan may be modified by the realities of classroom life, lack of time, or unexpected external requirements, but it will provide a time frame for assessment (see Chapter 9).

When assessment is done influences the type of information gathering and recording you will do. Initial "sizing up" (Airasian, 2001; Gage & Berliner, 1998) calls for efficient procedures, such as sensitive group observation, checklists, written parent reports, and child-generated performance samples. Ongoing assessment allows greater depth, using procedures that may take more time, such as recording observations through short narrative records or participation charts. Figure 3.4 summarizes when teachers carry out three types of assessment.

Before the School Year Starts

Do as much as possible before the school year starts. Determine school and center expectations. If tests or other information-gathering procedures are required, find out what they are and when they are scheduled. Mark the dates on a master planning calendar. Learn about reporting expectations. If parent conferences are at set times, schedule those times, because you will need to summarize information, review portfolios, and prepare for reporting. Organize filing and record-keeping systems (see Chapters 6 and 9). Study existing records, information from

Figure 3.4   Timing of Assessment

Before the School Year Starts	Determine expectations Organize filing and record-keeping systems Study existing records Study information from parents Study materials from previous years Review assessment measures you have used in previous years
During the School Year	Initial ("sizing-up") assessments Continuous appraisals Periodic assessment Before-and-after themes of study or projects As needed to address specific concerns As mandated Portfolios (Chapter 6)
During the School Year, outside of Class Time	Summaries (Chapter 6) Profiles (Chapter 6) Portfolios (Chapter 6)

parents, and transition materials from previous programs. If tradition, time, and resources permit, visit children's homes.

Make tentative plans for the different times you will be gathering information: required assessment; ongoing, continuous appraisals integrated with teaching and learning; periodic ones, including initial, interim, and final summaries and assessments; assessments before and after major units of study, themes, projects, or investigations; and "as needed" to address specific problems or concerns. Teachers collect different information, using different procedures, at these times. They also make assessment serve two purposes, such as when a major project or unit of study coincides with the end of a reporting period.

Assess to Fulfill Requirements

The number and type of tests and assessments that are required will vary depending on the age and grade level of the children, what entity funds and regulates the program, current laws and regulations, and school and community traditions. When they are given will also vary.

Assess Day by Day

"Assessments make the most sense if they occur on an ongoing basis as particular skills and content are being learned" (Shepard, Kagan, & Wurtz, 1998, p. 7). Good teachers continuously appraise children and revise procedures and interactions accordingly. A teacher does not have to stop being a teacher to gather and record data. In fact, some of the best and most useful information is obtained while a teacher is taking dictation from a child; listening to a child read a story he has written; assisting with paints, papers, or modeling clay; helping with math story problems; conversing during snacks; leading a discussion; guiding playground activities; or working with manipulatives. Assessment is embedded in the interactive processes of teaching. For instance, Mr. Sena lays out the beginning of a pattern of rods of differing lengths for Tui, to see if she can discern and continue the pattern. She does not perceive the pattern he started, but does continue the line of rods across the table. When Tui has finished, Mr. Sena lays out another, much simpler pattern for her, bringing the task closer to her level. For Cecile, sitting beside Tui, he may increase the difficulty of the pattern, because she so clearly enjoys studying and mastering the complex and varied patterns Mr. Sena starts for her. Sketches and notes about the children's work go in the files. Just as important, Mr. Sena immediately integrates the information into his interactions with the children and makes written or mental notes about future ways to help children grasp the concept of pattern based on today's appraisal.

Let's look at another example of integrating assessment and learning. Miss Gardner is helping her primary pupils with cooperative learning processes. Today she'll be surveying "sharing ideas and materials" and moves among the groups with a recording sheet. Such an approach tells little about the children's abilities to use that skill in other settings, but it tells her a lot about whether the children have the skill and can use it or whether she needs to reteach and review. Ongoing observation may increase children's motivation to practice and master the skill, because knowing something is important enough to observe and document may enhance its value to the learner. Miss Gardner also has the groups briefly evaluate their own cooperative work, naming and documenting two things they did well and one thing they need to do better (Johnson, Johnson, Holubec, & Roy, 1984).

Assess Periodically

If continuous assessment is done conscientiously, there may be little need for additional data gathering; summarizing existing documentation may be sufficient. However, focused initial, interim, and final assessments on one or more goals in developmental or curriculum areas sometimes are required. This does not imply the need for testing or for stopping other activities to "assess." Rather, the focused information gathering takes place as part of classroom activities. Over several days, children may demonstrate their abilities to solve measurement problems in mathematics and science or represent ideas through art and construction.

Initial assessment occurs when a new group, part of a group, or a new child begins. It yields information on a child's or a group's initial status—ability, attitudes and dispositions, prior knowledge and understanding, and skills and habits in relation to what the school or center emphasizes—to provide basic information for planning classroom activities and experiences. This initial reading or sizing up (Airasian, 2000; Gage & Berliner, 1998) should be done as soon as possible, but held tentatively, as all first impressions should be. Interim assessments are usually done halfway, or one-third and two-thirds of the way through the time the children are in the classroom. If children begin in September, a January or February "How are we doing?" allows for midcourse correction. Final assessment is done toward the end of a group's time with a particular teacher or teachers. It is a summing up before a youngster moves on to another teacher, unit, or school.

Centers and schools with nontraditional yearly schedules—year-round schools or child care centers, and child development centers or preschools that operate for a relatively short time—modify assessment times to fit their schedule.

Assess Before and After a Concentrated Emphasis

Assess before making final plans for any sustained unit, project, or topic, and again at its conclusion. Determine what children already know and can do, and consider their thinking and reasoning in relation to whatever is being planned. At the conclusion, summarize assessment information collected during the project, and, if necessary, look again to determine what children have learned, in what ways they have developed, and what continuation activities are needed.

Appraise children's interests, attitudes, and level of understanding of the essential elements of the topic, which may be quite different from recall knowledge. Consider what concepts the children hold about the topic and how it relates to other learnings. Look at the pattern of errors and the size of the gap between "where they are" and "where they are to go."

Let's look at one way to appraise before beginning a unit of study, theme, or project. Concept "webbing" or "mapping" is often recommended as a way for teachers to organize the concepts and relationships in a topic (Katz & Chard, 1989). It can also be used to assess how children organize their thinking, which is equally important for teachers to know.

Mr. Waner is planning an integrated unit on insects to work toward district standards in science, reading, writing, and mathematics in his combined first and second-grade class. He brings to class insects in a terrarium and colorful insect posters and books. He and the assistant observe and note what the children do: who approaches; who avoids; who asks what questions; which children say, "Yuck, I hate bugs"; which display considerable prior knowledge; and other indicators of interest, attitude, and knowledge. Such an approach allows him to do a preliminary appraisal of how suitable the topic is for this group. After several days of informal observation and recording, Mr. Waner plans a class discussion to find out what the children can say about insects and what they would like to learn.

As discussion proceeds and the chart develops, Mr. Waner begins to have a good idea of the current knowledge, attitudes, and interests of this group and its individual members, including a wealth of misconceptions and negative attitudes. He may or may not note names beside children's contributions on the chart. He'll play the tape after class to fill in contributions and nuances of expression he may have missed.

Only after Mr. Waner has studied his previous notes and information from the class discussion will he make a decision about how to approach a project on insects. He may decide to proceed with the full group, paying special attention to children's feelings and attitudes. He may decide to scale back, letting those children with a special interest conduct their own investigation, and plan to desensitize and give positive experiences to the fearful ones. He may do something else with the insect topic. What he will *not* do is proceed with the plans laid out in the "suggested unit" or the topic of study he developed in science methods class. He will adjust, modify, and shape planning based on his assessment of the children's knowledge about and attitudes toward insects.

Assess to Get Information about a Specific Problem or Concern

Concerns about specific children, a subgroup, or the total group don't always correspond to units of study or reporting periods, nor is continuous assessment always adequate for problem solving. Regardless of whether it fits the "assessment schedule," take a closer look as needed. Suppose a usually attentive, interested second-grader becomes restless, inattentive, and aggressive or anxious and clingy. If illness is not the cause, turn to other sources for information to shed light on this unusual behavior and ways to help the youngster. Problems outside the classroom, such as parental separation, death, divorce, job loss, moving, a birth in the family, and innumerable others may influence children's behavior. Simply observing the child won't give you the necessary information.

Children who move frequently from one school or center to another present a special problem. If adequate records are sent with them, continue from there. More often, children come with minimum enrollment information. Integrating them into the life of the classroom is top priority. What you can assess depends on when children enter and how long they stay. When children leave your classroom, try to send a file with something of value in it to inform the next teacher.

Some Final Thoughts

Although we have teased apart aspects of classroom assessment and curriculum for study and discussion, in the classroom there is no such distinction. They are merged. Questions of why, what, when, and how to assess are also closely related. Assessment is not an invariant linear or time-bound sequence in which you do the first step at the beginning of the year and the last one at the end of the year. On the contrary, information collected early in the year may result in immediate program modifications. Ongoing continuous assessment keeps teachers and the program sensitive and responsive to children. A teacher may quickly "size up" (collect data on) a particular situation, understand its meaning, and use the information on the spot. For example, a sensitive teacher leading a group discussion may see and hear the children whispering, nudging each other, yawning, playing with a neighbor's hair, or making faces at someone across the circle. She collects this information (actually, it forces itself on her), understands its meaning to be "this group discussion is off-target," and uses that interpretation as a signal to switch to something more appropriate. Another teacher reading a counting book to a small group of children finds that when he asks, "How many balloons does the clown have?" the children either simply sit, or say, "Blue and red." He collects enough information to confirm his suspicions that they either don't know what "how many" means or don't know how to count, and switches his request to one that helps them learn both things: "Let's count together to see how many balloons the clown has." This is assessment to enhance development and learning at its best.

Summary

Thinking about assessment as a series of decisions helps simplify a complicated process. Basic decisions pertain to why, what, and when to assess. Teachers also decide how to collect and record information and how to organize, summarize, interpret, and use it. This chapter focused on basic decisions—why, what, and when.

Assessment helps determine children's status and progress in growth, development, and learning. This information is used to guide classroom program planning and decision making, to identify children who might benefit from special help, and to collect and document information for reporting and communicating to parents and children; other professionals; and funding, regulatory, and advisory groups. Decisions about what to assess may be influenced by the need for information from major developmental domains, the expected outcomes of the program, the need to know something about the uniqueness of each child, classroom or individual problems or concerns, and practical considerations.

The timing of assessment determines much of its utility, so a tentative plan should be in place and preliminary tasks done before school starts. Different types of appraisal take place at different times. Continuous assessment is integrated with ongoing classroom activities. Periodic assessment or summarizing existing information takes place initially, midway, and for a final "summing up." Focused appraisals take place before and after a concentrated curriculum emphasis or when the need for specific information exists. Assess as needed to study a problem or concern.

For Personal Reflection

1. Teaching experience is a practical consideration in making assessment decisions. Appraise your own teaching experience. In what ways might the amount and type of your experience influence the assessment decisions you make?

2. Assessment can help you discover children's unique "approaches to learning." If teachers looked at your attitudes, values, habits, and learning styles as an adult learner, what do you hope they would find and take into account?

For Further Study and Discussion

1. Secure samples of the report cards or progress reports for parents that local school districts use. Analyze these for (a) likenesses and differences in type of reporting, (b) guidance they might give a teacher about what should be assessed, and (c) balance and comprehensiveness of the curriculum.

2. Interview the teacher of a neighborhood school or center to find out what assessment of children is done (a) in his or her classroom and (b) throughout the school. (If you are already teaching, interview a teacher from another type of school.) In what ways is the information used? When does the teacher assess? Combine what you find out with that of other students to see if there are any likenesses, differences, or general conclusions you might draw.

3. The kindergarten teacher at Hillside Elementary, a 25-year veteran teacher, organizes the reading portion of the kindergarten curriculum around a simple approach—letters of the alphabet. The first full week is "A" week, and so on. Evaluate this approach from the standpoint of assessment.

Suggested Readings

Airasian, P. W. (2000). *Assessment in the classroom: A concise approach* (2nd ed.). Boston: McGraw-Hill.

Herman, J. L., Aschbacher, P. R., & Winters, L. (1992). *A practical guide to alternative assessment.* Alexandria, VA: Association for Supervision and Curriculum Development.

Morrow, L. M., & Smith, J. K. (Eds.). (1990). *Assessment for instruction in early literacy.* Englewood Cliffs, NJ: Prentice Hall.

National Association for the Education of Young Children & National Association of Early Childhood Specialists of State Departments of Education. (1991). Guidelines for appropriate curriculum content and assessment in programs serving children ages 3 through 8. *Young Children, 46,* 21–38.

Schickedanz, J. A., Schickedanz, D. I., Forsyth, P. D., and Forsyth, G. A. (2001). *Understanding children* (4th ed.). Boston: Allyn & Bacon.

Shepard, L. A., Kagan, S. L., & Wurtz, E. (Eds.). (1998). *Principles and recommendations for early childhood assessments.* Washington, DC: National Educational Goals Panel.

Shore, R., Bodrova, E., & Leong, D. (Issue 5/March 2004). Child outcome standards in pre-K programs: What are standards; What is needed to make them work. *Preschool Policy Matters.* Available online at www.nieer.org.

CHAPTER 4

Documenting: Collecting Information

One way to improve assessment of children is to use "multiple measures" or "windows." Tests alone, teacher observations alone, children's work alone, or any other assessment data alone do not yield reliable and adequate information. When important decisions are being contemplated, such as formation of work and play groups, referral for a possible developmental problem, reporting to parents, or action for a behavioral concern, multiple measures should be used. The assessment data, or evidence, that teachers use to guide day-to-day planning and interaction with children can be less rigorous, because such plans can be changed (Shepard, Kagan, & Wurtz, 1998). Even there, a second look from another perspective may reveal strengths or needs not always apparent from one measure. In addition, regular early childhood educators are expected to be active participants in assessing and planning for special needs and high-risk children, where multiple measures are required (CEC, 2005; Taylor, 2000). Chapter 4 explains how to document using multiple sources and procedures in varying contexts—how to open "multiple windows."

Chapters 4 and 5 draw another essential distinction between two interrelated but separate processes: collecting information and recording information.

Collecting and recording are often thought of as the same. Ask teachers how they find out about children's progress, and you may get an answer such as "We have a checklist," or "Anecdotal records." Checklists and anecdotal records record and preserve information. They are records, not ways of collecting information. Information was collected using systematic observation or watching what children did. Keep these two steps separate to open up options both for learning about children and for recording what you discover.

There are many ways of obtaining information about children and as many ways of recording that information. Teachers are free to mix and match these methods as appropriate. Information can be recorded several ways. An observation of problem-solving strategies can be recorded either on an anecdotal record or a rubric. Information collected in different ways can be documented with the same recording technique. A checklist could record reasoning strategies observed in a cooperative science project, elicited by teacher questions, or reported by a child after building with blocks.

This chapter focuses only on collecting information, not recording it. Consult Chapter 5 for the recording process.

Multiple Windows

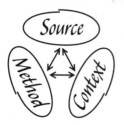

Teachers gather information about children through many "windows"—combinations of sources, methods, and contexts. Think of a house with many windows looking out on a panoramic view. To see the entire panorama, you must look through each window because each includes and excludes part of the view. From one window you see the mountains but miss the lake. From another, you see only part of the lake but get a good view of the meadow. It is the same with assessment. Different ways of finding out yield distinct pictures or pieces of information. No one source of information tells everything. One method reveals aspects of a child's behavior that another does not. One context facilitates certain behaviors whereas another does not. Journals, dictation, stories, conversations with other children, responses to questions from adults, and wordplay provide indications of and evidence about a child's language development. If a journal is the only source of information, the picture of language capabilities is incomplete.

In addition, one window or measure "is likely to provide a less valid estimate of a student's achievement than is some combination" (Gage & Berliner, 1998, p. 654). Any single assessment is an estimate of a child's or group's status and is not an exact indication of performance (Airasian, 2001). Using multiple windows results in better and more complete information about children (NAEYC/NAECS/SDE, 2003) and increases reliability and representativeness (Cronbach, 1990). It frees teachers from the rigidity imposed by overreliance on one approach and decreases the possibility for errors. Three aspects of classroom assessment can be varied to provide multiple windows or perspectives—multiple measures:

1. The source of information—the child, other children, parents, specialists, other adults, or records about children
2. The method of obtaining information—systematically observing, eliciting responses from children, collecting products from classroom activities, or eliciting information from parents and other adults

3. The context, setting, or situation for the appraisal—outdoors or indoors, at a desk or on the floor, in the classroom or a testing room, using paper and pencil or manipulative materials, alone or in groups, or with familiar classroom staff or strangers (see Figure 4.1)

Sources of Information

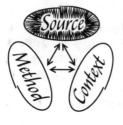

The source of information refers to who or what provides information about children. The primary sources are the child; parents, specialists, classroom assistants and volunteers, and other adults; and records from other teachers, specialists, or other sources. Sources provide information directly from children or indirectly through the eyes of other people. Both serve important purposes and, together, give a diverse, well-rounded picture of a child. Assess the variety of Jeremy's fine motor skills by asking him to fold napkins at snack time; by listening to his gleeful report of tying his shoe; by watching him build with Mary and Tony; by noting when his dad says, "Jeremy helped string snow peas for dinner"; and by reviewing records in which Jeremy's previous teacher recorded that he can use scissors. Each source presents distinct, valuable information about Jeremy.

The Child as a Source of Information

The most authentic and direct way of obtaining information is by watching, analyzing the work of, talking with, and listening to *that child.* Assessing a child functioning in a group yields information about the child and the group available in no other way.

Opportunities for obtaining information from children occur as natural outcomes of day-to-day classroom interaction. After reading a story about friendships, a teacher discusses it with a small group of children and later records their conceptions of "a friend." A child's construction with math manipulatives reflects a sense of number and pattern. Activities in which children cooperate, talking and explaining their thinking as they work and play, offer rich assessment opportunities.

Figure 4.1 Multiple Assessment Measures

Multiple Assessment Measures

Sources	Child/Children
	Other adults
	Records
Methods	Observe children
	Elicit responses from children (discuss, question, interview)
	Collect products
	Elicit information from other adults
Contexts	Any classroom activity
	Any school or center activity
	Routines of daily living

Children volunteer information about their own activities, making comments about what they like and dislike and what they understand. Sometimes these self-reports are unprompted and unsolicited: "I've done this before," or "I have one like this at home," or "I know how to do this." At other times children respond to questions: "What would you like to learn about tornadoes?" "What is the most interesting thing you have done this week?" "What do you know about Martin Luther King, Jr.?" Self-assessments convey the child's self-image as a learner. Even though young children may have difficulty articulating or demonstrating internal thought processes and feelings, their reports reveal information difficult to obtain in any other way.

Parents and Other Adults as a Source of Information

Other people—parents, specialists, teachers, aides, and other school personnel— are an indirect source of information about child behavior.

Insights from other people, particularly parents, improve and deepen a teacher's understanding of a child. Meimei seldom talks in school and never participates in singing or fingerplays during group time. The teacher learns something important when parents report, "When Meimei comes home from school she tells us everything she did. She sings the songs and chants the words to all of the fingerplays." Children may not display their most mature behavior at school, or they may reveal a different side of their personality to a particular teacher.

Parents provide a special perspective. They have known their children better and longer than anyone else. They have information about events occurring at home that might affect a child's behavior in the classroom. They may see a side of the child that is not revealed at school. Parents provide insights about home culture and home/school differences that are essential for teachers in today's multiethnic, multicultural classroom.

Other teachers or aides may observe a "different" child because they supervise other activities or have a unique relationship with a child. For instance, a child who is quiet and subdued during any reading activities or journal writing may be a full participant on the playground during free play, leading other children in rough-and-tumble games. The playground supervisor has a different perspective than the reading teacher.

Teachers obtain information from other professionals, including speech and language specialists, nurses, and psychologists. By working together, participating in formal meetings and staffings, and reading records, teachers gain important additional insights. Observations of a child by different staff members in different contexts and at different times provide a rich multidisciplinary perspective on a specific child (Hills, 1992).

Records as a Source of Information

Records include attendance records, intake records, health and school history records, progress reports, report cards, narrative reports from previous teachers, inventories, checklists, parent questionnaires, and results of standardized tests. Some programs archive a cumulative portfolio that documents growth year after year (Hebert, 1998). The type, quality, and quantity of information in records depends on the program's policies and procedures.

Some teachers choose *not* to look at records until they know a child and have made their own assessment. Others regard records as important background in knowing children's prior experiences. The "don't look at the records" approach has several drawbacks. The transfer of records is one way to help children make a smooth transition from one setting or grade to another (Love & Yelton, 1989). A professional teacher should be able to weigh such information against other evidence, regard it as tentative, and combine it with other information and perceptions to assess a child quickly and accurately. Other people's insights and knowledge can augment a teacher's, if only because there is disagreement. Previous accomplishments are not forgotten and the continuity of learning is reinforced. Children frequently move from one school to another and one community to another. It is not fair to children or parents to have to start totally anew in each setting. Finally, time, money, and energy are invested in screening, diagnostic, achievement, and health tests and in other records. They should be used.

Methods of Collecting Information

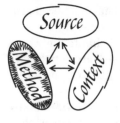

The method of assessment is the "how" or way information is gathered; it can be formal or informal (Goodwin & Driscoll, 1980). Formal methods are usually research instruments, clinical techniques, or standardized tests such as screening or achievement tests with limited uses in classrooms. Although they may yield useful information, formal methods require the teacher to have special knowledge and expertise for correct interpretation. Informal methods involve normal classroom activities and are directly relevant to classroom decision making and keeping track of progress toward developmental goals.

There are many informal methods to obtain information about children. This section covers four major ones: observing children, eliciting responses from children, collecting products from classroom activities, and eliciting information from parents.

Observe Children Systematically

The most common way of gathering information about children is watching and listening to them. All teachers, of course, observe the children with whom they work. Some observation is routine and informal—Eseme got a haircut; Omar spent most of the time playing with blocks. Some is intuitive or "sensed"—the children are losing interest; Brad is tired. But there is a type of observation that is systematic, focused, and used for collecting information. Teachers cannot take in everything happening with a group of 15 to 20 children. Simply looking does not guarantee *seeing*. Attention must be directed to a child, a particular pattern of behavior, a situation or problem, or progress toward an identified goal. This kind of observation is called "systematic observation."

Systematic Observation

STRENGTHS

- Children do not have to read and write to be assessed.
- Children can be minimally aware that their behavior is observed.
- Classroom routines and activities do not have to be changed.
- Children are assessed in the setting relevant to the event.

- It is the most direct and valid way to obtain information about some behavior. For example, a teacher must watch and listen to children interacting to find out how they negotiate taking turns.

LIMITATIONS

- Some important aspects of development, such as attitudes, values, and other mental processes, cannot be assessed by observing behavior.
- Systematic observation requires focused attention and is difficult to do while interacting with children.
- Personal elements that may color an observer's perceptions can never be completely eliminated.

Guides for Systematic Observation

Be unobtrusive. Select a place that allows full view and hearing but does not interfere with what you are trying to observe.

Be as objective as possible. There are many suggestions for increasing objectivity in Chapters 2 and 9.

Focus observation on a specific child, behavior, situation, concern, or identified goal. It is not possible to see everything at once.

Observe verbal and nonverbal behavior. Listen for verbal behavior—the actual words said and the way they are said, including intonation, enunciation, and pronunciation. Simultaneously, watch nonverbal behavior such as body stance and movement, motor responses, gestures, and facial expressions.

Suspend judgments, conclusions, and other interpretations of meaning until after observation.

Elicit Responses from Children

Teachers and children converse, discuss activities, and exchange questions and answers in daily classroom interaction and assessment. Teachers save time by focusing on needed information in a direct request to a child instead of waiting for spontaneous evidence. Teachers can also use instructional conversations or dialogues to explore children's thinking processes, problem-solving strategies, reasoning, and concerns about almost anything (Berliner, 1987; Ginsburg, 1997).

Alternative assessment has added several specific assessment approaches to traditional oral and written responses to adult prompts. These include performance assessment, dynamic assessment, interviews, conferences, and discussions. A brief description of each of these is given in the section that follows. Teachers seldom have time to conduct in-depth interviews with individual children. However, they can incorporate many interview techniques into instructional conversations and dialogues. For instance, teachers can probe the thinking behind a child's responses, or help determine what a youngster can do with assistance. In all "instructional conversations" or "instructional dialogues," especially those being used for assessment, teachers must give careful thought to the questions or statements they use and what they expect children to do. Sometimes the most important question is not the initial one, but the follow-up to a child's response. Guides for developing appropriate questions, prompts, and expectations conclude this section.

Performance Assessment. *Performance assessments* allow pupils to demonstrate what they know and can do in a real-life situation. They reflect the recent emphasis on real-world problem solving (Airasian, 2000). To see if children can solve a problem, the teacher asks them to solve one. The children may count to determine "how many" will be needed if each child gets one, or as part of a game (Kamii, 1990). They may read books and write about them to demonstrate literacy. Performance assessment can focus either on a process (such as oral reading) or a product (such as a piece of writing), or both. For example, a first-grade teacher can assess both writing process and product. He first observes a pupil writing and notes how the child holds and manipulates the pencil, positions the paper, and sits; then he judges the written product's letter formation, legibility, and spacing.

Early education teachers rely heavily on performance assessment because of young children's limited communication skills. Teachers may observe and assess naturally occurring behavior or set up structured performances (Airasian, 2000).

Dynamic Assessment. *Dynamic assessment* is a specific way of eliciting information from children, using Lev S. Vygotsky's concept of the Zone of Proximal Development (ZPD) (1978). Instead of seeing a child's performance as only what the child can do independently, dynamic assessment probes skills that are on the verge of emergence; they can be tapped as teacher and child interact. Teachers try to identify learning strategies a child already uses as well as instructional processes most likely to promote future learning (Berk & Winsler, 1995; Lidz, 2003). The hints, prompts, cues, and questions the teacher uses are recorded along with the child's responses. Examining the assistance that makes a difference in the child's ability to perform a task tells about the child's current level of understanding and skill and gives direction for future teaching. Dynamic assessment provides information at both levels of the ZPD: the lower, or unassisted, level and the upper, or maximally assisted, level. It integrates assessment with responsive teaching. According to Shepard (2000),

> This type of interactive assessment, which allows teachers to provide assistance as part of assessment, does more than help teachers gain valuable insights about how understanding might be extended. It also creates perfectly targeted occasions to teach and provides the means to scaffold next steps. (p. 10)

Melissa is at the beginning stages of learning about the sound–symbol relationship. Ms. Mansfield and Melissa look at a picture of a horse in a meadow with "horse" written underneath. Ms. Mansfield points to the word. Melissa looks at her expectantly. "I wonder what this word is," Ms. Mansfield says. "Sun," replies Melissa, looking at the sun in the picture. "This word starts with an . . . ," prompts the teacher. "H . . . is it tree? Pony?" asks Melissa. "H. . . . ," prompts the teacher. "Oh, horse," says Melissa. Ms. Mansfield notes that Melissa uses picture cues to try to read, doesn't connect the sound of *H* to the word without prompting, but once prompted, thinks of a word that both makes sense and has that beginning sound. By prompting with *H,* Ms. Mansfield exposed more knowledge about the sound–symbol relationship than she would have if she had just stopped at the child's response to "I wonder what this word says," or "This word starts with an. . . ."

Using a developmental continuum or a sequence of the likely next steps in learning as a guide, teachers plan prompts and hints to provide assistance as the child needs it. Assistance can be with specific skills and knowledge, or with broader strategies such as problem solving and seeing relationships (Bodrova & Leong, 2001a).

Interviews, Conferences, and Discussions.   *Interviews, conferences,* and *discussions* are other ways to elicit information. An interview usually involves a planned sequence of questions; a conference implies discussion, with teacher and pupil sharing ideas. Interviews can be conducted on almost any subject and at any level of complexity, but they lend themselves to open-ended and varied questions. "What are some things that are easy for you to do?" "What did you like about our field trip?" or "Explain your thinking" are queries that reveal unique approaches to learning and insight into individuals. They also help children learn how to give extended responses to an adult.

Conferences are usually conducted in relation to work a child has done, such as writing, science, or mathematics, but they are appropriate for almost any topic. Teacher and child discuss the work, each one contributing insights and suggestions. Conferences can reveal pupils' level of understanding and confidence (Stenmark, 1991). They are widely used in helping pupils analyze and reflect on their own work.

Eliciting Responses from Children

STRENGTHS

- Eliciting responses focuses both teacher and child on a specific behavior. Instead of waiting until a child spontaneously says, "That is the letter *J,*" teachers save time by asking.
- It is a more effective and reliable means of checking understanding than using incidental, nonverbal cues (Berliner, 1987).
- It can probe the level of a child's understanding, clarify answers, identify misconceptions, and help children learn and demonstrate complex thinking skills.
- Dynamic assessment integrates assessment with teaching and points the way to effective scaffolding of a child's learning.
- Interviews, conferences, and discussions can give insight into children's feelings and attitudes as well as into their knowledge and thinking processes.
- For children who read and write, eliciting responses through informal classroom tests provides information directly linked to classroom activities.

LIMITATIONS

- If a child does not respond, you do not know that she *could* not, only that she *did* not.
- A child's response may reflect social factors, not "knowledge." Cultural differences in adult–child interaction between the home and school may influence responses. Children who have difficulty answering may lose self-confidence and fail to respond although they know the answer. A child may guess or answer what she or he thinks the teacher wants to hear.
- The way a question is framed influences responses. Children may not know how to respond to confusing or misleading questions.
- Unless sensitively done, questioning may be perceived by children as drill or a recitation session.

Guides for Eliciting Responses from Children

Construct oral or written response prompts (questions, requests, statements) to elicit the desired level of performance. Teachers ask questions; make requests, statements, and suggestions; give directions, hints, and clues; present tasks or problems; and give nonverbal cues to elicit responses from children. The wording and form of these prompts determine the response. For instance, assessment questions frequently call for a factual, one-word or limited-word response. "What is the name of this animal?" "Where did the children in the story go?" "What happened after. . . ." Prompts that encourage children to combine, apply, and evaluate what they know will reveal and encourage complex thinking. Prompts that encourage children to *construct* responses, to say, write, graph, draw, or otherwise demonstrate what they know are appropriate as soon as youngsters have the necessary knowledge and skill. The following distinctions will help you target prompts to the level of response you want:

- *Recognition versus recall response levels.* Asking the child to choose the correct answer from an array taps *recognition:* "Is this one bigger or smaller than this one?" "What do we call the animal we saw on our walk—a squirrel or a chipmunk?" At the *recall* level, children must give the correct answer without the benefit of alternatives to choose from, as in "What is two plus two?" or "Who is this book about?" Children, like adults, are usually able to recognize information before they can recall it (Berk, 2006; Bukatko & Daehler, 1992; Steinberg & Belsky, 1991).

- *Receptive versus expressive response levels.* Requests at the *receptive level* call for a motor response, such as "Point to a circle" or "Go around the tree, and then up the ladder." *Expressive-level* questions and statements direct children to express, produce, or state ideas in words, such as "Tell me the name of this shape." Generally, receptive-level questions are easier to answer than expressive-level questions.

- *Convergent versus divergent response levels.* *Convergent questions or statements* request a specific verbal or nonverbal response and have correct answers: "What color is this?" "If I had two apples and I gave you one, how many would be left?" "Put this animal next to his home." "Mavis, show me you can climb this ladder!" "Point to the *L.*" "Write your name right here." *Divergent questions or statements* are appropriate when eliciting a child's opinion, thoughts, reasoning, or feelings; they do not have specific correct answers. "As you read, think of some reasons the animals in this story try to solve their problem in different ways. We'll discuss these reasons when you finish." "What did you like about our trip to the zoo?" "Help me think—what are some ideas we could have in a story about a bear?" Divergent questions or statements are phrased to indicate that several answers or responses are appropriate.

- *Levels of cognitive complexity.* Bloom's Taxonomy (Bloom, Englehart, Furst, Hill, & Krathwhol, 1956) suggests levels of cognitive complexity that are helpful in selecting questions and statements. The taxonomy lists cognitive processes in order of increasing complexity (see Figure 4.2). The levels beyond knowledge are the complex thinking and reasoning abilities alternative assessment can tap (Herman, Aschbacher, & Winters, 1992).

Determine how children will respond. Teachers can request an individual response—one child at a time—or a group response—all children together. Responses can be verbal, nonverbal, or written. A verbal response would be saying the answer aloud. Nonverbal responses are any motor action or physical re-

Figure 4.2   Levels of Cognitive Complexity

....

Knowledge. The ability to recall, remember, or recognize an idea or fact. "What is the name of this shape?" "Point to the letter *B.*"

Comprehension. The ability to translate or explain in your own words. "Explain in your own words what a mammal is." "Tell me the names of some things having a *circle* shape."

Application. The ability to use information, applying it to new situations and real-life circumstances. "Use your math skills to divide up this pizza." "Use your reading skills to figure out which of these words rhymes with *look.*"

Analysis. The ability to break information into parts. "Compare a tiger to a pet cat." "What is the difference between a triangle and a square?" "What information do you need to solve this problem?"

Synthesis. The ability to assemble separate parts into a new whole and recombine information from various sources into a new form. "Let's make your own poem using words starting with *B.*" "Make your own pattern from these cubes."

Evaluation. The ability to make judgments about information using a standard or a set of criteria. "Could this really have happened?" "Explain why you think the ending of this story was a good one." (Bloom et al., 1956)

---

sponse, such as pointing to, nodding, holding up a hand, or performing the behavior or skill. A written response entails drawing, circling, checking, or writing an answer. For example, a child could be asked to say the name of the animal, point to the animal, or circle a picture of the animal.

In many performance samples, children are told exactly what to do and how to do it, such as, "Jump on your left foot five times without touching the floor with your right foot." The criteria are transparent (Gage & Berliner, 1998).

Present prompts (questions, statement, problems) in ways that make it easy for children to respond.

- Frame questions and requests clearly, directly, and explicitly.
- If a specific response is required, include it in the directions. Say "Jump up and down" or "Tell me what you like about the story." Avoid being indirect—"Would you like to show me the capital letters?"—or vague—"How many times can you jump up and down?"
- Brief prompts, preferably one at a time, are easier for children to follow than long multiple requests.
- Make sure children understand the question or request. Use some practice items to confirm that they understand.
- Have more than one way to ask the same question. If one way does not work, try another.
- Allow "think time" before expecting a response.
- Respond to children's answers in ways that encourage them to continue.

Use sound test construction principles to construct or select any paper-and-pencil tests.   As children become proficient at reading and writing, written responses are used to appraise knowledge in reading, writing, spelling, and math. These include written performance samples, activities, practice papers, and informal tests made by teachers or taken from teacher resource books. Informal tests for beginning writers usually ask children to identify the correct answer from an array by checking, circling, underlining, drawing a line to it, or making an *X*. These tests have fewer items and more picture cues. Questions are read aloud or are printed on the test. As children get older, they read directions and questions, then construct and write answers.

The younger the child, the less valid and appropriate are written tests. Young children's fine motor skills may interfere with writing. Weak reading and writing skills cause poor performances even when children know the answers. Children lose their place, mark the wrong question, don't follow the directions, and do other things that have nothing to do with their knowledge. When written tests are used, teachers need to help children learn test-taking skills.

There are two major types of items: selected response and constructed response. Selected response items include true/false, multiple choice, matching, and fill in the blank. Constructed response items for primary children request short written answers. These items are closer to real-life experiences.

Guides for and examples of the various types of test items appear in Figure 4.3. Evaluate tests from teacher resource guides using the same criteria. In addition, check to make sure the test matches what has been taught.

Collect Work Products from Classroom Activities

Many classroom activities result in a product or object that provides valuable evidence of a child's status and progress. Although the clay snake Josefa made will not be saved, the fact that she can make snakes shows small muscle development. Jacob and Mara have built an elaborate town using interlocking plastic blocks. The town is evidence of task persistence and social skills—cooperation and negotiation used in building a joint structure. A comparison of Kyra's self-portraits at the beginning and end of the year reveals growth in cognitive representation. These items are important assessment windows that are often lost in the rush of cleanup or sent home without a second glance (Kuschner, 1989). Retain this evidence as documentation of learning (see Chapter 6).

Work Products

....

STRENGTHS

- Classroom products capture information that would be time consuming and difficult to put into words.
- A child's use of materials reveals information about several aspects of development, steps in learning, and progress toward a goal.
- Products or artifacts are easy to collect, because they are the outcome of many classroom activities.
- They can be collected for groups and individuals.
- They can be collected and compared over a period of time.

LIMITATIONS

- Much important development and learning does not result in a product. For example, a child who has learned to take another child's perspective will not have a product to show for it.
- Children will have unique products, making it difficult to get a sense of classroom needs.
- Overemphasis on assessment of products may shift the classroom focus away from "process" to "product."
- It is difficult to know which and how many examples to save.

....

Figure 4.3 Guides for First- and Second-Grade Written Tests

Type of Test Item	Example	Guides for First and Second Grade
Yes/no or true/false Statement to be judged yes/no or true/false	Yes No 1. Dogs are mammals.	• Use short statements without *and* or *but*. • Make the statements positive.

Multiple choice Stem with alternatives	First grade beginning of the year:
	1. Why did the family go for a swim?
	    a. It was a cold day.
	    b. It was a hot day.
	    c. It snowed.
	
	End of first/second grade:
	1. Little Red Riding Hood was going to visit _____.
	    a. her dog
	    b. the three little pigs
	    c. her grandmother
	    d. her teacher
		• Use a stem that is a statement to be completed or a question; questions are easier for young children.
		• Keep the wording in the choices to short sentences or phrases.
		• Students should be able to understand the question or problem by the stem alone.
		• Have only one correct response.
		• Avoid using *none of the above* or *all of the above*.
		• Avoid using the word *not* in the stem.
		• Construct plausible alternatives that have about the same number of words.
		• Place alternatives in varying order, with the correct item in different places.
		• Avoid grammatical clues (articles or verbs).

Matching Two columns of items to be matched	1. I'm she is 2. she's is not 3. isn't I am 4. who's I have 5. I've who is	• Have the same number of items in each list; one item in one column matches one item in the other with no extra words in a column and no double matches. • Keep the same type of words in the same column (e.g., all contractions in one column, all words that correspond to the contractions in the other). • Have no more than five items in each column.
Fill in the blank Sentence with missing word	1. There are 3 _____ . 2. There are 2 _____ . 3. There are 4 _____ . ponies cats dogs	• Use one blank per word. • The missing word should be a critical word or concept. • Place possible choices at the bottom or next to the item; have the same number of choices as items.

(continued)

Figure 4.3   Continued

Type of Test Item	Example	Guides for First and Second Grade
Short answer Child writes the answer in his/her own words	1. Why did Grandpa want to make the toy?	• Use direct questions rather than incomplete sentences. • The answer should be able to be concise, usually one or two sentences. • Teach the characteristics of an acceptable answer. • Develop a scoring rubric for grading.

Guides for Collecting Work Products

Develop a plan for selecting products.   For example, plan periodic sampling for those items meant to show progress. Collect a variety of products in different media to document all developmental and content areas. Choose products based on how well they show what a child has learned or experienced. Look for "break-through" samples—products that show particular growth and development. Do not worry if products are not neat or pretty. Choose products because of the process they show. Figures 4.4 and 4.5 show two children's abilities to represent events and objects. Troy constructed seemingly unrelated objects, some of which require a label to be recognized. His dictation consists of one or two word names for the objects. Jennifer's picture of the swimming race shows a purposeful and successful use of paper strips to represent objects in the event, and her dictation captures the whole story. There are also differences in fine motor skills, as evidenced by the use of glue, paper, and pencil.

Choose products because they demonstrate a child's unique approach to a problem or conceptualization of something. Marta, for example, makes intricate patterns with whatever materials she has. Tyler, using the same materials, will create something about favorite TV shows.

Set up a system for storing and summarizing products.   Record the child's name, the date, and the reason for saving directly on the product or on an entry slip attached to it. Store pieces in chronological order. Cross-reference group products. See Chapter 6 for more ideas on how to choose and organize work products.

Elicit Information from Parents

Information from parents is available in many forms: informal conversations and communications, conferences, home visits, forms and questionnaires, and involving parents in assessing their own children. All involve personal communication: asking questions, discussing concerns, attentive and active listening or reading, and responding. The following section suggests a wide variety of ways to set up parent–teacher communication related to assessment. Try those appropriate to your situation. Not all parents cooperate, but many do, benefiting everyone. Continued efforts by teachers result in increased parent involvement (Epstein, 1987).

Figure 4.4 Troy's Product

Figure 4.5 Jennifer's Product

Parents and Other Adults as Sources of Information

STRENGTHS

- Parents can provide information and insights about their children's behavior away from the school and classroom.
- Parents can share information about home/school, cultural, and linguistic differences.
- Other people's experiences and insights increase knowledge of a child. Parents have a long-range perspective of their child from birth to the present. Specialists with expertise in a specific area can augment a teacher's understanding of a child.

LIMITATIONS

- Other people's biases can distort a teacher's perception of a child.
- If parents are not familiar with the purpose of assessment, they may place pressure on the child to perform in a specific way.
- Specialists are usually brought in only for selected cases.

Guides for Eliciting Information from Parents and Other Adults

Be respectful of parent and community culture, customs, and language. If some parents are not comfortable speaking, reading, or writing English, use their primary language. If parents are not comfortable reading and writing, talk. Use sensitive, responsive discussion and listening techniques.

Advise parents about what information will be helpful. Some teachers simply ask parents, "What would you like me to know about your child?" Similar open-ended questions are listed in Figure 4.6. Many parents do not realize that family events may influence a child's behavior at school and that teachers can be more understanding if they are aware of a particular situation. Provide examples of what is helpful and why: significant events, such as the birth of a baby, moving, illness, marriage, divorce, or the death of a pet; daily ups and downs, such as illness, disruptions in sleep patterns, or a "bad morning."

Use existing communication opportunities. Background information on enrollment forms may give details such as previous schools, family composition, custody arrangements, health concerns, and allergies. Attach a short set of questions to the school enrollment form, and ask that they be relayed back to the appropriate classroom. Send questions home in communication folders, newsletters, or as a special request. Use kindergarten roundups, back-to-school nights, parent meetings, and parent–teacher conferences as opportunities to get information.

Informal exchanges are frequent in a small community or school where parents deliver or pick up their children. Have a specified place for exchanging messages to take full advantage of this opportunity. Some schools and centers have a place for comments on or near the daily sign-in/sign-out forms. In others, teachers plan the day so they are available to talk. Telephone calls help overcome distances when children ride buses, walk to school alone, or are dropped off at the school. Voice mail, answering machines, e-mail, and Web pages provide other opportunities.

Many programs have joint teacher–parent goal setting for the child at the beginning of the year. Parents list expectations of themselves and the teacher

Figure 4.6   Open-Ended Requests to Elicit Information about a Child from Parents

"What do you hope your child will get out of being in this program?"
"What are your child's current play (reading, learning) interests?"
"What are your child's strengths?"
"What special needs should we be aware of?"
"What do you do as a family?"
"We would like to know about your child's friends and friendships at home and in the neighborhood—ages, what they play, how they get along."
"What other things would you like us to know?"

Figure 4.7   Items Used for Joint Parent–Teacher Goal Setting

"I would like to see my child doing more of the following:"
"I would like to see my child doing less of the following:"
"At school, I would like the teacher to help my child with the following:"
"At home I would like to help my child do the following:"
"Ways in which we can work as partners in the child's total education:"
"I would like to know more about my child's . . . "

and then respond to prompts such as those listed in Figure 4.7. The parents and teachers keep copies of the expectations and at the end of the year give their perspectives on how the child has progressed.

Be diplomatic to get needed information related to a problem or concern. Some teachers describe what they see at school and then solicit parents' insights, similar experiences at home, and other information that will help them understand and determine a course of action. Be honest about concerns, but be open to parents' perceptions and viewpoints.

Have parents do some assessment and documentation.   Develop a few non-threatening tasks that parents and children can do at home. Give clear directions, including suggestions about appropriate timing, keeping tasks casual, and sensing when to stop. Figure 4.8 provides examples of ways parents can help with assessment.

Figure 4.9 is an example of a reading log that parents and children can keep at home. Parents keep the log for children who are not yet readers and writers. Children who read and write keep their own log, noting whether parents read the book to them or whether they read it themselves. For beginning writers, enlarge the cells. Explain and give examples of what goes in the "comments" section. When the page is full, place it in the child's portfolio.

Determine other teachers' and specialists' knowledge of children in a professional manner.   Avoid the sometimes unprofessional exchange of opinion in a teachers' lounge, "talking about," or labeling a child.

Refer to Chapter 11 for more suggestions.

Figure 4.8   Ways Parents Can Participate in Assessment

The teacher can send home a request with directions, any necessary materials, guides that might be helpful, and directions for what to record and how to return information to the school or center. Ideas for parent participation in assessment follow.

Interview the child:
"What are your favorite things to do at school? Least favorite?"
"What are your favorite things to do at home? Least favorite?"
"What are your favorite television shows (books, computer games, sports, and so forth)? Why?"
"What is your favorite thing to eat? Tell me how to make it and I will write it down."
"What are some things you are learning (have learned) at school?" (Use only if the school is making an effort to help children become aware of and remember what they are learning.)
"Tell me some things you know about (proposed topic of study)."

Help document strengths and needs:
Tape record the youngster reading aloud at home to get reading samples for portfolios.
Help the child keep a log of books read to the child and books the child reads independently.
Answer teacher-prepared questions about homework, noting the type of help the parent gave the child:
"How long did the assignment take?"
"How difficult was the assignment? Easy? About right? Difficult?"
Note study habits with which the child needs help.

Contexts for Assessment

The context, or setting, is defined by tangible factors in the environment, such as physical space or people (Bentzen, 2000; Boehm & Weinberg, 1997). It has a powerful effect on children and adults; any variations affect the outcome of assessment and influence the type of behavior and interaction that occurs (Barker, 1968). It is context that determines whether or not a performance assessment is an "authentic assessment." The context can increase child motivation and personal involvement, which, in turn, affect the complexity and maturity of responses (Cazden, 1972). Behavior during an interesting, involving activity differs from behavior during an uninteresting activity. Likewise, if a child feels at ease in a setting, the child will perform better. Anxiety in an unfamiliar, strange situation may cause uncooperative behavior, such as acting silly or refusing to respond. Context is a key factor in determining how a child will act (Bodrova & Leong, 1996).

Consider the following factors when choosing a context for assessment: physical space, materials, activities, people, and amount of teacher structure.

Characteristics of the Context

Physical Space.   The arrangement of physical space can increase the frequency of certain behavior and minimize distractions. For instance, put climbing

Figure 4.9 Reading Log Maintained at Home

....

Reading Log

Name _____ Date Started _____

Name of Book and Author	Who Read? Child = C Adult = A	Dates Start	Finish	Comments*

*Comments can include impressions, opinions, or reactions to the book or writing; revealing associations between events in the book and prior knowledge or experience; reflections on the plot or themes in the book; or other personal reactions. Write as much as you would like.

equipment in a line to increase the likelihood that children will use the pieces in sequence and will climb, swing, and balance. Also, children are less apt to interrupt each other's progress if there is an implied order.

Materials. Adding new materials or changing the ones normally present will affect assessment. A new book in the reading area, new mystery rocks at the science table, or other subtle variations often produce changes in behavior. Adding one or two props in the dramatic play area may encourage a child to join in who would not ordinarily do so.

Activities. Activities have a direct impact on behavior. More large muscle skills are observed in certain activities, such as outdoor play, a game of tag, or a movement activity, whereas artistic behavior occurs more often in others. Pick activities that are sufficiently involving and interesting. Activities that are a usual part of the classroom may be too familiar to elicit interest and involvement. To attain the level of involvement and interest necessary for a good assessment, modify familiar activities. Sometimes activities not commonly associated with a specific behavior are novel enough to increase child interest.

For example, counting jumps in an outdoor activity may be more involving and interesting than the usual counting tasks with manipulatives.

For children younger than age 7, the activity most likely to elicit complex and mature behavior is play (Bodrova & Leong, 1996). Watch a child playing or pretending. Perhaps a child does not listen while the teacher reads a story to the group. However, when she is playing school with a friend who pretends to read, she listens attentively for 10 minutes.

People. Children's behavior is influenced by the number of people present and who they are—friends, peers, adults. Group behavior is more than the sum of individual behaviors; a complicated dynamic exists within the group that influences social interaction. The personality, interests, and behavior of each individual influence the functioning of the whole. For example, a child's academic ability and social status may influence participation in cooperative groups. At the same time, group interaction affects individual behavior. For instance, Stacy's strong desire to have other children do what she wants influences group interaction. She makes constant efforts to get children to play her way, dominates conversations, and tries to keep other children from talking. Stacy's behavior in turn is influenced by Jason, who follows her lead, and Marta, who resists. Subgroups within a larger group also have an effect on interaction, such as when two best friends dominate a cooperative learning group by constantly rejecting other children's suggestions.

Amount of Teacher Structure. Contexts range from those with little teacher intervention to structured settings where teachers directly modify and control the environment. In most assessments, teachers provide some sort of structure, ranging from putting out new materials, to organizing an activity, to participating in activities. For informal classroom assessments, it is helpful to think of distinctions in terms of the amount of teacher structure—materials introduced or activities planned. Structured activities flow with normal classroom interaction patterns and are not noticeably different from them. To observe cooperative behavior, set up a cooperative game. During the game, you will see more examples of cooperation than usual, yet children view the game as a normal part of classroom life.

Examples of Contexts for Assessment

Many contexts lend themselves to assessment. Some are obvious, such as using the manipulatives area to assess small motor development or the book area for literacy skills. Others are overlooked, although they are excellent contexts for appraisal. Consider the following:

1. *Daily routines.* Assess during snack, cleanup, lunchtime, transitions, and other daily routines.
2. *Outdoors.* Watch children as they play in organized games or alone. Many aspects of development can be observed, including large muscle and social development, language use, and problem solving.
3. *Dramatic play.* Dramatic play can be a context for assessing social, language, and cognitive development, as well as fine motor skills.
4. *Learning centers.* Children can be assessed or assess themselves as they work in learning centers. By collecting learning center products, the teacher has a record of what the children have done. Children who read

and write can be taught to assess themselves by filling out charts and rating scales, or by tape recording comments.

5. *Classroom meetings or large groups.* An often overlooked context for assessment occurs when the class gathers together. Teachers can assess group functioning and individual participation as well as specific knowledge and skills.

6. *Cooperative group activities.* Groups in which children learn together are the ideal context for assessing the social and content goals for those groups.

7. *Independent work.* Observe children as they work alone, noting such things as posture, movement, facial expressions, tension or comfort, ability to concentrate, and so on.

Guides for Selecting Assessment Contexts

Make sure children feel at ease.

Think about each factor in the setting separately: physical space, materials, activities, people, and amount of teacher structure.

Use physical space to increase desired behavior and minimize distractions.

Do not use distracting materials.

Make the context interesting and realistic enough to engage children.

Remember that the size and composition of the group influence interaction.

Choosing the Appropriate Assessment Window

Because so many possible combinations of sources, methods, and contexts exist in an early childhood classroom, a teacher can vary the assessment window often. As you decide which combination to use, identify the behavior to be assessed; use authentic assessment windows; maximize the frequency or chance of seeing a behavior; and use multiple sources, methods, and contexts.

Identify the Behavior to Be Assessed

The focus behavior guides the choice of source, method, and context, so identify, as explicitly as possible, the behavior you decide to assess (see Chapter 3) and what you want to learn about it.

Two illustrations clarify this: If a teacher is interested in how children function in small groups during dramatic play, the teacher should choose the children playing in a *group* as the source of information. Observation is a good *method* for assessing social interaction, because it can be done without interfering with group dynamics. To pick the best *context*, the teacher must consider the number of children, materials, and composition of the group, such as ages and friendships of members.

If "using inches, feet, and yards to measure" is the focus behavior, the most authentic *source* of information is the child. The best *method* is to elicit information in a performance task that focuses attention on specific facts and behaviors. Any *context* in which children can demonstrate these skills would be good, such as measuring the sidewalk, measuring objects to be used in a cooperative construction, or determining their own height.

Use Authentic Assessment Measures or Windows

Consider whether the source, method, and context will produce an authentic assessment. Use direct sources of information, except when you cannot obtain information from the child or group or when the perspectives of parents and other adults are your focus. If you are assessing a behavior that usually occurs in a specific setting, use that context. Obviously, an authentic assessment of cooperative learning is a cooperative learning activity. Although cooperation also occurs in dramatic play, it is not the same kind that takes place in cooperative learning. Appraisals should tap the identified behavior as directly as possible.

Maximize the Chances of Seeing a Behavior

Assessment windows should maximize the chance of seeing focus behaviors. To determine how many children can classify objects by one attribute, choose activities in which children sort and classify objects. One person or source may see behavior more frequently than another source; for instance, the playground supervisor sees more gross motor behavior than the reading specialist. Certain settings tend to restrict interaction and limit certain types of behavior. Spontaneous play happens more often during dramatic play than in a teacher-directed activity. Certain activities are more engaging and elicit better, more reliable samples of behavior. Contexts affect motivation—children might be more motivated to add during a toss–catch and answer session than during a paper-and-pencil test.

Use Multiple Assessment Measures or Windows

Multiple assessment measures ensure a richer, more balanced perspective of a child. Using multiple assessment windows to gather information improves reliability and validity for the entire process (Airasian, 2000; Sattler, 2001). Any weaknesses of a particular source and method will be offset by the strengths of others.

No formula exists for deciding how many different assessment windows are necessary. Teachers must use their own judgment. Consider the following general guidelines:

- To assess progress, at least two assessment windows must be similar. A drawing collected at the beginning of the year should be compared with a drawing collected later, not with a painting. Compare the same skills or behaviors in a similar context.
- Whether a window is overused depends partly on the total number of appraisals being made. If five samples of problem solving will be collected, no more than two or three of them should come from the same source, method, or setting. If ten assessments will be made, then three or four of the same method are acceptable.

Figure 4.10 shows the wide variety of assessment windows available for assessing what children know and can do in different development and curriculum domains (Airasian, 2001; Gage & Berliner, 1992; Meisels & Steele, 1991).

Figure 4.10 Assessment Windows Used to Appraise Major Early Childhood Goals

Large Muscle/Gross Motor
- Systematic observations of child in movement during movement activities, outdoor play, physical education
- Self-reports or elicited information about a child's favorite games, activities, or apparatus and why they are favorites
- Systematic observations of a child's skill level
- Evidence of participation in large muscle activities
- Performance sample of an obstacle course combining several skills
- Performance sample of one specific skill
- Evidence of the length of participation in active physical exercise without tiring
- Performance sample of mimicking of progressively harder patterns of movement (following a song, videotape, or teacher)
- Descriptions of after-school and weekend physical activities from parents

Small Muscle/Fine Motor
- Systematic observations and examples (products) of a small muscle skill, such as fingerplays or use of writing instruments, modeling clay, manipulatives, crayons, paints, pencils, chalk, clay, paste, or other material that requires small muscle use (these can be spontaneously generated or elicited by the teacher)
- Spontaneously generated work products and performance samples of cutting
- Spontaneously generated work products and performance samples of scribbling or printing of letters and numerals
- Examples of constructions with small manipulatives, such as cubes, pattern blocks, pegs, seeds
- Computer printout of child's work with a draw/paint program (product)
- Systematic observation of child's ability to use keyboard, mouse, and accessories
- Samples of child's stitching (product)
- Systematic observations of use of hand tools and implements (may be videotaped)
- Child sketches of own constructions
- Performance samples of constructions (build a bridge from this side of town to the other, build a tower that is this high)
- Self-portraits drawn at the beginning and end of the term
- Systematic observations of self-help skills made by the teacher
- Reports from parents about self-help skills seen at home

Cognitive Development
- Elicited information about a child's knowledge or thinking processes (using a web or semantic map to record information)
- Elicited information or self-reports of what a child was thinking in a particular operation, project, or process (Why did you sort the shells that way?)
- Self-reports, elicited information, or work products showing a child's ability to present information in graphic form
- Systematic observations or performance samples of puzzles, problems solved, and how they were solved
- Work samples from different subject matter areas
- Performance samples of a child's ability to carry out basic cognitive processes—classify, pattern, seriate, think, and represent using symbols; sequence; use number concepts and operations; observe; compare and contrast; and others
- Self-reports or elicited descriptions of memory strategies (e.g., list made by child)
- Self-reports or elicited descriptions of a child's understanding of a process, such as how a favorite food is made

(continued)

Figure 4.10   Continued

- Performance samples of specific knowledge or skills
- Work products, such as reports, practice papers, displays, presentations, models, or other end products of project work
- Performance samples of problem solving with teacher- or child-recorded information
- Self-reports of games the child has made up or played and how to play a known game (knowledge needed, strategies used)
- Systematic observations, elicited descriptions, or self-reports of things child uses to aid own thinking (use of fingers, self-talk, monitoring thinking processes)
- List of hints at different levels that helped the child solve a problem; list of hints that were not helpful
- Descriptions of error patterns found on practice papers and performance samples
- Descriptions of child's favorite problem-solving games and puzzles from home
- List of the "How does this work?" and "Why?" questions children ask their parents

Language and Literacy Development
- Systematic observations and performance samples showing communication competence
- Evidence of comprehension and use of specific concepts, vocabulary, constructions
- Evidence of time spent reading or looking at books, times in book center
- Self-report or record of books read or books read to child at home or school
- Self-report or elicited listing of favorite books
- Performance sample of child reading aloud to another child, parent, aide, volunteer, or the teacher (may be recorded on audio- or videotape)
- Evidence of child's understanding of functional uses of print (e.g., signs, maps, letters, newspapers, lists, books, teacher recordings, photographs)
- Work products such as copies of final and draft copies of child compositions—songs, poems, stories, recountings, samples of journal entries
- Performance sample showing a child's phonemic awareness or letter knowledge
- Performance samples of storytelling, retelling, or reading of own writing (recorded on tape)
- Performance samples of writing—successive drafts or stand-alone samples
- Group compositions or experience charts
- Performance samples showing a child's conceptions about print
- Parent reports of favorite books or reading activities at home

Personal and Social Development
- Teacher observations and recordings of specific aspects of a child's interactions with peers
- Evidence of friendship and affiliation abilities
- Self-reports or observations of a child's skills in cooperative work groups, class projects, and outings
- Evidence of a child's choices of activities for a specified time
- Evidence of participation in and contributions to various activities requiring peer interaction
- Evidence of a child's ability to organize self and others to accomplish task
- Evidence of a child's uniqueness and personal style, interests, and dispositions
- Elicited information about friendship (what it means to be a friend and have a friend) and social problem solving (How would you handle this problem?)
- Observations of positive initiations with others or of negative, inappropriate interactions
- Descriptions from parents of the child's friendships and affiliation abilities at home
- Elicited or self-reports of a child's conception of self (Who am I?)
- Systematic observations and self-reports of a child's level of motivation during different types of activities

Figure 4.10   Continued

. . . .

Attitudes and Dispositions (about almost everything)
- Evidence showing time spent at a given activity or task
- Evidence showing a child's choices of activities, books, projects, food
- Elicited information and self-reports of "favorite" activities, books, songs, subjects, things to do at home and on playground—and why
- Evidence of a child's uniqueness in approach, attitude, and disposition
- Self-reports or elicited information of the number of books read, puzzles completed, maps made, pictures drawn, or skills mastered
- Knowledge and skill in a particular developmental or subject area
- Parent reports, reports from other teachers about a child's attitudes and dispositions
- Description of motivation levels, attitudes, and dispositions observed during performance samples in a specific area

Specific Content Areas
- Performance samples of a child's ability, designed to elicit specific skills, concepts, or processes
- Practice papers and other work products: science, math, or integrated project journals or reports
- Evidence of the relationships between concepts, processes, and strategies for use (may be documented by webs or semantic maps)
- Descriptions of specific skills, concepts, and processes

Other Important Assessment Windows
- Attendance and tardiness records
- Child's reflections on own development
- Observations of who sleeps at nap time and for how long (preschool)
- Observations of who is tired or hungry in the morning
- Observations of a child's preferred study time (morning or afternoon), quiet time, reactions to noise or new situations, and other learning style characteristics

Summary

. . . .

To fairly assess individual children, teachers use multiple measures or "windows." They gather information using different sources, methods, and contexts. The child, parents, other adults, and records are sources of information. Observe; elicit responses from children, parents, and other adults; and collect and analyze products of classroom activities to use a variety of methods. Vary physical space, materials, activities, and people to achieve different contexts or settings.

Each approach has strengths and limitations. To choose the most appropriate combination of source, method, and context for a given assessment, use these criteria: choose a combination that is as authentic as possible, that is appropriate to the purpose, and that maximizes the chance of seeing a behavior. Use a variety of approaches to avoid overdependence on one source, method, or context.

Using different assessment measures requires certain skills and attitudes of teachers. These are described in the Guides sections throughout this chapter. Teachers must be sensitive and skilled in talking with parents and children; they must be respectful of community culture, customs, and language. With parents, use existing communication opportunities to elicit their perspective, have them do some assessment, and help set goals. With children, use authentic performance tasks; interviews, conferences, and discussions; and dynamic assessment strategies. Ask a range of questions to stimulate both memory and the reflection that prompts complex thinking and reasoning. Use a variety of questions, requests, and prompts at different levels of difficulty and complexity to increase the accuracy and amount of information from children.

For Personal Reflection

1. Context, or setting, is one of the variables that teachers must consider in assessing children. Think of times and situations in which context influences what you do. What aspects of those settings are influential? Physical space? Materials? Activities? People? Structure? In what ways do they exert their influence?

2. Teachers often have strong opinions about studying records made by other people as a source of information about children. Examine your own beliefs about records. What are some of the reasons for those beliefs?

For Further Study and Discussion

1. Mr. Lee is interested in finding out how many of his children can count by 1s, 2s, and 5s. Identify three different assessment windows to gather the information. Explain your choice of sources, methods, and settings.

2. Mr. Bonatti wants to know if Marcia exhibits the same amount of physical and verbal aggression in other settings as she does in the classroom. Identify three possible sources, methods, and settings for obtaining this information. Explain your choices.

3. Write convergent and divergent questions or statements calling for a response about a book a child has just read. Write a question or statement at the receptive and expressive levels about a concept. Write a question or statement at the recall and recognition levels about the concept of an insect. Use Bloom's Taxonomy to develop questions and statements about the concept of food.

Suggested Readings

Airasian, P. W. (2000). *Assessment in the classroom: A concise approach* (2nd ed.). Boston: McGraw-Hill.

Bentzen, W. R. (2000). *Seeing young children: A guide to observing and recording behavior* (4th ed.). Albany, NY: Delmar.

Boehm, A., & Weinberg, R. (1996). *The classroom observer: Developing observation skills in early childhood settings* (3rd ed.). New York: Teachers College Press.

Ginsburg, H. P. (1997). *Entering the child's mind: The clinical interview in psychological research and practice.* Cambridge, U.K.: Cambridge University Press.

Helm, J., Beneke, S., & Steinheimer, K. (1998). *Windows on learning.* New York: Teachers College Press.

Popham, W. J. (1999). *Classroom assessment: What teachers need to know* (2nd ed.). Boston: Allyn & Bacon.

●●●

CHAPTER 5

Documenting:
Recording Information

Information collected and recorded during an appraisal is the original assessment record or primary data record (Engel, 1990). Accurate and complete primary data records are essential to ensure the trustworthiness of information. Such records preserve information so it can be consulted, studied, and combined with other evidence to show progress, reveal patterns, and provide perspective that may be lacking in daily interactions with children. Records of what children have done and learned are the basis for communicating with other people. Teachers depend on records to help them remember what children know and can do (Leong, McAfee, & Swedlow, 1992). During an average school day, teachers have 1,500 interactions with children (Billups & Rauth, 1987); they cannot rely on memory.

Recording information in a systematic way helps focus attention on each child's development, on important educational targets, and on the way authentic assessment and good instruction are linked. The discipline of documenting—collecting and recording information—makes us better observers and teachers.

This chapter is divided into two sections: (1) description and examples of recording procedures; and (2) selecting an appropriate recording procedure.

Teachers and researchers have developed a bewildering array of recording techniques that fall into three basic types: those that describe; those that count, time, or tally; and those that rate or rank whatever is under consideration. Figure 5.1 shows the most frequently used procedures in each type. Other procedures usually involve a combination or variation of the basic types.

Descriptive records are "pictures" of a behavior that are written, drawn, photographed, or tape recorded, as in anecdotal records or sketches. Counts or tallies note the number of times a behavior occurs, usually on a checklist of some type. Rating scales or rubrics record information by ranking or rating attributes on a continuum relative to other individuals or a predetermined standard. Figure 5.2 compares the information from one incident recorded using the three procedures: describing, counting, and rating.

We include only basic recording tools that are feasible for teachers to use, and we encourage you to vary them and use others to meet your own recording needs. Current word-processing programs make it easy to develop forms tailored to a specific need.

Description and Examples of Recording Procedures

This section describes, gives examples, and lists the strengths and limitations of selected recording tools useful in early childhood settings. They are grouped according to type: those that describe, those that count, and those that rate or rank. Other procedures—combinations and variations—conclude the section.

Procedures That Describe

Procedures that describe preserve raw data in a form that is closest to what actually happened in narrative records, such as descriptive narratives, anecdotal records, and jottings; diagrams, sketches, and photographs; and audio and video records.

Figure 5.1   Types of Recording Procedures

	Recording Procedures
Procedures That Describe	Descriptive narratives, anecdotal records, jottings Diagrams, sketches, photographs Audio and video recordings
Procedures That Count	Checklists Participation charts Frequency counts
Procedures That Rank or Rate	Rating scales Rubrics

Figure 5.2   Comparison of Information Recorded as a Description, Count, and Rating

Description	Count or Tally	Rating
Standing in front of class, C says with a loud voice as she points to each word in her journal, "My Friend Jana."	3/12/06 reads dictated story 3/12/06 points to words while reading 3/12/06 speaks with confidence	Shows confidence 1 3 ⑤ Enjoys writing 1 ③ 5 Enjoys reading 1 ③ 5

Narrative Records: Descriptive Narratives, Anecdotal Records, and Jottings. Narrative records are detailed, storylike descriptions of what occurred. The amount of detail and length of the entry are the primary differences among descriptive narratives, anecdotal records, and jottings. Descriptive narratives, sometimes called *specimen descriptions,* or *specimen records,* are the most detailed. They are like video recordings—continuous records of everything said or done during an assessment, written as the behavior is observed. They may include many types of behavior and activities, as well as several children and adults (see Figure 5.8). Descriptive narratives are seldom used by classroom teachers because of their responsibilities to the total group. To document questions and responses in interviews and discussions, audiotape the conversation and transcribe it.

Figure 5.3   Descriptive Narrative Record

Item(s) Sociodramatic play

Child M. Pierce & D. Smits   Date 5/12/06   Time 10:00 am

Observer Franklin   Setting dramatic play area

Marica and Dolores are standing next to the sink. Dolores hands Marica an apron. They both tie the aprons around their necks like capes. Dolores grabs the yellow mop and Marica takes a purse. Dolores begins to march around the room. "Follow me everybody," she says, pushing the broom up and down like a majorette. Marica, still in the dramatic play area, starts addressing an empty chair. "You have been sooooooo bad. I'm going to make you eat mushy mushy mush mush. Here." She walks back to the sink, turns several pots over, rummages around. Dolores returns--holding Kathy's hand--and says to Kathy, "You come play with us, O.K.? We need a baby. Want to be it?" Kathy looks away toward the sink, and lets go of Dolores' hand, and says "What is this?" . . .

Notes/Interpretation

Few roles. Talk is primarily statements. Beginning to assign roles.

Anecdotal records are focused, short, narrative accounts of a specific event (Bentzen, 2000; Goodwin & Driscoll, 1980; Irwin & Bushnell, 1980). They are widely used to document unique behaviors and skills of a child or a small group of children. Figure 5.4 shows examples of anecdotal records documenting problem solving. Dates and children's names are noted on the actual record.

Jottings are short notes about significant aspects or characteristics of a behavior or event. They take less time to write than descriptive narratives and anecdotal records but preserve important details by using phrases and abbreviations, leaving out words, and taking other shortcuts. Because they take little space and are quickly recorded they can be used in the "Comments" or "Notes" sections of checklists, participation charts, and other forms, or they can be recorded in a group matrix record, as shown in Figure 5.5. Jottings are often added to children's work products as an explanatory annotation. Following are some examples of jot-

Figure 5.4   Examples of Anecdotal Records

At small-group time, Latoya wanted a bigger piece of playdough. She tried to take some of Karol's but Karol said, "No." The adult asked Latoya if she had another idea for getting more playdough. Latoya turned to Karol and said, "Let's add our playdough together and then we'll both have a hugest piece." Karol agreed and they put their two pieces together.

Getting ready for outside, J. J. put his snowpants on backwards, took them off, turned them all the way around, and put them on backwards again. He looked down at them and said, "Oh well, I guess it's backward day!" He then put on his coat and went outside.

Reprinted with permission from High/Scope Educational Research Foundation. Courtesy of Beth Marshall. Children's names have been changed. The ability to solve problems is an expected outcome of High/Scope's approach.

Figure 5.5   A Record Using Jottings

Item(s) _Counting skills_

Group _PM Kindergarten_   Date _1/5/06_ to _4/10/06_

Observer _Wong_

Name	Rote	Meaningful	Notes
Beck, A.	1/22/06___ To 5 no errors 5–10 w/prompt	3/25/06___ To 3 Prompts not used	
Benny, D.	1/22/06___ To 20 no errors To 50 w/prompts	2/22/06___ To 20 no errors To 50 w/prompts	Has number conservation for 3, 4, & 5

tings: "Runs around obj. easily, arms balanced, jumps rope, attempts jumping jacks." "Responds correctly and without hesitation."

Narrative Records

STRENGTHS

- Narratives require a minimum of equipment and preparation.
- Notes can be varied in length and detail.
- Written accounts preserve the context and sequence of events.

LIMITATIONS

- Written accounts take more time and attention than other methods.
- Writing can detract from ongoing interaction with children.
- Recording done after the event may be unreliable.

Guides for Making Narrative Records

Record exactly what you see or hear in the order in which it happens. Use words that convey distinctions in behavior. For example, children not only "say" something but they may also shout, whisper, scream, speak loudly, or speak softly. Do not interpret or summarize while recording. See the section Be Fair and Impartial in Chapter 2.

When possible, record as the event is happening. If it must be recorded later, note a few words to help you remember what happened, and reconstruct the event accurately as soon as you can.

Include all the information necessary to understand the description. This will vary with what is being recorded and may include context, what happened before the event, who was involved, what happened afterward, and other details, depending on the focus of the observation and what transpired.

Date each entry.

Diagrams, Sketches, and Photographs.   Not all records have to be in written form. Diagrams, sketches, and photographs preserve important details of products and processes otherwise requiring lengthy written descriptions. Older children can sketch and take pictures of their own work. Figure 5.6 is a teacher's sketch of a child's block construction. Figure 5.7 is a sketch a kindergarten child did of his own block construction.

Special types of diagrams used to record children's knowledge and learning about concepts or processes are called *webs, concept maps,* or *idea maps.* Webs and semantic maps document one child's thinking or the ideas of a group. Children are asked to state what they know about a specific topic or idea. As ideas emerge, the teacher asks questions to find out what a child means by an idea and to find out the relationship between ideas. For example, when a child says, "Insects are alive," the teacher may ask, "What does alive mean?" or "How do you know they are alive?" Correct information and misconceptions are both recorded. Like ideas are placed in relationship to each other in a diagram, forming a web of ideas (see Figure 5.8). Webs can be used to document knowledge or processes, and they can be recorded by teachers or children.

Figure 5.6 Diagram/Sketch Made by the Teacher of a Child's
Block Construction

....

Item(s) Small block construction

Child Morgan, T.   **Date** 5/14/06 **Time** 9:00

Observer Schulhammer   **Setting** Manipulatives

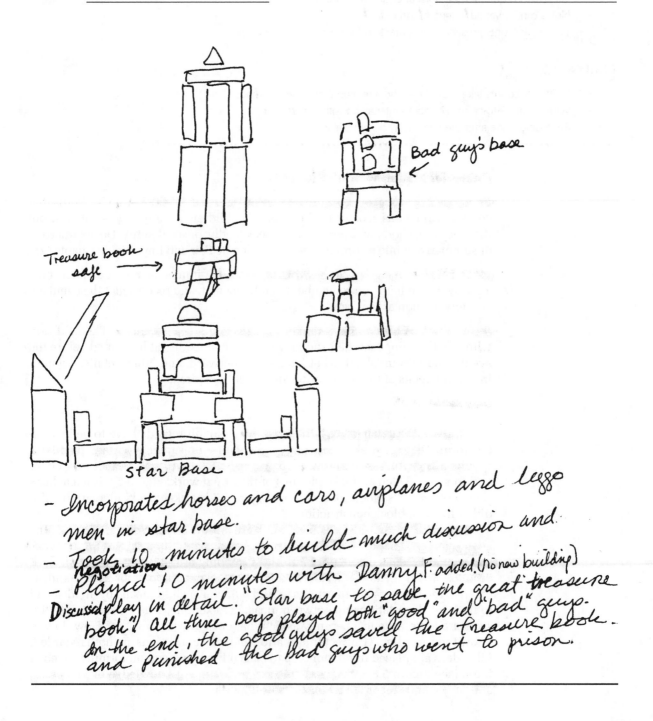

Bad guy's base

Treasure book safe →

Star Base

- Incorporates horses and cars, airplanes and lego men in star base.
- Took 10 minutes to build – much discussion and negotiation
- Played 10 minutes with Danny F. added. (no new building)
Discussed play in detail. "Star base to save the great treasure book." All three boys played both "good" and "bad" guys. In the end, the good guys saved the treasure book and punished the Bad guys who went to prison.

Figure 5.7 Diagram/Sketch Made by a Kindergarten Child of His Own Block Construction

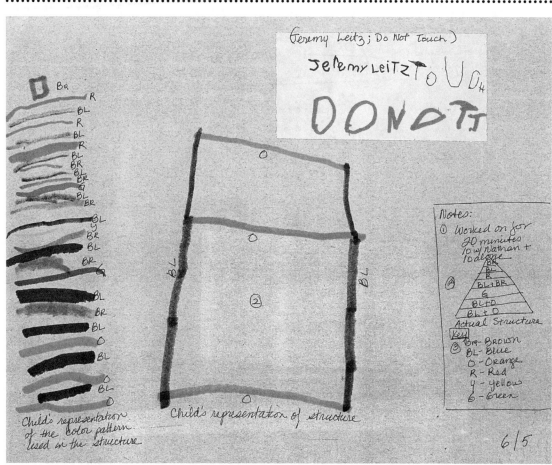

Photographs, Diagrams, and Sketches

STRENGTHS

- Graphic records (diagrams, sketches, photographs) capture evidence about a product that can't be saved, such as a model, display, or construction.
- They can preserve details of a process, such as changes made to a design or revisions in thinking.
- Graphic records can be used to record individual or group work in almost any developmental or curriculum domain.
- Photographs and sketches are quick and easy and require little advance preparation.
- Concept maps or webs record a child's or a group's current knowledge and the relationships among elements in it.

LIMITATIONS

- Graphic records require a written annotation to provide context and detail.
- Photographs are expensive.
- Children need time to get used to the camera.

Figure 5.8   Web

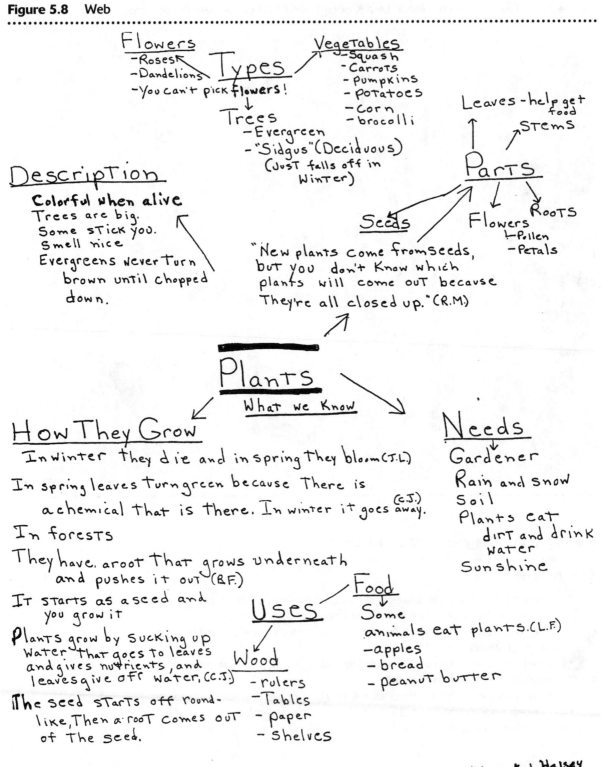

Flowers
- Roses
- Dandelions
- You can't pick flowers!

Types

Vegetables
- Squash
- Carrots
- Pumpkins
- Potatoes
- Corn
- brocolli

Trees
- Evergreen
- "Sidgus" (Deciduous)
  (Just falls off in Winter)

Leaves - help get food
Stems
Parts
Roots
Flowers
- Pollen
- Petals

Description

Colorful when alive
Trees are big.
Some stick you.
Smell nice
Evergreens never turn
  brown until chopped
  down.

Seeds

"New plants come from seeds, but you don't know which plants will come out because They're all closed up." (R.M.)

Plants
What we Know

How They Grow

In winter they die and in spring they bloom. (J.L.)

In spring leaves turn green because there is a chemical that is there. In winter it goes away. (C.J.)

In forests
They have a root that grows underneath and pushes it out (B.F.)

It starts as a seed and you grow it

Plants grow by sucking up water that goes to leaves and gives nutrients, and leaves give off water. (C.J.)

The seed starts off round-like, then a root comes out of the seed.

Uses

Wood
- rulers
- Tables
- Paper
- Shelves

Food
Some animals eat plants. (L.F.)
- apples
- bread
- peanut butter

Needs
Gardener
Rain and snow
Soil
Plants eat dirt and drink water
Sunshine

Class K-1, Halsey
3-30

Audio and Video Records. Recording devices capture complex performances that give authentic evidence of the integration and application of learning. Presentations, exhibits, demonstrations, displays, dramatizations, reading aloud, explaining and summarizing a project or investigation, and other integrating activities are candidates for recording. Assessment of needs and progress in oral language and literacy is easier when speech is captured for later analysis (Rhodes & Shanklin, 1992). Use video records to preserve both speech and action and to serve as a backup and supplement to other methods of recording. Both methods allow teachers to be included and are a useful, sometimes jolting, record for teacher self-evaluation. Audio records are useful for recording parent comments, especially if parents are not comfortable writing information.

Children, teachers, aides, parents, or other adults can record activities in a center, during individual or small-group activities, or with the entire class. In fact, at many school exhibits or class demonstrations, the number of video cameras may almost equal the number of families present.

Audio and Video Records

STRENGTHS

- Audio and video recordings retain exactly what occurred, including the setting, interactions, and other variables.
- They can be listened to or viewed repeatedly by different people.
- They record events that occur too quickly or are too complex to write down.
- They provide backup evidence for other records.
- They are an easy way to involve children and parents.

LIMITATIONS

- The amount of data preserved can be overwhelming.
- Audio and video equipment and the process of recording may disrupt classroom activities until children get used to it.

Guides for Making Audio and Video Records

Focus on specific assessment situations. It is tempting to record "everything" but time consuming to review all.

Place recorders so they are unobtrusive.

See Chapter 9 for more suggestions.

Procedures That Count or Tally

Counts or tallies preserve information about the presence or absence, frequency or number of occurrences, or duration of a behavior. Appropriate behaviors to tally have an identifiable beginning and end (Cartwright & Cartwright, 1984), such as building a structure or talking. Counts or tallies document expected, anticipated behaviors or products. Behaviors and products are identified before the assessment begins, and a recording form is developed that contains only selected items. For example, during a math assessment, counting and making patterns, both expected behaviors, are placed on the tally record. Unexpected events—those not identified beforehand—would not be recorded. Although a wonderful example of cooperation occurs spontaneously during the math assessment, it would not be recorded on the math tally.

Behaviors must be mutually exclusive or nonoverlapping. For example, aggression and shoving overlap because shoving could be counted both as aggression and as shoving. It would be better to use shoving and biting, two mutually exclusive behaviors.

Behavior tallies use either sign systems or category systems (Boehm & Weinberg, 1997; Irwin & Bushnell, 1980). Sign systems are representative of a larger set; a few behaviors that are indicators or *signs* of a skill are appraised instead of every behavior. Being able to hold a pencil is a sign that a child is probably able to hold a crayon, marker, or a watercolor paintbrush.

A category system is exhaustive—all possible behaviors are categorized and recorded. Parten's breakdown of play (Parten, 1933) is a category system that records play behaviors in four categories: solitary, parallel, associative, or cooperative. Time samples and duration samples are used primarily in research or when a specialist is assessing a child. The recording tools most useful in the classroom are checklists, participation charts, and frequency counts. Chapter 9 provides additional information on the use of these tools.

Checklists. Checklists are a practical, versatile way to document many behaviors, skills, attitudes and dispositions, and even products. They can record inferences or teacher judgments, such as a child's confidence when speaking in front of a group. They preserve information from any area of development— physical, cognitive, and social—or curriculum, such as social studies, science, or art. They can be developed, compiled and stored on a computer using standard word-processing software. Because they are so adaptable, they are widely used, especially to record literacy and mathematics skills.

Checklists can originate from standards, instructional objectives, or developmental sequences. Items may record specific skills or different levels of performance. For example, a checklist might record a child's ability to recognize, point to, say, or use a concept.

Checklists can be modified to fit specific classroom needs and to collect information from an individual or group. Checklists can be filled out gradually; not all children have to be assessed at the same time. Also, checklists can document appraisals made at different times and thus create a progress record.

Figure 5.9 is an example of a checklist using a grid system. Figure 5.10 is an example of a published checklist.

Checklists

STRENGTHS

- Large amounts of information are recorded quickly.
- Checklists are versatile and easily analyzed, interpreted, and quantified.
- Completion of checklists can be ongoing—spread over several days or longer.
- Checklists can track a child's progress as well as achievement at a specific time.
- Other adults can be trained to use checklists.

LIMITATIONS

- Checklists may oversimplify complex behavior and learning.
- Checklists that contain too few representative items must be interpreted cautiously.

Figure 5.9 Checklist for Recording Individual Performance on a Group Record

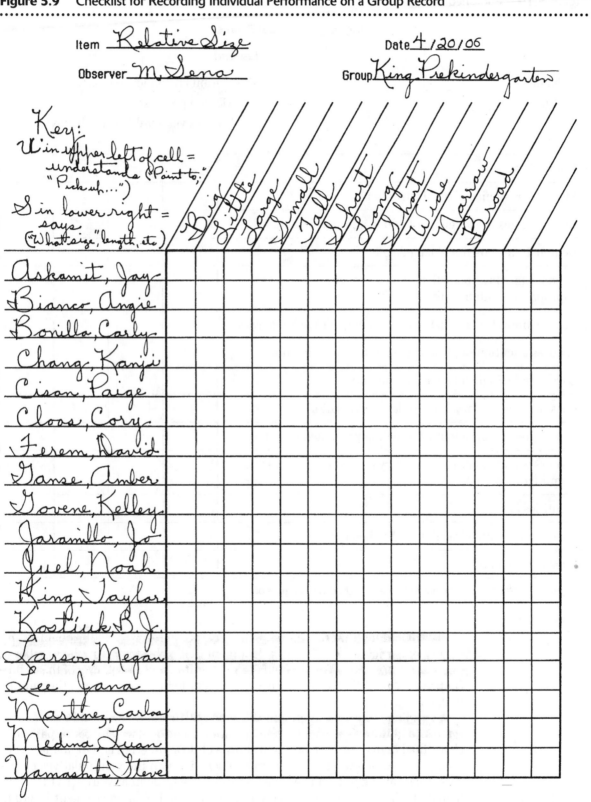

Figure 5.10 Published Checklist

....

Ongoing Individual Profile

Legend

Name _____

Age _____

✓ Exhibits behavior regularly

+ Making progress

* Has not yet exhibited the behavior

Vocabulary				
Moves in response to oral instructions.				
Demonstrates the language of action and movement.				
Demonstrates positional language.				
Matches the position/action/movement with the appropriate written word.				
Demonstrates the understanding of comparative language.				
Focuses attention on, listens to, and responds to others.				
Uses simple English language structures.				
Uses new vocabulary in everyday conversation.				
Makes predictions about what will happen next in a story.				
Discusses and acquires vocabulary related to concepts in meaningful context.				
Identifies facts.				
Uses information to retell what has been read.				
Interprets symbols.				

Rigby Kinderstarters: Assessment and Evaluation. Used with permission.

Participation Charts. Participation charts can record both the quantity and quality of participation. They can document that a child joins in, the number of times and activities in which the child is involved, and the quality of the child's contributions. Participation charts can be recorded by the teacher, other adults, or the children.

A participation chart highlights different participation rates and provides insight into children's preferences, dispositions, and patterns of participation. A chart filled in over several days will show a child's preferred activity pattern. For example, over one week, Leigh worked exclusively in the manipulatives or science areas during free choice time and did not engage in any art activities. Participation charts can document the degree and quality of engagement in group discussions or cooperative learning activities, such as whether a child's contributions are relevant, irrelevant, or disruptive. Participation charts also identify activities or areas of the room that are overused or underused. They clearly document the teacher's pattern of communication, such as a tendency to solicit or favor comments and contributions from a few children rather than all. Participation charts called *room scans* record which areas children are involved in at different times of the day (see Figure 5.11).

Figure 5.12 shows a child-recorded participation chart, and Figure 5.13 shows a chart recorded by a teacher.

Participation Charts

STRENGTHS

• Participation charts are a simple, quick way of recording quantity and quality of participation.
• Children can report on their own participation. Other adults in the classroom can record children's participation.

LIMITATIONS

• The rate of participation may not reflect how much a child is learning. A child who is observing and listening may be absorbing as much as children who are talking or doing.
• Participation charts may give the impression that participation is the child's responsibility, when it is a complex performance influenced by many factors.

Frequency Counts.   A frequency count or event sample tallies *each* time a behavior occurs and documents the number of times or rate of occurrence. Frequency counts are practical ways to record behaviors such as social initiations and responses to others, aggressive and disruptive behavior, and a child's requests for help from teachers or peers. If Marcia raises her hand three times, the record would read "| | |." Frequency counts may document behavior during a specified period, such as ten minutes, during group time, or for an entire day. Focus on a limited number of children and behaviors.

Define the behaviors to be tallied on the record. Counts of the same behavior conducted at different times can be recorded on the same form. Divide the space used for the tally into three columns as shown in Figure 5.14. List the dates of the assessment in the left column, and record a tick mark for each occurrence in the center column. A column for totaling each tally is on the right.

Frequency Counts

STRENGTHS

• Frequency counts are useful for documenting the rate or changes in the rate of frequently occurring behaviors.
• Recording can be done unobtrusively during classroom activities.

LIMITATIONS

• Frequency counts do not document the sequence of events or antecedent and consequent events.
• Infrequent behaviors cannot be adequately documented.
• Frequency counts are usually limited to one child and no more than three behaviors at a time.

Figure 5.11   Room Scan Participation Chart

Date____/____/____

Observer_____   Group_____

Make one tally mark /
for each 15 minute
scan.

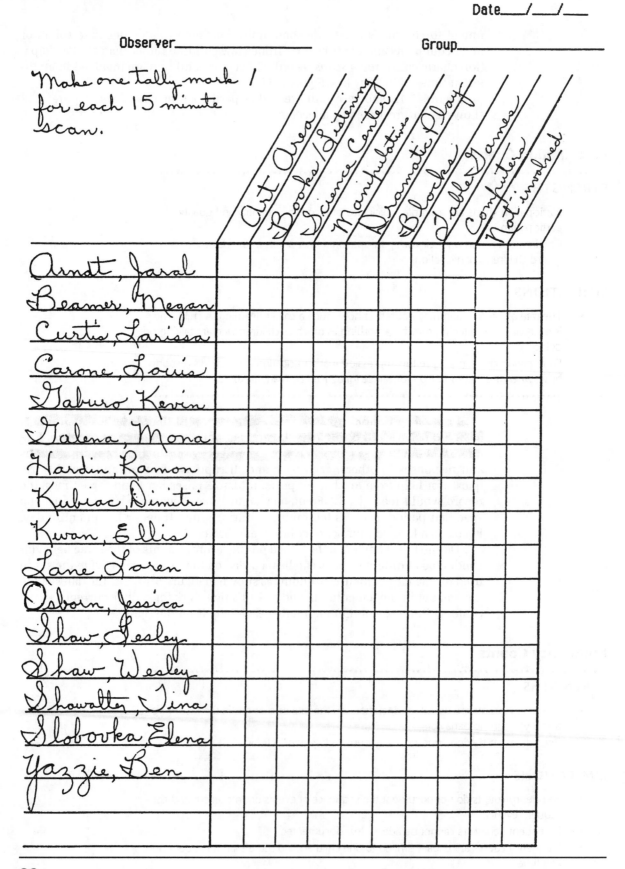

	Art Area	Books/Listening	Science Center	Manipulatives	Dramatic Play	Blocks	Table Games	Computers	Not involved
Arndt, Jaral									
Beamer, Megan									
Curtis, Larissa									
Carone, Louis									
Gaburo, Kevin									
Galena, Mona									
Hardin, Ramon									
Kubiac, Dimitri									
Kwan, Ellis									
Lane, Loren									
Osborn, Jessica									
Shaw, Lesley									
Shaw, Wesley									
Showalter, Tina									
Slobovka, Elena									
Yazzie, Ben									

Figure 5.12 Participation Chart Recorded by Children

Item(s) <u>Participation Chart</u>

Group <u>Entire class</u>   Date <u>3/12/06</u> Time <u>9–10:00 am</u>

Observer <u>Child Recorded</u>   Setting <u>Outdoor hunt & study</u>

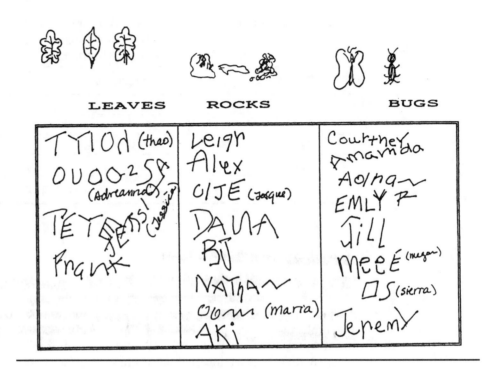

Figure 5.13 Participation Chart Recorded by a Teacher

Item(s) <u>Participation in Cooperative Learning Task</u>

Group <u>Albie, Baker, Thomas, Zucher</u>   Date <u>3/23/06</u> Time <u>10:25</u>

Observer <u>Wickelgren</u>   Setting <u>Science project</u>

Name	Collects & contributes materials	Participates in discussion	Participates in final project
Albie, T.	IIOOIII	ⅢOI	I
Baker, J.	IIIO	OOIIIII	I
Thomas, F.	OOIIOI	OOOIOO	I
Zucher, A.	OIIIOI	OIOO	I

Code: I   relevant contribution
        0   irrelevant contribution
  Blank   no contribution

Figure 5.14   Frequency Count

Item(s) <u>Aggressive Behavior</u>   Dates <u>3/5/06</u> to <u>3/8/06</u>

Child <u>Munja, K.</u>   Time <u>12:45</u> to <u>1:00 pm</u>

Observer <u>Delos</u>   Setting <u>Outdoor play</u>

Frequency count: Number of times child deliberately hurt another
                 child, including: hitting, biting, pushing,
                 shoving, kicking, slapping.

Date	Frequency	Day Total
3/5	~~THH~~	5
3/6	II	2
3/7	~~THH~~ III	8
3/8	~~THH~~	5

4-DAY TOTAL: 20

Procedures That Rate or Rank

Rating scales and rubrics record judgments and summaries by assigning a rank or standing on a continuum relative to other individuals or a predetermined standard. They attempt to capture complex performances and thinking, such as writing, oral presentations, problem solving, or scientific investigations. They can document "global" or "holistic" evaluations of children's behavior or work (see Figure 5.15) as well as fine distinctions in quality (see Figures 5.16 and 5.17). Ratings and rankings should be based on solid assessment evidence, not impressions and opinions. One of the great advantages of rubrics is that they detail the qualities that go with each rank.

Rating Scales.   Rating scales (Figure 5.15) typically expect the rater to evaluate an individual on the characteristics under consideration, then rank the individual along a predetermined continuum from low to high frequency or quality. Words or numbers define levels of the scale. Some typical scales include:

- Advanced, Proficient, Partially Proficient, Needs Development
- Exceeds Standard, Meets Standard, Progressing toward Standard
- Never, Sometimes, Usually, Always
- Satisfactory, Unsatisfactory
- Grading—A, B, C, D, F—is the most familiar rating scale and is used to "grade" politicians, products, and services in addition to students' performances in school.

Rubrics or Descriptive Rating Scales.   A rubric presents clear criteria—rules or guidelines—by which a complex performance can be judged. Such rules are typically used in judging diving, figure skating, and gymnastic competitions. A *scoring rubric* "consists of a fixed scale and a list of characteristics describing performance for each of the points of the scale" (Marzano, Pickering, & McTighe, 1993, p. 29). The scale often specifies what is acceptable performance. Figure 5.16 is an example of a scoring rubric for the standard "expresses ideas clearly."

Figure 5.15 Rating Scale

Retelling Procedure 2

Directions: Indicate with a checkmark the extent to which the reader's retelling includes or provides evidence of the following information.

Retelling	None	Low Degree	Moderate Degree	High Degree
1. Includes information directly stated in text.		✗		
2. Includes information inferred directly or indirectly from the text.			✗	
3. Includes what is important to remember from the text.			✗	
4. Provides relevant content and concepts.			✗	
5. Indicates reader's attempt to connect background knowledge to text information.		✗		
6. Indicates reader's attempt to make summary statements or generalizations based on text that can be applied to the real world.			✗	
7. Indicates highly individualistic and creative impressions of or reactions to the text.			✗	
8. Indicates the reader's affective involvement with the text.		✗		
9. Demonstrates appropriate use of language (vocabulary, sentence structure, language conventions).			✗	
10. Indicates reader's ability to organize or compose the retelling.			✗	
11. Demonstrates the reader's sense of audience or purpose.		✗		
12. Indicates the reader's control of the mechanics of speaking or writing.		✗		

Interpretation: Items 1–4 indicate the reader's comprehension of textual information; items 5–8 indicate metacognitive awareness, strategy use, and involvement with text; items 9–12 indicate facility with language and language development.

From Morrow, L. M. (1998), Retelling Stories as a Diagnostic Tool. In *Reexamining Reading Diagnosis: New Trends and Procedures,* edited by Susan Mandel Glazer, Lyndon W. Scarfoss, & Lance M. Gentile. Newark, Delaware: International Reading Association, pp. 128–49. Reprinted with permission.

Teachers working with this rubric would analyze information pertinent to that standard and decide what statement on the scale best describes the child's performance at a particular time.

Figure 5.17 is an example of a rubric used for scoring in the Child Observation Record (COR), developed by High/Scope (1993). Teachers use evidence

Figure 5.16   Rubric for Scoring "Expresses Ideas Clearly"

A.   **Expresses ideas clearly**

4   Clearly and effectively communicates the main idea or theme and provides support that contains rich, vivid, and powerful detail.

3   Clearly communicates the main idea or theme and provides suitable support and detail.

2   Communicates important information but not a clear theme or overall structure.

1   Communicates information as isolated pieces in a random fashion.

From R. J. Marzano, D. Pickering, & J. McTighe, *Assessing Student Outcomes: Performance Assessment Using the Dimensions of Learning Model.* Alexandria, VA: Association for Supervision and Curriculum Development. Copyright © 1993. Reprinted by permission of R. J. Marzano.

documented during children's daily activities to make a judgment about which statement applies.

Specifying important aspects of a complex performance presents many challenges. What is acceptable performance at a given age or developmental level, or even in relation to a standard? As with any rating scale, the intervals between points on the scale may not be equal. Attaching numerical values to children's work is difficult, at best. The items on the rubric often represent only one of many

Figure 5.17   Rubric for Scoring "Solving Problems"

B. Solving problems		Time 1	Time 2	Time 3
Child does not yet identify problems.	(1)	_____	_____	_____
Child identifies problems, but does not try to solve them, turning instead to another activity.	(2)	_____	_____	_____
Child uses one method to try to solve a problem, but if unsuccessful, gives up after one or two tries.	(3)	_____	_____	_____
Child shows some persistence, trying several alternative methods to solve a problem.	(4)	_____	_____	_____
Child tries alternative methods to solve a problem and is highly involved and persistent.	(5)	_____	_____	_____

Notes:

_____

_____

_____

Reprinted with permission from High/Scope Educational Research Foundation. Copyright © 1992.

possible indicators of progress toward the standard, often the most obvious one. For example, efforts to specify various levels of classification may entirely overlook the fact that children need to learn to classify on bases they select and specify, as well as those specified by someone else.

Rating Scales and Rubrics

STRENGTHS

- Rating scales are a quick and systematic way to record inferences, judgments, and evaluations, including qualitative aspects of complex performances.
- Rating scales and rubrics can be constructed so that raters agree on the meaning of the descriptive terms, fostering greater consistency among raters.
- They are a quick way to record the opinion of others.
- Well-constructed rubrics are easy to translate into curriculum.

LIMITATIONS

- Good rating scales and rubrics are difficult to construct.
- People may differ in their understanding of a scale, or tend to rate toward the center of the scale.
- Rater biases may affect responses.
- Even the best rubrics cannot include all relevant characteristics.

Other Procedures

Some recording processes can be used to keep track of almost anything. These include narrative writing by teachers and children, computer record systems, and children's work products. Chapter 6 details ways of preserving work products in portfolios.

Narrative Writing. Teachers and children record inferences, conclusions, judgments, and reflections in their own words in journals, logs, reports, summaries, reviews, and other work products. Children dictate or write their reflections and judgments.

Some teachers keep daily or weekly chronological journals of their reflections about their teaching practices, concerns, and impressions. They record notes about children, plans for the future, or achievements, or they reflect on past and present experiences. Journals may help teachers improve their own teaching by encouraging self-reflection (Lay-Dopyera & Dopyera, 1987). Reflection on events may result in insights that would never occur in a busy classroom (Hannon, 2000).

Computer Record-Keeping Systems. Three types of computer systems are currently in use: those that track children's performance on a specific computer teaching program; those that organize and store information about children and help teachers develop and print summary reports; and those that assess and analyze children's behavior, then make suggestions for instruction.

Available programs teach early reading or math skills, record student responses, and create student profiles ready to be printed. Their focus is primarily on limited aspects of reading and math that lend themselves to a gamelike format.

Several commercial assessment systems have computer-based recording and information management systems that correspond to manual systems. Teachers enter data they have collected and recorded in other ways into the computer, where it is stored, ready to be summarized or analyzed. This can be a time-consuming step. In some cases, teachers enter information directly using personal digital assistants (PDAs) or laptop computers. Because the unique contribution of most systems is in summarizing and managing information that teachers have already collected and recorded, we discuss them in Chapter 6.

Selecting a Recording Procedure

The appropriateness of a recording procedure depends on the purpose of the assessment, what is being assessed, amount of detail needed, and practical considerations.

Purpose of the Assessment

Whether teachers describe, count, or rate depends on how a record will be used. Descriptive records may be best if the purpose is to share information with parents. For a teacher's use, a count or tally may suffice. A program or school may mandate the records needed for official purposes, such as referral or reporting progress.

What Is Being Assessed

Certain behaviors and products are best captured by a description, others by counts or ratings. The most appropriate way to preserve what a child says is to record the actual words. A count is a good way to keep track of the number of times a child participates in group discussion or the presence or absence of skills and subskills. Attitudes and dispositions may be documented on a ratings scale or rubric or can be inferred from descriptions and tallies.

Amount of Detail Needed

Records capture varying levels of detail or amounts of raw information. Writing down exactly "who said what" and "who did what" preserves more detail than "had an argument." Tallying discrete units of behavior, such as appropriate and inappropriate initiations and responses to other children, preserves more detail than a tally of "social interaction" as one broad category.

The amount and type of detail needed depends on how a record will be used and the area of development or curriculum being assessed. Records that document problems and concerns, or for determining program placement, should contain as many specific details as possible about important behaviors. Detail may be less significant for everyday planning. Focus description on those aspects of performance that are relevant. For example, knowing a child pronounced "Robert" as "Wobert" is significant when appraising language development but less so when examining motor development.

More detail is not always better. Unnecessary detail is distracting. In documenting if a child understands how to measure time, the way she is standing and whom she is talking with are not important. Too little detail makes a record inaccurate, so noting only the child's understanding of minutes leaves out important information about hours and other time concepts.

Teachers can adjust recording procedures to fit the level of detail needed. Descriptive records are easiest to adjust—write or draw more or fewer details or take more or fewer pictures. Because they require little preparation, adjustments can be made during recording. Increase the detail of tallies by counting smaller subcategories, components of skills, or units of behavior. Instead of counting "prosocial" behavior, count the number of appropriate and inappropriate initiations to others, number of responses to other children, and number of social conflicts resolved successfully. Because tallied behaviors are identified before assessment starts, adjustments to procedures will be difficult to make while recording.

Practical Considerations

Teachers must weigh practical considerations when selecting a recording procedure. These include preparation time, amount of attention needed to record data, and whether to use group or individual records.

Preparation Time versus Recording Time. Some procedures require much preparation time before assessment starts but take less time to record. Rating scales and rubrics take lots of time to prepare, especially those designed to be used by people other than the teacher. Items must be carefully phrased, and the scale must be developed. Counting and tallying procedures also require preparation to identify behaviors, determine the level of detail, develop descriptions of what will be observed, and prepare recording forms. Recording on rating scales, counts, and tallies is quick—a circle, a check, or a tick mark.

Procedures that require little preparation, such as anecdotal records and narrative descriptions, take more time to record. The recorder must have enough time to write the information, not simply check or circle an item.

There are trade-offs either way. Think through the time available for recording during class. If you have sufficient time to make detailed recordings in the classroom, then those procedures may be best. However, when classroom time is limited, invest the time in preparation to keep recording during class at a minimum.

Amount of Attention Needed to Record Data. Procedures that require a teacher's total focus for recording information are difficult, if not impossible, without the presence of other adults helping in the classroom. For example, to write an accurate, descriptive narrative of group interaction in a complicated project, one person must do nothing but record. Procedures requiring moderate amounts of teacher attention can be done without the aid of other adults if teachers are interacting intermittently with children. During an art activity, the teacher interacts with children, steps back to make short notes describing fine motor coordination, and then returns. Making a record becomes part of the flow of interaction. Because some procedures require only making a mark or pushing a clicker, a teacher can record as he talks and works with children. For instance, as a teacher leads a group discussion, he can check names of children who participate.

Procedures recorded outside of classroom time do not take time away from teaching but rely on teacher memory, which may or may not be accurate. An example is an anecdotal record written at the end of the day about an incident that happened just before lunch. The many events between lunch and three o'clock will make remembering the details of that incident difficult. Do not depend on these procedures to record important classroom information, but use them as a supplement to routine recording procedures.

Consider classroom resources when choosing a procedure. If an aide or another adult is present, attention-intensive techniques may be feasible. Teachers who don't have extra help may opt for procedures that can be used while teaching or interacting intermittently (see Figure 5.18).

Group versus Individual Records.   Information for all the children in a group can be recorded so that the whole group's achievements can be seen quickly; one sheet of paper may suffice, or each child can have a separate record. Although both types are used in most classrooms, practical considerations limit the number of separate individual records a teacher can make.

Concisely recorded and displayed information about each child in the class is called a *group matrix record* (see Figure 5.9). Group matrices are the most efficient way to document appraisals of all the children in a classroom. One group record can display data collected during one or several appraisals, done at one time or spread over a period of time. It can also serve several purposes: primary data record, a list of who has and has not been assessed on a particular item, and a group profile or summary (see Chapter 6).

Individual records document one child's performance or behavior. They usually are used for unique or in-depth information about a child or small group (see Figure 5.19, and Figures 5.3 and 5.6). To get a picture of the group as a whole, the information has to be transferred to a group profile or summary, which requires another step.

Practical considerations suggest that when the knowledge or behavior under consideration lends itself to a group record, that might be a wise choice.

Figure 5.18   When Recording Procedures Can Be Used

Procedures Difficult to Use While Interacting	Descriptive narratives Anecdotal records made while behavior is occurring
Procedures Easy to Use When Interacting Intermittently	Jottings Diagrams, sketches, pictures Rating scales Duration counts Time samples
Procedures Easy to Use When Interacting	Checklists Participation charts Frequency counts Audio recordings Video recordings Collecting work products
Procedures Recorded outside of Classroom Time	Anecdotes recorded after behavior has occurred Teacher journals and logs Computer tracking systems

Figure 5.19 Individual Record

....

Item(s) <u>Cognitive Development</u>

Child <u>M. Harvey</u>   Date <u>1/27/06</u> — <u>8/2/06</u>

Memory

Said "I put it in my memory bank," as he touched his
forehead. 2/2/06

Observed M repeating the words of the song to himself after
the song was over. 2/25/06 (Good example of practice)

During classification activity, M repeats the "big and small"
in a sing-song voice over and over as he puts the objects in
the groups. Was able to group 15 objects into big and small
red circles and big and small green circles. 2/26/06

Summary

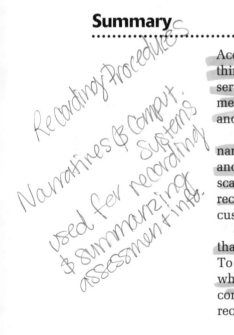

Accurate and complete primary data records are essential to ensure the trustworthiness of authentic assessment. Records preserve information for future use, serve as the basis for communicating with other people, and help teachers remember what children know and can do, helping them become better observers and teachers.

Examples of practical classroom recording procedures include descriptive narratives, anecdotal records, jottings, diagrams, sketches, photographs, audio and video recordings, checklists, participation charts, frequency counts, rating scales, and some rubrics. Narratives and computer systems can be used both for recording and for summarizing assessment information. Work products are discussed more fully in Chapter 6.

Recording procedures can be grouped into (1) those that describe; (2) those that count, time, or tally; and (3) those that rate or rank the item being assessed. To select a recording procedure, teachers consider the purpose of the assessment, what is being assessed, the amount of detail needed, and practical classroom considerations—such as the amount of preparation time, attention required to record, and whether information is recorded by groups or individuals.

For Personal Reflection

1. Much current writing on assessment suggests that teachers keep a journal or log documenting their own experiences with child assessment, and then evaluate and reflect on those experiences. Thoughtfully consider that suggestion, weigh its advantages and disadvantages, and then write your opinion concerning it.
2. One way for teachers to learn to use the many recording procedures is to start using them one or two at a time, practice and learn these, then go on to others. Reflect on your own knowledge and experience. Which

procedures have you already mastered (if any), and which do you have yet to learn? Decide which one you will learn next, and why.

For Further Study and Discussion

1. You are planning an assessment of social interaction during a cooperative learning activity. You are particularly interested in whether children can organize themselves into a group, follow directions, help each other, and resolve disputes. What two recording procedures would be appropriate for the situation? Justify your choices.

2. You are planning an assessment of math skills—understanding "more than/fewer than." Give two alternative recording procedures appropriate for this situation. Explain why you chose these two procedures. Identify the disadvantages and advantages of one of the procedures.

3. Watch a videotape of several children interacting. The first time you watch, write a descriptive narrative of what you see. The second time you watch, count the social initiations that children make to each other, such as invitations to play or bids for attention. Compare the two methods. Which would be most useful to a teacher interested in social development? Why? Which was easiest to record?

Suggested Readings

Bentzen, W. R. (2000). *Seeing young children: A guide to observing and recording behavior* (4th ed.). New York: Delmar Publishers.

Boehm, A. E., & Weinberg, R. A. (1996). *The classroom observer: Developing observation skills in early childhood settings.* New York: Teachers College Press.

Cohen, D. H., Stern, V., & Balaban, N. (1997). *Observing and recording the behavior of young children* (4th ed.). New York: Teachers College Press.

Helm, J., Beneke, S., & Steinheimer, K. (1998). *Teacher materials for documenting young children's work.* New York: Teachers College Press.

Helm, J., Beneke, S., & Steinheimer, K. (1998). *Windows on learning.* New York: Teachers College Press.

Marzano, R. J., Pickering, D., & McTighe, J. (1993). *Assessing student outcomes: Performance assessment using the dimensions of learning model.* Alexandria, VA: Association for Supervision and Curriculum Development.

Nicholson, S., & Shipstead, S. G. (2002). *Through the looking glass: Observations in the early childhood classroom* (3rd ed.). Upper Saddle River, NJ: Prentice Hall.

CHAPTER 6

Compiling and Summarizing Information

Teachers compile and summarize classroom data to integrate and distill information from different sources, contexts, and methods; reduce it to a manageable size; and keep past assessments accessible for continued analysis and interpretation. Similarities and patterns in behavior emerge only when several appraisals are integrated. As teachers compile and summarize information from the classroom, they begin to understand specific children and a specific group of children.

As the year progresses, the number of records increases—more than anyone could possibly commit to memory. "The wealth of data provided by continuous assessment of student behaviors . . . can be overwhelming, even if systematically recorded. . . . Only through [checklists, profiles, and other means of summarizing] can the vast amount of information on each child be reduced to manageable proportions" (Athey, 1990, p. 180).

Summaries keep past appraisals accessible so they can be analyzed and interpreted in light of the new information that is gathered. Instead of looking through all previous appraisals, the teacher looks at distilled data, saving time and effort.

Three complementary ways of compiling and summarizing information are discussed in this chapter: portfolios, group profiles, and individual profiles.

Portfolios

Description and Definition

Portfolios are part of almost every alternative assessment system and are popular with teachers, children, and parents at all levels of education. They have generated widespread interest, development, and use. A portfolio is an organized, purposeful compilation of evidence documenting a child's development and learning over time. It is not a "method" of appraisal or assessment but a way of keeping together and compiling information from many methods. It exhibits to the child and others the experiences, efforts, progress, and accomplishments of that child, showing a person's unique capabilities as well as accomplishments shared with others. In the process, portfolios provide a basis for evaluation and a guide for further learning and development.

Physically, a portfolio is a folder, file, box, computer disk, or other container that stores evidence of a pupil's learning (see Chapter 9).

Conceptually, a portfolio is an evolving concept rather than a term with an agreed-on, precise definition. Valencia and Place (1994) identify four major types of portfolios:

- The showcase portfolio shows a pupil's best or favorite work.
- The evaluation portfolio contains mostly specified and scored material.
- The documentation portfolio holds evidence of children's work and progress, which is selected to build a comprehensive description of each child.
- The process portfolio contains ongoing work for a larger project, usually chronicled and commented on by the pupil.

People select different types depending on their purposes and what will best serve a particular group of teachers and children (Murphy & Smith, 1990).

Portfolios are well suited to organizing, storing, and preserving informal, authentic data about all aspects of young children's development. Portfolios

- Are flexible and adaptable. They can be varied to suit the age and development of children, the developmental or curriculum domain, school or center goals, or other considerations.
- Capture many dimensions of children's development and learning
- Focus on children's strengths—what they can do
- Help children assume responsibility for their own learning
- Lend themselves to samplings over time from a variety of assessment windows
- Involve children in selection of and reflection on items as appropriate to their development and the item under consideration
- Can contain information that is common to every child in the group, as well as that which is unique to each child
- Provide for dynamic, ongoing assessment, not static reports, grades, or scores
- Are a rich source of information for communicating with and about children and their learning

Purposes

Portfolios fulfill most of the basic purposes of assessment: determining children's status and progress, informing instruction, providing information for reporting and communication, and preliminary identification of children who might benefit from special help. Portfolios often serve additional purposes, which influence what is included and how the portfolio is organized (Arter, 1990; Arter & Spandel, 1992). If the purpose is to show growth over time, representative or best work is included at several points in time. If the portfolio is meant to show how children plan and carry out a project, a record of all activities, assignments, field trips, meetings, drafts and revisions, displays, and reflections on the processes and products might be kept. Other purposes include motivating children and promoting learning through reflection and self-assessment (Murphy & Smith, 1990). "Composite" portfolios tell the story of a group's efforts, progress, or achievements, such as those of a kindergarten or second grade (Arter & Paulson, 1991).

Portfolios serve teachers as well as children. The reflection, discussion, and interaction generated among teachers as they examine, compare, and interpret children's portfolios are as important as the content (Hebert, 1998; Murphy & Smith, 1990). Portfolios remind teachers that assessment is ongoing and can enhance children's learning (Valencia, 1990; Wolf, 1989). Portfolio development and conferencing can increase communication among child, teacher, and parent. Many teachers develop their own portfolios, complete with reflection and self-assessment, to guide and document their personal and professional growth.

Basic Approaches to Portfolio Building

There are four basic approaches to portfolio building: requiring specific items; requiring evidence in given developmental or curriculum areas but not specifying the items; collecting individual, often spontaneous, samples from ongoing classroom activities; and combinations of the preceding three.

Required Items. Required items, "core" items (Meisels & Steele, 1991), or "common tools" (Valencia & Place, 1994) specify certain items to be collected for all children in a given class or at a given level. Teachers assess the same thing in the same way within designated time intervals or collection periods, such as crayon self-portraits done at the beginning and end of the year or child responses to a uniform drawing or writing prompt. The Kamehameha Elementary Education Program specified the measures used in six aspects of literacy in kindergarten through third grade (Au, 1997). These included samples of responses to literature to document reading comprehension, teacher observations and logs of voluntary reading, and running records to identify word-reading strategies. The first grade Integrated Language Arts Portfolio in Juneau, Alaska, required a teacher checklist on reading and oral language development, a student reading attitude survey, one sample per quarter of text that a child could read, two writing samples per quarter, open-ended tests of reading comprehension, the number of books read, a checklist of language arts skills, and scores on a year-end standardized test (Arter, 1990). Specific requirements such as these ensure appropriate documentation for all children on important goals, and guide teachers as they learn portfolio development.

Required Evidence. Required evidence portfolios specify certain types of things, such as a sample of creative art; a sample of the child's ability to represent events, objects, or actions; a language sample; or evidence of fine motor development, but leave exactly what is collected up to the teacher and child (Valencia, 1989).

Individualized Sampling. Individualized sampling relies on selection from ongoing classroom work or activities. These systems are more open, allowing the teacher, child, or both to select work and other documentation (interviews, observations, children's interactions, participation in given activities) that exemplify how children feel, act, or think. They show each child's unique approach, progress, and understandings (Chittenden & Courtney, 1989). They may show a child's "favorite," "best," or "most-improved" work. There is no requirement to collect similar items for each child except as the items reflect progress toward important goals. Some schools using this approach include only items selected by children.

These portfolios identify and document an individual child's unique interests, knowledge, skills, dispositions, and "style" of development and learning—their "personal signature" (Eisner, 1991, p. 17) or "approach to learning" (Kagan, Moore, & Bredekamp, 1995). Such insight can be extracted from other documentation but is more likely to be identified, recognized, and valued in a portfolio.

Combinations. Required core items or indicators plus optional individualized items selected by the teacher and child seem most appropriate for young children. They combine systematic documentation pertaining to important goals with the opportunity to capture evidence that occurs spontaneously and may be unique to that child or that situation. Teachers experienced in portfolio development say the right combination evolves (Hebert, 1998).

Selection of Content

A portfolio is not simply a folder of student work or a catch-all file of checklists, notes, test results, and other information and records. It must be thoughtfully planned and organized.

Appropriate Types of Items. Portfolio items vary with the age and development of children, goals of the program, the curriculum or developmental domain under consideration, the type and purpose of the portfolio, and teacher preferences. Figure 6.1 suggests some possibilities. No school or center would use all of those listed but would select a combination to provide "multiple windows"—different sources, methods, and contexts—on a child's accomplishments.

Item Selection. Unless they are involved in large-scale assessment, teachers in a given school or center usually have much latitude in identifying portfolio items. When they discuss and agree on what they are going to put in a portfolio, they are more likely to know what to collect and to actually do it. Indiscriminate additions to a portfolio quickly become overwhelming, but a too-scanty portfolio will not have enough information to be useful and certainly will not provide multidimensional evidence of a child's progress over time.

Items should be *informative, easy to collect,* and representative of *meaningful* classroom activities (Meisels, Jablon, Marsden, Dichtelmiller, Dorfman, & Steele, 1994). *Informative* items reveal several aspects of a child's learning and development. Work included in the portfolio should occur regularly in the classroom, so

Figure 6.1 Types of Items Appropriate for Portfolios
....

Work will be done in different ways at different ages and levels, and for different developmental and curriculum areas. Teachers and children may develop many imaginative variations on these basic types. For more ideas, see Figure 9.2 (p. 165).

- Work products done on paper—samples of cutting, drawing, any art medium, printing, practice papers, pasting, writings—initial drafts, editing, final drafts. Dictations by nonwriters.
- "Journals"—math, science, writing; children's drawings, scribbles, collages reflecting their experiences and growth.
- Records of data collection and presentation in math, science, social studies, health.
- Sketches of a child's work, made by the child or an adult (block structure, pattern blocks, sand, any 3-D work). Sketches of the plan for that work.
- Photographs of a child engaged in significant work or play.
- Photographs of exhibits and displays prepared by child or group.
- Audio and video records.
- Printouts of work done on computer—draw/paint, math, writing programs, games.
- Participation chart—what a child did on a given day or during a given period. Include qualitative information.
- Logs of activities and results (books read to or by child; parents can help).
- Time sample or count of what a child did on a given day or period.
- Interviews—audio/video/written. Elicit reports or descriptions of a process— how to make a favorite food, getting to school, making friends, playing a game, or "favorite" activities, books, things to do. Child can draw it and then dictate explanation to an adult.
- Structured observation, performance assessment, or dynamic assessment results. Do one or two children a day.
- Anecdotal records or jottings grouped according to the portfolio categories, and/or affixed in chronological order. Use Post-its, gummed labels, or quarter sheets of recycled office paper (tape them on).
- Awards, certificates, citations.
- Parents' comments and goals, notes from parent–teacher and child–teacher conferences; drawings and dictated or written messages to parents from children.

---

it is *easy to collect*. Classroom activities that result in high-quality portfolio items are *meaningful* and interesting to the children.

Who chooses items to go in the portfolio—teacher, child, or both? In what proportions? Much depends on the age, developmental level, and previous experience of the children. Preschool and primary children cannot assume major responsibility for their own portfolios, even though they may play an active role. Three- and 4-year-old children are unlikely to be discriminating in what they want to include, and the portfolio could be full or empty at the end of a month; second-graders may be able to make many choices. Teachers must judge how much choice and access young children have, and monitor them to ensure that important information is not missing (Hebert, 1998; Maeroff, 1991).

Age and Developmental Level of the Children. The portfolio concept must be adapted to the developmental level and prior experience of each group and, in some cases, each child. Children who read and write proficiently will have different portfolio items than those who are emergent readers and writers. Children who read and write fluently will be able to do and record more self-assessment and reflection, and with assistance they can take far more responsibility.

Organization of Content

There is no single way to select and organize portfolio content, as long as content relating to major developmental domains and the expected outcomes of the program are included.

Categories or Domains for Portfolio Content. Divisions might be the traditional developmental domains of physical, cognitive, language, and social/emotional development; subject matter such as health and safety, social studies, science, mathematics, and language and literacy; or report card categories. Teachers who are only beginning to use portfolios may focus on only one domain, such as language and literacy, or one aspect of literacy, such as emergent writing, where there is much information on appropriate items to collect, guides for evaluating processes and products, and excellent information to help teachers (see Appendix Figure A.7). The Work Sampling System (Meisels et al., 1994; 2003), which spans preschool through fifth grade, uses seven categories or domains:

Personal and social development
Language and literacy
Mathematical thinking
Scientific thinking
Social studies
The arts
Physical development

Some items will be difficult to categorize: They may not fit any of the categories, or they may fit several. A primary student's written report of an interview with the school cooks reveals much about the reporter's fine motor coordination, thinking processes, task persistence, and understanding of social roles and interdependence in the school community, as well as listening and writing competence. If the report is a result of a cooperative group effort, each child's contribution will need to be recognized. If an item is selected for a primary purpose, with other aspects being secondary, file it in the primary category. For example, if the primary purpose of the report was to check on listening and writing competence, it would be filed under language and literacy development. If the primary purpose was to document children's developing understanding of the way we organize ourselves as social groups, it might be filed under concept development or social studies.

Teachers who keep anecdotal records or jottings in individual children's portfolios simply arrange them in chronological order, perhaps coding them with colored pens or stickers as primarily related to social interaction, language, or another category. Gummed labels can be arrayed on a sheet of paper for storage.

Check frequently to ensure that all developmental or subject matter areas are adequately documented for all children. Place a list of any requirements at the front of each portfolio to keep track of which items are in place and which remain to be collected. An example is shown in Figure 6.2. Before duplicating such a

Figure 6.2 Portfolio Record Form

....

Portfolio Record

Grade _____ Child _____ Teacher _____

Domain	Sample 1	Sample 2	Sample 3
Physical and Motor			
Social and Emotional			
Language and Literacy			
Cognition and General Knowledge			
Approaches to Learning			

form, write in any required items, so that each child's portfolio has the same requirements. As items are inserted, note the date in the appropriate cell. As optional or individual items are collected, note what they are and the date they were added.

If a portfolio has an excess of creative art and journal samples, with few entries about physical or social development, determine why, and begin to build a more balanced portfolio. The imbalance may be caused by the fact that some important school goals, such as motor and social development, do not result in an "easy to collect" product, but must be documented in other ways. Or the imbalance may reflect an imbalanced curriculum and schedule.

Because portfolios lend themselves to the collection and storage of work products, make sure that children's thinking and learning processes are also documented. Even though performance samples and work products may make up the bulk of the portfolio, any classroom assessment procedures are appropriate to include and will probably be necessary in order to obtain adequate information about children's progress.

Self-Reflection and Self-Assessment. Developing children's abilities to reflect on and assess their own actions and work is an integral part of portfolio development. Three- and 4-year-olds will be limited in their ability to reflect on what they have done. Older children will be more capable, particularly if they have been coached and encouraged for several years. If not, they can learn. Don't ask children to reflect on everything; they soon tire of overanalysis. When 5-year-old Monique was asked to tell why certain books were her favorites, she said of the first, "Basically, it's just a very funny book"; of the second, "It has a sad ending and then it comes out nice"; of another, "It's just nice—it's like a lullaby to me"; and then, "Can I go now?"

Self-reflection and assessment start children on the long path to assuming responsibility for their own actions and learning. Appropriate prompts help children think about what they have learned or practiced during a particular activity (see Figure 6.3). Teacher or child may record the responses and attach them to the item.

Model, discuss, and practice developmentally appropriate reflection and self-assessment just as you would any other thinking process. Don't be dismayed at early responses that miss the mark. An entering kindergartner may say that what he likes about the picture he has drawn is "It's pretty 'n' stuff." A year later he may be able to spot letters that are formed incorrectly, explain why, and work

Figure 6.3 Sample Prompts for Self-Assessment and Reflection
....

"Tell me what you did."
"Tell (or show) me how you did it."
"Why did you decide to . . . ?"
"What were you thinking when you . . . ?"
"Tell me more about this and your thinking (feelings) as you did it."
"What do you like about this picture (structure, painting, writing)?"
"What would you do differently if you were doing this again?"
"Why do you want this to go in your portfolio?"
"What did you learn while you were doing this?"
"What problems did you have while doing this? How did you solve them?"

toward conventional forms; another year later he may revise his own writing and justify the revisions.

Children's reflections contain insights, understandings, and delights that don't reveal themselves in other ways. One second-grade teacher had worked all year to teach children the criteria for good writing and was now having children choose a piece to go in their portfolios. Anna had chosen one that met all the criteria. Delighted, the teacher asked her why she had chosen that one. Anna's response: "It reminds me of my dog." It was not the expected response but one that captured the essence of good writing.

Relationship of Portfolios to Other Types of Assessment

A portfolio differs from a youngster's personal file and cumulative record (Paulson, Paulson, & Meyer, 1991), but its relationship to other types of assessment and documentation varies from setting to setting, as do the contents of the portfolio. In some cases, portfolios are the only systematic documentation and compilation of children's work. In others, portfolios are only one part of a comprehensive alternative assessment system. Meisels and colleagues at the University of Michigan developed such a system for children in preschool through fifth grade (1994). It consists of three complementary elements: observations by teachers using developmental guidelines and checklists, collections of children's work in portfolios, and summaries of this information in summary reports. Developmental checklists "document the broad scope of a child's learning" (Meisels et al., 1994, p. 13) in relationship to state and national standards; portfolios contain in-depth information about how a child works, and the nature and quality of that work; summary reports integrate, summarize, and evaluate information about each child from the checklists and portfolios.

We recommend that portfolios complement and supplement other documentation, such as individual and group records. It is difficult to incorporate into a portfolio everything you need to know about a child, and it is even more difficult to determine how to plan for a group when documentation is based solely on individual portfolios.

Increasing the Information in Each Portfolio Item

Make each item that goes in the portfolio as informative as possible: Identify and annotate work products, photographs, or sketches; if the items are required, develop procedures and instructions that maximize information; and select spontaneously generated items for what they reveal about the child as well as their uniqueness.

Identify and Annotate Each Item. Identify each work product with the child's name and the date. Whenever possible and pertinent, include the teacher's name, setting (outdoors, writing center, enrichment math), time of day, grade or group, and any other relevant information. Date items with a rubber stamp, or let children copy or generate their names and the date as functional practice in letter and numeral formation.

An annotation is a reflection, comment, or explanation that makes the significance of an item clear and adds relevant information not otherwise available. Teachers, children, or both may annotate items. Annotations might include the following:

- Reason the item was selected
- Task variables: setting, assigned or voluntary, assisted or independent, amount and type of assistance, directions, materials available, time and effort expended
- Written or dictated reflections, descriptions, remarks, and assessments
- Responses to questions or prompts (see Figure 6.3)
- Analysis of what the work shows about the child's learning and comparisons with previous work
- Explanation of why the item is significant as an example of the child's work
- Child's personal responses or observations, such as making a connection to prior knowledge and experience, pride, interest, or preference

Annotations should clarify the situation in which the item was developed and its significance. For instance, did Ben compose the simple but beautiful poem handwritten in his portfolio, or did he copy it from a bulletin board or book? Did Cory plan, research, and write her report on porcupines in class or at home, where she had guidance from her parents and computer technology for research, composition, and revision? Was the topic assigned or chosen? Children change schools, teachers change, and people other than classroom staff will have no way of knowing the situational elements that give meaning to a portfolio item unless it is recorded.

Annotations include observations by teachers. For example, in assessing fine motor skills and use of tools, teachers make observations about children's grasp, strength, and coordination. This information is not evident from the product itself, but is important in understanding the product and should be noted.

Identify and annotate or "caption" (Kingore, 1993) the portfolio item by writing on the item itself (Figures 6.4 and 6.5), on all-purpose record forms (Chapter 9), or on a separate portfolio entry slip (Figure 6.6). Fix the item and the entry slip together, and they are ready to file.

Affix photographs of children engaged in significant work to 8½ × 11 inch portfolio entry slips (see Figure 6.6) with glue stick, rubber cement, or another appropriate adhesive. Identify, annotate, and file. If there is a delay between picture taking and developing, fill out the form when the picture is taken, so you won't forget the reason you took it. For additional insight, let the child pictured study it, and dictate or write the significance to her of what is shown.

Half sheets of paper are adequate for most entries, but photographs need a full sheet to allow for comments and explanations.

The entry slip has several advantages. It reminds everyone to caption portfolio items; children's work is not intruded on by analytical remarks; there is adequate space; and observers can note significant process variables (pencil grasp, use of a model, concentration, time spent) while children are working, thus saving time. Children who write can fill out some or all of the entry slip. One school calls these "reflection tags" and has plenty of them available for children and teachers (Hebert, 1998).

Develop Instructions and Procedures to Maximize the Information Gained from Each Item.   Portfolio items can be made more informative by having children demonstrate several things in one item. For example, if you ask a child to draw a picture of a person, ask her also to tell you about the picture and then to print her name on the paper. Instead of only the picture, you will have a writing sample, language sample, coordination observation, ability to follow instructions, observation, and opportunities for many other insights.

Figure 6.4 Informative Portfolio Item: Fall

Develop consistent instructions and procedures for performance tasks. In the "draw a person" task, are the children allowed to choose whatever drawing instrument they want, or are they assigned one? Think through these seemingly small details, and make decisions; the details affect performance. Duplicate and attach the instructions to the portfolio entry slip, or duplicate them on the entry slip. At the least, they should be written on the product, as in Figures 6.4 and 6.5: These simple, easily collected work products contain a wealth of information about Brian, far more than the picture alone. They reveal his familiarity with drawing instruments and their characteristics; his small muscle development; his

Figure 6.5 Informative Portfolio Item: Spring

knowledge of print; and an understanding of his own capabilities, language, and progress from October to May. Just as important in the long run is the beginning of reflection and self-assessment—shown in how he remembered the way he used to draw people and realized that he had progressed. These figures also reveal how duplicated instructions and conditions would have lessened the teacher's task, allowing her to record observations and comments as the events occurred.

Select Spontaneously Generated Items for Information as Well as Uniqueness. Rich and informative items for portfolios result from children's sponta-

Figure 6.6   Portfolio Entry Form

Child _____ Date __/ / /__

Context/Setting _____

Comments/Significance _____

_____

Use a form such as this for portfolio items that are not totally self-explanatory. Doing so identifies and annotates—"captions"—items so their meaning is not lost. Half sheets work well for artwork and writing, but you need a full sheet for photographs. You may also want heavier paper for photographs.

Photographs can be of work a child has done—modeling with clay, wood sculpture, block buildings or arrangements, sand modeling, outdoor play, patterns, and other products. Or they can be of a child working on something of significance. The trick is to photograph something "of significance"—something that displays important learning or accomplishment on the part of the child, captures a characteristic approach to learning, shows achievement of a goal or standard, or demonstrates an aspect of development that you are trying to nurture.

Comments or reflections on portfolio items can be made by the child, teacher, or both. They should explain or highlight what is significant about the item—why it is included in the portfolio. Comments might include

- Dictated or written remarks by the child
- Child self-assessment or reflection
- Reasons the item was chosen
- Observations by the teacher (directions given, process used, approach to work, use of tools, length of time worked)
- Analysis of what the work shows about the child's learning
- Comparisons with previous work
- Personal responses or observations

neous work and play—often revealing capabilities far beyond what we anticipate, because they are not constrained by adult direction and expectations. Look for these as priceless portfolio additions, add any needed explanations, and study them for what they reveal.

Jeremy is in kindergarten and has diagrammed the process of making cookies, which he did a week ago (see Figure 6.7). The task was a self-appointed one, done at the writing center. His work shows the following attributes:

- The sequence of steps is clear, distinct, accurate, and in order.
- Because the cookie making was done the week before, Jeremy had stored the steps in memory and was able to retrieve them.
- Left-to-right progression on the top row gives way to a flow-type representation that retains horizontal orientation.
- The product combines several types of representation into one schematic diagram—including drawing, writing, dictation, circles demarcating the discrete steps, and arrows showing the flow of the process—a more complex task than any one or two combined.
- Conceptualization of the representation was the child's; he had no model.

- Pictures and print are linked in meaning.
- Some steps are represented by print only, such as "Kut out," revealing understanding that print alone will carry the meaning.
- Clear concepts of a "word" are demonstrated. No words are run together.
- Abstract concepts of time, temperature, and measurement are incorporated in the correct places and linked with the correct units of measurement (cups, degrees, time). Estimation of numbers of units (2 to 3 minutes, 70 degrees) are far afield.
- Invented spelling shows almost perfect sound–symbol correspondence. Conventional spelling is used in several words.
- Formation and placement of letters are still being learned. Uppercase and lowercase letters are intermingled. Uppercase *L*s are backward.
- Control of small hand and arm muscles and coordination skills show in the size of drawing and lettering, the control over placement of arrows, and the small illustrations. Such control is beyond normal expectations for kindergarten.
- Language is used to explain and inform another person; understanding that language can direct and control actions is demonstrated—the "re-sape" book tells you what to do.

Figure 6.7   Kindergarten Child's Schematic Diagram of the Process of Making Cookies

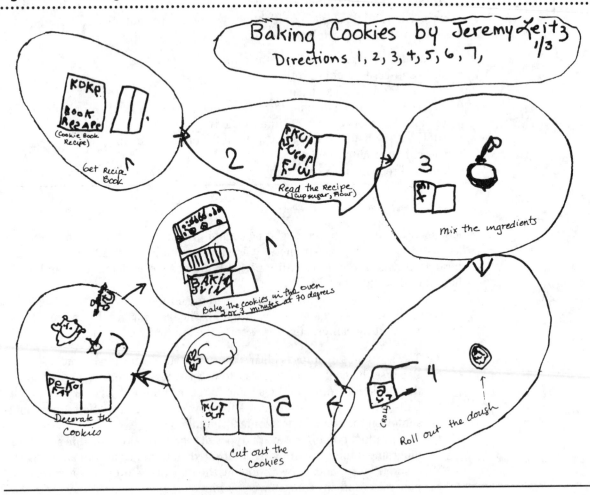

- The entire diagram demonstrates knowledge of function of print and ability to communicate and explain intent. Trying to determine the significance of what appeared to be a book in each circle, the adult inquired about it. Jeremy answered, "We use the recipe book each time," pointing to each step in the process. Other explanations of intent were dictated to and written by the adult.

Analysis of even one work product such as this, demonstrating print literacy, representational and sequencing processes, cognitive development, and use of fine motor skills, tells far more about this youngster than a test would, especially when coupled with answers to adult requests for explanation. If comparison is needed, compare the product and its interpretation to developmental expectations in cognitive development, literacy, and fine motor skills; to school and center objectives; or to similar work the child has done previously, such as earlier drawings captioned with his own printing. By any measure, the work is high quality for kindergarten. Not every work product will offer this much insight into a child's capabilities, but usually there is more information available than we take time to understand.

The Place of Technology

"Electronic portfolios" help create, preserve, and store children's work using digital technology. Software is available from several commercial companies. With a digital camera or color scanner, teachers or children can enter graphics, illustrations, photographs, and pictures directly into portfolios stored and managed by the computer. Text can be created or imported, including reflections and comments by teacher and children. Sound and movement features are available for narration or for saving speeches, music, drama, and other movement performances. Selected items or entire portfolios can be stored for viewing by parents or next year's teachers. The long-term storage and tracking possibilities could be useful for following children's progress from one grade or school to the next. One tech-savvy teacher combined still shots and video clips from a digital camera with explanatory text to make a PowerPoint presentation for parent conferences.

Group and Individual Profiles and Summaries

Group and individual profiles are ways to compile, summarize, and organize assessment information in instructionally meaningful ways. Taking time—a teacher's most precious resource—to summarize assessment information has several benefits. Working with the data calls for reflection—thoughtful, analytical consideration of whatever is at issue. As you summarize, think of each child, the group, what is going on in the classroom, what you hope to achieve, and what may need to be modified. There is little time for this in day-to-day classroom activities. Without reflection, assessment, and consequently instruction, may not be linked to meeting children's needs. In addition, summarizing data ensures that no child and no important dimension of development is neglected. Finally, summarization helps you focus on this group, these individual children. Patterns of strengths and needs emerge that are not apparent in a busy classroom.

There is no set time for compiling summaries. If the children are learning measurement—linear, weight, volume, and perhaps other units—and you've assessed individual children, it makes sense to get that information summarized to give some idea of the group's understanding (see Figure 6.8).

Individual profiles are usually done as progress reports for parents and school records or when an individual child must be considered in depth.

Because summarization is the first step in, and a part of, interpreting and using assessment information, keep two references nearby: the standards, goals, or other outcomes you are aiming for; and the developmental patterns in the Assessment and Analysis Guides in Appendix A.

Published Summary Forms

Schools and centers using a published curriculum (such as High/Scope or a specific reading or mathematics approach) or a published assessment system (such as the Work Sampling System) usually use the summary forms that align with that curriculum. School district or state curriculum frameworks may include forms for summarizing children's progress.

Figures 6.8 through 6.10 are representative pages from three widely used curriculum and assessment approaches. These firms also supply forms for narrative observations and summaries, and provide electronic assistance in summarizing and managing information.

To use electronic data management, teachers enter information they have collected about children, usually in the form of a rating scale. The information management program then summarizes the information for each child and for the class. Some software links a child's profile to suggested classroom activities and provides key formats, words, and phrases teachers can use to generate progress reports for each child or for the class. Some software generates reports that can be used for accountability reporting. Some software scores and stores data online. High/Scope's Child Observation Record (COR) (www.highscope.org/Assessment) and Creative Curriculum's Assessment Toolkit (www.teachingstrategies.com) are examples of curriculum approaches that align with an assessment system using computer technology to summarize and manage information about children. The Marazon System (www.marazon.com) and the Galileo Preschool (www.ati-online.com) provide profiles that can be used for planning suggested activities. The Work Sampling System (www.pearsonearlylearning.com/index2htm) provides a more general classroom-based summary and analysis aligned with a state's standards or a specific program's expected outcomes. The Dynamic Indicators of Basic Early Literacy Skills (DIBELS) (Moats, Good, & Kaminski, 2003) is an example of a standardized early literacy test that summarizes information, analyzes it, and provides specific intervention suggestions.

Published summary forms seldom yield enough detail for instructional purposes. They summarize a general assessment of a child's progress in language and literacy, mathematics, scientific thinking, or social and physical development. Such summaries are appropriate for reporting to parents and for accountability purposes. Teachers usually need more specific information to guide planning. For example, in mathematics, science, and language development, children are expected to compare and contrast objects, people, events, and ideas in increasingly complex and accurate terms. Which terms do which children understand. Which terms do they use. Which terms do they need to learn? The guides that follow help teachers develop their own methods to summarize such specific information in instructionally meaningful ways.

Figure 6.8 **Portion of a Summary Form for an Individual Child.** This example is from the Work Sampling System Kindergarten Developmental Checklist 4th ed., 2003. Other child development domains are on other pages of the form (not included here).

E	Measurement	F W S
1	Orders, compares, and describes objects by size, length, capacity, and weight. (p. 16)	Not Yet ☐☐☐ / In Process ☐☐☐ / Proficient ☐☐☐
2	Explores common instruments for measuring during work or play. (p. 16)	Not Yet ☐☐☐ / In Process ☐☐☐ / Proficient ☐☐☐
3	Estimates and measures using non-standard and standard units. (p. 17)	Not Yet ☐☐☐ / In Process ☐☐☐ / Proficient ☐☐☐
4	Shows awareness of time concepts. (p. 17)	Not Yet ☐☐☐ / In Process ☐☐☐ / Proficient ☐☐☐

F	Data collection and probability	F W S
1	Begins to collect data and make records using lists or graphs. (p. 17)	Not Yet ☐☐☐ / In Process ☐☐☐ / Proficient ☐☐☐

IV Scientific Thinking

A	Inquiry	F W S
1	Seeks information through observation, exploration, and descriptive investigations. (p. 19)	Not Yet ☐☐☐ / In Process ☐☐☐ / Proficient ☐☐☐
2	Uses simple tools and equipment to extend the senses and gather data. (p. 19)	Not Yet ☐☐☐ / In Process ☐☐☐ / Proficient ☐☐☐
3	Forms explanations and communicates scientific information. (p. 20)	Not Yet ☐☐☐ / In Process ☐☐☐ / Proficient ☐☐☐

B	Physical science	F W S
1	Identifies, describes, and compares properties of objects. (p. 20)	Not Yet ☐☐☐ / In Process ☐☐☐ / Proficient ☐☐☐

C	Life science	F W S
1	Observes and describes characteristics, basic needs, and life cycles of living things. (p. 20)	Not Yet ☐☐☐ / In Process ☐☐☐ / Proficient ☐☐☐

D	Earth science	F W S
1	Explores and identifies properties of rocks, soil, water, and air. (p. 21)	Not Yet ☐☐☐ / In Process ☐☐☐ / Proficient ☐☐☐
2	Begins to observe and describe simple seasonal and weather changes. (p. 21)	Not Yet ☐☐☐ / In Process ☐☐☐ / Proficient ☐☐☐

V Social Studies

A	People, past and present	F W S
1	Identifies similarities and differences in people's characteristics, habits, and living patterns. (p. 23)	Not Yet ☐☐☐ / In Process ☐☐☐ / Proficient ☐☐☐
2	Demonstrates beginning awareness of state and country. (p. 23)	Not Yet ☐☐☐ / In Process ☐☐☐ / Proficient ☐☐☐
3	Shows some awareness of time and how the past influences people's lives. (p. 23)	Not Yet ☐☐☐ / In Process ☐☐☐ / Proficient ☐☐☐

B	Human interdependence	F W S
1	Begins to understand how people rely on others for goods and services. (p. 24)	Not Yet ☐☐☐ / In Process ☐☐☐ / Proficient ☐☐☐

2	Describes some people's jobs and what is required to perform them. (p. 24)	Not Yet ☐☐☐ / In Process ☐☐☐ / Proficient ☐☐☐
3	Begins to be aware of technology and how it affects life. (p. 24)	Not Yet ☐☐☐ / In Process ☐☐☐ / Proficient ☐☐☐

C	Citizenship and government	F W S
1	Demonstrates awareness of the reasons for rules. (p. 25)	Not Yet ☐☐☐ / In Process ☐☐☐ / Proficient ☐☐☐
2	Shows beginning understanding of what it means to be a leader. (p. 25)	Not Yet ☐☐☐ / In Process ☐☐☐ / Proficient ☐☐☐

D	People and where they live	F W S
1	Expresses beginning geographic thinking. (p. 25)	Not Yet ☐☐☐ / In Process ☐☐☐ / Proficient ☐☐☐
2	Shows beginning awareness of the relationship between people and where they live. (p. 26)	Not Yet ☐☐☐ / In Process ☐☐☐ / Proficient ☐☐☐

VI The Arts

A	Expression and representation	F W S
1	Participates in group music experiences. (p. 27)	Not Yet ☐☐☐ / In Process ☐☐☐ / Proficient ☐☐☐
2	Participates in creative movement, dance, and drama. (p. 27)	Not Yet ☐☐☐ / In Process ☐☐☐ / Proficient ☐☐☐
3	Uses a variety of art materials to explore and express ideas and emotions. (p. 27)	Not Yet ☐☐☐ / In Process ☐☐☐ / Proficient ☐☐☐

B	Understanding and appreciation	F W S
1	Responds to artistic creations or events. (p. 28)	Not Yet ☐☐☐ / In Process ☐☐☐ / Proficient ☐☐☐

VII Physical Development and Health

A	Gross motor development	F W S
1	Moves with balance and control. (p. 29)	Not Yet ☐☐☐ / In Process ☐☐☐ / Proficient ☐☐☐
2	Coordinates movements to perform tasks. (p. 29)	Not Yet ☐☐☐ / In Process ☐☐☐ / Proficient ☐☐☐

B	Fine motor development	F W S
1	Uses strength and control to accomplish tasks. (p. 29)	Not Yet ☐☐☐ / In Process ☐☐☐ / Proficient ☐☐☐
2	Uses eye-hand coordination to perform tasks effectively. (p. 30)	Not Yet ☐☐☐ / In Process ☐☐☐ / Proficient ☐☐☐
3	Uses writing and drawing tools with some control. (p. 30)	Not Yet ☐☐☐ / In Process ☐☐☐ / Proficient ☐☐☐

C	Personal health and safety	F W S
1	Performs self-care tasks competently. (p. 30)	Not Yet ☐☐☐ / In Process ☐☐☐ / Proficient ☐☐☐
2	Shows beginning understanding of and follows health and safety rules. (p. 30)	Not Yet ☐☐☐ / In Process ☐☐☐ / Proficient ☐☐☐

Sidebar (right margin): K 4th Edition — CHILD — DATE OF BIRTH — TEACHER — SCHOOL — FEMALE ☐ MALE ☐ — Observation Periods — FALL — WINTER — SPRING — The Work Sampling System, Kindergarten Developmental Checklist

ISBN 1-57212-240-4 © Pearson Education, Inc., publishing as Pearson Early Learning. All rights reserved. The Work Sampling System is a registered trademark of Rebus Inc.

Figure 6.9 **Summary Form for a Class or Group.** This example is from High/Scope's Preschool Child Observation Record (COR) 2nd ed., 2003.

C O R

Class Summary

In the columns below, enter the Category Averages and COR Total scores for each child in the group from his or her Child Information and Developmental Summary form. To obtain Class Averages in each Category, add the Category Averages in each column and divide the result by the number of children in your class. To obtain Class Growth in each category from Time 1 to Time 2, subtract the Time 1 Class Average from the Time 2 Class Average. To determine percentage growth, divide the Time 2 Class Average by the Time 1 Class Average, and then subtract 1 (e.g., if your result is .243, this indicates 24% growth). To calculate growth from Time 2 to Time 3 or from Time 1 to Time 3, follow the same steps.

Class: ______
Name: ______
Teacher: ______

Scoring Period:
Time 1 ___/___/___ to ___/___/___
Time 2 ___/___/___ to ___/___/___
Time 3 ___/___/___ to ___/___/___

	Initiative			Social Relations			Creative Representation			Movement & Music			Language & Literacy			Mathematics & Science			COR Total		
	Time 1	Time 2	Time 3	Time 1	Time 2	Time 3	Time 1	Time 2	Time 3	Time 1	Time 2	Time 3	Time 1	Time 2	Time 3	Time 1	Time 2	Time 3	Time 1	Time 2	Time 3
1																					
2																					
3																					
4																					
5																					
6																					
7																					
8																					
9																					
10																					
11																					
12																					
13																					
14																					
15																					
16																					
17																					
18																					
19																					
20																					
21																					
22																					
23																					
24																					
25																					
Category Totals																					
Class Category Average																					
Class Growth: Time 2 – Time 1																					
Class Growth: Time 3 – Time 2																					
Class Growth: Time 3 – Time 1																					

P1214

ISBN 1-57379-192-X

Preschool Child Observation Record (COR), (p. 1, 214) by High/Scope Educational Research Foundation, Ypsilanti, MI: High/Scope Press. © 2003, High/Scope Educational Research Foundation. Used with permission.

Description and Definition of Group Profiles

Group profiles show class performance on one or more items. They focus on the range of class behavior and identify clusters or subgroups of children with similar strengths and needs. They also condense information about the entire class's performance in one area of development or on one assessment for the entire group.

Group profiles summarize the qualitative and quantitative variations found in the behavior of individuals in a group. Qualitative variations include the following: one child throwing a ball accurately and another simply throwing; one child telling a story with little sequence and another telling a detailed, sequential story; one child drawing a human figure with only a circle for a head and another drawing a body with arms, legs, fingers, and even eyelashes. There may be different levels of complexity, as in the case of a child who sorts by one attribute and one who produces a complex matrix when sorting. Quantitative variations refer to the number of behaviors performed. In dramatic play, one child uses two themes and plays three roles, whereas another child uses only one theme and one

Figure 6.10   Portion of a Class or Group Summary Form. This is from The Creative Curriculum Developmental Assessment Toolkit for Ages 3–5, 2001. Other child development domains are on other pages. "F" stands for "forerunners" of the behavior under consideration.

	The Creative Curriculum® Developmental Continuum for Ages 3-5								Class Summary Worksheet		

The Creative Curriculum® Developmental Continuum for Ages 3-5 — Class Summary Worksheet

PHYSICAL DEVELOPMENT — Fine Motor / COGNITIVE DEVELOPMENT — Learning and Problem Solving

Columns: 19. Controls small muscles in hands; 20. Coordinates eye-hand movement; 21. Uses tools for writing and drawing; 22. Observes objects and events with curiosity; 23. Approaches problems flexibly; 24. Shows persistence in approaching tasks; 25. Explores cause and effect; 26. Applies knowledge or experience to a new context. Each with F, I, II, III.

CHILDREN: André, Ashley, Chris, Christopher, Emily P., Emily S., Jacob, Jose O., Jose V., Joshua, Kayla, Luis, Madison, Matt, Michael G., Michael W., Nicholas, Samantha, Taylor, Vanessa

CHECKPOINT TOTALS — Fall*, Winter*, Spring*
*Fill in the box with the color you are using for each checkpoint

From Dodge, D. T., Colker, L. J., & Heroman, C. *The Creative Curriculum® Developmental Continuum for Ages 3–5 Class Summary Worksheet* (p. 3), by Teaching Strategies, Inc., 2001, Washington, DC: Author. Copyright 2001 by Teaching Strategies, Inc. Reprinted with permission.

role. One child volunteers many ideas in a cooperative learning activity, whereas another volunteers only a few.

Purposes of Group Profiles

Group profiles are primarily planning tools used to identify children's needs and strengths so that differentiated instruction can be planned. Instead of guessing at what children know and can do, a teacher uses a group profile to identify clusters of children with similar interests, strengths, needs, or levels of performance. Knowing this, she can plan for and respond to the group's needs.

Group profiles evaluate the entire class's growth and achievement. By comparing a group profile made before a concentrated emphasis to a profile made after, a teacher can gauge what children learned from the experience. Mr. Gonzales assessed children prior to a project on the solar system and compared this assessment to the profile made after the project. He found that only a subgroup of children who already knew the most about the solar system learned from the unit. The group profile helps him discover which children did not benefit and to analyze why. Group profiles help teachers evaluate their own teaching techniques and improve their effectiveness.

Guides for Selecting and Organizing Content of Group Profiles

To construct a group profile specific to a given classroom, select or make an appropriate blank grid, such as shown in Figures 9.14 or 9.15 (pp. 176 and 178). List the children's names on the left side, then follow the guides below.

Determine what will be profiled. What is profiled depends on the teacher's planning needs. Figure 6.11 shows a form ready for recording observations of children's social pretend play. Figure 5.9 (p. 85) shows a form ready for recording children's *understanding* and *use* of terms used to describe size. When information from assessment has been recorded, it can be used to display, or "profile," the group's strengths and needs, identifying children who need help in learning certain things.

When possible, convert existing group records into profiles. Use a different colored marker for each cluster or subgroup, and circle or highlight performances falling within the same cluster.

If necessary, create a separate form for the group profile. Sometimes information is on individual records, one record per child, but you need a group profile. This often occurs when making a group summary using work products, portfolios, or anecdotal records. Place the identified divisions or clusters in columns, and write the names of children in that cluster in the appropriate column.

Place a key on each profile, identifying clusters or subgroups. For color coding, write the color used for each cluster at the top of the page.

Divide the range of behaviors. Make divisions that have significance for teaching—what and how you are going to teach. Following are some examples:

- Use children's needs as the basis for categories, such as "needs introduction," "needs practice," and "needs more challenge."
- Use groupings that describe different levels of mastery, such as "no evidence," "developing this," and "controls this"; or "beginning to," "does this," or "has mastered this."
- Use subskills to divide the range of behavior. Examples are "can snip," "cut one whole cut," "cut on a straight line," and "cut on a curve."
- Base clusters on levels of performance, such as "expressive" or "receptive language," "recognition" and "recall."
- Use content as a basis for clusters, such as "addends" in mathematics.
- Use the steps identified in skill acquisition. For example, use the skill levels described in literacy development: "emergent reader," "early reader," "independent reader," "fluent reader."
- Use levels of performance identified in appropriate rubrics.

Compile and use group profiles as soon as possible. Because group profiles are used for classroom planning, they are of little use when they are several weeks old.

Use group profiles when you plan. Use the profile to determine activities for specific children or groups of children. Compare group profiles over time to determine needed changes in instruction.

Figure 6.11 Form for Recording Observations of a Group of Children's Social Pretend Play

Observe over 1 week. Note: Check mark (✓) = Yes

Date: ⎯⎯⎯ ⎯⎯⎯ Name	Props			Roles			Themes			Social Skills			
	Has a pretend scenario	Plays with realistic props	Uses props symbolically	Identifies role (Mommy, baby, etc.)	Plays more than one role	Plays with objects as actors	Incorporates multiple themes	Incorporates new themes from field trips, literature, etc.	Incorporates literacy in theme (reads books in center, writes, etc.)	Solves social problems that emerge in play	Plays with all children. Does not exclude others	Resumes play after interruption (next day or within same period)	Incorporates teacher suggestions and support

Description and Definition of Individual Profiles

An individual profile integrates information from classroom assessments into a summary of a particular child's capabilities. Summaries can focus on one dimension of development or provide an overall picture of the child.

There are several types of profiles. The two typically used by teachers are checklists and written summaries. The checklist is usually divided into categories and subcategories based on skill acquisition, goal statements, or report cards. Checklists have the strengths and limitations of all such instruments. In particular, they allow for little information other than what is on the list. See Figure 11.4 (p. 204) for an example.

Written, ongoing summaries can be noted on columnar record forms such as those used in many programs for recording anecdotal records. See Figure 9.6 for an example. The headings would be the development and learning domains emphasized in a particular program. In each column, a summary statement about a child's status and progress is written and dated. To support the entry, make notes about where to find the evidence on which that statement is based. Teacher concerns, reflections, and things to monitor can also be included. As development occurs, new summaries are added. When the time comes to synthesize information into a progress report, historical and current data across the areas emphasized by the school are readily available. Indeed, in a pinch the recording form can serve as a summary.

Purposes of Individual Profiles

Individual profiles document a child's capabilities and behavior patterns, provide information for planning, and show when information is missing. They are a broad view of where the child is and where the teacher hopes the child will be, focusing on the entire forest and not individual trees—the child's general capabilities, neither isolated skills nor specific content. They chronicle an individual child's progress as information about patterns of interests, development, and interaction emerge. Individual profiles help teachers study extremes, uniqueness, and stylistic approaches that are difficult to see when looking at one assessment. In short, they help teachers know and understand each child.

Individual profiles help teachers plan to meet individual strengths and needs. When compiling Peter's profile, the teacher notices that he never participates in art activities, but he does like numbers, counting, and manipulatives. The teacher can use this identified interest to entice Peter into the art area. A teacher can identify a child who is having trouble making friends or doesn't participate in conversations and plan activities to help. Individual profiles also help teachers check for missing documentation.

An individual profile is helpful for narrative summaries, report cards, cumulative files, and collaborative work. Narrative reports based on evidence gathered throughout the year instead of those things the teacher remembers are more accurate. See Figure 11.2 (p. 202) for an example of a progress report for parents.

Guides for Selecting and Organizing Content of Individual Profiles

Limit the number of educational and developmental categories on the profile. Six to ten areas the same as or similar to those used for portfolios and group profiles would be sufficient for most classrooms. Create a form with the same categories for each child in the class.

Use categories that are similar to those on the portfolio record and summary reports. Plan the profile so it helps you with report cards and year-end summaries. Key it to the portfolio so that the profile summarizes the information in the portfolio. If state or district standards are used, reference them.

Use a consistent referencing system for supporting evidence. Write the date of the primary data record followed by its type and location in your files. Use the same abbreviations throughout. Keep the primary data records organized and coordinated with the profile. For example, if the primary data record is stored in the child's portfolio, note it by writing "portfolio." The reference note allows anyone to go back to the original record.

Use all available information. Include relevant work samples, group assessments, anecdotal records, performance samples, any elicited information, group and individual projects, participation charts, frequency counts, and any information contained in children's portfolios.

Compile information one area at a time, one child at a time. Review all of Maria's assessments and products relating to cognitive development, then her assessments for language development, continuing until her profile is complete. After finishing Maria's profile, move on to Phil's. By compiling profiles one child at a time, you gain an understanding of that child as an individual. This will not happen if you work on several children's profiles simultaneously.

Summarize trends demonstrating growth or a breakthrough in learning. Compare assessments collected at different times. Look for convergence of indicators showing a trend in development. Entries can summarize progress or movement from one place on the developmental sequence to another. Entries might show that a child has moved from one cluster to another in a group profile or how a pattern of behavior has changed. For example, at the beginning of the semester, Luis showed great distress when his mother left him, but by the third week in school, he no longer cried.

Summarize unique child characteristics. Describe attitudes and dispositions, such as persistence and motivation levels, that cut across different assessments. Leslie's persistence and motivation are obvious when you look at the times she tries to build a large city with blocks during one assessment. Only after the structure collapses eleven times does she settle for a smaller structure. Look for similar behaviors in different contexts. Not only is Leslie persistent in block building but she also approaches other tasks in the same way.

Include behaviors or areas to monitor. Make entries on which you want to follow up. The profile can serve as a reminder or "tickler" file. Mr. Zatus is concerned because Mia is quiet and doesn't participate in class. He notes this on the profile to help him remember to check her progress in class interaction.

Update the profile at specific times. Enter information early in the year to compare with information gathered later. Review contents of individual profiles several times a year—at midyear, end of the year, and prior to reports and parent conferences. At midyear, review additions and make new entries. At the end of the year, review the profile, adding entries to document growth since midyear and to describe status at the end of the year. The more often you update the profile, the more useful it will be in the classroom.

As patterns of behavior change, note those changes in the appropriate column. Also note your inferences and reflections. If new information indicates that an inference or behavioral trend was incorrect, cross it out and note the new interpretation.

Make entries in chronological order. To determine changes in patterns of behavior, compile information in chronological order.

Summary

Teachers compile and summarize information to integrate and distill information from different sources, methods, and contexts; reduce it to a manageable size; and keep past assessments accessible for continued analysis and interpretation. Three complementary ways of compiling and summarizing are portfolios, group profiles, and individual profiles.

Portfolios present a thoughtful, organized compilation of evidence documenting a child's development and learning over time. There are four basic types of portfolios: the showcase portfolio, which shows a pupil's best or favorite work; the evaluation portfolio, in which most of the contents are specified and scored; the documentation portfolio, which holds evidence of a child's work and progress selected to build a comprehensive description of the child; and the process portfolio, which contains ongoing work for a larger project. Portfolios fulfill most of the basic purposes of classroom assessment.

There are four basic approaches to portfolio building: requiring specific items; requiring evidence in given developmental or curriculum areas but not specifying the items; collecting individual, often spontaneous, samples from ongoing classroom activities; and combinations of the preceding three. Appropriate portfolio items vary with the age and development of the children and the goals of the school. Good portfolio entries are informative and easy to collect. Items should be identified and annotated so their significance is clear. Helping children learn to select, assess, and reflect on portfolio items is central to the process. The information available from portfolios can be increased by identifying and annotating each item, developing procedures and instructions to maximize information, and selecting spontaneously generated items for information as well as uniqueness.

Forms and charts to help teachers compile and summarize assessment information are available from publishers, or teachers can construct their own. Group profiles summarize the range of behavior within a classroom and identify groups of children with similar strengths, needs, or interests. They are most useful for planning activities for the class as a whole.

Individual profiles keep track of a child's growth relative to classroom goals and objectives. They summarize basic child capabilities in terms of broader educational and developmental outcomes and are not merely a catalog of isolated skill/performance/content behaviors. They are used to plan for meeting individual needs, to write progress reports for parents, and for official purposes.

For Personal Reflection

1. We suggest several ways that teachers who are beginning to develop portfolios for children can gradually learn the process: Start with one developmental or curriculum area, one specific subject, one learning process, or some other aspect of development and learning that can be assessed.

Assess your own interests, experience, and skills. What approach would best suit you at this point in time?

2. Suppose you were to begin now to construct a portfolio to showcase and document your own development and learning. What categories would it have? What would you want to include? Explain your reasoning.

For Further Study and Discussion

1. Identify the advantages and disadvantages of the four approaches to portfolio building: required items; required evidence; individualized, unique samples; and combinations. In what ways might the advantages and disadvantages be different for a beginning teacher and an experienced teacher?
2. Identify three pieces of evidence you would gather to build a portfolio for a preprimary classroom in the domains of small muscle development, math and science, and language and literacy. Use the assessment and analysis guides in Appendix A.
3. Identify three broad aspects of development and learning that you would include on an individual profile for first grade. Identify three appraisals you would use to document growth for each of these.

Suggested Readings

Clemmons, J., Laase, L., & Cooper, D. L. (1993). *Portfolios in the classroom: A teacher's sourcebook.* Jefferson City, MO: Scholastic, Inc.

Hamilton, R. N., & Shoemaker, M. A. (2000). *AMCI 2000: Assessment matrix for classroom instruction.* Portland, OR: Northwest Regional Educational Laboratory.

National Education Association. (1993). *Student portfolios.* West Haven, CT: Author.

Northwest Regional Educational Laboratory. (1994). *Portfolio resources bibliography.* Portland, OR: Author.

Shaklee, B. D., Barbour, N. E., Ambrose, R., & Hansford, S. J. (1997). *Designing and using portfolios.* Boston: Allyn & Bacon.

Stone, S. J. (1995). *Understanding portfolio assessment: A guide for parents.* Reston, VA: Association for Childhood Education International.

Wortham, S. C., Barbour, A., & Desjean-Perrotta, B. (1998). *Portfolio assessment: A handbook for preschool and elementary educators.* Olney, MD: Association for Childhood Education International.

• •

CHAPTER 7

Interpreting Assessment Information

Assessment is of little use unless teachers know what the information means and how to use it to help children develop and learn. This chapter focuses on analyzing, interpreting, and understanding collected information. Chapter 8 suggests ways to use that understanding to make classroom activities and procedures support children's growth, development, and learning. The two steps may merge as teachers skillfully adjust materials and interactions to immediate needs of children. In other cases, it may be difficult to make sense of the information and even more difficult to decide what actions to take based on the interpretation. Both processes call for professional knowledge and judgment, because it is in these steps that a crucial blending takes place. Teachers take information that has been systematically collected, recorded, and summarized, then combine it with understandings, insights, and intuitions that come from day-to-day interactions with children. It is in this blending of objective information and sensitive judgment that assessment of children in its truest sense takes place (Barnett & Zucker, 1990).

There are two major steps in analyzing and interpreting assessment information: (1) ensuring the authenticity and trustworthiness of the data, and then (2) understanding what it means.

Ensure the Authenticity and Trustworthiness of the Data

Teachers work to make assessment reliable, valid, fair, and adequate (see Chapters 2, 4, and 5). Before you interpret information, check again to make sure:

- There are *enough* samples.
- Samples are *representative* of what is being assessed.
- Samples are *balanced*, employing different sources, methods, and contexts.
- Evidence obtained in different ways *converges*.
- Information is *consistent* over time, sources, contexts, and methods (sometimes, however, a significant inconsistency can emerge here).
- Evidence corresponds to *reality*—it is generally compatible with other aspects of the child's development and learning, and makes sense in comparison with other children of about the same age and developmental level.

As you move from documenting children's actions to interpreting what they mean, the following additional safeguards will maintain quality and trustworthiness.

To Determine Progress, Compare Performance at Two or More Points in Time

The points should be far enough apart to reveal development and learning. The interval depends on what is being taught and assessed. Make sure opportunities to learn have been provided in the interval. Measurements should be comparable: Writing samples should be compared to prior writing samples, and oral reading to prior oral reading.

Work from Compilations and Summaries

One or two summary sheets that profile each child's progress toward major goals synthesize information from many sources and make it readily available for interpretation and further use. Use recorded information, and do not rely on memory alone (Barnett & Zucker, 1990).

Look for Patterns, Including Patterns of Errors, Rather Than Isolated Instances

As you compile information on any behavior, stable patterns will usually emerge. Attendance and tardiness are simple examples of the way patterns offer insights about children, families, and schools (Almy & Genishi, 1979). Absences on the first or last days of the week may signal a situation at home, such as weekend visitations to a noncustodial parent or weekly trips away from home. Some families may not have developed the habit of getting children to school regularly and on time, or there may be transportation difficulties. If this is the child's first year in a group, the youngster may catch every sickness that is "going around." There may be problems with resistance, stamina, or lack of medical care. Because children who are sick a lot will miss a lot, the pattern will give you clues to follow up on. Such consistent patterns of behavior can alert teachers to children who need help.

Consider a Child's or a Group's Unique and Individual Patterns of Development, Temperament, Interests, and Dispositions

Morgan's mom told you that he was "deliberate" in his development—in no hurry to sit up, teethe, walk, talk, or do anything else. His kindergarten teacher remarked, "He does things in his own good time." This type of information can help you understand the data you have collected. Carita's tendency to be a perfectionist is evident, because she avoids activities she is not good at and struggles for perfection—even to the point of tears—in things that are important to her. Children's unique interests and prior knowledge may become evident as you attempt to understand what certain information means. The children in Donna Frank's class had no interest in dinosaurs, a unit Donna always counted on to intrigue students. Looking further, she found that most of the children had thoroughly investigated dinosaurs the previous year.

Identify Areas of Concern

Consider if the child's current functioning and progress are of concern to the child, parents, you, or other school staff. If so, look in depth at the developmental or curriculum area of concern, take a broader look at all developmental areas, assess the skill or behavior in a different context, or recheck for indicators of the need for special help. Consult available specialists.

Suppose a youngster has difficulty following directions, is inattentive during story time, seldom plays with other children, either indoors or out, and responds inappropriately in conversations and discussions. Classroom staff and other children have difficulty understanding her speech. The youngster is frequently absent. Clearly, available information identifies a concern. More and different information is needed to determine the sources of the problem and develop a course of action. What do parents see at home? Are there clues in the youngster's medical records or developmental history? Are there situations in which the youngster follows directions and pays attention; are there situations in which she simply cannot follow what is going on? What does the speech and language specialist say?

Interpret and Understand the Meaning of Assessment Findings

Understanding the meaning of assessment information requires teachers to examine evidence from a number of different perspectives. The first one is cautionary: Generate several hypotheses about possible meanings, but hold them tentatively so that you are open to alternative explanations. The other three are basic guidelines or approaches for analyzing the information about children. The examples highlight each guideline separately, but as you work with summary and primary information, you will use them simultaneously. Think of children's understanding and performance as falling within a band or interval, rather than at a specific point on a scale; compare their understanding and performance to developmental or curriculum expectations (goals, objectives, standards); and analyze information for evidence of the learning processes and strategies they are using. All these approaches will yield information relevant to promoting children's learning.

Generate Multiple Hypotheses about Possible Meanings, but Hold Them Tentatively

Avoid thinking in terms of certainties and absolutes. There is no simplistic formula for interpretation—if a child does X then it means Y and only Y. Information may have several meanings, depending on what aspect you focus on. Human development is complex and not always easy to understand. Consider all aspects that are relevant to classroom decisions. Documentation of a child's efforts to solve a real-life arithmetic problem may have one interpretation if you are analyzing error patterns, another if you are judging disposition to use arithmetic, and still another if you are concerned with developmental level. Consulting with colleagues may provide additional insights and help maintain focus on children's progress and needs rather than blaming a child, her home, or last year's teachers for any problems (Johnston, 2003).

Interpretations should reflect only what you actually know. For example, if a child does not do what is expected in an assessment, we only know that. We do not know that he could not do it. Positive results can be trusted more than negative results. If a child does something—reads aloud, throws a ball overhand, helps a classmate, contributes to a class discussion—we know the child has that capacity. We do *not* know the child's capacity to perform tasks that are *not performed* or are *performed poorly* (Lidz, 2003).

Children change rapidly. Our knowledge of child development changes, affording new insights into the meaning of things children do and new ways of looking at their behavior and our responses to it. Even under the best of circumstances, the assessment information we have is only a small sample of what any child can actually do—a sample based primarily on school- or center-related behavior, which may or may not reflect a child's total competence. Some of the most important information about children and their achievement may be difficult to document: motivation, drive for mastery, willingness to expend effort, and family support and encouragement.

Keep a broad view of the child. Focusing too closely on aspects of development or learning that are considered important in a given program may not reveal children's other strengths. The strong emphasis on language and literacy in most early childhood programs may conceal children's strengths in mathematics, science, the arts, or social relationships.

Analyze Performance as a Band or Interval within Which a Child Is Functioning

Development is best thought of as a continuum, moving toward more complex and mature behavior (Bodrova & Leong, 1996; Vygotsky, 1978). Whatever a child has done or is doing indicates where he is within a larger band or interval that reflects the upper and lower limits of his capability at this point in time (Airasian, 2001; Gage & Berliner, 1998). There are several reasons why an interval describes children's performance better than a specific point or score: error in measurement, normal variation in development and learning, the nature of developmental processes, and the influence of the amount and nature of assistance.

Error in Measurement.   Expect some error in the information you have. For example, performance or situational tasks often require children to give an oral or motor response. If children do not respond, we cannot conclude that they cannot, only that they *do* not. Accurate estimates of a child's oral language ability are difficult to obtain. The upper level of the band or interval may be higher than the samples. Children are quite sensitive to external influences such as hunger, illness, distractions, or problems at home, which can lead to measurement error. In addition, adults make errors as they document children's behavior.

Normal Variation in Development and Learning.   There are wide variations of what can be considered "normal" in development and learning—normal variations in when behaviors are acquired and the rate or speed of acquisition (Berk, 2006). Child development norms and sequences are usually drawn from large numbers of children, and no individual child is expected to "fit" exactly. For that reason, published guides to children's development usually indicate a range or interval, rather than a fixed point. Children have unique and individual patterns of development. "Normal" children begin walking at anywhere from 9 to 18 months—a tremendous variation in a short life span. If such differences exist in a universal, biologically linked developmental milestone, we can expect at least as much variation in other aspects of development and in children's performance relative to expected child outcomes.

The Nature of Developmental Processes.   Children's development is dynamic. It changes from day to day and week to week. What a child cannot do today, she may do tomorrow, especially if given appropriate assistance. Children may regress because of illness, stress, or other factors. Development may proceed unevenly, both within a given developmental domain and across domains. The pupil whose versatile vocabulary revolves around family and friends may need help learning abstract concepts. A youngster who is developing quite normally in other areas may lag in social skills.

The Influence of the Amount and Nature of Assistance.   In addition to general measurement and development guides that establish the principle "think of a band or interval" rather than a point or score, consider the amount and nature of assistance a child receives to establish the Zone of Proximal Development (ZPD)—the specific type of zone described in Chapter 3. In this concept of development, the ZPD has two limits. The lower level is a child's independent performance—what the child can do alone. The higher level is the best the child can do with maximum assistance (Bodrova & Leong, 1996). Within this zone are different levels of partially assisted performance.

A child's ability to make use of suggestions and prompts gives clues to his thinking processes, level of functioning, and the range of tasks he is ready to learn (Bodrova & Leong, 1996; Campione & Brown, 1985; Vygotsky, 1978). Dynamic assessment techniques try to explore a youngster's ability to profit from assistance in doing a task (Campione et al., 1991; Cronbach, 1990; Feuerstein,

1979; Lidz, 2003). Look for development and learning that are in a formative stage and give prompts, suggestions, and hints to see what a youngster does with such help.

As an example of how a teacher gives and interprets children's use of assistance, suppose you bring in a variety of seashells for children to examine, sort, and group in whatever way they want. Some children may immediately grasp the possibilities, and then group and regroup in imaginative and perceptive ways. They don't need any hints; in fact, suggestions might stifle their creative approach to the task. Some children may perceive nothing but a bunch of shells. They are oblivious to hints and suggestions, either verbal or nonverbal. But another group may initially see nothing or only the most obvious groupings, and then quickly pick up on the slightest hint. Subtly shaded construction paper placed beside the shells will lead children into sorting and ordering by fine differentiations in color. A row of shells ordered by size will set them to grouping by size. A remark such as "Look how deep the ridges are on this shell" will lead to examination and grouping by definition of the ridges. It is these children who can benefit the most from adult assistance to lead their development (Bodrova & Leong, 1996; Rogoff, 1990). The assistance of the colored paper and hints by the teacher are within their ZPD.

Document and interpret the meaning of how children use prompts, hints, and suggestions. Those who do not pick up on the hints may need experiences at a simpler level or more assistance. Those who are beyond the hints may need amplification of the classification ideas within their Zone of Proximal Development, or tasks and assistance that will provide more challenge.

We cannot understand the meaning of what a child does unless we know something of the amount and nature of assistance received.

Consider the Influence of the Total Sociocultural Context on Children's Actions

We cannot interpret children's behavior apart from their sociocultural context (Goodenow, 1992). The sociocultural context encompasses the who, what, when, and where of the interaction: who the child interacts with, what materials are used, and the time and setting. Look for two things: ways the context may be hindering development and learning, and ways the context may be supporting development and learning. Both help us understand children's actions as well as what to do in the future.

Hindrances can include placement of furniture and equipment in a way that gives children the wrong signals about what to do, such as an arrangement that encourages children to visit with each other instead of finishing tasks, or to run wildly around the gym or playground instead of using equipment. It may involve choice of materials: books, games, activities, and songs that children are no longer interested in; materials that are too difficult or too easy; or materials that promote aggressive behavior. Adults may expect children to be accomplished in doing things that they are just beginning to learn.

General supports include clear guidance concerning what children are supposed to do, setting up the environment to promote desired behavior, and having enough appropriate materials ready, as well as specific supports that enable a youngster to do whatever she is supposed to do: making sure children can see and hear, reducing distractions, coaching and practicing expected behavior, and providing effective mediators to help youngsters learn.

Study the context as well as the child so that you can identify hindrances and decrease them, as well as identify supports and increase or modify them as needed.

Compare Evidence to Developmental or Curriculum Expectations

Expected developmental and curriculum outcomes help determine "what to assess" (see Chapter 3). At this point, you will look back to those expected outcomes as a basis for interpreting assessment information.

Compare Evidence to a Current General Sequence of Development.   Developmental guides or continua establish our current state of knowledge and understanding in basic child development domains: physical, social/emotional, cognitive, and language. The assessment and analysis guides in Appendix A summarize that knowledge for easy reference. Compare a child's or children's performance to the guidelines in the appropriate domain. Determine the child's approximate place in the continuum, which prior developments have been mastered, and which later developments are emerging or evident. A caution: Use the developmental continua as guides, not as strict milestones. Remember that these continua are not exact, nor do they cover every aspect of development. In addition, there are gaps in our understanding of how some domains develop.

Determine whether the progress the child is making is appropriate, or if opportunities to learn and develop need to be modified. Many development and curriculum goals take a long time to achieve. Don't panic if a November check reveals that a youngster (or a classroom of youngsters) is a long way from year-end goals. Determine where children are on the continuum of progress to help decide if current curriculum approaches are sufficient or need modification.

Look at how checking for developmental and curriculum status and progress works, using simplified examples. Figure 7.1 shows two observations of Shana's dramatic play made approximately 3 months apart. Next to it is the developmental sequence for that type of play. Comparing the first observation, made on September 23, with the developmental chart, the teacher concludes that Shana's behavior seems closest to parallel play. Consulting other evidence, her teacher finds one or two examples of social play, and some turn-taking, but not much.

To determine progress over time, compare the child's performance on samples of the same type of behavior taken at two or more points in time. Look at both the entries for Shana, the first made on September 23 and the second on December 27 (see Figure 7.1). Shana talks directly to other children and interacts more in the second sample than in the first. The sample taken in September resembles parallel play. The sample from December closely matches simple social play. Shana is not yet exchanging toys, nor is she involved in complementary roles involving back-and-forth interactions. Other evidence about Shana's play and interactions on the play yard, in the block area, and with manipulatives reveals similar behavior. Shana has progressed one level on the developmental continuum, is developing at a rate comparable to her peers, and is in line with the developmental sequence.

If you are interpreting a group profile, determine the range of development and learning—the most mature or advanced behavior and the least mature or advanced behavior. Compare these two extremes with development or learning charts to determine if they are in the expected age ranges. Compare clusters of behavior in the profile to the typical expectations as shown in the charts.

Figure 7.1 Comparison of Two Assessments of a Child's Play Behavior to a Developmental Sequence for Play

Selected Excerpts from Social Developmental Records of Shana Maas

Developmental Sequence for Peer Play 2½ to 6 Years of Age (Adapted from Howes, 1980)

9/23—Dramatic Play
Dresses as Mom. Announces "I'm going to wash dishes. I'm making dinner." Washes plate, pot, silverware and puts in drainer. Looks at child next to her, who picks up towel. S. picks up a towel, too. They don't interact.

12/27—Dramatic play
Dressed up w/heels and purse. Chairs lined up for playing bus. S. takes first chair. "This is my bus. I'm gonna drive. Gabriella, give me your money. Go sit down." G. says "Can I drive?" S. does not respond, but starts bus, making driving noises.

Level 1: Simple Parallel Play
Close proximity but doesn't engage in eye contact or any social behavior.
Level 2: Parallel Play Mutual Regard
Engage in similar activities and occasionally look at each other. May involve imitation.
Level 3: Simple Social Play
Direct social behavior to one another. Activities not coordinated.
Level 4: Complementary/Mutual Awareness Play
Take turns with objects. No verbal exchange.
Level 5: Complementary/Reciprocal Social Play
Engage in complementary conversation. Back and forth turn-taking with social interaction.

Figure 7.2 shows two examples of classroom appraisal of a group's status and progress in fine motor development. Evidence on cutting with scissors was recorded on a checklist. Notice that in the assessment made on September 11, the behavior ranges from snipping to cutting on a curved line. Several children have similar skills: Shana, Danny, and Gabriella cut on a straight line; Jerry and Fran cut on a curved line; only Bobby snips.

Compare the assessments of September 11 and December 18. The range has changed. In the first sample, the range was from snipping to cutting on a curved line. In the second sample it is from cutting on a straight line to cutting on a curved line. In addition, the children cluster differently. In the first sample there were three clusters: Bobby snips; Shana, Danny, and Gabriella cut on a straight line; Jerry and Fran cut on a curved line. In the second sample this has changed: Bobby and Gabriella cut on a straight line; Shana, Jerry, Fran, and Danny cut on a curved line. Work products in the children's portfolios and jottings made during observations of art and center activities provide further evidence of their progress. A third sample, taken near the end of the year, should reveal even more.

Is that progress enough, or do the children need additional fine motor experiences? Several had never used scissors before coming to school. This is where interpretation comes in. The expected developmental sequence for cutting, shown in Figure 7.3, offers one piece of information for gauging progress. Another is the program goals. Should the children be able to cut out figures and move paper and scissors accurately by the end of the year? Interpreting the meaning calls for integrating all these considerations, collecting more information as needed, and making a judgment about its meaning.

Figure 7.2 Classroom Appraisal of a Group's Status and Progress in Fine Motor Development

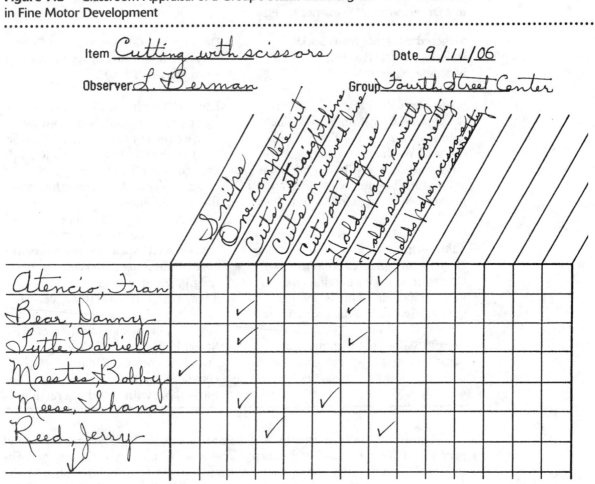

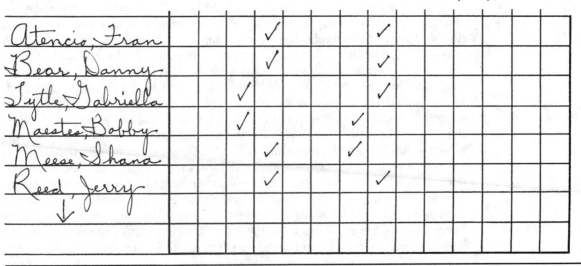

Figure 7.3 The Developmental Sequence for Cutting with Scissors

Level 1: Snips. May hold paper and scissors incorrectly.

Level 2: Makes one complete cut with the scissors. May hold paper and scissors incorrectly.

Level 3: Cuts on a straight line. May hold paper correctly, scissors incorrectly.

Level 4: Cuts on a curved line. Holds scissors and paper correctly.

Level 5: Cuts out figures.

Compare Outcomes to Curriculum Goals, Objectives, and Standards. To understand assessment results, compare them to expected outcomes, however they are stated. Some goals, objectives, and standards are quite broad and require further specification before assessment or interpretation of assessment results can occur. Some are stated so that direct rather than general comparisons are possible, especially if they identify specific objectives, knowledge, or skills.

Suppose that a goal states that "children should be able to compare objects, events, and experiences in the physical and social world." This goal is a comprehensive one, encompassing language and the major subject matter areas, as well as basic learning strategies (Marzano, Pickering, & McTighe, 1993). It is relevant for learners of all ages. The specific expectations will change depending on children's age and development. If expectations for early childhood are that children will understand and use terms of contrast and comparison, such as "same as," "different from," "like," "alike," "unlike," "not the same," "similar," and "dissimilar," linked with appropriate descriptive terms (shape, size, color, number, location, function, direction, and so forth), then you know what to help them learn, what to assess, and to what to compare their performances.

Standards can be used in the same way. The National Council of Teachers of Mathematics (NCTM) designated Patterns and Relationships as one of the key categories of mathematics standards. A related *content standard* explained that

> In grades K–4, the mathematics curriculum should include the study of patterns and relationships so that students can . . . *recognize, describe, extend, and create* a wide variety of patterns [italics added]. . . .
>
> Pattern recognition involves many concepts, such as color and shape identification, direction, orientation, size, and number relationships. Children should use all these properties in identifying, extending, and creating patterns. . . . Identifying the "cores" of patterns helps children become aware of the structures. For example, in some patterns the core repeats, whereas in others the core grows. (NCTM, 1989, pp. 60–61)

Because preschool and primary children experiment, construct, repeat, and identify patterns of all types, it is fairly easy to collect evidence to compare what children do with the standard.

Let's look at an example. Leslie and the other children in her first-grade class were to create ABAB (every other one) patterns on lines marked with an *X*. Leslie's paper (see Figure 7.4) indicates she has met the standard of "creating" a simple ABAB pattern in two dimensions. The next step is to ask Leslie to reflect on and explain what she has done. The recorder notes her explanation. It is clear that she can also *recognize* and *describe* the AB pattern, including pointing

Figure 7.4   Leslie's ABAB Patterns

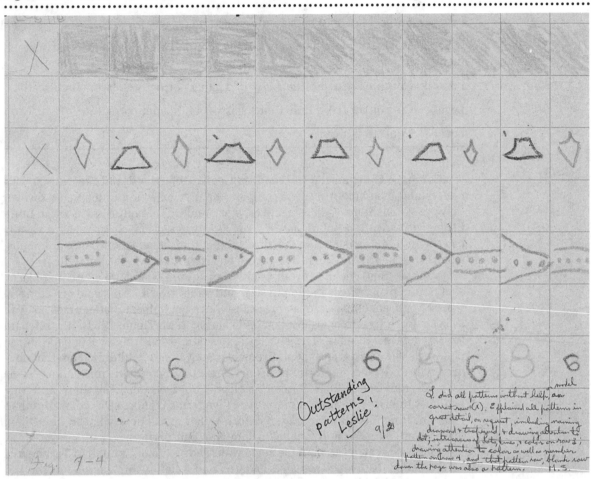

out that the rows of patterns alternating with a blank row make an ABAB pattern vertically down the page. A structured performance assessment with manipulatives indicates that she can *extend* the pattern as well. Comparison with the standard tells us that this child has met the standard for simple ABAB patterns and is ready for other work with varied patterns: amplification using different modalities, such as actions or sounds; challenge through introduction of more complex repeating patterns or different types, such as patterns that "grow"; application to other situations by working with material in which the pattern is less obvious; or other variations on patterns and relationships. The standard and the implied benchmark (by fourth grade, students should recognize, describe, extend, and create a wide variety of patterns) provide a basis for comparison and a guide for planning further experiences.

Rubrics.   Because most standards are usually broad and include a number of complex behaviors, educators develop rubrics to help them judge children's progress toward the standard and related benchmarks.

If you have gathered evidence related to the behavior described in the rubrics, it is not difficult to identify a youngster's level of functioning, and thus

Figure 7.5   Example of a Rubric

....

Works toward the achievement of group goals.

---

4   Actively helps identify group goals and works hard to meet them.

3   Communicates commitment to the group goals and effectively carries out assigned roles.

2   Communicates a commitment to the group goals but does not carry out assigned roles.

1   Does not work toward group goals or actively works against them.

From R. J. Marzano, D. Pickering, & J. McTighe, *Assessing Student Outcomes: Performance Assessment Using the Dimensions of Learning Model,* Alexandria, VA: Association for Supervision and Curriculum Development. Copyright © 1993. Reprinted by permission of R. J. Marzano.

where she may need help. For example, look at the rubric in Figure 7.5. The item, working toward the achievement of group goals, is an important nonacademic one, and observations of children working in groups will give you the information you need to score it. For analysis and instructional purposes, the numbers are not important. The descriptions of behavior identify what a child does and does not do. There are additional examples and more information on rubrics in Chapter 5, pages 90 to 93.

Analyze Information for Clues to Learning Processes and Strategies

Understanding children's learning strategies does not focus on outcomes such as the ability to read a selected passage; add, subtract, multiply, and divide; or correctly interpret another's social intent. Instead, it addresses thinking and learning processes, which are difficult to capture and interpret. These learning strategies and processes—such as the ability to relate present learning to prior knowledge, construct "theories" and generalizations, transfer learning to another situation, or use prompts, hints, and clues—apply to all development and learning. For instance, many of us have tried to "unlearn" a faulty tennis or golf swing. Faulty prior knowledge interfered with learning the correct way.

As knowledge of cognitive processes and their development expands, more emphasis is being placed on helping children understand and use effective learning strategies. Learning is not always a linear, sequential process but can proceed in fits and starts. Concepts are refined and redefined as the learner progresses from being a novice to being an expert. Knowledge, strategies, and thinking processes change at different stages of the learning process (Rogoff, 1990). Even when a barrier in children's learning processes is identified, such as interference from cultural differences or prior knowledge, appropriate action is not always clear. However, commands to "try harder" and "apply yourself" are no substitute for figuring out what is causing problems for children and doing whatever is possible to help them overcome those problems.

Development and learning processes often reveal themselves in children's behavior: the errors they make; the way they use prior knowledge; the explanations they give; the way they make use of prompts, hints, and suggestions; and the way they progress from simple skills and knowledge to complex, coordinated patterns of actions and thinking.

Examine Underlying Mental Processes.   Young children are acquiring the skills that allow them to focus their attention, remember deliberately, and regulate their own cognitive and social behavior (Bodrova & Leong, 1996, 2006). They learn to be less reactive and more thoughtful and deliberate. The lack of these metacognitive abilities manifests itself across all developmental domains. For example, the 4-year-old who has a hard time concentrating in group time, waiting in line, and playing cooperatively with others, and who turns the block area into a bowling alley, may be having trouble with underlying self-regulation skills. Because he is so reactive, his attention and actions are driven by what catches his fancy at that moment. He cannot inhibit his behavior, concentrate, or act with mental deliberateness, considering the consequences of his actions before he acts. Although a teacher may work on this behavior as it appears as an isolated action in group time, play, or other activities, the underlying reactiveness is the root problem.

To determine whether children need help and practice in developing underlying cognitive skills, observe them in different contexts. Compare them. Which situations tend to produce more mature behaviors, and which ones produce the least mature behaviors? Children with reactive behaviors often do well when they become engrossed in an activity of their own choosing and have trouble breaking away. When they are not engrossed, they may flit from one activity to the next. They have trouble ignoring distractions and sticking to the task at hand, and may perform better in a one-to-one relationship with objects, peers, or the teacher.

Analyze Error Patterns.   Errors should not be thought of as "random, careless, or lazy behavior of a student but . . . as rooted in a complex and logical process of thought" that is amenable to correction (Glaser, 1987, p. 333). Children make errors because they have misconceptions or partial understandings. Error analysis is regularly used in teaching reading and is helpful in any content or performance area. For example, children who are having difficulty regrouping in mathematics may make errors that show teachers the source of their difficulty.

Check the number, type, and pattern of errors to see if they fit any of the following categories (Gage & Berliner, 1992):

1. Systematic error patterns have a consistent pattern. The child makes the same mistake over and over. Systematic errors usually mean that a child does not understand a rule or fact and consistently misapplies it. Interpretation may vary with the level of development. Very young children may simply require time and experience, as in the systematic overregularizations that young children make in learning language. In other cases, skilled questioning, explanations, or appropriate material or experiences can help break a pattern that more time and experience may not correct. Think of the social skill of entering and becoming part of a group. Many children (and adults) make the same mistakes over and over and would benefit from coaching and modeling.

2. Random error patterns do not have a predictable pattern. They usually mean the child is guessing because he has no facts or rules to apply. To understand random error patterns, teachers have to sensitively probe the child's thinking. The cause of the pattern may vary depending on the child. For example, children may not have the prior experience or knowledge to enable them to respond reasonably. Some urban children may know little about plants, hills, valleys, rivers, and other aspects of the natural world.

Rural children's knowledge of urban life may consist of what they see on television. Neither group will have accurate facts or rules to apply. Teachers may have to provide experiences and teach or reteach the information or skills.

3. Skip error patterns are "goofs." They are not of concern unless they become an established pattern. You can suspect that hurrying, disinterest, loss of concentration, or anxiety caused these errors.

Determine Prior Knowledge and Its Relationship to Current Understanding and Performance.   Children's beliefs, knowledge, and past experiences provide the base for current learning (Glaser, 1987). Look at Renata, whose experience with pets was limited to cats, dogs, rabbits, guinea pigs, and other furry creatures. When the teacher introduced a pet turtle, Renata described him as having "bumpy fur"—a logical extension of her prior experiences. Because of the wide diversity in young children's backgrounds and experiences, teachers cannot assume shared knowledge about anything. Probably no other aspect of children's development and learning is as subject to influence from families, communities, previous schooling, and other experiences. This prior knowledge can help or interfere with new learning (Winne & Marx, 1987). If children approach new information or skills without prerequisite skills or background, lack of knowledge will interfere.

Compare what children know to what you have taught or will be teaching, to assess their familiarity with the knowledge or skills. Analyze a "map" or "web" constructed from children's responses to identify misconceptions or preconceptions that need to be considered. Review records of skill development. For instance, children who learned one type of letter formation at home or in a previous school may show interference as they attempt to learn a new system. Study children's answers or explanations for indications of prior knowledge and understanding and whether they have linked that knowledge to present learning. Disinterest may mean either lack of knowledge or mastery. For example, children's difficulty with arithmetic story problems is related to their inability to transfer computation skills to a different situation. "Children need to learn skills in finding or creating similarity across contexts" (Rogoff & Gardner, 1984, p. 961). Adults may need to guide children to help them create links between what they already know and what they are trying to learn. "Remember when we learned how to measure and graph your growth? Today we are going to start learning how to measure and graph the growth of plants."

In analyzing learning processes, you may detect problems or facility in different types of application and transfer:

Negative transfer occurs when prior learning impedes new learning. The child uses a familiar response in a situation that calls for a different one or uses intuitive understandings that are counter to what should be learned. For example, social behavior that is accepted in the home or community may interfere with learning a different type of social behavior at school.

Positive transfer occurs when prior knowledge and skills help children learn new skills. The links between old and new learning help children remember and perform better. We may identify either positive or negative transfer as children try to apply to new situations what they know and can do.

Intuitive theories or preconceptions may also interfere with present learning (Ginsburg, 1997; Glaser, 1987). In their efforts to make sense of the world, children construct their own theories, which can be inaccurate or incomplete, about why things are the way they are. Teachers can address some of these preconceptions directly if they can identify and interpret them accurately. Dominique was playing a computer game that presented him with simple addition problems:

$$
\begin{array}{ccc}
11 & 13 & 16 \\
\underline{+1} & \underline{+1} & \underline{+1}
\end{array}
$$

As Dominique entered his answers—3, 5, and 8—he became increasingly upset. The computer wouldn't accept them. Only as the teacher examined the pattern of error did Dominique's "theory" about addition become clear. She was able to address it directly and help him learn how addition worked. Looking only at the number of right and wrong answers does not reveal the kind of help he needs, but analysis of errors does. Children may develop their own theories about the meaning of other people's actions—often misreading social cues or transferring the understanding of one set of social cues to a situation where that understanding does not apply. Boys who exhibit aggressive behavior may be misinterpreting friendly social cues as being aggressive (Dodge, Pettit, McClaskey, & Brown, 1986; Dodge & Somberg, 1987).

Analyze Explanations and Descriptions.   Learning involves active construction of knowledge by the learner (Bredekamp & Rosegrant, 1992, 1995; Mayer, 1992). Teachers gain insight into how children select, organize, and integrate information by listening to children's explanations to each other or from teacher–child interaction.

Children's responses to "How did you get that answer?" "Explain how you did that," "Why do you think that?" and other similar questions give clues to many aspects of development and learning. Children may be able to do something but not describe or explain how or why (Berk, 2006). Some children may give explanations that seem perfectly logical to them, but indicate a level of development dominated by perception and an inability to think about several variables at once. Such a situation is revealed in the following interview with a child who is experimenting with things that sink and float:

Teacher: Why do you think some things float?

Child: Just 'cause they have to float. A puppet would float because it's light. A fat person can float.

Teacher: Can a skinny person float?

Child: Yes, 'cause it's light.

Teacher: But is a fat person light?

Child: No, the fat person can float if it holds still. The wooden cabinet can't float 'cause it's too heavy.

Analysis of responses reveals the quality and level of children's thinking and reminds us how much children have to learn and how incomplete their knowledge and understanding are. Analysis of interview responses may also reveal children's current thinking processes and problem-solving strategies (Ginsburg, 1997).

Asked "How do you know that's a male lion?" a child may be unable to elaborate beyond "I saw it on TV" and establish her level of learning at recognition. Another may immediately identify the lion's distinctive attributes, showing a higher level of knowledge. Listening to children's responses to "Why would someone do that?" or their perceptions of a classroom or playground incident can help you understand their social knowledge.

Cognitive research suggests that the difference between many poor and good problem solvers lies in the activation of appropriate strategies and the ability to monitor thinking process (metacognition) (Gardner, 1991; Mayer, 1992). Poor students may have the requisite knowledge and skills but fail to use them correctly or at the appropriate time. These students lack flexibility and may stick to one strategy even when it does not lead to successful solutions. Children's descriptions and explanations in response to questions such as "Tell me the ways you tried before you got this answer" often reveal aspects of their metacognition.

Look for Qualitative and Quantitative Differences. Assessment information can help us understand changes in what a youngster knows and can do and how she expresses that in the journey from beginning to proficient learner. Beginning learners may be inconsistent. There are qualitative as well as quantitative differences (Glaser, 1987). For example, a beginning learner may have only a vague and incomplete understanding of a term such as *mammal*. Her fragmented knowledge, incomplete understanding, and thought process are better described as a "complex" of ideas, rather than a true concept (Hanfmann & Kasanin, 1937; Sakharov, 1990; Vygotsky, 1962). As she organizes her scattered ideas into a true concept, she can define *mammal* in her own words, apply the very specific and narrow concept correctly to novel instances, and explain the relationship of a mammal to other members of the animal kingdom.

To analyze a child's level of performance, compare the documented behavior to a breakdown of the important components of the learning. For instance, patterning requires that learners be able to match one to one, perceive similarities and differences among items, and identify the significant features of the pattern. When Steven tries to repeat an alternating pattern of two red circles and three blue squares, he gets the first two circles correct, then places a blue square, red square, and yellow square in the row. Steven has some of the essential skills. He identifies the repeating nature of a certain number of circles and squares and matches one to one, but he omits the element of color in the squares. By comparing his performance with the essential components, the teacher identifies the components he can and can't do.

We ask children to do tasks that require integrating several subskills into a complex behavior. Analysis of children's performance on the various components will aid understanding. In some cases, a child may have trouble performing one of the subskills. A child who can't catch a ball while she is standing can hardly be expected to catch a ball while she is running. If she can't hop, she can't skip. In other cases, a child may have the subskills but be unable to combine them. He may read isolated words and identify word meanings but can't read a passage and explain its meaning. Sometimes the number of steps required simply overwhelms the learner, and he cannot proceed. An incomplete performance may mean that the number of things the child must attend to is overwhelming.

Identify the component subskills, their relationship, and the child's performance on each. Analyze where the child is having problems, and why.

Summary

Interpretation is a high-level process that requires analysis of information, integration of that information with other data, comparison with developmental guidelines and curriculum expectations, and making valid hypotheses about what it all means. Doing so blends objective information with sensitive judgment to yield a true assessment.

To ensure trustworthiness of the information, check for fairness, validity, and reliability. Make sure there are enough representative and balanced samples; that evidence obtained in different ways converges; that samples are consistent over time, unless the inconsistency itself is of significance; and that the assessment corresponds to reality. To maintain quality during analysis and interpretation, follow these guidelines: to determine progress, compare performance at two or more points in time; work from written documentation, compilations, and summaries, not memory; look for patterns, rather than isolated instances. Consider a child's or a group's unique and individual patterns of development, temperament, interests, and dispositions. For areas of concern or where more information is needed, look in depth, look more broadly, look in different contexts, or recheck.

As you analyze and try to understand information, use these guidelines:

- Generate multiple hypotheses about possible meanings, but hold all interpretations and hypotheses tentatively.
- Think of performance as a band or interval within which a child is functioning, not as a specific point on a scale.
- Compare outcomes to developmental or curriculum expectations.
- Analyze information for clues to learning processes.

For Personal Reflection

1. This chapter suggests that the sociocultural context of the classroom can either support or hinder children's performance. Reflect on classrooms you have observed and worked in. What evidence of this principle have you seen? What are its implications for you as you document and interpret children's performance in your own classroom?

2. Think of a time when your prior knowledge of a subject was not recognized by someone teaching you. Looking back, what are some ways your knowledge could have been determined, then recognized and put to good use?

For Further Study and Discussion

1. Look at the example of the range of performance and clustering of cutting skills shown in Figure 7.2 (p. 132). What are possible interpretations of this information (a) if children are 3 years old and in their first year of preschool and (b) if they are age 5 and in kindergarten? Based on these interpretations, outline appropriate classroom strategies relating to these children's cutting skills.

2. You are getting ready to check children's progress in language development. The records include periodic samples of children's drawing and writing; lists of books they like to "read" or listen to; checklists at two points in time on their comprehension of concepts of space, time, and attributes of objects; and performance samples on tasks that required following oral directions given by an adult. What other information might be

needed before you have enough representative samples to interpret children's progress in language? Outline a strategy to obtain that information.

3. Secure one or more work products from a preschool or primary child. Analyze them for information about that child. Explain and justify your interpretation. If you cannot get work products, do an in-depth analysis of Figures 4.4 and 4.5 (see p. 63), and then compare and contrast the two products.

4. Interview both a beginning teacher and an experienced teacher who are using classroom assessment to see how they interpret the information they collect. Compare and contrast their responses. What are some implications for you at this point in your teaching career?

Suggested Readings

Bodrova, E., & Leong, D. J. (1996). *Tools of the mind: The Vygotskian approach to early childhood education.* Englewood Cliffs, NJ: Merrill.

Bredekamp, S., & Rosegrant, T. (Eds.). (1992). *Reaching potentials: Appropriate curriculum and assessment for young children* (Vol. 1). Washington, DC: National Association for the Education of Young Children.

Bredekamp, S., & Rosegrant, T. (Eds.). (1995). *Reaching potentials: Appropriate curriculum and assessment for young children* (Vol. 2). Washington, DC: National Association for the Education of Young Children.

Ginsburg, H. P. (1997). *Entering the child's mind: The clinical interview in psychological research and practice.* Cambridge, U.K.: Cambridge University Press.

Levine, K. (1995). *Development of prewriting and scissor skills: A visual analysis.* Boston: Communication Skill Builders.

Rogoff, B. (1990). *Apprenticeship in thinking: Cognitive development in social context.* New York: Oxford University Press.

Tharp, R. G., & Gallimore, R. (1988). *Rousing minds to life: Teaching, learning, and schooling in social context.* New York: Cambridge University.

Wortham, S. C. (1995). *The integrated classroom: Assessment–curriculum link in early childhood education.* New York: Macmillan.

••••••••••••••••••••••••••••••••••••

CHAPTER 8

Using Assessment Information

The primary purpose of classroom assessment is to maximize children's development and learning. For the classroom teacher, this means aligning what is done in the classroom with what assessment reveals: where children are in their learning and development and what they have yet to attain. Bringing these two elements together is a challenging artistic process, not a mechanical one. Teachers can't say, "If Jeanne can't do this, turn to page 59 for activities" or "Recycle this group through Unit 8." Solutions are more complex than that. Knowing a child's strengths, needs, and interests does not always tell you what to do next. Thoughtful, sensitive, artistic planning is the best process teachers have for using assessment information in a way that directly benefits children and weaves the many threads involved in teaching into whole cloth.

Activities, content, grouping, instructional interactions, and the other elements that make up classroom learning and teaching must be grounded in children's current abilities and potential, as determined by assessment, and designed to lead them on (Stiggens, 1997). Unless teachers plan to use assessment results, the insights and information are likely to be lost in the rush of classroom events.

Teachers can link assessment with developmentally appropriate curriculum and differentiated instruction, no matter what planning process they use. The basic principles that follow apply to almost all developmental areas or curriculum goals, are drawn from the broad age span of early childhood—3 to 8 years old—and reflect the differing classroom organizations and emphases of the various levels. Suggestions and examples are representative and are neither prescriptive nor exhaustive. Our intent is to show teachers ways in which information from assessment can inform and improve classroom practice through planning strategies, individual and group strategies, and curriculum and classroom modification strategies. Specific examples of how assessment information can be linked to planning appropriate experiences for children conclude the chapter.

Planning Strategies

Planning allows for reflection on what to do with assessment results and gives an opportunity to outline a course of action that may involve changes in the environment and in teaching processes and procedures.

Plan and Organize the Intended Changes

Although much planning is never written (Clark & Yinger, 1987), translation of assessment results into differentiated instruction and activities to help children learn probably requires more planning than teachers can carry in their heads. Projects and investigations, for example, integrate assessment results, information about how children learn, and important developmental and learning outcomes. However, projects and investigations require a high degree of planning and organization to achieve the expected results (Helm & Katz, 2000; Katz & Chard, 1989; Morine-Dershimer, 1990).

Think through and outline what you plan to do, make notes or attach a card to remind you, revise a lesson in a science or social studies guide to incorporate the problem solving and critical thinking that assessment shows is needed, or script sample questions to ask children working on multilevel activities so that each one has appropriate interaction with an adult. Do whatever is necessary to guide and remind you and other adults in the classroom of any modifications you intend to make.

Refer to Assessment Information as You Plan

Study the summary sheets and class profiles for logical, flexible groupings and subgroupings. Review notes and children's work to remind you where they need help and where they are progressing satisfactorily. Check the assessment plan to determine if you need to collect one of the core items for the portfolio, or plan a performance check on the children's abilities to estimate and measure as a part of their ongoing work in science and mathematics.

Allow Time for Reflection

Allow enough time for thoughtful consideration of and reflection on assessment results. Don't try to plan everything at one time. Make preliminary notes to provide a framework, then gradually fill in details, incorporating insights from periodic and ongoing assessment and from other people working in the classroom.

Plan Ways to Meet Children's Assessed Needs

When a particular need is identified, it is unlikely to be met through incidental learning or the passage of time alone. For instance, children who are rejected by their peers should receive help before that rejection is set in stone and the possibilities for social integration are lost (Staff, *Harvard Education Letter*, 1989). Youngsters whose backgrounds have not provided them with the experiences, language, and dispositions to tackle academic tasks are unlikely to pick them up.

Deliberately Incorporate the Wealth of Information, Resources, and Strategies Available to Support Young Children's Learning

Knowledge about young children's development and learning is expanding rapidly, but unless teachers plan to use that knowledge, they will continue to do things the same old way. Be open to trying different approaches.

Suppose you've always regarded outdoor time as a time for everyone to enjoy strictly unstructured, unplanned play. Assessment reveals that the children whose large muscle skills were already good when they entered school are getting better, and the ones who need to improve haven't. It's time to rethink the approach to outdoor time, using information that shows that children benefit from appropriate instruction in physical and motor development (Gallahue, 1993; Poest, Williams, Witt, & Atwood, 1990).

Assessment often reveals children who are having difficulty discriminating symbols important in mathematics, problems in reading, maintaining attention, remembering or problem solving (Berk, 2006). What will help the youngster who is having difficulty discriminating mirror-image letters, such as *b* and *d*? Experiences with print in actual reading situations rather than as isolated letters may make a youngster more sensitive to these and other reading-specific perceptual cues (Casey, 1986). Because this suggestion is compatible with the language and literacy approach the school is using, plan for it.

Theories about helping children learn through appropriate scaffolding and guided participation in the Zone of Proximal Development have enormous implications for teaching and learning in early childhood (Belmont, 1989; Berk & Winsler, 1995; Bodrova & Leong, 1996). Planning for how this will happen helps teachers implement these subtle and sensitive instructional approaches.

Plan for and with Other People in the Classroom

Many early childhood classrooms have classroom assistants, aides, parent and grandparent volunteers, older children, and specialists at given times. Extra people make more learning opportunities possible, but these must be planned.

Involve regular classroom personnel in planning. They may offer different perspectives on ways to meet assessed needs.

Using assessment results to help children learn almost always requires greater specificity in planning for other people than most teachers are apt to do. Plan where adults will be and what they will say and do to support children's learning. An example: As you assess, it is clear that several children need lots of help with social interaction. Classroom disruptions affirm that conclusion almost daily. You work out a plan of action designed to prevent some of the disruptions and simultaneously teach children appropriate behavior. Because all classroom adults need to be consistent if the plan is to work, coach other adults.

Assessment almost always reveals children who are at the cutting edge of some new learning and who have a range of tasks they are ready for. It shows where a child is currently functioning and perhaps gives some insights on the direction of growth and interest. Plan dialogue and activities to enable the child to move to a higher level. Pair an adult or a child who is competent in a given skill with a child who is on the verge of becoming competent, and show the "expert" how to assist the "novice" as they work together. For instance, children might not be able to set a table or prepare snacks on their own but can do so with assistance. Children who are still learning the social and organizational skills to dramatize a favorite story can benefit from adult assistance. Planning ensures that props, space, time, and a coach are available.

Demonstrate and explain to other people what they are to do. Use index cards to jot reminders and prompts to yourself and assistants about how to word requests, directions, and explanations to align with a child's level of learning. For example, it is often difficult to get children to *use* new vocabulary words. How can we interact with children who are ready to get them to use language such as "same shape as," "not the same shape as," "different sound than," "same texture as," "not the same size," "different temperature than"? We do not need to form language groups to do this, but rather to change the way we interact with children, to *intentionally* converse with them in ways that support their language learning. As teachers, most of us need reminders of how to do this; so do other people.

Balance What You Might Like to Do with What Is Possible

Set priorities for individual children and the class. Make easy changes first. Changing time schedules in a self-contained classroom to be more compatible with children's development and ways of learning is relatively easy. Changing the teaching of reading from one long-established approach to another method may take longer.

Start with obvious and critical needs. If assessment reveals that the youngster you thought was comprehending English is not, an obvious and critical need exists. If assessment reveals that a youngster frequently disrupts or is rejected in classroom activities, an obvious and critical need exists.

Individual and Group Strategies

Assessment usually reveals many strengths and many things "yet to learn." There will be developmental or curriculum areas in which only individual children need challenge or assistance, areas in which several children could benefit, as well as areas in which all children will benefit from additional opportunities to learn and develop but at different levels. Balancing the needs of individual children with those of the total group is one of a teacher's most challenging tasks. Current instructional practices and research offer many guidelines and clues but no definitive answers. We consider situations in which one or two children may need specific attention, when several children would benefit, and when the entire group will benefit, as well as mixed-age classes.

For One or Two Children

Sometimes one or two children require specific help, either because they are still learning or because they need challenge. Usually their needs can be met by providing opportunities for learning with the entire group, in a small subgroup, or by providing multilevel activities. It is seldom necessary to remove children from the group. You might plan a specific activity that would be appropriate for several children, including the one or two that need help. Sit beside the youngster(s) who need attention, and as you work with the entire group, give appropriate help. Maybe that consists of counting balls of modeling clay, when the others are well into understanding "fewer" and "more." A few opportunities for individual attention will often work wonders with a child who is on the verge of grasping an idea.

Sometimes opportunities must be closely tailored to needs and interests. If a child is having difficulty, analyze assessment results for clues to the problem. If a second-grader is having difficulty alphabetizing words because she does not fully understand *before* and *after* as they apply to position in a sequence, help her learn those terms, going back to experiences with concrete materials if necessary. If the difficulty stems from uncertainty about the order of letters in the alphabet, provide practice to make alphabetical order automatic and fluent.

Children who need challenge deserve the same thoughtful consideration. Multilevel activities, project work, and cooperative groups enable them to enjoy the benefits of group interaction. Individual activities can challenge, extend, broaden, and elaborate their development and learning into areas they might not otherwise explore: creative problem solving, scientific investigation, composing music or poetry, mastering games of strategy and skill. Amplification (Zaporozhets & Elkonin, 1971) of children's knowledge can bring depth and breadth of understanding at their own level of development. "Challenge" need not be synonymous with acceleration.

Sometimes individual children are reluctant to participate in activities such as vigorous outdoor play, art, dramatic play, focused skill development, or oral presentations. Look first for obvious reasons: Is the play too boisterous and competitive? Are the skills beyond the child's developmental level? Are there gender signals that keep a boy or girl away? Is the reluctance simply this youngster's initial reserve in entering into a new activity? Are sociocultural differences operating? Evaluate the child's current level of functioning and skill for possible clues to the reluctance. Plan activities the child likes and in which she is successful, and relate or extend them into other areas, such as gradually combining the block area and dramatic play area or setting up attractive, versatile art, science, or writing materials that engage the child's interest.

Perhaps observation of participation confirms what others have found—that children may not be engaged in large muscle activities, even though they are outside (Poest et al., 1990). Rearrange active, physical play apparatus and put it in a prominent place on the play yard. Plan noncompetitive games and activities to discourage inappropriate competitiveness, often disheartening to the children who need the most encouragement. Select or alter activities so children do not have a long wait for a turn. Join in to guide and provide a model.

In all situations, provide support, guidance, informal instruction, and encouragement, but also help the youngster improve skills that will make participation easier (Bodrova & Leong, 1996; Rogoff, 1990). Help children who can't throw and catch to learn how. Teach oral presentation skills gradually, and let children practice with one other person or a small group until they are comfortable, gradually assuming more responsibility for their own performance (Rogoff & Gardner, 1984). Adapt classroom interaction processes to recognize community and cultural practices, such as allowing more time for responses or time for pauses in speech (Gage & Berliner, 1992).

For Several Children

Class profiles usually identify several children who are having difficulty with the same skill, who need more opportunity to practice, or who need challenge because they are quite proficient. Use a variety of flexible grouping strategies. Some of the options are friendship groups, interest groups, achievement groups, interdependent cooperative groups, work and study skills groups, self-selected groups, informal skill groups, formally assigned skill groups, random groups, groups of one or two, and others. For instance, groups of two can form author/editor pairs in which each child learns important writing, reading, editing, and discourse skills. Two children can "pair and share" to give an opportunity to discuss, report, or share without the deadly routine of round-robin "show and tell" or reporting. Children who write can be paired with children who are still dictating. If children are having difficulty entering a peer group, let them play and work with some younger children. Aggressive children may be less aggressive with older or larger children. Pair a shy child with a friendly, outgoing one, and form small groups in which less outgoing children feel welcome (Wittmer & Honig, 1994).

Avoid assigned, unchanging ability or skill groups that may stigmatize and track children by narrowing their opportunities to learn (Manning & Lucking, 1990; Oakes, 1991; Slavin, 1987). Group children on functional competence and need related to specific developmental or learning areas, not on overall perception of ability or achievement. With skillful planning, subgroups can be formed, accomplish their purposes, and then the children can proceed to another activity unobtrusively.

Interdependent cooperative learning groups mix children with differing skills and knowledge so children learn from each other; the group itself becomes a way to learn both social and academic skills (Newman, Griffin, & Cole, 1989).

"Choice" activities can be geared to the needs of one group, and others can participate if they wish. Children who have mastered a certain development or learning often enjoy and benefit from repetition, just as they reread favorite books. If the activity involves adult–child interaction, adults can vary the level of interaction to the child's need. For example, in a game designed to help children learn the concepts "more," "less," and "equal," some children might simply be hearing and repeating the terms, whereas others would be using them spontaneously or in conversational interchanges.

Mixed-Age Classes

Typical early childhood groups are grouped by age. Mixed-age classes open up new possibilities for meeting children's assessed needs. There are indications that social development, particularly leadership and prosocial behavior, is enhanced. Interaction between less able ("novices") and more able children ("experts") may have academic and social benefits for both. Children who are slightly older and more proficient may be operating in another child's Zone of Proximal Development and thus be able to provide the appropriate amount of modeling and guidance to help the learner (Katz, Evangelou, & Hartman, 1990). Children will need some specific guidance if the benefits of this approach are to be realized. Katz and associates (1990) suggest that children be helped to ask for and give assistance; that teachers guard against exploiting older children as helpers and discourage stereotyping by age; that children be sensitized to their peers' emotional needs and help them know how to respond; and that children be helped to know their peers' interests, needs, and capabilities. The opportunity to help another student can increase the "expert's" motivation as well as the actual learning (Webb, 1983). Many of these same strategies will work in any group, which will always have mixed abilities and interests.

For the Entire Group

Sometimes almost all children in a group will benefit from experiences provided to a total group: class meetings, group or circle time, music, dance, movement, aerobic exercise, group discussion and problem solving, listening to books being read aloud, and many other activities. Even activities traditionally thought of as self-selected or individual may have components that involve the whole group. For example, some physical development experts suggest that outdoor playtimes begin with a group "warm up," with everyone walking, then walking briskly, before children proceed to their chosen activities. Everyone should also participate in a "cool down" as a transition from outdoor play to the next activity. An "individually appropriate" activity does not mean that children do everything as individuals.

Attractive, interesting learning centers are another way to make learning experiences available to every child. Children work in these at their own level as they are interested and have time. Monitor participation. If some children don't participate, try modifications in placement, materials, competing activities, time, and adult involvement before deciding the approach doesn't work. Participation doesn't have to be daily but can be over a period of time.

As an alternative, children can be expected to participate in certain learning centers sometime during each day. For instance, children who are learning to express themselves in writing might be expected to write in their journals or work in the writing center sometime during the day. The choice of when and what to write is theirs. Children involved in project work can be expected to solve certain mathematical problems related to the project. They may not all do it at one time or in the same way, but all will have the experience.

Child-selected or free choice activities can also reach all the children in the group, provided they are interesting enough and children have an extended period of time to work through their choices. Monitor participation to make sure children who need the experience get it.

Children can also be assigned to groups that rotate to appropriate activities at set intervals, although it is difficult to make such groups flexible enough to accommodate young children's varying interest levels and task orientations.

Children can participate in "everyone needs to do this" as individuals. Choose interesting and intrinsically rewarding activities, and offer them often. Computers, tricycles, reading or looking at books, writing, puzzles, art, scientific observations, and many problems based on manipulatives can be individual activities.

Curriculum and Classroom Modification Strategies

Making the curriculum responsive to children's strengths and needs as determined by assessment requires modification of classroom activities.

Allocate Time and Space in Different Ways to Achieve Different Results

Teachers make most of the decisions about how much time to spend on a goal, subject, or activity. They decide on the space arrangement in the room. These easily manipulated variables can help make the classroom more responsive to children's needs. They are one way to give more or less emphasis to a particular activity or curriculum area. However, the effect of time and space on children's involvement and learning has to be carefully monitored so that more does not become "too much."

To solve problems created by crowding during the opening class meeting, you spread the children out so they can't possibly nudge, push, or bother each other, and inadvertently create a different problem. The children are so scattered you cannot maintain their attention, they can't see visuals—even "big books"—and the feeling of being a group is lost.

Suppose assessment indicates that most of the children would benefit from extensive work and play with math manipulatives. You decide to leave 1-inch interlocking cubes out for children to use whenever they want. Monitoring reveals that use increases immediately, then falls off as the cubes blend into the shelves. Replanning, you try another approach. Interlocking cubes, attribute and pattern blocks, and other math manipulatives will be rotated, with the time for rotation guided by the level of use.

A related problem is that of too little time. Integrate learnings so children learn several things simultaneously. Children do not distinguish one area of development or one subject matter from another. Reading, writing, listening, speaking, and literature can be learned simultaneously. Science, mathematics, problem solving, symbolic representation, physical development, and other learnings are merged as children work, play, and experiment with manipulative equipment, water and sand, weighing and measuring, cooking, music, movement, and art. Such integration, combined with the use of learning centers, individual activities, and small flexible groups, allows teachers to do away with rigid time periods and creates a classroom that allows children to work at their own paces and explore topics "in-depth" both within a day and over longer periods of time. Children who need plenty of time and practice for mastery of key concepts and skills are not left behind.

Select and Arrange Materials in Response to Assessment Results

Equipment, supplies, and activities should encompass the range of capabilities found in the group. A group profile reveals the range: Three children don't grasp the idea of pattern; two can copy and extend almost any pattern and also create their own. Two children are reading; two cannot recognize any letters, not even the first letters of their names. Four children can construct and read their own maps; three don't know what maps are. The other children are at all points in between.

Fortunately, almost any activity, content, or process in which young children are involved can be made either simpler or more complex (Hendrick & Weisman, 2005). Multilevel activities and materials enable each child to achieve success and continued learning. Some of the very best material for children's learning is open ended: counting cubes, blocks, pattern and attribute blocks, modeling clay, books, drawing and writing materials, movement, music, art materials, and many others. Plan to adapt the same basic material and activities to meet the assessed needs of particular children. Teachers often have to open up different possibilities for children, such as supplying accessories, signs, and suggestions for extended block play.

Any classroom with children who need language and literacy development should have a prominent, changing, and varied display of books, functional signs, posters, and other written material keyed to children's interests and backgrounds. Youngsters who are learning to sort and classify need many opportunities to explore a wide variety of structured and natural materials on their own and to solve specific classification problems. Emerging literacy—at whatever age—calls for writing instruments and paper of all kinds to be placed strategically around the room. Children who are learning to share resources in a cooperative learning group shouldn't each have a box of crayons, a pair of scissors, and identical books. Materials and activities should be gender-neutral or clearly include both boys and girls. Plan procedures that ensure equal access to computers, science and math apparatus, dolls, blocks, and challenging physical games. Avoid activities that may be gender stereotyped.

Use Any Apparent Sequence

Although not everything can be sequenced, it makes sense to use known sequences. Give children experiences to help them understand a concept before they are expected to comprehend and then say the words that stand for that concept. Make sure children understand directions before they are expected to follow them. Show children how to share and take turns before admonishing them to do so.

Some sequences are fairly evident from the way children develop. Larger manipulatives (beads, pegs, interlocking blocks, parquetry) are usually easier to use than small ones; mixing, pounding, squeezing, and rolling modeling clay directly with the hands is easier than with tools. Tracing inside a cut-out template is easier than tracing around the outside. Whole-hand fingerplays are easier than ones calling for individual finger movement, which in turn are easier than complicated, two-hand coordinated ones. Many adults have difficulty alternating index finger and thumb to make the eensy beensy spider climb! Printing large letters without regard for lines is easier than printing on lines. Cutting out a circle is easier than cutting out an angled figure.

By understanding the direction and sequence in which a skill develops, teachers can provide scaffolding to ensure that children grow increasingly independent. The term *scaffolding* refers to the support that teachers, materials, other children, or interactions between the child and others provide to help the child perform a task. But just as we remove scaffolding from a building when its walls are able to stand alone, so the teacher must plan ways of making the child gradually responsible for performance of the task. Scaffolding has another implication—that the teacher knows what the end skill is going to look like and how to get to it. Thus the support is given in such a way that it fosters the child's ability to eventually perform independently. Both the support and its removal are provided in a conscious manner (Bodrova & Leong, 1996).

For example, a teacher provides a scaffold for a child's counting by holding her hand and showing her how to move it as they point and count together. As they work, the teacher begins to "fade"—to omit a number to see if the child can say it on her own. When the child seems able to say the numbers by herself, the teacher only points with the child. In the next step the teacher doesn't point but simply watches the child point and count aloud, progressing from assisted, or scaffolded, counting to independent counting.

Children can provide scaffolds for each other, too. A second-grader who is having trouble remembering the story he is trying to write may have a buddy whose job is to help him remember what he wants to say. By talking through the story with the "say-back buddy," he is able to write a more complicated story than he would have by himself. As this second-grader becomes a more fluent writer, he will need less scaffolding by his buddy. He will have moved from assisted, or scaffolded, writing to independent writing.

Look at the Need for Possible Change in Procedures

Suppose participation charts show that more than half the children seldom talk during class meetings, group discussions, circle time, or any teacher-led activity—not an uncommon finding. Before starting to work with the children, examine adult patterns of interaction—calling on volunteers or those children who readily respond, answering our own questions, or allowing so little wait time that thoughtful children are still thinking when the next question comes. Plan interaction techniques to get more children to participate, such as beaming questions to the group, calling on all the children, and valuing their responses.

Rethink and Restructure to Meet Children "Where They Are"

Many children don't match the curriculum guide, activities handbook, or expected sequence of goals and objectives. We've got different kids! Professional teachers must know curriculum theory and child development well enough to simplify, delete, extend, elaborate, and embellish curriculum content and processes so they are developmentally and individually appropriate for the children. Teachers have to know how to construct curriculum when no guides exist.

Examples of Using Assessment Information to Guide Instruction

Examples of ways teachers use assessment information to inform and guide instruction are given throughout the previous chapters. The intent is to show possibilities, not to prescribe a single approach. The simple examples that follow are chosen from typical curriculum areas in early childhood education. For other examples, see the research and instructional strategies in the extensive literature available on children's learning. Guides for nurturing children's emergent literacy are particularly rich in their implications.

Play

Mr. Frankel's assessment during dramatic play revealed that Tony, LaTessa, and Jerry sometimes engaged in play that became angry and sometimes physically violent. His attempts to let the three of them work it out usually led to crying and disintegration of the play. If he were to remove all the props they argued about, the playhouse would be bereft of any props at all. When asked what they could do next time to avoid an argument, all three children seem to be able to state reasonable alternatives: "We should use our words"; "I shouldn't hit him." But once they are at play, bickering stops only when Mr. Frankel enters the dramatic play area and directly intervenes. These youngsters need to learn better strategies for interacting with one another instead of practicing inappropriate ones. Without intervention it is likely that they will *not* learn or practice positive social skills. Mr. Frankel considers two options: child planning and "social tutoring."

Children can plan their play before they begin (Bodrova & Leong, 1998b). As they plan, the children develop a common theme, choose the props they will use, and identify their roles. The children can do this on paper, by drawing (not in detail, but simply as a reminder) what they plan to do, as shown in Figures 8.1 and

Figure 8.1   Child's Plan for Play—Dictated

play with horses at blocks

Figure 8.2   Child's Plan for Play—Dictated

play babies in play house

8.2. Have the children who plan to go to the dramatic play center decide what they will play and what props they need. Assist the planning if children need coaching on how to pick an appropriate theme or divide roles without arguing. If they can plan independently, have them show and explain the plan after it is done. We have yet to see children plan to fight! They always plan to work together and to have fun.

Planning avoids many of the arguments that children have over objects or roles. If there is only one ballerina costume, children can work out a solution. When children enter the play area with a solution to the "one costume" problem ahead of time, they usually do not fight or argue when they get there. Planning avoids conflict over roles, such as who will be the doctor. Appealing related roles can be suggested (receptionist, technician, nurse), or different types of doctors (surgeon, heart doctor, X-ray reader). Doctors need patients, too!

Planning allows the teacher to stay out of arguments when children get upset. Asking "Was this part of your plan?" is often enough to stop the altercation and get everyone back on track.

More important in the long run, planning helps children learn to think ahead, interact, solve potential problems, and make their own play more productive. They begin to imitate and practice the advanced social skills that the teacher wants them to learn. This thoughtful, deliberate approach will lead to advanced cognitive skills as well (Bodrova & Leong, 1996, 2001b).

The teacher can also pair Tony, LaTessa, and Jerry with other children who have more advanced social skills or with an older child from another room. Each child can play separately with the "social tutor" so they do not overwhelm him or her.

Small Muscle/Fine Motor Development

Assessment of kindergarten children's fine motor development identifies several who are having difficulty cutting. They can't hold either paper or scissors to make them work. One parent explained that crayons, pencils, markers, and scissors were off limits to the children in their house because they marked on the walls and messed up the house. Other parents had difficulty providing food, let alone scissors and paper.

Plan opportunities for all types of fine motor development. Incidental learning, such as is made available in unplanned manipulative play or art, probably will not be enough. Have a center or area that focuses on needs, or incorporate skill development into appropriate existing functional areas or centers. Develop an office area with rotary and push-button telephones, paper and pencils, scissors, a keyboard, and other office tools. Develop a center with writing, drawing, and cutting tools. Vary the manipulatives area to provide needed skill building. Incorporate "real-life" materials to add interest, variety, choice, and practice with a variety of fine motor motions—paper punches and fasteners, nuts and bolts, wrenches, screwdrivers, hand drills, and egg beaters, all types of fasteners and closures—any appropriate tools to help develop strength, dexterity, coordination, and control.

Plan specific assistance for those youngsters who are still learning to use scissors. Show them how to hold both scissors and paper "thumbs up" and to say "thumbs up" to remind themselves. Put a dot on the paper in the place where the thumb is supposed to go. Start with strips of paper, gradually making them wider as children learn. Make essential practice interesting and functional. When children need practice to advance from snipping to a smooth single cut, have them cut straw for the horses and cows, or pretzels, carrots, and celery sticks for a pretend snack. Let children snip or punch confetti for a parade or collage. The paper strips they cut can be used by the whole group for a special collage, three-dimensional representations (strips pasted on top of strips to make their own creations), or bulletin board decorations. The adult's job is not to withhold assistance, but to coach those children who need help in learning certain skills and then to let the children take over. There is quite enough for children to learn on their own. Watch the awkward and laborious way many older children and adults write with pen and pencil, and providing young children guidance and practice in fine motor skills will take on more meaning.

Early Literacy Development

Assessment of a typical state standard for preschool, "name writing"—the child's ability to write his/her own name—reveals a wide range of ability in your classroom. You have assessed children individually during center time by asking each child to write his or her name on a sheet of paper so you can tell who is in the center. It has taken two days to watch each child's attempt at name writing. One group of children are like Megan and Estefan who can already write their first names easily. Another group of children are like Martin who writes his name backward "nitraM" but knows all the letters. Some children know only some of the letters of their name, like Chris who knows only the "C" and "i." Awan is typical of another group of children. He does not recognize his name and cannot write any of the letters. Every morning children sign in by writing their own names next to the date on their individual sign-in sheet. Each sheet has 5 lines, one for every day of the week. Children know that after the sign-in, they have free choice. Since you do not have to supervise each and every child, you have time to work with some children individually.

You scaffold the name writing by having a model of each child's name for them to recognize and copy, working with the children individually, and modifying their name tags to provide support for them when you are working with another child. The model is a "name tag"—a 6-inch strip of tag board with the child's first name written in capital and lower case letters. The child's last name is on the back. Each name tag has the scaffold that particular child needs and no more. The name tags are placed in a different spot at the sign-in table each day, so children have to identify their names. The examples that follow illustrate ways to provide scaffolds for children at varying levels of ability:

- Awan cannot recognize his name or write any of the letters. On Awan's name tag, paste his picture temporarily right next to the first letter. Draw a line under the "A" with a wipe-off marker. When he walks in, you help Awan find his name tag. When he finds his picture, point out that another way find his name is to look for the letter "A" that you have underlined. Help him write that letter. The next day, encourage him to look for the letter and not just his picture. Then turn the picture under and see if he can find his name using the first letter only. If he cannot, tell him to see if his picture is attached to the name tag. That way he will know if it is his name without your help. (If there are two children whose names begin with "A," use the first two letters or more instead of just the first.) Encourage him to write the "A" and to try writing the other letters. Add supports similar to those on Chris' tag as Awan progresses.

- Chris writes some letters of his name. Place Chris' name tag with the first name up. When Chris signs in, point out that he knows how to write "C" and "i" and have him try to write the letters "h" "r" and "s," as you point to the name tag. If he cannot write the "h," show him how and underline it with the marker to help him remember. When he can write "Chi," erase the line under the "h" and move onto the next letter "r." Children like Chris might learn two and even three letters at a time. Underline each of the letters you want him to remember. On following days, give verbal prompts and demonstrate writing as needed.

- Martin knows the letters of his name but writes them in order backward: "nitraM." On Martin's name tag (first name up) use a wipe-off marker to draw a dot under the first letter of his name and an arrow extending from the dot to the last letter of his name to indicate the direction he is to write. When Martin signs in, put a dot and arrow on his sign-in sheet so that it matches his name tag. Encourage him to start at the dot with the letter "M" and then write the "a" next, and then the "r" next, etc., indicating the direction of the arrow. The next day, give a verbal prompt. As soon as you think he understands the direction he is to write, remove the arrow. When he can write his name without support, erase the dot. Martin will then be ready to write his last name.

- For children like Megan Johnson and Estefan Ramirez, who can write their first names correctly from memory, start the activity with the last name displayed on their name tags. When they sign in, tell them to write their first and last names. Once children can write their first and last names, put the name tags away because you want them to write their names from memory.

Johnson

Ramirez

Provide supports that are temporary and remove them as soon as children can perform by themselves. There are many other activities to help children practice name recognition and name writing. For example, children who need practice recognizing their names can play with puzzles made by cutting their names into individual letters. Children can then put the letters of their names in order. Dismiss children by displaying a name tag one letter at a time until the child recognizes his/her name. Have children find their place at lunch by placing their name tags in different locations on the table. Functional practice in different contexts will also help. Children can sign in to be the next in line for playing at a center. They can sign their names on participation charts or charts that show what food they like or their favorite color. Children can write their names on artwork and other papers. Your assessment of the level of the child's ability to write his/her own name is the first step in planning and implementing effective support for learning.

Summary

Teachers can use assessment information to help children develop and learn by employing a combination of thoughtful planning, meeting individual and group needs in a variety of ways, and modifying the classroom and curriculum to be more responsive to assessed needs. Plan intended changes and adjustments; refer to assessment files and summaries during planning; allow time for reflection; plan strategies and activities to meet children's assessed needs; incorporate current knowledge and resources; plan for and with other people in the classroom; and balance what you might like to do with what is possible.

Meeting the needs of individual children within the context of a classroom is a challenge. A variety of approaches are needed for using assessment results when one or two children need specific attention, when several children would benefit, when an entire group would benefit, and for using assessment results in a mixed-age classroom.

Modify and adjust the curriculum and classroom to meet children's needs: select and arrange equipment, materials, and supplies in response to assessment results; use appropriate sequences for simplifying or increasing complexity; consider the need for possible changes in classroom procedures; and rethink and restructure curriculum if needed.

Within the context of a developmentally appropriate curriculum, plan specific activities and intentional teaching to help meet children's development and learning needs. They are unlikely to be met by incidental learning alone. Several examples showed how this can be accomplished.

For Personal Reflection

1. Making full use of aides, assistants, and volunteers is suggested as a strategy to meet instructional needs identified by assessment. Reflect on your own knowledge, attitudes, skills, and feelings regarding planning for, guiding, and coaching other adults in the classroom.
2. People plan in different ways. Some do all their planning in one block of time; others spread it out, entering plans as insights occur to them; others use different approaches. We recommend that you allow time for reflection on assessment results and classroom processes as you are planning. Examine your own planning style. When will that reflection take place?

For Further Study and Discussion

1. Interview one or more teachers to learn how they plan to meet the assessed needs of children in their classrooms. Within your adult learning group (college class or staff development group), interview representatives from both preschool and primary levels. As a group, or as individuals, analyze their responses. What conclusions can you draw?
2. Assessment has revealed several needs within a kindergarten group: three children are having difficulty entering a play or work group, either indoors or out; four youngsters are obviously lost when discussion turns to comparisons of likenesses and differences. Specifically, they neither

comprehend nor use the terms *the same as* and *different from;* two children are having difficulty classifying objects or pictures of objects on any
basis except observable attributes (color, shape, size). Select one of these
needs, and plan a course of action to help children within the context of
a developmentally appropriate curriculum.

3. After conducting several assessments, you find three clusters of children
with similar skills. Cluster 1 needs practice hopping, cluster 2 has already mastered the skill, and cluster 3 cannot hop at all. Discuss how you
might develop multilevel activities that will benefit all of the children.
Describe several ways you could work with the children.

Suggested Readings

Berk, L. E., & Winsler, A. (1995). *Scaffolding children's learning: Vygotsky and early
childhood education.* Washington, DC: National Association for the Education of
Young Children.

Bodrova, E., & Leong, D. J. (1996). *Tools of the mind: The Vygotskian approach to early
childhood education.* Englewood Cliffs, NJ: Merrill.

Bredekamp, S., & Rosegrant, T. (Eds.). (1992). *Reaching potentials: Appropriate curriculum and assessment for young children* (Vol. 1). Washington, DC: National
Association for the Education of Young Children.

Bredekamp, S., & Rosegrant, T. (Eds.). (1995). *Reaching potentials: Transforming early
childhood curriculum and assessment* (Vol. 2). Washington, DC: National Association for the Education of Young Children.

Copley, J. V. (2000). *The young child and mathematics.* Washington, DC: National Association for the Education of Young Children and National Council of Teachers
of Mathematics.

Copple, C., & Bredekamp, S. (2006). *Basics of developmentally appropriate practice:
An introduction for teachers of children 3–6.* Washington, DC: National Association for the Education of Young Children.

Helm, J., & Katz, L. (2000). *Young investigators: The project approach in the early
years.* New York: Teachers College Press.

Neuman, S. B., Copple, C., & Bredekamp, S. (2000). *Learning to read and write: Developmentally appropriate practices for young children.* Washington, DC: National Association for the Education of Young Children.

CHAPTER 9

Organizing for Assessment

Knowing what to assess, when to assess, and how to collect and record assessment information provides teachers with different options to use when appraising children. How do you pull all of these things together to create a workable classroom assessment process? This chapter discusses three elements that will help you get started: integrating assessment with teaching, developing an assessment plan, and organizing files and forms.

Integrating Assessment and Teaching

The key to classroom assessment is embedding it in regular classroom activities. The following guidelines provide a general, practical approach, followed by tips about specific assessment opportunities found in most preschool and primary classrooms.

General Guidelines

Assessment can be overwhelming if you attempt everything at once. Schedule activities so you have time to assess. Begin gradually, starting with easy assessment techniques that are appropriate for the children. Stay organized and current. Make assessment a regular part of classroom living, and enlist the aid of other people.

Schedule Activities So You Have Time to Assess.   Help children learn to work and play on their own as well as in interaction with an adult. Teach them how to move to their next activity, get help, regulate their own behavior, and solve problems on their own or with a classmate.

Help children understand that assessment is part of teaching. One team of primary teachers enlisted the children's help. Each teacher developed a visible signal that showed she was documenting learning—a pair of old sunglasses perched in the hair or a bright bandanna around the neck. When the children saw these signals, they knew an important aspect of teaching was going on and did not interrupt. If required assessments are scheduled, plan other activities accordingly.

Begin and Proceed Gradually.   It is easy to attempt too much. Only you can know your other personal and professional commitments; prior knowledge and skill; teaching load; and center, school, and parent expectations. Start with one developmental or curriculum area, and focus on it until you are comfortable with the process. Or start with four or five children, adding more as you learn. Don't try to get an anecdotal record on each child every day, but get one on two or three children a day.

Start with Easy, Appropriate Techniques.   Start with assessment techniques that are relatively easy and developmentally appropriate. Children who are reading and writing will produce many products to provide evidence of their learning. Collect and work with these while you are learning how to analyze reading and writing processes—a more challenging task.

Stay Organized and Current.   Many teachers take a few minutes at the end of each day to file notes, completed charts, and other information. Certainly, it should be done once a week. Summarize when there is enough information to warrant it. Keep information current enough to be useful in the classroom. Last month's notes are needed to document progress but are no help in planning tomorrow's or next week's activities.

Make Assessment a Normal Part of Classroom Life.   One of the big advantages of classroom assessment is that activities do not have to be suspended for a week of testing—whether screening, readiness, or achievement. Information is collected along the way. The intent is to have gathering and recording information "seem so much a part of the ongoing classroom procedure, so focused on [children's] learning" that the children are hardly aware of it (Almy & Genishi, 1979, p. 9).

- *Place supplies for recording in each activity area.* Keep a stack of paper or prepared checklists near areas where routines are carried out. If parents bring children to school, put paper and pen in the transition spot. Slip a pencil, index cards, or a small spiral-bound notebook in your pocket when you go outdoors. The spiral wires of the notebook make a convenient storage place for a short pencil. Keep well-organized supplies near learning centers where children write subject matter journals, maintain reading logs, plan projects or play, or write or dictate stories; they will do much of their own documentation. Have your own recording supplies in several places so it is easy for you to make a note, mark a checklist, or fill out a rating scale as you supervise and work with children.

- *Gather information regularly so everyone gets used to it.* If you teach primary grades and plan to use short paper-and-pencil tests, give them frequently, not only before report card time. If performance samples are used as evidence of learning, use them often in interactive teaching, not only at "assessment time." Interview and have conferences with children routinely, so they don't feel put on the spot. Photograph and record regularly so children don't "mug."
- *Be unobtrusive.* Learn to gather and record information deftly; sit or stand nearby rather than hovering. When appropriate, fade into the background. Store recording forms in key places where you can sit or stand to see the whole room. A few minutes of recording while the children are working and playing will yield much useful information. Place recording devices so they are not the center of attention.
- *Be matter-of-fact when children ask what you're doing.* "I'm writing what we do and say so I can remember." "I'm keeping track of what we've learned and have yet to learn." "I do this to help me teach better." Keep an extra clipboard with scrap paper on it for those children who want to scribble or write their own records in imitation. Some children may do their first functional "writing" that way—a nice example to go in a portfolio.
- *Maintain "dual focus"* (Kounin, 1970) so you can monitor the activity of a group of children as you record or play a learning game while simultaneously checking length or level of participation. Maintaining dual focus is the ability to attend to two or more things at once—a skill that will improve with practice. It helps keep the classroom going while a teacher records information. Some suggestions: Face into the room or play yard, place yourself so you see as much of the space as possible, scan the area frequently, and keep your ears and other senses attuned to the tone of the group.
- *Establish the habit of retaining some work products early in the year, helping parents and children understand the reasons.* Exhibit some in the classroom, halls, and display cases; keep some for portfolios; and send some home. If a child feels strongly about taking something home, it's probably wise to let her. We have no way of knowing what an item means to a child, and one of the advantages of having many examples is that undue importance is not attached to any one. If necessary, make a photocopy.
- *Maintain credibility.* Don't retain a number of items only to dump them in a wastebasket that children or parents will see. If you dispose of some, do it discreetly.

Enlist the Aid of Other People. Specialists, classroom aides and assistants, volunteers, parents, and interns can be an integral part of the assessment process, gathering information from their own perspectives. Coach all nonprofessionals on confidentiality as well as what they are to do. Only professional school personnel should handle confidential information, but volunteers can check how far children can kick a ball, throw a beanbag, count objects, or "count on." Aides or volunteers can write a brief, objective description of several children a day to help get acquainted and to contribute their perception of the children. They can take dictation, observe small groups, help children record reading samples, check type and level of participation in almost any activity, and do other assessment tasks. They can help with classroom activities while you are assessing a small group of children. They can bridge language and cultural differences between the classroom, home, and community.

Children can record their attendance and their participation in learning activities; identify and date their work; place portfolio items in a basket or work folder; check spelling and arithmetic; keep reading logs; and perform numerous other assessment-related tasks. More important, they begin to take responsibility for their own learning.

Developing a Plan

Teachers need a plan for incorporating assessment into teaching activities. Planning keeps assessment systematic, aligned with expected outcomes, and makes it easier to embed appraisals in ongoing activities. It allows teachers to spread the assessment process out over the year and gather information gradually. Teachers avoid arriving at family conference time with a lot of information about some children and no information about others. There will be no hurried effort to get adequate information and good opportunities for gathering information will not be missed. Planning also allows you to key collecting, compiling, and summarizing assessment information to end-of-semester and end-of-year evaluations. Records will accumulate that will help you with parent conferences and reports.

The section "When to Assess" on page 43 has several planning suggestions. We suggest you review that material when you develop your plan. Enter all required assessments, reporting times, and assessment-related activities into a master calendar. Even with required assessment, and the assessment that may accompany literacy, mathematics, or science materials and guides, there will be development or curriculum domains where you need more information. The sections that follow give a way of thinking through what and how to assess when you need to look in depth at a specific area of learning.

Figure 9.1 shows one way of planning. Teachers systematically work through the basic assessment decisions: why, what, and when to assess, and how to collect and record information. At first, they consciously consider and write the plans. As assessment becomes routine, some steps are done mentally and more quickly. Experienced teachers find that some steps always have to be written—either noted on monthly or weekly classroom plans or on a shorter form than the one presented here. For example, what to assess and the assessment window to be used are usually written.

Considerations in Planning for Assessment

Purpose of the Assessment.   Write the purpose of the assessment at the top of the planning form. Because assessment can serve several purposes, choose one primary purpose that will influence other choices for the plan. For example, if the primary purpose is to keep track of children's progress, collect information from the children at different times. If the purpose is to plan an upcoming project

Figure 9.1 Example Assessment Plan to Assess Status and Progress in Literacy Development for Preschool and Kindergarten

Assessment Plan: _____ August 20 to June 20 _____

Purpose of Assessment: _____ Monitor Status and Progress _____

Area of Development/Curriculum: _____ Language Skills _____

What to Assess	When to Assess	Assessment Window and Recording Procedure
Reading: 1. Book handling: Knows front and back of book, holds book right side up, turns pages 2. Tracks print: Points to words as reads, sweeps finger under long words, sweeps to the next line. 3. Understands function of print: Notices words and letters, attempts to read logos, signs, and other environmental print. 4. Recognizes letters and words: Can put fingers around a letter, put fingers around a word, point to letters in name, point to letters in a word, identifies letters by name, reads name, reads some words partially or completely.	Beginning, midyear and end of the year for 1 & 3. As occurs for 2.	1. Performance samples during daily small-group literacy activities. Documentation on group matrix checklists. 2. Anecdotal records during play. 3. Parent reports elicited during parent conferences.
Writing: 1. Scribbles and draws in play to stand for print. 2. Dictates stories slowing down voice to match teacher writing. 3. Uses letters to stand for sounds, uses invented spellings. 4. Can conventionally spell some simple familiar words: the, is, are.	Beginning, midyear, and end of the year for #2. As occurs for 1 & 3.	1. Anecdotal records during play. 2. Performance samples during center time associated with play activities or during small group literacy activities. 3. Work samples gathered throughout the many writing opportunities during the day.
Attitudes and Dispositions: 1. Enjoys books. 2. Chooses to look at books during free time. 3. Uses books to find out information. 4. Is eager to write during writing activities. 5. Uses writing during play and other activities that are not literacy activities.	During literacy and other activities.	1. Observe during free play time. 2. Observe during literacy activities.

or theme, collect information before, during, and immediately after the project. Listing a purpose does not preclude using the information for other functions, if appropriate.

Development and Curriculum Domains.   Identify the general area of development or curriculum that you plan to assess and write it in the appropriate blank. Have at least one assessment planning form per area; if the domain is large, you may need several. For example, language may be divided into spoken and written language, or reading and writing.

What to Assess.   In order to assess, teachers have to be specific about what "social/emotional development," "physical fitness," or "geographic concepts and skills" mean to the children. As in specifying child outcomes, large and complex areas of human behavior and learning have to be organized and analyzed to get to "indicators" of learning. For example, social development might include subcategories such as positive peer interaction, friendship-making skills, and cooperative learning skills. But what are the specific cooperative learning skills we are able to assess. We can observe and gather evidence about whether a child can "accept another's ideas," "contribute to the group," or "reject an idea diplomatically." As another example, map knowledge and skills are important aspects of geography. They can be appraised by seeing if a child "points to a street on a map," "draws own fantasy map," "draws representational maps," "states what information can be found on a map," or knows "what maps are used for."

Statements of expected outcomes for children (standards, essential learnings, or curriculum frameworks) usually have this organization and analysis done. You can use their divisions and subdivisions of content, including items you can assess, if they fit. If you are developing your own, use guides such as those found in Appendix A. To keep clear the relationship of a specific behavior to larger goals, identify those goals on the planning form.

When to Assess.   In the next column, identify approximate times or "collection periods" for assessment. Write either the actual month of the assessment or the general schedule. Consider what you have already identified as the purpose, the area, child capabilities, and specific learnings. Verify completion of assessment by checking the item when you have assessed it.

Assessment Window and Recording Procedure.   In the third column, describe the assessment window you will use—the source, method, and context—and the recording procedure. Consider how you will embed the assessment in your classroom activities, and pick a source, method, and context that are appropriate given the resources you have in your room. Figure 9.2 presents some examples, and there are more listed in Figure 4.10 (pp. 71–73). Decide how you will record the information (Chapter 5) and note that on the planning form. If putting together a complex obstacle course is not possible unless you buy new equipment, then this is not appropriate. Be practical! (For more guidance, refer to Chapter 4.) Write the assessment window in the column *Assessment Window and Recording Procedure*.

Sample Assessment Plans

Figures 9.1, 9.3, and 9.4 are examples of assessment plans that might be developed in preschool and primary classrooms. Figure 9.1 shows a plan to document status and progress in the area of language development for a preschool through

Figure 9.2 Typical Recording Procedures for Different Assessment Windows

Type of Window	Recording Procedure
Observations, elicited responses, self-reports, descriptions, performance samples	Jottings, checklists, expanded checklists (with jottings), frequency counts, timed samples, video- and audiotapes, diagrams and sketches (webs or semantic maps), descriptive narratives, and anecdotal records
Evidence of participation or time spent doing activity	Participation charts, duration samples, checklists, room scans
Work products	Product itself, checklists, sketches, diagrams, rating scales, self-assessments, videotapes, audiotapes (record supplementary information about behavior or processes with jottings or narrative)
Information from parents and other adults	Descriptive narratives, jottings, rating scales, audiotapes, parent responses to prepared questions

first-grade classroom. Figure 9.3 is a sample plan for assessing a social studies theme, and Figure 9.4 is a sample assessment for basic concepts in science, mathematics, and social studies. Note the variety of assessment windows—sources, methods, and contexts—as well as the variation in the timing of assessment.

Using the Plan

Consult the assessment plan often as you organize and plan classroom activities for the week or day, just as you would for a semester or unit classroom plan. Look at the *When to Assess* column. Should you be planning an assessment of a specific area? Look at the activities and projects you are considering. Ideally, assessment fits into the project or topic of study that is under way. Systematically review and revise the plan as necessary.

Organizing Files and Forms

Being well prepared and organized helps teachers appraise children as an integral part of teaching. Workable, efficient filing and storage systems save time and keep valuable records from being misplaced, lost in a stack of papers, or accidentally tossed out. Few teachers use all available recording forms and organizational systems; they pick, choose, or adapt those most appropriate or preferred by a center or school. Experiment to see which systems work best. Consider the age

Figure 9.3 Example Assessment Plan in Social Studies for Preschool or Primary Classroom

Assessment Plan: ___October___ 20__

Purpose of Assessment: ___Plan Classroom Activities___

Area of Development/Curriculum: ___Social Studies Theme: My Family___

What to Assess	When	Assessment Window and Recording Procedure
1. Knowledge base about the family: Has studied families before? Can identify who is in own family including extended family (grandparents, uncles, and aunts). Can discuss similarities and differences.	Before theme After theme	1. Large-group activity—discuss what we know about families. Document on a concept map. 2. Elicited responses to open-ended questions about families. Document on group matrix, checklist.
1. Knowledge base about family artifacts: Can describe what an artifact from daily life is and how it is used. Can discuss similarities and differences between family artifacts.	Before theme During theme	1. Parent questionnaire before activity asking for help in finding an artifact with child and describing child's understandings about family artifacts. 2. Work product from an activity in which children draw a picture about their artifact. Include jottings.
Attitudes and Dispositions 1. Pride in own cultural identity. 2. Curiosity, enjoyment, and empathetic awareness of cultural differences and similarities. 3. Appropriate responses triggered by cultural differences.	During theme As occurs	1. Several activities around the artifacts theme. Document child participation using a participation chart. 2. Observe specific instances when children voice pride, enjoyment, curiosity, and empathy. Document on individual anecdotal records.

Theme and ideas adapted from Derman-Sparks, L., & A.B.C. Task Force (1989). *Anti-bias curriculum: Tools for empowering young children.* Washington, DC: National Association for the Education of Young Children.

of the children, the expectations of the program, what recording is required and what is optional, and personal preference. Representative examples follow.

Notebooks, Files, and Portfolios

Notebooks and files help keep track of different types of information.

Notebooks and Record Books. Class roster and attendance record books are usually issued by the center or school. Most have a place for children's names on the left and day and week divisions across the page. Daily attendance is marked in the appropriate column.

Loose-leaf notebooks are a convenient way to organize some records for individual children, as well as summary information about a group. Label the di-

Figure 9.4 Example Assessment Plan to Assess Status and Progress in Cognitive Development—Classification for Preschool Classroom

Assessment Plan: <u>September</u> 20__ to _____<u>June</u> 20__

Purpose of Assessment: _____<u>Monitor Status and Progress</u>

Area of Development/Curriculum: _____<u>Basic Concepts: Science, Mathematics, Social Studies</u>

What to Assess	When	Assessment Window and Recording Procedure
1. Classifies objects into two groups: Classifies spontaneously using consistent attribute; can say attribute. Classifies given an attribute; can say attribute. Can reclassify into another grouping spontaneously; can say attribute. Can reclassify given new attribute; can say attribute.	Every two months: Sept., Nov., Jan., March, June	1. Performance sample. Document on a group matrix with jottings. 2. Work products, such as drawings or descriptions of the child's classifications.
1. Makes patterns: Makes simple ABAB pattern spontaneously; can voice pattern. Copies simple ABAB pattern; can voice pattern. Makes more complex patterns spontaneously, ABCABCABC or a pattern rotated in space. Can graphically express pattern on paper.	Beginning, midyear, end of year As occurs	1. Performance sample. Document using a sketch with notes. 2. Patterning activities. Document using anecdotal records for children who participate.
Attitudes and Dispositions 1. Enjoyment of classification and pattern making.	During activities: beginning, midyear, end of year	1. During selected ongoing classification and patterning activities. Document using a participation chart or antecdotal records.

viders and tabs alphabetically according to the things you are going to keep track of, such as social development, literacy, mathematics, large muscle development, or dramatic play. When the summary sheets are prepared, punch and place them in the binder in chronological order with the latest entries to the front. To store recording forms for individual children, tab the dividers with children's names and alphabetize them according to last names.

If you use notebooks, you'll want either two notebooks or a thick notebook with two major divisions, one for individual children's records and one for group records. You'll want a suitable bound or loose-leaf notebook to keep a journal of your own reflections and development.

Files.　Some administrative files are kept in a central office. What teachers keep in the classroom varies. At the least, you'll need personal files and portfolio files for the children.

Keep personal files for each child in a file drawer or cabinet that is not accessible to children or unauthorized adults. Contents vary, but this file is the place for results of any standardized screening or diagnostic tests, reports from specialists or other teachers, sensitive information from parents, medical information (if not in a separate health file), lunch payment status, social security number, custody arrangements, and any other information that could be construed as private in nature. Set up files alphabetically by children's last names. Leave plenty of space so that items can be added, with the most recent entry toward the front. Some teachers keep all assessment information in standard file folders.

If you plan to make notes and records on index cards, and wish to keep them separately, you'll need a card file with blank tabbed dividers.

Portfolios.   Portfolios require at least two storage systems for collecting and organizing children's work: a "work folder" and a more permanent portfolio. The distinction between these influences the handling and storage systems. Children temporarily store work in progress or completed work that a teacher needs to see in a work folder. Younger children put their work in labeled baskets or shallow "tote" trays. By kindergarten or first grade, children can do their own filing in folders that are clearly marked and accessible. File folders in a open file holder work well (see Figure 9.5). Place it where children can easily reach their own files. Teachers quickly review children's progress daily or weekly, note observations, discuss them with children, make decisions about items or information that should be transferred to the portfolio, and send the remainder home. Because items are not personal or private, work folders are left out so teachers and children can add to them.

Portfolios require more space and flexibility. Legal size (11 × 14 inches) hanging files organized in an open portable stand work well (see Figure 9.6), because they can store the larger items young children generate. They come with plastic indexing tabs. Roll-away racks and some plastic file "crates" hold letter-size folders (8½ × 11 inches) one way and legal size (11 × 14 inches) the other (see Figure 9.7). Have extra files for supplies such as checklists, address labels, and portfolio entry forms. Include a "to be filed" folder, at least one folder for group work, and a miscellaneous file. Different-colored file folders are highly visible dividers for developmental or subject matter domains.

Bins provide easy access but fill up quickly (see Figure 9.8). Some teachers use a large expanding file envelope for each child (see Figure 9.9). They are available in both standard and legal sizes. The fold-over flap and enclosed sides keep items from getting misplaced.

If the budget allows for none of these, strengthen with tape the corners of a corrugated cardboard box—one that reams of paper come in is ideal—and fold large construction paper to make file folders. Leave an inch sticking up on one side for children's names. Smaller boxes, such as pizza or shirt boxes, can store an individual child's portfolio. Roll and store group projects such as murals, maps, or graphs in a map cylinder or with rubber bands. Or fold and place them with other documentation of group projects in files behind the portfolios.

Forms

Examples of several forms and charts that teachers use are on the following pages. A school or center may have prepared recording forms that match their goals and objectives. Select two or three you think will be most useful, and prepare enough for several weeks' trial, after which you can make modifications or try others. Try starting with blank half-sheets and grids. Make copies of the forms you plan to use, file them, and then put some in several convenient places close

Figure 9.5   Open File Holder
for Working Portfolio

Figure 9.6   Portable Stand
for Hanging Files

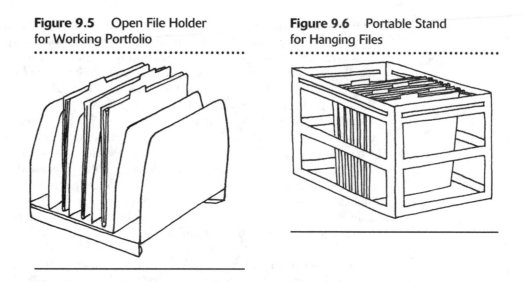

Figure 9.7   Roll-Away Racks for Hanging Files

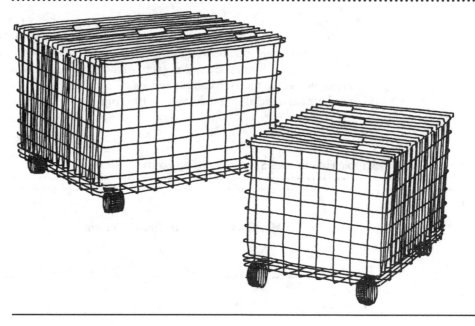

Figure 9.8   File Bin

Figure 9.9   Individual File Envelopes

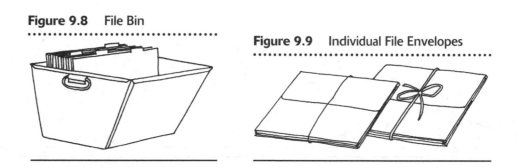

to the point of use. Use small notepads, gummed labels, self-sticking notes, or "recycled" office paper cut in fourths for quick jottings. Many commercial assessment systems supply all forms, including printed Post-it notes.

Prepare a standard heading for forms, including a place for the child's name or group's designation (Pueblo Primary School, second year), observer's name, the date including year, and setting (see Figure 9.10). Add time of day if that is important. The slash marks on the date line help people remember to include the year. If codes or marks will be used, add a place for a key. You may remember what the symbols "X," "/," or "+" meant, but someone else won't know.

The consistent format helps people learn what information goes where and reminds them to fill in complete information. A note without a child's name or a date is useless. All observers and interviewers should initial or sign records. An alternative is to have a rubber stamp to make the heading. This is especially useful for small sheets of recycled office paper.

Half-Sheets of Paper.   Use half-sheets of paper with a standard heading at the top for anecdotal records, quick notes, sketches, notes about performance tasks, portfolio entry slips, and information from other adults about individuals or a small group.

Index Cards.   Copy the standard heading on index cards, and keep several stacks available to use for notes or sketches, or punch a hole in one corner and place a stack on a bookring. For a more systematic use of index cards, prepare them using a different color for each area of interest—developmental or content areas, activity centers, experiences, or whatever you are documenting. Place one card for each child for each area on the ring. When one or more observations are

Figure 9.10   Sample Full- or Half-Sheet Recording Form

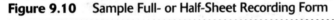

Mankota Early Childhood Center

Child _____   **Date** ____/____/____   **Time** _____

Observer _____   **Setting** _____

Group _____   (if needed)

made, remove the card and file it. The remaining cards act as a reminder of children yet to be observed in a particular area. Duplicate simple forms such as participation charts or columns directly on large index cards. Index cards are convenient because they are stiff enough to write on, but they are costly.

Grids, Matrices, Charts, and Checklists. Various types of grids, matrices, charts, and checklists are widely used, because they quickly document so much information in so little space. They are especially useful for recording and profiling information about a whole group, or a lot of information about an individual child. Chapter 5 identified, described, gave examples, and listed the strengths and limitations of the recording tools classroom teachers typically use. General guides for modifying the basic grid format, selecting and placing items to be assessed, and efficient recording follow; examples appear in both Chapters 5 and 9. In addition, refer to forms marketed by commercial assessment systems. Some are ingeniously constructed to help record and display an enormous amount of information.

A sample blank grid is shown in Figure 9.11. Simply change the heading to use it for an individual child.

Modify the spacing of rows and columns to accommodate the recording procedure you want to use. For example, for abbreviated notes and jottings, enlarge the cells to 1 × 1½ inches (Figure 9.12).

Instead of copying the class list by hand on each of these forms, use a computer to make the form and list simultaneously. Or make a master list with spacing identical to the grid or chart, and make several copies. Tape one to each of the forms, and copy as many as you need. Delete or add names, then realphabetize as children depart and enter.

You can use a class list and simple grid to make sure you have information about each child. Jot the items being documented across the top, children's names down the left side, and check the appropriate square as an observation is recorded, a performance task documented, or a required portfolio item collected. When all children have been checked, move on to other items. Tape such a list to a counter, desktop, side of a cabinet, or other convenient spot as a reminder of who is left to assess.

Guides for Constructing and Using Checklists

Choose items that are representative indicators of the development being assessed. In using a developmental continuum to select items, choose a few items above and a few below what would be expected for the children in your classroom.

Group like items and put them in a sequence, if appropriate. Leave spaces between groups.

Divide behavior into observable subskills, levels, or steps. For example, instead of "knows numerals," list three observable actions: "points to or places fingers around numeral on request," "says name of numeral on request," and "volunteers name of numeral."

State items in the positive to avoid confusion. For example, instead of "doesn't jump on left foot," use "jumps on right foot" and "jumps on left foot."

Leave a space for "Comments." You will want to note interesting, unique, or contextual information about the child, the item, or the situation.

Figure 9.11   Sample Blank Grid for Group of Children

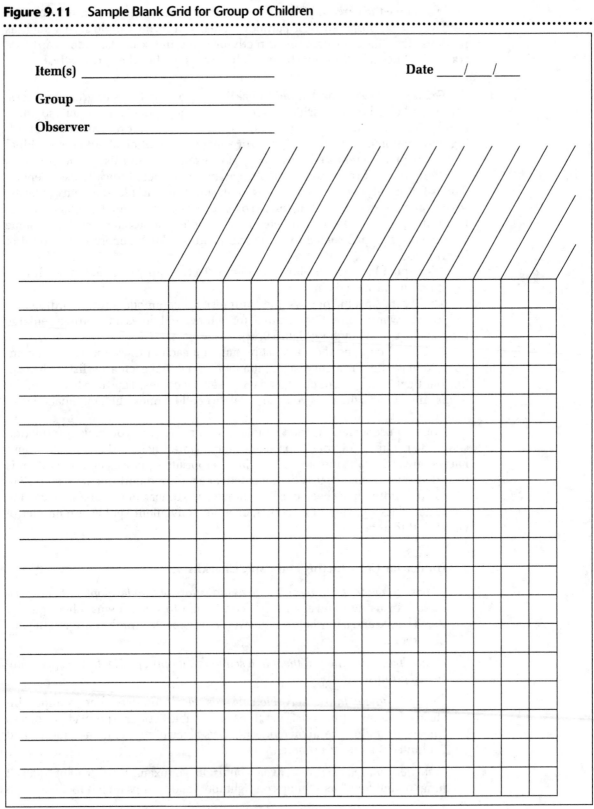

Figure 9.12 Sample Blank Grid with Large Cells

Area of Development _____   Date ___/___/___

Observer _____   Group/Child _____

The way a checklist is marked can increase its value. Develop and use a consistent marking system. Put a key on the checklist so you and others are sure how to record and interpret information. Experiment to find marking systems that fit the kind of information you collect and that work for you. Some teachers mark only the presence of a behavior. Others use coding systems that capture other information, as well. Some examples are as follows:

- For items attained or mastered, mark checklists used only once with a checkmark, *X*, or yes/no. Checklists completed over several days or weeks should include the date the child performed the item.
- If items are not assessed because a child was absent or the target behavior was not observed, leave the space blank or mark *A* for *absent* or *N/O* for *not observed*.
- For items performed partially or at different levels of proficiency, mark a slash for beginning level and make the / into an *X* when the child masters the item. Or mark *B* for *beginning* or *P* for *partial*. Or highlight the blank with a specific color indicating partial achievement, then write over the highlighting the date the child achieves mastery.
- If items are attempted but not performed appropriately, highlight the blank with a specific color or a code such as a circle. When the child performs the behavior or skill, write the date over the code.

Guides for Constructing and Using Participation Charts

Use a special chart if children are to record their own participation (see Figure 9.13 and Figure 5.12, p. 89). Leave extra space, and teach them what they are to do.

When children can participate several times, as in group discussions, use multiple tally marks as needed (see Figure 5.13, p. 89).

Use codes to document the quality of participation, such as R for relevant, I for irrelevant, and D for disruptive.

Guides for Constructing and Using Frequency Count Records

Identify and list specific indicators of the behavior to be counted on the record.

Divide the space into three columns as shown in Figure 5.14 (p. 90). List the dates of the assessment in the left column, the tally in the center, and the total on the right.

Tally directly on the form or tally unobtrusively on a wide piece of masking tape taped to the inner side of your wrist or a 3 × 5 inch index card held in one hand. If you are counting only one behavior and one child, use a wrist clicker. Tallies recorded on masking tape, cards, or clickers must then be transferred to a conventional form—a separate step.

Columns.   For recording some types of information about individual children, full sheets of paper with columns are useful. Figure 9.14 shows one setup for an individual profile of major child development areas. Change the column headings to reflect content areas (literacy, art, science) or learning processes (representation, communication, classification) that might be emphasized in various programs. This form lends itself well to abbreviated notes or jottings.

Figure 9.13 Sample Form for Child Reporting of Participation, by Center

Art Area

Make a check beside your name if you worked in this area today.

Armano, Tony _____
Bustos, Seri _____
Curtis, Sarah _____
Dawson, Carl _____
Foreman, Akala _____
Kubiac, Jody _____
Lucero, Angie _____
Makaves, Sierra _____
Markum, Josh _____
Namaste, Ashley _____
Poste, Alfonso _____
Ramirez, Jana _____
Rostukus, Paul _____
Rutledge, B.J. _____
Shonka, Troy _____
Tran, Kwan _____

Other Aids

Computers. Computers quickly generate grids, checklists, and other forms. They keep the class roll current and alphabetized, so it can be printed on frequently used forms, charts, and address labels. They can keep a copy of all paper forms and charts filed and ready to print. They store and manage images from digital cameras. Some programs for personal digital assistants (PDAs) allow direct entry of observations.

Cameras and Audio and Video Recorders. Cameras and audio and video recorders are powerful tools for capturing information about children. Before

Figure 9.14 Sample Columnar Recording Form for an Individual

Longview Early Childhood Center

Child _____ Year _____

(Date and initial each entry)

Personal/Social	Spoken Language	Written Language	Learning Processes	Knowledge Base	Large Motor	Fine Motor

school begins, find out which, if any, are available to keep or use in your classroom. If you don't know how to use the equipment, learn on simple cameras or tape recorders. Then learn to use another. Learning one tool a year will rapidly boost your confidence and skills. These tools will be most useful if they can be kept in the classroom.

Low-Tech Solutions. Teachers have developed ingenious and practical ways to organize for assessment. Here are a few of their ideas.

• *Clipboards.* Get a couple of full-size or several half-size clipboards, tie a pencil or pen to the clip, insert a stack of blank forms, and you have a portable recording surface for indoors or outdoors. Metal box-type clipboards have storage space inside for extra paper, forms, pens, or pencils. Hang the clipboards on the wall or on the end of a cabinet, and they will be readily accessible but out of the way. Have an extra or two for the children to use. In some classrooms each child has a half-size clipboard to document project work, experiments, or other learning.

• *Self-Sticking Notes, Labels, and Colored Dots.* Self-sticking notes and gummed address labels are convenient for short notes about a child or group. Some teachers use sheets of computer labels with each child's name already printed, an automatic check on whether you have made a record for each child. Make notes during class time, and then later stick them to the appropriate product, folder, or form. Colored dots identify different development or curriculum areas.

• *Writing Implements.* Keep sharpened pencils or working pens beside the blank forms and index cards. Some teachers wear pens on a long yarn loop around their necks or attached to their belts, or wear smocks, aprons, or shirts with pockets for paper and pencils. If you plan to use colored pens or pencils to designate separate development or learning domains or children who need certain experiences, have a good supply.

• *Rubber Stamps.* Use a rubber stamp to quickly date children's work or teacher recordings. If printed headings are not feasible, a rubber stamp can put the same information on any size paper or card, or the back of a photograph.

• *Counters and Timers.* Counters, stopwatches, and timers are useful for tallying and timing behavior. Wrist "clickers" are available at most teacher supply houses.

• *Self-Reports.* If children are to mark their own participation in centers or activities, they need appropriate forms. Figure 9.13 shows an efficient one. While children are learning to recognize their names, use symbols or pictures beside the names. Mount the backing separately in each center, and change the listing of children—every day for young ones and once a week for older ones who can manage different daily headings. To keep track of each child's activities, prepare something as shown in Figure 9.15 for each child to complete daily. Children can also print their names or initials to report participation, as shown in Figure 5.12 (p. 89). Change the listing to correspond to the major areas in each classroom and outdoor play area. Older children need plenty of paper and implements to record what they have done. Journal paper, forms for reading logs, and entry slips for portfolio items should be readily available.

Figure 9.15 Sample Form for Child Reporting of Participation, by Child

Child_____	Week_____				
	Mon.	Tues.	Wed.	Thurs.	Fri.
Art					
Blocks					
Computer					
Dramatic Play					
Language Games					
Manipulatives					
Reading/ Listening					
Writing					
Science					

Summary

Teachers learn to integrate assessment with instruction by scheduling activities so that they have time to assess, proceeding gradually, staying organized and current, making assessment a regular part of classroom activities, and enlisting the aid of other people.

Use an assessment plan to record decisions about what, when, and how to assess. Identify the purpose of the assessment first, and then decide what will be appraised and when. Identify some possible assessment windows and recording procedures. Consult the assessment plan as you create daily and weekly materials and activities. Review and modify the plan as you proceed.

Prepare and organize files, forms, and other necessary aids for systematic storing of information about children to make classroom assessment easier. Choose file systems and forms to suit the purpose for which the information is being collected, the age and developmental level of the children, school and center expectations, and your own preferences.

For Personal Reflection

1. Authentic classroom assessment can be overwhelming if you try to begin everything all at once. Review the general guidelines for integrating assessment with teaching on pages 160 to 162. Examine your own comfort level and competence related to assessment, and decide how and where you will begin. Justify your decisions.
2. Planning and organization are essential for integrating assessment with teaching. Reflect on and identify your own strengths and needs in planning and organization.

For Further Study and Discussion

1. Mr. Stanley is interested in assessing how children communicate and use language as a tool in his classroom. Suggest how this assessment could be integrated into the routines of daily living, outdoors, and while the teacher is interacting with the children. Which of these would be the best context? Why?
2. Ms. Tan is interested in assessing her kindergartners' familiarity with books. Give suggestions as to how can she integrate assessment of these skills during the routines of daily living, when children are working or playing on their own, and when she is interacting with children. Which of these would be the best context? Why?
3. Develop an assessment plan for social development in a preschool. Using Appendix A, identify two skills that would be appropriate for children of 3 and 4 years of age. With documentation of progress as the purpose, fill out an assessment plan giving two assessment windows that are appropriate. What recording procedures would be best? Why?

Suggested Readings

Almy, M., & Genishi, C. (1979). *Ways of studying children.* New York: Teachers College Press.

Bennett, J. (1992). Seeing is believing: Videotaping reading development. In L. Rhodes & N. Shanklin (Eds.). *Literacy assessment in whole language classrooms, K–8.* Portsmouth, NH: Heinemann.

Helm, J. H., Beneke, S., & Steinheimer, K. (1998). *Teacher materials for documenting young children's work.* New York: Teachers College Press.

Helm, J. H., Beneke, S., & Steinheimer, K. (1998). *Windows on learning.* New York: Teachers College Press.

National Education Association. (1993). *Student portfolios.* West Haven, CT: Author.

Stenmark, J. K. (Ed.). (1991). *Mathematics assessment: Myths, models, good questions, and practical suggestions.* Reston, VA: National Council of Teachers of Mathematics.

CHAPTER 10

Standardized Tests: What Early Childhood Teachers Should Know

[handwritten margin notes: screening, achievement, diagnostic, aptitude, Readiness, inappropriately, How they can predict future]

The primary role of a teacher in the classroom is to provide instruction. In order to do this, teachers need to use assessment to guide classroom decisions and to monitor whether instruction is effective. Although this "assessment for instruction" is paramount, teachers are also asked to participate in standardized testing—something that is separate and apart from the type of assessment we have been discussing in this book. There has been a change in the use of standardized testing with young children, because these tests are being used for a wider variety of purposes. Standardized tests are administered to gauge whether children are making progress toward state and national standards or to check on acquisition of essential literacy skills. Overall, standardized testing in kindergarten and in first and second grade is becoming more common. These changes are causing much concern on the part of measurement specialists and early childhood educators. Consequently, it is more important than ever that early childhood teachers know about standardized tests so they can be sure these tests are used and interpreted appropriately. In this chapter we describe standardized tests and what early childhood teachers need to know about them.

The Difference between an Assessment That Has Standardized Procedures and a Standardized Test

accommodations

time
space
library/quiet room

The word *standardized* means that the procedures for an assessment are the same for each and every individual who is assessed. Each person is asked the same question or asked to do the same thing in the same way. Standardized procedures include asking children to cut on a line, on a curve, and then cut out a figure using the same kind of scissors and the same kind of paper. Children can be asked to spell the same list of words or answer the same math problems. Standardized procedures are useful when you wish to make comparisons between one performance and another performance at different times. You can compare a child's performance in January to one in May, or you can compare one child's performance to that of other children. If standardized procedures were not used, it would be difficult to gauge a child's progress. Bernie cuts with an adult scissors in September and uses a child scissors in March. When his teacher compares the two samples, she cannot tell if the changes in Bernie's performance were because of his learning the skill of cutting or the fact that the scissors were less cumbersome. If she had used the same scissors and the same paper at both times, then differences between Bernie's first and second performances would be attributable to growth in small muscle development. Many published inventories and checklists that are used every day in the classroom have standardized procedures in this sense. An assessment may have standardized procedures without being a "standardized test."

Definition of a Standardized Test

A *standardized test* is a test with specific characteristics. Standardized tests are constructed following a specific set of statistical and psychometric guidelines that are described in the *Standards for Educational and Psychological Testing* (American Educational Research Association [AERA], American Psychological Association [APA], & National Council on Measurement in Education [NCME], 1999). A standardized test is accompanied by a test manual that gives information about how the test was constructed, the demographic profile of the population used to develop the scoring system, and how the test's reliability and validity have been established. Most standardized tests are published and sold by commercial testing companies. However, not all published assessment instruments have undergone the rigorous process that would make them standardized tests.

A standardized test usually has a scoring system that compares an individual's scores to the scores of a specific population of people. The population might be all first-grade readers, children who have mastered addition, or preschool children aged 2 ½ to 5 years of age. Depending on how the results are analyzed and reported, the test is either *norm-referenced* or *criterion-referenced*. In norm-referenced tests, the child's score is compared with the average scores of the population used to design the test, for example, the average kindergartner. Criterion-referenced standardized tests use a defined criterion for performance instead of the average score of a group of people. The criterion-referenced test allows a comparison of a student's level of performance to a preestablished level of mastery. Tommy is "partially proficient" in the second-grade content area standards for mathematics. In this case, the population is used to establish the cut-off scores for proficiency instead of being used as a comparison group for the child's scores.

The standardized test manual describes specific procedures for administration—exactly how the test should be given. Deviations from these directions may jeopardize the integrity of the test. Certain sections of the test may be timed so that all children have the same time constraints. All of the materials used during the test are identified. The room arrangement may even be described, such as where the children sit and whether normal classroom features, such as bulletin boards, have to be covered. Children make their responses in specific ways, such as bubbling-in or circling answers on special forms. Many tests have specific security requirements so that no one can look at the tests prior to or after administration.

Many well-known published inventories and checklists, widely used in classrooms, do not qualify as standardized tests. One such example is miscue analysis checklists published in literacy books or as stand-alone instruments. These may have norms and some standard criteria to be used in assessment, but they lack the required rigor in establishing reliability and validity, and they often have many nonstandard elements, such as using a different book with each child. Publication of an inventory or test is not the same as meeting technical criteria. This is not to cast aspersions on these types of classroom assessments; it is meant only to underscore the fact that they are not standardized tests and their interpretation should take this into account.

Limitations and Inadequacies of Standardized Testing

Standardized tests are the focus of much of the criticism aimed at inappropriate assessment. Critics target the tests themselves, their overuse and misuse, their unsuitability for a diverse population, and their undue influence on education.

Technical and Educational Inadequacies

Many tests for young children do not meet technical standards described in the Standards for Educational and Psychological Testing (APA, AERA, & NCME, 1999). Educational inadequacies of standardized tests can stem from outmoded theory of what and how children learn used in test development (Shepard, 2000). Many standardized tests are based on the idea that testing children on isolated elements of skills is the best indicator of final performance. This view is at odds with current knowledge, which emphasizes that children actively construct knowledge and that skills tested in isolation may not be indicators of final performance. Vygotskians would go even further to say that, when a child is asked to perform a task independently, a test provides only a partial picture of this child's performance. To obtain a complete picture, the child also should be tested in a situation in which he is offered various hints and cues, such as during dynamic assessment (Bodrova & Leong, 1996).

Overuse and Misuse

Educational institutions and individuals spend enormous amounts of time and money on tests and testing—money that might be used in other ways. It is estimated that children in second grade spend a total of a month on test preparation and standardized testing per year, squandering precious learning time. Misuse of tests costs children even more. Children can be placed in the wrong program or denied educational opportunities based on tests results, turning testing into a "high-stakes decision." One glaring example is the use of tests for the purposes of retention, which research now shows does not have positive effects on development. A meta-analysis of 44 independent studies of retained versus promoted students showed consistent results—children who were retained did not gain significant advantages by being held back a year (Holmes & Matthews, 1984). In addition, retention had a negative impact on self-esteem and child motivation. Testing may result in children being placed in categories or labeled in ways that do not enhance their development and learning.

Unsuitability for the Population

Evidence is strong that many tests and testing procedures are unfair to poor children, youngsters from any racial or ethnic background other than the middle-class majority, English-language learners, divergent and creative thinkers, and just about any group one might wish to investigate (FairTest, 1990; Kamii, 1990; National Association for the Education of Young Children, 1988; Perone, 1991; and many more).

It is difficult to find standardized tests suitable for assessing literacy or school readiness for English-language learners. If children cannot understand the directions or the questions in a literacy test, the test score will not represent literacy knowledge, but English proficiency. Research indicates that it takes English language learners four to seven years to acquire "educational" English, the type used in tests (Hakuta, Butler, & Win, 2000). Children may be able to engage in everyday conversations in the classroom, but may not know the grammar or vocabulary used in the test. Many children cannot be tested in their native language because test makers have not made a Farsi or a Hindi version of the test, for example. Words, directions, concepts, and vocabulary with the same levels of usage must be found to make the tests equivalent. Even when the test is available in the child's native language, as in the case of Spanish, the test may be written in a specific dialect of Spanish, for example using "Mexican" as opposed to "Guatemalan" dialect. Furthermore, even if children are familiar with the dialect, there are still problems. Tests use "educational" Spanish rather than colloquial Spanish with vocabulary familiar only if the child was taught concepts in Spanish. For this reason, many children score poorly in both English and Spanish versions of the same test, missing different items on each.

Young children have problems taking tests of any kind, even individual tests administered by skilled psychologists (Bagnato & Neisworth, 1991). They may see no point in playing adult "games," especially with strangers in a strange situation (Kamii, 1990). They have particular trouble with group-administered, paper-and-pencil tests, because young children are easily distracted, bored, or made uneasy; they also have trouble following directions and marking or "bubbling in" responses. They may act silly or refuse to participate. Traditional tests may be particularly inappropriate for young children with special needs, the very population with which they are used the most (Bagnato & Neisworth, 1991).

One-shot testing is poorly suited to the way children grow. Children's development and learning proceed unevenly, with spurts and regressions. Some children may suddenly "put it all together" and achieve unexpected insights. Some children progress in tiny increments that few tests are sensitive enough to detect, yet progress is real and significant for that child.

Undue Influence on Education

Knowing they will be judged on how well children score, teachers may teach and shape instruction to fit the test, not necessarily the content of greatest worth. This practice, often unconscious, may narrow and distort the curriculum to items most amenable to testing or to those that fulfill the purposes of the test (Meisels, Steele, & Quinn-Leering, 1993; Shepard & Graue, 1993). Tests intended for national distribution may not be congruent with local curriculum. At the least, teachers have to take extra time to teach children test-taking skills such as keeping their place and making precise markings.

All too often tests are used as the primary approach to accountability—the way schools and centers report to their patrons what and how well they are doing. Scores from tests are used to compare schools, districts, and states; racial and ethnic groups; and the current year with previous years—as a way of judging quality and effectiveness. Such comparisons lead to distortions and misunderstandings of the properties of tests, as humorously exemplified by the "all above average" children of the mythical town of Lake Wobegon. Test scores are reported in precise numbers, often leading to an "illusion of precision" (Lidz, 2003).

Few people would abolish the use of all tests, even with young children. Early screening and identification of correctable physical problems, developmental delays, or other factors that place children at high risk for school failure enable many children to receive appropriate treatment (Meisels, Steele, & Quinn-Leering, 1993). Individual clinical tests provide valuable information to guide important decisions, such as whether a child has special needs (Cronbach, 1990). In addition, tests may be the best way to assess certain kinds of learning, such as basic knowledge about a particular topic (Stiggins, 1995). Most early childhood educators advocate delaying use of group-administered, standardized, multiple-choice, norm-referenced tests until children are in third or fourth grade, and discontinuing tests that lead to delayed entry to kindergarten or first grade (NAEYC & NAECS/SDE, 2003).

Types of Standardized Tests

Standardized tests fall into three broad categories: achievement, aptitude, and screening and diagnostic tests. These categories are used by educational psychologists and researchers, but in actual practice the lines between them are blurred. Readiness tests are a good example of this blurring. They are aptitude tests, designed to predict future performance, but are often used to assess what children have learned in a program—the purpose of achievement tests. With any test, we should not make interpretations that are invalid or that overreach what the test is designed to show.

Standardized Achievement Tests

Achievement tests are designed to measure what children have learned in school in general or in a specific area, such as reading or math. Items for these tests are chosen to be a representative sample of the knowledge that should have been learned at that grade. Achievement tests are designed by culling concepts and facts from the most commonly used textbooks and curriculum materials for a given grade. Test makers use teams of content specialists in the respective curriculum area to make up the items for the test. These items are then administered to large samples of students of that grade level. Some well-known examples of achievement tests are the California Achievement Test (CAT), the Iowa Test of Basic Skills (ITBS), and the Stanford Achievement Test. The state standards tests, such as the Colorado Student Assessment Performance Tests or the New York Regents Exams, use state populations and state standards as the basis for items.

You have probably read a great deal about achievement tests in the popular media. Achievement tests are used to show that children are above or below the state or national average or when states give schools "report cards." Such use is questionable. Although it is important to have a measure of how a child is doing relative to other children of the same grade level, a child's score on an achievement test is only a "snapshot" of that child's knowledge and may not be an accurate estimate of the child's true knowledge. A score may not be a relevant indication of achievement unless a child's classroom experience matches the curriculum used in developing the test. The relevance of the score in showing the child's knowledge also depends on whether the child's characteristics are the same as those of the children in the population used by the standardized test makers. The more like the child the population is, the more reliable the score will be. Those problems aside, achievement tests allow us to see whether a child knows the same amount as her counterparts in other areas of the country.

Standardized Aptitude Tests

Aptitude tests or ability tests are intended to predict future performance or success in a given area of training or in an occupation. They are often used for program placement, career decisions, or to measure general intellectual functioning, such as an Intelligence or IQ test. In early childhood classrooms, readiness tests, such as the Metropolitan Reading Readiness Test, are examples of aptitude tests. Examples of IQ tests that are designed for young children include the WISC-R, the WPPSI, the MSCA (McCarthy Scales of Children's Abilities), and the Stanford-Binet.

There is considerable controversy about aptitude tests in general and their use in early childhood specifically. A single test given only once might not even provide an indication of a child's ability, much less of his or her potential ability. Many psychometricians argue that there is little if any distinction between aptitude and achievement tests, because both test the child's level of current knowledge (Anastasi & Urbina, 1997; Bracey, 1998). As discussed in Chapter 2, there is danger in making high-stakes decisions based on one test without considering results from multiple assessment measures. In addition, the predictive ability of some tests, such as reading readiness tests, has been attacked by a number of psychometricians (Shepard & Smith, 1986), because they do not conform to rigorous guidelines for test construction. A number of groups advise against the use of standardized aptitude tests alone to determine school readiness or reading readiness. At best, the score on an aptitude test is only one piece of information that should be used.

Standardized Screening and Diagnostic Tests

Standardized screening tests, sometimes called developmental screening tests, are used to identify whether a child is at risk of a possible learning problem or handicapping condition and are usually administered as a first step in a sequence of assessments. Items for developmental screening tests are usually rather broad, surveying abilities in large and small muscle coordination, perception, language, and cognitive development. Because they do not require formal training in special education, they can be given by classroom teachers and their aides. Developmental screening tests that are commonly used include the Denver Developmental Screening Test (DDST), the McCarthy Screening test, the DIAL-3, and the Early Screening Inventory (ESI).

Screening tests are also used to identify children who are at risk for learning to read. The Dynamic Indicators of Basic Early Literacy Skills (DIBELS) (Moats, Good, & Kaminski, 2003), the Phonological Awareness Literacy Screening Assessment (PALS) (Invernizzi, Sullivan, Meier, & Swank, 2004; Invernizzi, Jeul, Swank, & Meier, 2004) have versions for children prekindergarten through the primary grades. The DIBELS and the PALS are administered three times a year to determine a child's rate of acquisition of literacy skills, and if that places her at risk for reading failure. The Get Ready to Read Test (Whitehurst & Lonigan, 2001) is designed to be given to 4-year-old children. Get Ready to Read is available online (www.getreadytoread.org) and can be given by parents and teachers. All three tests have suggested activities to help children learn the knowledge and skills that are tested. Although developed as screening tests, these instruments are frequently used to gauge the effectiveness of early childhood literacy interventions. A word of caution: these tests do not supplant developmental screening.

A diagnostic test is designed to actually identify the specific problem a child might have. It is used to plan interventions. Someone who is trained in giving, interpreting, and using the test information in interventions administers diagnostic tests. Access to the tests may be restricted to teachers who attend special training sessions or who have specific academic degrees. Most of the time, the person who administers a diagnostic test is a special education teacher, school psychologist, speech pathologist, or occupational therapist. Classroom teachers are seldom involved in diagnostic testing, but may be involved in carrying out the recommendations based on the test results. Examples of diagnostic tests include the Test for Auditory Comprehension of Language and the Woodcock-Johnson Psycho-Educational Battery.

The Early Childhood Teacher's Role in Standardized Testing

In the course of your career as a teacher, you will be involved in standardized testing in some way. You may serve on a committee to choose a test that will be used in your program. You may have to administer a standardized test or supervise other adults who are giving tests. You may have to prepare children to take tests to ensure that the testing situation does not negatively impact their performance. On rare occasions, you may have to score a test. (Most tests are sent to a computer center for processing, so teachers do not score them.) You may have to explain what a test score means to parents and children.

The sections that follow describe what classroom teachers usually need to know about standardized tests. To choose a test, you must know how to determine whether a test is reliable and valid. You must know how to administer a test and possible pitfalls when doing so. You must know how to explain different kinds of test scores. You will be asked to interpret these scores for yourself and for parents. The Finding out More about Standardized Tests section at the end of the chapter will help you increase your knowledge about these concepts.

How to Find Out if a Standardized Test Is Reliable and Valid

To find out if a standardized test conforms to AERA/APA/NCME standards, look for critiques of tests in the *Mental Measurements Yearbook* (Spies & Plake, 2005) or *Test Critiques*, Volumes I–XI (Keyser & Sweetland, 2006), textbooks such as *Assessment of Exceptional Students* (Taylor, 2000), and Web sites such as http://ericae.net. Test publishers make available information in the test manual or in the test's statistical report to help people make informed decisions about their tests. Choosing a test can be compared to buying a car; you don't have to know everything about auto mechanics, but you do have to be an enlightened consumer to make the right decisions. Similarly, teachers do not need to be expert psychometricians, but they need to know how the concepts of reliability and validity apply to standardized testing, because these are the major criteria used to determine whether a test is a good one. Not all published tests are good tests. For a review of the general definitions of reliability and validity see Chapter 2.

Reliability Applied to Standardized Tests.   The first major criterion of a good test is that the resulting score is accurate or reliable (see Chapter 2). The test maker proves that a test is reliable by providing statistical estimates of "error" in the score and by conducting a reliability study. The test critique and the test manual will both contain information about these studies, including the demographic characteristics of the population used for the studies.

In order to understand how reliability is determined, it is first necessary to introduce three psychometric concepts: true score, confidence interval, and standard error of measurement. For more information on the concepts and how they are computed consult a textbook on tests and measurement. When we test children, we hope that their performance on the test represents exactly what they actually know and can do in the area being tested. However, all test scores are an imperfect snapshot of actual ability. Present as a part of any child's actual score—called the observed score—is some "error." Error in an observed score can be caused by the fact that the child guesses on some items and gets them correct. In this case the child was lucky but doesn't really know the material. The observed score, thus, is an overestimate of the child's real knowledge; giving the child credit for something he doesn't really know. On the other hand, a child may have the knowledge and understanding but somehow fail to choose the correct option. Such errors can be caused by fatigue or a lapse in attention during part of the test. In this case, the mistake is not caused by lack of knowledge, so the observed score underestimates what the child really knows. The term *true score* is used to describe the score that represents the child's real level of knowledge without error—neither an over- nor an underestimate of what the child knows and can do. Hypothetically, this true score could actually be obtained if you could give a test many times to the same child. Eventually, after all of these multiple test administrations, the errors would balance out and the average score of all these tests would be the true score. But children take a test only once so psychometricians use the actual or observed score to estimate the true score.

The *standard error of measurement (SEM)* is the statistical approximation of the variation of the observed score from the true score—an estimate of "error." The smaller the SEM, the less variation is caused by error, and the more reliable the score. Conversely, the larger the SEM, the more variation is due to error, and the less reliable the score. If you know the SEM for a given test, then you can estimate a confidence interval around each observed score. The *confidence interval* around the actual score contains the hypothetical true score. For example, if the SEM is 5 and a child's actual score on a test is 125, then we can say that his true score is likely to fall within a confidence interval between 120 and 130. The true score lies within a band formed by adding and subtracting the SEM from the observed score (see Figure 10.1). The implication of the concepts of the true score, confidence interval, and standard error of measurement is that a child's score is only an estimate of a child's ability and always contains "error." Teachers should keep these in mind when interpreting scores for parents as well as when deciding whether a test is sufficiently reliable to use.

There are four ways to establish reliability: test–retest, alternate-form, split-half, and internal consistency. In the *test–retest reliability* method comparisons are made between tests given at different times to the same person. A person's score should not vary a great deal if the test is an accurate, reliable measurement of performance. In norm-referenced tests, a comparison is made in the rank of a specific student obtained on the first testing occasion and that rank on the second testing occasion. In criterion-referenced tests comparisons are made between scores on the first and second test, not the student's ranking relative to other children. To determine exactly how reliable the test is, a correlation, a statistical measurement of the strength of relationship between the two test administrations, is calculated. The closer the correlation is to 1.0, the more reliable the test. Coefficients of between .80 and 1.0 are indicators of acceptable levels of reliability for a standardized test. Both the correlation between the two test administrations as well as the time interval between test–retest administrations should be reported in the test manual. The closer the administrations are in time, the more likely the correlation between them will be high, because students remember the test items, rendering the test–retest reliability figures less meaningful.

The second way of establishing reliability is the *alternate-form reliability* method. In alternate-form reliability, the test makers create two forms of the same test that are as equivalent as possible, covering the same content with the same type of questions. Reliability is determined by correlating the scores on the two forms of the test. Again, for norm-referenced tests, the correlation between the scores on

Figure 10.1   Confidence Intervals (SEM = 5 with two actual scores of 125 and 150)

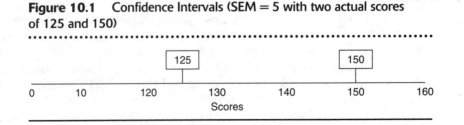

both forms should be high; for criterion-referenced tests, the student's scores should be similar on both forms. The time interval between test forms is less important than in the case of test–retest reliability.

Reliability can be established using *split-half reliability* and using *internal consistency reliability* methods. In split-half reliability, the test maker divides the test in half and compares one half to the other. Establishing split-half reliability can be complicated by the way a test is organized; in some cases the test has to be split by sections rather than using the more common way of comparing all odd numbered items to even numbered items. Both the manner of splitting the test as well as the correlation between the two halves would be reported in the test manual. Internal consistency reliability is computed using a statistical formula that is too complicated to discuss here, but can be found in an introductory text on tests and educational measurement.

Validity Applied to Standardized Tests.   The second major criterion for a good test is that it is valid (see Chapter 2). In addition to showing that the test is reliable, test makers or the test critique also describe the method used to determine the test's validity. There are two major threats to the validity of a test. The first is that validity was not established according to the standards (APA, AERA, & NCME, 1999), and the second is that the test is used for a purpose for which it is not designed. For example, using a standardized screening test to show achievement gains in a classroom would not be a valid use. Using an achievement test to diagnose learning problems would also be an invalid use. Thus, validity is not only influenced by the way the test is constructed, but is also affected by the way it is used.

There are several types of validity: content validity, criterion (concurrent/predictive) validity, and construct validity. *Content validity* is the degree to which the test covers a representative sample of behaviors in the area that is being tested. The manner in which this was established should be described in the test manual or critique. For example, subject matter experts often review test items to establish content validity. The number of experts used, their qualifications, and whether the experts agreed with each other should be reported. The procedure used to ensure that the items were representative of the subject area being tested should also be described. For achievement tests, the manual should identify when the experts were consulted and the date of publication of the classroom materials used in test creation, because the content covered in a specific grade level changes with time (Anastasi & Urbina, 1997). You should be satisfied that the test makers have used accepted procedures to establish content validity.

Criterion validity, also called *concurrent* or *predictive validity*, indicates whether the test is effective in predicting an individual's performance. This type of validity is of concern for aptitude tests especially when the tests are used to select individuals for a program, such as a school readiness test. One way to establish validity is by following children who took the test over time. For example, a reading readiness test could be validated by a follow-up research study following children into the next grade to see if the children who received high scores on the test learned to read earlier than those children who received low scores. Thus, a valid reading readiness test should predict something about the child's future achievement in reading. Similarly, children identified as being at-risk for developmental delays on a screening test should have more delays in later grades if the test has predictive validity. Comparing the scores on one test with the scores on another accepted test is yet another way to show criterion validity. Children who score high on one test should also score high on the other test.

Construct validity is the most difficult kind of validity for a lay person to understand. Construct validity addresses the extent to which a test measures a theoretical attribute or characteristic that it says it measures. For example is there such a thing as an attribute we can identify as "school readiness" or "IQ," and can that attribute be studied and measured? Unlike height and weight, many of these attributes cannot be measured directly, but their existence is inferred using other measurements. This is especially critical for the aptitude tests, because they test a general ability in a context that is by design different from the context where this ability will be demonstrated later (e.g., a child is tested for school readiness before he encounters any of the school-related tasks). Construct validity is determined in a number of ways, one of which is to compare the test results to another test, which assesses the same theoretical attribute or characteristic. Another method is to test hypotheses about how high-scoring versus low-scoring students would behave or would show the characteristic (Anastasi & Urbina, 1997).

How to Administer a Standardized Test

You will probably be asked to administer a test or to supervise others giving a test. Standardized tests have prescribed directions for giving the test, arranging the room, and scoring to ensure that every test administration is exactly the same. Consequently, it is important to follow all of the directions as closely as possible. Be sure to read the test manual ahead of time. If the test manual specifies what you have to say to the children, practice reading the directions until you can say them without stumbling. Go through the entire test until you can read it easily. Check to see that the children have everything they need—pencils, paper, and so on. If there is a testing kit, check to make sure all items are in the kit. When kits are shared, it is easy for small items to be left out. Think through how you might answer student questions. Usually, the manual will have examples of frequently asked questions and appropriate answers.

You can probably remember being nervous taking standardized tests. There is evidence that even young children can become anxious during testing, sometimes reflecting their parent's concerns (Gage & Berliner, 1998). As a teacher you have to follow directions carefully, but at the same time you want the children to feel at ease in the testing situation. Your reactions can influence the child's answers in a way that can jeopardize the standardized nature of the test. If one test giver praises children profusely and another is cold and distant, children's answers may be more of a response to the adult than the test. The test manual usually has guidelines for what to do, but if no guidance is given, follow these suggestions. In general, the test giver should remain positive, but not give too much praise. Smiling, saying "OK," and nodding are ways of responding that convey an accepting, positive attitude on your part. Do not say or give an indication of whether a response was correct or incorrect. Give approval for trying to answer. When children make mistakes that upset them in some way, you can comment on the difficulty of an item or the fact that the children are not expected to know everything; for example, tell the child, "That was a hard one" (Cronbach, 1990).

Familiarizing children with the testing format can alleviate anxiety and at the same time make the test results fair. This kind of coaching is not the same thing as teaching to the test. Test manuals often come with special test preparation exercises so that children can get used to following the directions and marking the scoring sheets. In addition there are a number of articles that can guide you (Caluns, Montgomery, & Sarlman, 1999; Chicago Public Schools, 2000). Familiarity with the format will increase the children's chances of getting answers correct, because they know what to do. It will also increase their feelings of ease.

The test manual will also give policies about guessing. Most children in preschool and kindergarten, as well as many first-graders, will not understand what guessing actually means and will guess anyway. Older children will probably want to know whether they should guess when they don't know the answer. If, however, after reading the test manual the policy is unclear, the general advice is that if it is a "wild" guess, you shouldn't answer the question, but if it is an "intelligent guess," that is you think you're right but you aren't positive, you should go ahead and guess. Using the practice sheet you can show children how to eliminate answers by talking through the questions and answers. You can model how one thinks about the choices on the test: "I know that B, C, and D are definitely not correct, so the answer must be A."

Take time to "establish rapport" or create a feeling of ease before you begin the assessment. Most of the time, you will probably give tests to children in your own classroom—children you know and are comfortable with. However, there may be times when you will test a child you don't know very well. For example, if your program requires screening prior to entry into the program, you may give a standardized test to a child you have only met once or twice.

How to Explain Different Types of Test Scores

Test results may be reported in several ways, as school/district/state reports, class reports, and individual profiles. The school/district/state reports are designed to show the public how students are performing compared to other children. These are usually organized by grade level and do not identify each classroom but aggregate classes. Class results usually show the scores of all of the children in the same class. Results are also given in individual scores and may have progress indicators or other indication of the skills in which a student showed a weakness.

Test makers use different types of scores in the results. In order to understand these scores, you must understand how scores are calculated as well as the meaning of percentile ranks, grade equivalents, and standard scores.

How Scores Are Calculated. The information about a child's test performance is reported as a score that identifies whether the child has reached a specific criterion or where the child stands relative to other children. First the child's answers are tallied. This tally is called the *raw score*—the actual number of correct and incorrect answers. Sometimes, the raw score is not a direct reflection of the number of correct and incorrect answers but also reflects different weights assigned to different answers. The raw score is usually not reported, because it is not meaningful unless it is compared to a set of criteria or to other children who took the test. Consequently, the raw score is converted into another kind of score. For criterion-referenced tests, the converted score indicates whether the child has attained the specified level of proficiency on the criteria. In norm-referenced tests, which comprise the majority of achievement tests, the raw score is converted into one of three types of scores: a percentile rank, a grade equivalent, or other scaled scores.

To understand norm-referenced scores, you have to know how psychologists determine norm-referenced scoring systems. These scoring systems are based on the idea of the *normal distribution,* which is also referred to as the *normal* or *bell curve.* This normal curve has important mathematical properties, which are used as the basis for statistical analyses and the creation of the scoring system. When

Figure 10.2 Relationship between Percentile Rank and Standard Scores (*z* scores, *t* scores, and stanine) in a Normal Curve (σ = standard deviation)

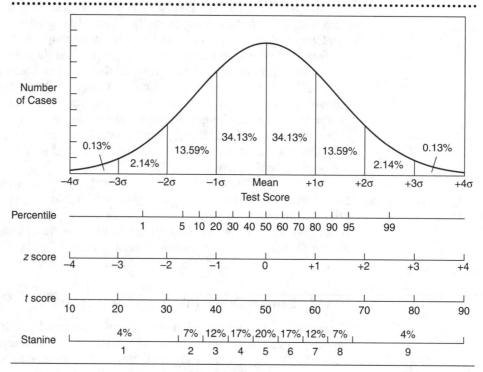

a test is given to many people, their scores tend to fall into a distribution or grouping in which a few people do really well or really poorly, but most people score in the middle range. The curve is symmetrical, with a single peak in the center (see Figure 10.2).

Several statistical terms are used to describe the shape of any distribution of test scores and in particular the normal distribution. The most commonly used statistics tell us about two defining features of any distribution:

- What is the most typical score? These statistics are called *measures of central tendency.*
- How much do other scores differ from this typical score? These statistics are called *measures of variance.*

The central tendency is described by the mean, the median, and the mode. The *mean* is the average score. The *median* is the score that is in the exact middle of the distribution. The *mode* is the most commonly occurring score. In a normal curve the mean, median, and mode are the same score.

In addition to the central tendency, the way scores vary within the distribution is described by the *standard deviation* (SD or σ). The standard deviation describes the variability of the distribution of scores in reference to the mean. In a normal distribution, 68.26 percent of the scores fall within 1 standard deviation above or below the mean. Another way to express this is to say the 68.26 percent of the scores are + 1 *SD* and −1 *SD* from the mean. Figure 10.2 shows the mean, the standard deviation, and the number of scores that fall within 1, 2, or 3 standard deviations from the mean. There are other measures of variance, used by psychometricians to understand a distribution; refer to a statistics textbook for more information about these other measures.

In most cases, the raw scores on a standardized test fall into a distribution that is close to the normal distribution. When the raw scores do not form a normal distribution, the normal curve is still used to assign scores. Just because the scoring system uses the normal curve as its basis doesn't mean that the actual skill that the standardized test is supposed to measure occurs in real life distributed in a normal curve (Cronbach, 1990).

Percentile Ranks. A *percentile rank* describes where a person stands relative to the norm used to develop the test. The child's raw score is compared to those of other children taking the test, the norming sample. The percentile rank is the percentage of people who scored at a similar level or less than you did. If Tina's score places her in the 30th percentile, it means that 30 percent of the students in the norming sample scored the same or less than she did. Ashley scored in the 90th percentile, which means that 90 percent of the people scored the same or below her score. Percentile ranks are used in achievement tests and tests that measure children's progress on state and national standards. Percentile ranks are often confused with percentage scores. A percentage score is a raw score showing the percentage of correct items the child answered. Percentile ranks, however, emphasize the child's standing relative to other children, not the number of correct items on the test. Because they are based on the normal distribution, there is an inherent problem with percentile ranks: Although they show one's position relative to other people, they do not show the amount of difference between the scores. For example, on a test that has 100 items, if your results are very low or very high, you may be placed in the next percentile only after you get 10 or even more items correct. However, if you score in the middle, even a difference of 5 items can place you in a different percentile.

Grade Equivalents. Some achievement test scores are presented as *grade equivalents,* as in the case of these two first-graders. Sarah scores at the 3.6 or third grade, 6-month level, and Michael scores at the kindergarten level. Of all the types of scoring discussed in this chapter, grade equivalents cause the most confusion. This is because grade equivalents do not mean that Sarah can actually read third-grade books. It means that she scored as well as children halfway through third grade on the first-grade test of reading achievement. The test contained the content and skills covered in first grade, not the content and skills expected in third grade. Grade equivalents actually tell us more about Michael, who is reading below grade level. We know that Michael is performing at a level that would concern both you and his parents. This is a distinction that confuses most people, leading parents to ask that their children be skipped to the upper grade level when test results are similar to Sarah's. What grade equivalents do tell us is whether the child is performing below grade level, at grade level, or above grade level.

Scaled Scores. There are several additional ways to convert raw scores. These are called *standard scaled scores.* These standard scores allow comparisons across tests, because they are based on the distance between a person's score and the mean score in the norming distribution or on percentile ranks. The main types of standard scores are z scores, t scores, and stanine scores. A z score expresses the distance from the mean in terms of the standard deviation. A z score of 0 is at the mean, $+2$ is two standard deviations from the mean, and -2

How much of time to dedicate to

is two standard deviations below the mean. With a *t* score, a score of 50 is at the mean, and 60 is one standard deviation above the mean. Note that with *t* scores there are no negative numbers. A stanine score (standard nine) uses percentile ranks that are presented as a nine-point scale. Consequently, the lower the stanine, the lower the percentile rank. Stanine 1 would correspond to percentile ranks of 0 to 4th percentile and a stanine of 9 would correspond to the 97th to 100th percentile. Stanine scores are rough approximations.

How to Interpret Standardized Test Results

Standardized tests give teachers little useful information for day-to-day classroom decisions. However, the tests can tell us something about general trends in our teaching. For example, results comparing your class to others in the district can give you insights about whether your class is keeping pace with the content being tested. Teachers should not be afraid to look at this data and try to figure out why there are discrepancies. The information can be useful in adjusting emphasis or changing curriculum content. There is one cautionary note, however: Because many of these tests are administered only in the spring, it is difficult to sort out whether the differences are caused by differences in instruction or content, or by differences in the population of children tested. For example, in one classroom 60 percent of the first-graders knew all of the sound–symbol correspondence of all of the letters in the alphabet on the first day of school, and in the classroom next door none of the children had that background knowledge. You would expect children in the first class to score higher on an end-of-the-year achievement test because they started out higher. This makes assessment by teachers even more important. Knowing this antecedent information helps you analyze the meanings of classroom scores you receive at the end of the year.

Classroom reports and individual profiles from standardized tests can aid in fine tuning instruction but must be examined with the following things in mind. The test results may be returned months after the test was taken. If so, first re-assess the child yourself, to make sure that the test still presents a true picture of the child. Second, profiles are often extrapolated from what test makers have predicted to be the most common or most likely progress, or most likely problems. Remember, you do not have two performances on the same standardized test to compare so you don't know the rate at which the child is learning; you only know how the child performed at the time he took the test. Subtest scores give detailed information about a child's performance on the components of the test. They may reveal a weakness or strength that is not apparent in the overall score. Class results are most helpful in planning for next year. They help you answer questions such as what things to do to make sure the class keeps pace with what is expected. You don't want to teach to the test, but to use test results as one piece of information to guide planning.

You will also discuss and explain children's standardized test scores to parents. In most cases, this is done in a parent–teacher conference with other assessment information. When results are presented in isolation, the meaning of the test scores may be overemphasized. A conference to discuss a single test score can unintentionally turn into a high-stakes decision-making situation. Check your school's policies and procedures for giving test results to parents.

Following are some additional guides for the conference. Prepare to explain general information about the standardized test—why it was chosen and how the population of children used to norm the test is similar to or different from the children in your class. You may want to include district information to explain what is being tested and how the test is being used in your school district. Explain to parents the strengths and limitations of any kind of standardized test—in particular, why specific test scores vary.

Because parents have varying backgrounds and experiences with standardized testing, be prepared for a wide range of questions. Percentile ranks, grade equivalents, and standard scores can be confusing. Explain the implications of the information as well as the score. Don't be afraid to say, "I'll have to check to find out more information" when you do not know the answer to a parent question.

Think through how you will use the information to improve your teaching of that specific child. When a test score is considered "high," explain how you will support further learning. When a test score is "low" and the child demonstrates several weaknesses, explain how that will influence your approach in the future. Parents will often ask what they should do at home to support instruction; be prepared to answer that question. Embedding standardized test results in classroom assessment results is the best way to report to parents. It allows you to align instruction and assessment and to use standardized test scores in a productive way.

Standardized Instruments Used to Measure Opportunities to Learn

Classroom environment scales are used to evaluate the quality of early childhood classrooms, measuring the opportunities to learn that are provided by the physical environment and the teacher. They are often mandated by state standards as a part of accountability procedures that monitor early childhood programs. Many of these instruments have gone through rigorous validity and reliability procedures similar to those of standardized tests given to children, but instead of measuring child outcomes, the instruments examine the materials, the ways the teacher interacts with the children, the kind and quality of activities, and how instruction happens. These classroom environment scales usually require a trained evaluator to administer the instrument. The Early Childhood Environment Rating Scale Revised (ECERS-R) is an example of an instrument designed to measure the general quality of the environment (Harms, Clifford, & Cryer, 1998). There are seven subscales: Space and furnishings, personal care routines, language-reasoning, activities, interaction, program structure, and parents and staff. Each item in the subscale is rated from 1 (inadequate) to 7 (excellent). Reliability and validity were established through a number of research studies. An example of an instrument that focuses on one content area is the Early Language & Literacy Classroom Observation (ELLCO) (Smith, Dickinson, Sangeorge, & Anastasopoulos, 2002). The ELLCO evaluates the opportunities to learn language and literacy that are provided in a classroom. It has three components: a literacy environment checklist, a classroom observation and teacher interview, and a literacy activities rating scale. Examples of other focused measures are the Supports for Early Literacy Assessment (SELA), which measures the literacy environment in a slightly different way than the ELLCO (Smith, Davidson, Weisenfeld, & Katsaros, 2001), and the Preschool Classroom Mathematics Inventory (PCMI) which looks at classroom opportunities to learn mathematics (Frede, Dessewffy, Hornbeck, & Worth, 2000). There are also classroom environment instruments that focus on the quality of the teacher's interactions with the children, such as the Classroom

Assessment Scoring System (CLASS) (LaParo & Pianta, 2001). Teachers may be evaluated or trained to evaluate others using one of these instruments.

Finding Out More about Standardized Tests

You may need to know more about standardized tests than we have covered in this chapter. College courses in tests and measurement explain in detail the psychometric and statistical concepts briefly covered here and will also provide more information about specific tests. Books that critique tests can be found in the reference section of your academic library. Two books of interest are the *Mental Measurements Yearbook* and the *Tests in Print* series, both published by the Buros Institute and updated periodically. The websites http://ericae.net and http://NIEER.org include definitions and information about standardized tests as well as a database for searching major test review sites, such as the Educational Testing Service (ETS) Test File and the Buros Institute of Mental Measurement's Tests in Print. The Web pages for the American Educational Research Association (AERA) at http://aera.net and the American Psychological Association (APA) at http://apa.org post position statements about testing and standards for tests on their Web sites. The APA site has a downloadable document about testing. In addition, most test publishers have their own Web sites where you can find a general description of the test, example test items, and sometimes documentation on reliability and validity.

Summary

Although the primary function of classroom assessment is to inform instruction, early childhood teachers are asked to participate in other types of assessment that serve other purposes and often involve standardized testing. In many cases early childhood teachers are asked to give standardized tests and to interpret test results. Standardized tests are tests that have been constructed according to specified psychometric standards and guidelines, compare students with a specific population, and have specified procedures for administration. The testing manual identifies how the test makers established reliability and validity. Standardized tests can be criterion or norm referenced, which consequently influences how scores are reported. Criterion-referenced standardized tests report whether a child has reached specific criteria, such as being proficient. Norm-referenced tests report scores as either percentile ranks, grade equivalents, or standard scores.

Standardized tests are a snapshot of the child's abilities and should always be considered as only one piece of information about the child's capabilities. The inadequacies and limitations of standardized testing should lead us to look at the scores with a healthy dose of skepticism.

For Personal Reflection

1. Most adults have taken many types of tests and assessment measures. Reflect on your experience with them. Do you consider any of them "unfair"? If so, why? Which measures do you consider adequate evaluations of what you learned or did not learn? Why? In what ways could the evaluation of your learning have been improved?

2. Reflect further on your testing experience. Were you ever nervous? What was it about the testing situation that made you nervous? Was the anxiety from you or from the expectations of others? What were things that you and others did to make you feel more comfortable?

For Further Study and Discussion

1. There is a difference between teaching to the test and preparing children for a test. Discuss what the differences might mean when you work with children in the classroom.
2. If it is possible, look at a standardized testing manual. How was reliability and validity determined? Do these meet the criteria described in this chapter?
3. With a partner, role-play a situation in which one of you is a concerned parent and the other person is the teacher. Here are some possible scenarios:
    a. John scores at the 25th percentile in reading, and the class on average scores from the 20th to the 60th percentile in reading. The parent wants to know what the score means.
    b. Lenore is in second grade but she scores at the 6.8 (sixth grade, eighth month) level in math. The parent wants Lenore to be skipped to sixth grade.
    c. Anita is in first grade but scores at the kindergarten equivalent. Should her parents be concerned?
    d. Miguel scores at the 88th percentile.

Suggested Readings

American Educational Research Association, American Psychological Association, & National Council on Measurement in Education. (1999). *Standards for educational and psychological testing.* Washington, DC: American Educational Research Association.

Anastasi, A., & Urbina, S. (1997). *Psychological testing* (7th ed). Upper Saddle River, NJ: Prentice Hall.

Bracey, G. W. (1998). *Put to the test: An educator's and consumer's guide to standardized testing.* Bloomington, IN: Phi Delta Kappa.

Bracey, G. W. (2000). *Thinking about tests and testing: A short primer in "assessment literacy."* Washington, DC: American Youth Policy Forum. Available online at www.aypf.org.

Caluns, L., Montgomery, K., & Sarlman, D. (1999). Helping children to master the trials and avoid the traps of standardized tests. *Practical Assessment, Research, and Evaluation, 6*(8), 58–69.

Chicago Public Schools. (2000). *Preparing young elementary students to take standardized tests.* Chicago, IL: Author

Sattler, J. (2001). *Assessment of children* (5th ed.). San Diego: Jerome M. Sattler.

CHAPTER 11

Communicating and Collaborating Using Assessment Processes and Results

Although the primary purpose of classroom assessment is to help children learn, assessment has other purposes.

Teachers report assessment results to students and to parents or guardians. In addition, they are frequently asked to report or to discuss assessment results with other educators and with diverse lay audiences. If the results are not communicated effectively, they may be misused or not used. To communicate effectively with others on matters of student assessment, teachers must be able to use assessment terminology appropriately to articulate the meaning, limitations, and implications of assessment results. Furthermore, teachers may have to defend their own assessment procedures and interpretations. At other times, teachers may need to help the public to interpret assessment results appropriately. (American Federation of Teachers et al., 1990)

Teachers of children with special needs communicate and collaborate with other teachers, specialists, parents, and community services. Assessing and guiding young children also has potential for enriching teachers' professional and personal lives as they attempt to understand children and themselves and help both develop and learn.

Communicating with Children

Teachers and children have conferences to discuss children's progress as an integral part of assessment and teaching. Assessment is not something administered to children, with the results returned from some distant place weeks later and then reported to their parents. Children edit and revise their writing in conference with their teachers. They are congratulated specifically on the restraint they show by using verbal conflict resolution. Drawing a happy face and saying "O.K.," which convey only general approval, are supplanted by helping children understand what they did that was appropriate and productive and what remains to be learned.

Some progress reports use pictures and simple words that children understand. Children build portfolios and explain their contents to teachers, parents, and others. Children assess and reflect on their own progress, as one youngster did as she was preparing to leave second grade (see Figure 11.1). Many schools have a policy of including children in all conferences with parents. However it is done, children should know what they have achieved and what they have yet to learn.

Communicating with Parents

Before Reporting

Communicating with parents about classroom assessment begins long before a parent conference is held or a progress report is sent home. If changes are planned, parents should be involved from the very beginning through task forces, planning committees, advisory panels, open forums, or other means. Moving from letter grades or other rankings to narrative or standards-based reporting, for example, requires the understanding and support of parents.

Regarding Assessment and Reporting.   Inform and involve parents. Solicit and consider their reactions to drafts of reporting forms and formats of parent conferences. Explain the reasons for assessment and the potential benefits to them and their child. Demonstrate the way changing concepts about how children learn to read, write, compute, and solve problems influence how teaching and assessment are done. Show and explain a portfolio and the reasons some

Figure 11.1   Self-Assessment by Second-Grade Child

Name _Torrey Stenmark_

Date _6/9_

School _Jackson—RE 6_

Key: 1. Needs improvement
2. Developing
3. Doing well, confident
4. Exceeds expectations

Reading	1	2	3	4
Initiates own reading				4
Chooses variety of materials			3	
Participates in discussion			3	
Uses comprehension strategies				4
Requests appropriate help			3	
Reads at or above expected level				4

Writing	1	2	3	4
Initiates own writing			3	
Participates in conferences			3	
Edits/revises as needed				4
Requests appropriate help				4
Writes at or above expected level			3	

Teacher comments:

Torrey's confidence, initiative, and desire to learn have increased her reading and writing skills. This self-assessment is quite accurate. —R. J.

Pupil comments/goals:

I don't really need much help in reading or witeing.

Parent comments:

Torrey really enjoys reading and writing.

P.S.

items will be kept for the portfolio. Anticipate and deal with questions and concerns before they arise.

Involve parents in assessment. They are a valuable source of information (see Chapter 4), and can support learning at school and home. Your purpose is to build parent understanding and to have home and school work together for the benefit of the child.

Collect Sufficient Evidence.   Judgments and conclusions communicated to parents should be substantiated and grounded in valid and reliable appraisals. Early childhood teachers often report on many things other than reading, arithmetic, and other "subjects." They judge dispositions and skills such as attention span, confidence, participation in group activities, social interaction, and work habits. Teachers should know what reporting forms they will use and develop ways to assess child progress on all items. When reporting time comes, adequate evidence will be in each child's files and portfolio to make fair and valid conclusions and to have examples to discuss with parents.

Ways to Report

Reporting to parents takes many forms, both formal and informal. Formal reports include parent conferences, written progress reports and letters, report cards or forms, summarized and interpreted children's portfolios, and test scores. Informal reports include sample work displayed or sent home, programs and exhibitions, informal conversations or notes, telephone messages, folders of sample work and reports sent back and forth between home and school, short notes or "happy-grams," Web pages, and others. Most programs use a combination. Formal reports are usually given more weight than informal ones, but anything communicated by teachers is likely to be taken seriously by parents. Informal reciprocal exchanges convey much useful information (Powell, 1989).

Prekindergartens and kindergartens rely heavily on parent conferences, samples of children's work, and informal communication, although many have formal rating scales. Primary grades usually have a report card or progress report. Parent conferences are typically scheduled at least once or twice a year and are always available on request.

In some early childhood settings, teachers are required to make *summary* or *summative* evaluations of children's progress. These evaluations compare a child's cumulative status, general strengths and weaknesses, or progress toward a standard or criterion or to other children (Gage & Berliner, 1998). When teachers compare a child's performance to a goal or objective, they are making *criterion-referenced* evaluations. Wendy has made satisfactory progress toward the goal of being responsible for her own work in the classroom. In *norm-referenced* evaluation children are compared with other children of the same age (as in using a developmental continuum or pattern) or to the other children in the class. Wendy's self-management skills are similar to those of other children her age but better than the average found in this second-grade class. Comparisons can also be made between past and current performances.

Many teachers find summary evaluations difficult and distasteful and would gladly do away with them altogether. They fear that ratings and reports can be disheartening for children and parents and encourage unhealthy competition (Juarez, 1996). "Putting less emphasis on comparisons is fine, but at some point a child and his parents have a right to know whether the child's progress is reasonable for his or her age and experience" (Maeroff, 1991, p. 276). The issues that early childhood teachers and schools face are (1) when is that point and (2) how shall progress be communicated. Two types of summary evaluations are used in early childhood programs: narrative reports and grades or ratings. Some programs require both, others only one, and some require none at all.

Narrative Reports.   Good narrative reports (Figure 11.2) emphasize strengths and communicate concerns and recommendations. They usually do not summarize all areas of growth but only the most significant. Comparisons are made

Figure 11.2   Typical Narrative Progress Report

....

Progress Report   **Date** 6/15/06

Child Turner, T.

Tina has made great progress in all areas of development. Most notable were gains in the areas of written language, thinking skills, knowledge base, and social development. At the beginning of the year, Tina was just beginning to label her drawings with scribbles that were horizontal, had repeated features, and spaces for words. Now she has begun to incorporate letters and has written words interspersed between the scribbles. I would expect her to increase the number of written words. She has begun to read back some of her stories, but for the most part, what she reads is not yet tied to what she has written—a normal developmental step.

In thinking skills, Tina is experimenting with numbers and with the idea that numbers remain the same even though the objects are arranged in different groupings. For example, she figured out that $4 + 1$, $1 + 4$, $3 + 2$, and $2 + 3$ all make 5.

Her knowledge of math facts has also grown during the year. Early in the year she was counting meaningfully by 1s to 20. She is now counting by 2s and enjoys experimenting with adding different one-digit numbers. I anticipate that this interest and enjoyment of math will continue.

Tina has also grown in her social skills. Her dramatic play is full of fantasy and very complex, showing both intellectual development and social development. She has shown instances of empathy and social problem-solving skills. She enjoys being with her friends and plays primarily with Tania, Mark, and Sonia. She participates in cooperative learning activities.

---

between the child's capabilities and program goals, standards, universal patterns of growth and development, or the child's previous performance. Comparisons with children in the same class are kept to a minimum. Narrative reports seem to lighten the "impact of comparisons among students and give the teacher an opportunity to bring up important areas to parents" (Hopkins, Stanley, & Hopkins, 1990, p. 325).

Recorded and summarized classroom assessment information is essential to accurate narrative reports. Summarize information that reveals the child's progress toward major classroom goals and objectives, as well as information on the individual child's uniqueness. Because other people will read and be influenced by the report, it must be fair, accurate, and impartial; report only what can be substantiated with data.

A consistent format helps organize the report, so that important information is included and easy to find. If the school or center does not supply a format, develop one. Figure 11.3 shows one page of a four-page "Family Report" with space for a narrative description of a child's progress, supporting evidence, and space for parent/guardian comments and observations. The report is designed to be used in a family conference. Figure 11.4 shows one page of a two-page kindergarten report card. An accompanying booklet explains the reporting system, which conveys information on the quality of a child's work in content areas; the student's work level (above, at, or below grade level); and student performance in relationship to the district's standard (exceeds, meets, progressing toward). The

Figure 11.3   Portion of a Narrative-Type "Family Report" Used with the High/Scope Child Observation Record (COR)
••

III. Creative Representation
Representación Creativa

Developmental summary:
Resumen del Desarrollo:

Supporting anecdotes:
Anécdotas que lo complementan:

Parent observations:
Observaciones del padre o madre:

IV. Movement and Music
Movimiento y Música

Developmental summary:
Resumen del Desarrollo:

Supporting anecdotes:
Anécdotas que lo complementan:

Parent observations:
Observaciones del padre o madre:

Preschool Child Observation Record (COR), by High/Scope Educational Research Foundation, Ypsilanti, MI: High/Scope Press. © 2003, High/Scope Educational Research Foundation, Used with permission.

ratings are entered into a computer, which then prints the report card in either English or Spanish. There is room on the back for teacher comments. Additional explanations are given in parent conferences.

Grading and Grades.   Grading is an official assessment that most kindergarten, first-, and second-grade teachers are required to do. Although most teachers dislike grading, it does not necessarily have the negative motivational

Figure 11.4   Portion of a Report Card Using Ratings Referenced to District Standards

<< Back to Main

Content Area Grades

H = High Quality
HS = High Satisfactory Quality
S = Satisfactory Quality
I = Improvement in Progress
N = Needs Improvement
U = Unsatisfactory Progress

Student Work Level

AG = Above Grade Level
G = Garde Level
BG = Below Grade Level

Student Performance Levels

4 = Exceeds Standard
3 = Meets Standard
2 = Progressing Toward
    Standard
1 = Limited Progress Toward
    Standard
/ = Not Introduced

Scale for Traits

4 – Always/Almost Always
3 – Usually
2 – Sometimes
1 – Almost Never

Kindergarten Report Card

Selected Term is **1**		Delete grades for selected term ☐

Print Grade card in English? ◉   Spanish? ○   Both? ○

Grading Period:	1	2	3
Reading	☐	☐	☐
Level at which student is working **	☐	☐	☐
Demonstrates alphabet knowledge	☐	☐	☐
Demonstrates phonemic awareness	☐	☐	☐
Demonstrates directionality in print	☐	☐	☐
Uses beginning reading strategies	☐	☐	☐
Demonstrates comprehension of stories	☐	☐	☐
Writing	☐	☐	☐
Level at which student is working **	☐	☐	☐
Writes own name accurately	☐	☐	☐
Writes effectively for a variety of purposes and audiences	☐	☐	☐
Math	☐	☐	☐
Level at which student is working **	☐	☐	☐
Number Sense	☐	☐	☐
Algebra	☐	☐	☐
Statistics/Probability	☐	☐	☐
Geometry	☐	☐	☐
Measurement	☐	☐	☐
Computation	☐	☐	☐
Science	☐	☐	☐
Level at which student is working **	☐	☐	☐
Life: Animals Two by Two	☐	☐	☐
Physical: Wood and Paper	☐	☐	☐
Earth Systems: Sunshine and Shadows	☐	☐	☐
Social Studies - Friends and Neighbors	☐	☐	☐
Level at which student is working **	☐	☐	☐
History	☐	☐	☐
Geography	☐	☐	☐
Civics	☐	☐	☐

Kindergarten Report Card. (2004). Adams 12 Five Star Schools, Thornton, CO. Used with permission.

consequences that teachers fear, and it can be a valid part of the total system of motivation in a classroom (Berliner, 1987). If standards-based rubrics are used for grading, the descriptions that determine each level of accomplishment can be quite useful in describing what has been achieved and what is yet to be learned (Marzano, 2000).

School policies vary. Some may have a grading handbook that specifies how to report grades: the grading system, the type of assignments to use for grading, and the reporting periods. Grading systems vary from a simple satisfactory/unsatisfactory to the traditional A, B, C, D, F. Many programs use terminology linked to their standards: advanced (exceeds the standard), proficient, partially proficient, developing. The trend is to use rating scales that identify children's level and quality of learning rather than simply an overall rank within the class. Assignments and evidence of progress used to compile the grade may be based on district curriculum, state or district standards, or left up to the teacher. Reporting periods may be once a quarter, trimester, semester, or some other regular interval. They can coincide with parent–teacher conferences or may be independent from conferences.

Likewise, there is no one accepted strategy for teachers to use to assign grades. To make grading fair and reflective of what children have accomplished and have yet to accomplish, use these guides:

- *Distinguish between grades compiled for reporting and teacher responses to classroom assignments, work products, and practice as children are learning.* Children need to know what they are doing right and wrong and how to improve as they attempt to learn. This feedback should not be a grade. Many good learning activities, such as cooperative projects, discussions, successive drafts of writing or investigations, and portfolios, do not lend themselves to grading. Children need opportunities to practice and learn without the pressure of grades.
- *Develop a grading plan.* A written plan will help overcome problems of subjectivity and unfairness (Marzano, 2000). First, identify the development and learning areas on which you are required to report: academic objectives, standards, and benchmarks, as well as learning approaches, such as listening and organizational skills. Be as specific as possible. Next, identify appropriate assessments to gather evidence of children's progress toward those goals. Choose different types of assessments, as described throughout this book. Choose those that represent a significant segment of achievement. For example, story retelling is a good check on children's reading comprehension—a significant aspect of learning to read. Finally, decide how much each assessment will contribute to the grade. There are two ways to do this: Assign points to each assessment, or assign each a percentage of the grade. For example, a performance assessment relating to practical math problems might be worth ten points or 10 percent; a computation test, fifteen points or 15 percent; and so forth. Modify the plan as necessary. Keep records from these assessments in a separate file so that you have them as evidence to refer to at "report card time."
- *Specify grading criteria in advance.* By doing so, you, children, parents, and the school are clear on what constitutes each rating. Grading handbooks or standards-based rubrics may be helpful.
- *Set up a grade book.* Use it to keep track of the results of the assessments you will use for compiling grades.

- *Use the same grading assessments for each child.* Make it as standard as possible by using the same materials, questions, and procedures.
- *Grade academic and nonacademic factors separately.* When parents see that their child received an "A" in math they expect that the "A" represents their child's achievement in math—what the child has learned and accomplished in the classroom. Although nonachievement factors such as effort (participation and work completion), behavior (following rules and teamwork), and attendance (absenteeism and tardiness) are important, they should not be counted in a content grade. When a child with a "C" on all graded assignments and tests is given a "B" because he is trying hard, the meaning of the grade is unclear. It can be perceived by parents and children as subjective and biased. Many report cards list effort, attitude, and other work and social habits separately.
- *Compare children's performance to a criterion: a specified goal or standard.* Do not grade "on a curve." Distributing grades according to a standard curve is not valid unless the number of pupils is large (sixty or more), and it may not apply to any one group (Gage and Berliner, 1998). Assigning grades by comparing to other children in the class does not reflect classroom instruction that aims to help each child achieve the stated standards.
- *Be as objective as possible.* The helping relationship teachers have with their pupils makes it difficult to judge them on a completely objective basis (Airasian, 2000). When grading tests, cover or ignore the child's name. Grade assignment by assignment and not child by child. For example, grade all of the tests, then all of the written assignments. Don't grade all of Megan's work and then all of Dylan's work.
- *Remember that grades and comments on official report cards are part of a child's permanent record.*

For more information see Marzano's *Transforming Classroom Grading* (2000), Airasian's *Classroom Assessment* (2001), and Stiggins's *Student-Centered Assessment* (1997).

Parent Conferences. In parent–teacher or parent–student–teacher conferences, all parties consider, discuss, and exchange evidence, thoughts, and recommendations face to face. As parents and teachers go through the documentation together, opportunities for explanation, questions, and responses arise from the records, work products, and other materials. The conference becomes a shared reflection and a look to the future rather than a cut-and-dried evaluation of a youngster's performance. Some guides follow:

Have a plan. Identify one or two desired outcomes for the conference; jot down ideas for a positive and personal opening (something positive about this parent's child); list the points you want to make, including the examples or evidence you will use to substantiate those points; and note some possible actions that parents and school personnel can take to sustain or enhance learning. If you need to, write reminders of ways to elicit parents' responses—"What do you see at home?" "Has this been your experience?" "What are your concerns?"

Communicate with parents, not to or at them. The process is one of people interacting with other people. Parents are a primary source of information about their children, and teachers listen as well as report. Even better is mutual sharing of information and insights. Parent conferences are ideal, but telephone conferences, voice mail, progress letters, home visits, informal sharing, and many other forms of communication achieve similar results.

Give parents a written progress statement that reports on major developmental and learning areas. In some schools and centers, parent conferences are held from teachers' notes, and parents receive nothing in writing. They should.

Be specific. Avoid vague generalities, such as "He is doing just fine. I wish all the children were responding as well" or "She is having a lot of trouble in reading." Classroom assessment supplies the evidence that explains what "just fine" or "having trouble" means for these children.

Keep language clear, simple, and free of jargon. Use terms that everyone can understand instead of "perceptual–motor," "auditory memory," "cognitive processes," and the many other terms we as educators use. Use no labels. Concentrate on what the child does. Offer enough explanation that parents see the significance of what you are discussing. For example, unless the clarity and organization in a child's report or journal are pointed out, a parent may focus on poorly formed letters or misspelled words. If the parent or guardian speaks a different language from you, arrange for a translator to be present.

Be selective. The amount of documentation you have about a child requires that you summarize and select what parents will want and need to know. Some children may wish to help in this process. Select a few items to make your points clear. A portfolio may be a good source.

Be clear, straightforward, and supportive. With the documentation that good classroom assessment provides, you can share children's strengths and needs in a way that parents respect and accept. It is no kindness to gloss over problems and concerns. In fact, if real concerns exist, you, the administrator, or the appropriate specialist should be working with parents immediately, so there are no surprises at conference or reporting time (Abbott & Gold, 1991).

Be prepared to answer parents' questions. Many schools send out preconference forms to parents to ask what they would like to discuss at the conference. Almost every parent, at some time or other, will want to know their child's relative standing in the class. Schools have worked hard to find alternative ways of reporting about children, but this question inevitably arises. Be prepared to tell or show what the typical child of that developmental level can do, and make your comparison to that hypothetical child, rather than to other children in the class. A different way to accomplish the same purpose is to save samples of typical work from past years that show parents the variations within the range of normal.

If parents have questions about the program, be prepared to answer them. Be ready to explain and show how children are progressing toward school and parent goals.

Be sensitive to the impact of what you are saying. Judgment of what is appropriate to say will vary with the family and child. Altered expectations, pressure, and even punishment can result from insensitivity to family dynamics. Teachers sometimes expect parents to give more help with school behavior problems than any parent can. If a child's parents knew how to keep her from disrupting class, they would doubtless do it. Indeed, sometimes there are no problems at home (Tuma & Elbert, 1990).

Use assessment results as the basis for home activities.   One of the most effective home–school collaborations is helping parents learn how to help their children (Epstein, 1987). Assessment results tell you what children need help with. You can get beyond "give her some help when she has trouble" or "help him with his homework" to being specific about what this family can do (Coleman, 1991; Gotts, 1984). Assessment results may also help you with the parent who needs to ease up on a child—an equally valid aid to some children's development.

Look ahead.   Together, decide on a home–school action plan to sustain progress and address any concerns. Allow no more than two or three items. List these, and provide a copy for the school and one for the family. Perhaps parents suggest that they can listen to a child read for fifteen to twenty minutes a day, get the backpack organized and ready to take to school the night before to help with "forgetfulness," or go to the library every week. What will you be doing at school? Reaching agreement and writing it down brings parents into the process of using assessment results for the benefit of their child.

Portfolio Conferences.   Reports to parents based on portfolios usually take two forms: (1) Children present and explain their portfolios to their parents or (2) portfolios focus or supplement parent conferences.

Child-led portfolio conferences.   At an evening or afternoon meeting, children show their individual portfolios to their own parents, explain to the parents how items were generated and selected, why they are important as evidence of learning, the self-reflections involved, and any other aspects of the portfolio the children wish to share. Children need a certain level of maturity and experience with portfolios to lead such a conference. With preparation, most second-grade pupils can participate. One school prepares in this way:

> Children spend several weeks talking about their portfolios . . . with their teachers, with peers, and often with older students. Specific lessons are focused on how to organize selections of work; how to place them in chronological order; how to think about work as evidence of competence in more than one subject area; how to compare earlier work with present work, showing the acquisition of more advanced skills; and . . . how to reflect on the portfolio as a whole. Students complete portfolio menus called "Ask me about" sheets. On these organizing sheets the students highlight the contents of their portfolios and emphasize learning experiences that are important to their portfolio story. (Hebert, 1998, p. 585)

In the process the children learn to assess their own work, take responsibility for their own learning, and acquire the metacognitive skills to interpret what they have done. Such portfolio events require commitment from school staff and have great benefits for all concerned.

Teacher-led portfolio conferences.   Portfolios bring many pluses to parent–teacher or parent–student–teacher conferences.

- A portfolio provides an objective focus for the conference.
- The documentation often speaks for itself.
- The portfolio items provide substantiation for conclusions, summaries, and recommendations.
- Going through selected items together facilitates explanations, questions, and shared satisfaction. As teachers point out what is significant in various items, they are educating parents.

Use the same basic approaches as for any parent conference, with additions specific to using portfolios.

Prepare the portfolio for sharing.   If children are not participating in the conferences, they can write or draw messages to their parents to put in the portfolios. Select the portfolio items you will use in the conference. Focus on those that illustrate the points you want to make. Tab the items so you can quickly turn to them. Supplement the captions with notes, if needed. Add a page for parent comments and reflections. Children can read what their parents said, and the comments can become part of the portfolio.

Let parents study portfolios on their own.   Plan a place and time before or after the conference for parents to look at portfolios on their own, because you will be sharing only a few items. Conference schedules seem to get off track, and this is a worthwhile use of time. The captions you and children have placed on items will explain their significance.

Exhibits and Displays.   Exhibits, displays, and performances of children's work are public compilations and summaries of what children have done, how they did it, and what they learned. This type of documentation is widely used in programs following the Reggio Emilia approach to education (Helm, Beneke, & Steinheimer, 1998; Hendrick, 1997). When the original Italian schools needed to make themselves known to their communities, they showed their work using attractive and informative displays and exhibits.

Reggio Emilia children and teachers document group and individual work using photographs, sketches, narrative reports, artwork in all media, transcriptions of children's conversations, audio- and videotapes, work products, and any other appropriate evidence. Examples that tell the story of the group's study and what they learned are attractively displayed on large poster panels, shelves, walls, or other space. With explanations and interpretations on captions and signs as needed, the displays communicate to children, parents, and other professionals, administrators, and communities the processes used and the results.

Most displays tell the story of what was done during a project—a systematic study of a topic. Teachers and children may also document other things about which they wish to communicate: types of representation, or important knowledge and skills. As with portfolios, there is no set way to compile and present classroom experiences.

As important as the exhibit is the process of gathering many and varied examples, reflecting on them with children and colleagues, and using them to inform future learning experiences.

Exhibits and displays need to be in a public place: a school hallway; the lobby; the library or entrance area; community libraries; shopping malls; town, county, or tribal council buildings; or wherever communities gather. Open houses, receptions, parent meetings, parent–teacher conferences, and other functions are opportunities for interested people to study the exhibits.

A different way of "going public" is through a Web site, which extends to relatives and friends beyond the immediate community. Current technology allows any flat paper surface—photographs, work products, graphs, concept maps, writing, math and science investigations—to be scanned and entered into a computer. Explanations, descriptions, and reflections can be entered directly to caption and draw attention to the focus of the display. Add an e-mail address for the class or teacher, and it becomes an interactive display.

Communicating and Collaborating with Other Professionals

Communication with other professionals and staff takes many forms: communication and coordination within the school or center; communication with other teachers, centers, and agencies to coordinate delivery of services and to ease transitions from one educational level or setting to another; and the communication and collaboration that are essential to identify and serve children with special needs.

Communication within the School or Center

Administrators in schools and centers usually require certain minimum reports from teachers: attendance, potential concerns, permission slips for special activities, and others as determined in the individual setting. Teachers involved in alternative assessment are almost always working with the support and understanding of the administrator, who should be kept informed. Do this indirectly using displays, bulletin boards, exhibits, invitations to hear reports, and other public ways as described earlier. Direct ways are also appropriate: a well-done portfolio explained by a child, outstanding progress by a child or group in any developmental or content area, a new form or way of documenting children's work that you think might be helpful to others, or simply an informal conversation about how it's going—what's working and what isn't.

Teachers, aides, assistants, specialists, administrators, and other school or center staff do not always agree on children's needs and how to respond to them. Often these disagreements are the result of deeply held convictions about how children learn (Smith & Shepard, 1988), but sometimes they happen because each person has only part of the necessary information. A classroom teacher may focus on a child's total functioning, a specialist may focus on deficiencies or strengths that become obvious in one-to-one therapy, whereas the teacher down the hall may know that part of the child's behavior which shows itself in play yard disputes. Although some elements of truth are present in all these perceptions, no single one is complete. Basic information from each source, discussed objectively and professionally, can help staff arrive at appropriate courses of action.

Communication with Other Schools and Centers

As children move from one setting to another, teachers should send and receive summarized assessment information about them to ease the transition and assure continuity in their education. Some forms have a section designated "information for the receiving teacher." Unfortunately, children from highly mobile families often leave abruptly, with no word of where they are going. Worthwhile assessment records should accompany children who are going from one level or setting within the same community to another. Transition from Head Start or private preschool to kindergarten, kindergarten to first grade, or among different preschool settings is smoother if information about children is sent and sought. Health and special services staff can use existing information as a starting point to ensure continuity of services for children and families (Administration for Children, Youth, and Families, 1986; IDEA, 2004).

Communication and Collaboration in Specialized Services

Schools and centers do not have all the resources to serve the diverse children and families with whom they work. Coordination and collaboration with other schools and centers, other public and private community resources and agencies, and other disciplines are essential (Committee for Economic Development, 1985, 1991; National Association of State Boards of Education, 1988). Collaboration with professionals from other disciplines, with different orientations, priorities, and possible constraints on what they can do, is part of the role of today's early childhood teacher. In certain areas of diversity, such as cultural, ethnic, or language, reaching out to the community may be the only way to get essential information.

Teachers who have children with disabilities in the classroom can call on specialists with relevant knowledge and skills. Such specialists are not always employed by the school or center but may be from another public or private agency or group, such as a mental health center, public health agency, local hospital, or nearby university. They help with prereferral strategies, identification, diagnosis, and the development of Individual Educational Programs (IEPs) and Individual Family Service Programs (IFSPs), the required plans for delivery of services to children with special needs. They can devise accommodations or modifications to assessment so children with disabilities can be fairly appraised.

The three major approaches to working with specialists are *interdisciplinary*, *multidisciplinary*, and *transdisciplinary* (Bagnato & Neisworth, 1991; Taylor, Willits, & Lieberman, 1990; Wolery & Dyk, 1984). These approaches are not mutually exclusive, but may occur simultaneously and complement one another.

A fourth, the *collaborative team approach*, is another way to help classroom personnel, parents, and specialists work together. We examine each of these, then the roles and responsibilities of classroom teachers, with emphasis on assessment.

Interdisciplinary Approaches. Interdisciplinary approaches bring together specialists from various disciplines, including teachers, parents or parent representatives, and, where appropriate, cultural specialists, to work as a team outside the classroom. Each contributes their unique perspectives on a particular child or problem, and then consult and work together to develop an appropriate course of action. Probably the best example of this approach is the "staffing" process used to consider evidence and deliberate on its meaning for children with special needs.

Multidisciplinary Approaches. Multidisciplinary approaches depend on specialists from several disciplines who usually assess and evaluate a child independently and submit separate reports. An in-depth medical or psychological evaluation and diagnosis of a child might well be of this nature. It is left to others to fit the various pieces together into a workable program for a child or center.

Transdisciplinary Approaches.   Transdisciplinary collaboration takes place "across" and involves all relevant disciplines. The approach minimizes disciplinary boundaries and promotes interactive collaboration and team consensus (Bagnato & Neisworth, 1991). "Play-based" assessment for children with special needs (Linder, 1993) is an example of transdisciplinary assessment.

Transdisciplinary approaches can be likened to team teaching, with the classroom teacher and one or more specialists working together to assess, plan, and carry out appropriate activities. The specialists may be in the classroom full or part time, depending on availability and need. Boundaries between the various specialties are minimized as the team works together. Advantages of transdisciplinary assessment include the following:

- Several professionals see and relate to children in the real-life setting of the classroom. Their observations and findings complement each other's.
- Two professionals in the classroom make authentic classroom assessment more feasible.
- Interpretation of the meaning of results benefits from joint deliberation and consideration.

Collaborative Team Approaches.   Collaborative teams focus on the needs of the student rather than the special diagnoses and services of a particular specialist. Teams share decisions about and responsibility for meeting children's needs across environments. They also conduct assessments and other educational services in natural locations such as the classroom, playground, or home. Each team member observes and interacts with children at different times and in different contexts. The team accepts that all team members have important knowledge and skills that can enhance educational outcomes for a given child (Gilles & Clark, 2001).

Team members are individuals who have a vested interest in the child's education or who can offer important insight into the educational program at any given time. Figure 11.5 lists some potential team members and their roles.

Collaborative teaming has the potential for meeting several criteria of valid assessment: looking at real skills in natural settings such as home, school, and community; measuring skills that are relevant to many developmental and learning domains; and using multiple measures (different sources of information, different procedures, different contexts) over time. The practical daily concerns and contributions of teachers and parents are less likely to be disregarded, because specialists work with them to focus on the child, not the specialty.

Roles and responsibilities of the teacher in team assessment.   The roles and responsibilities of the teacher are slightly different in these approaches, although some aspects remain the same. In all approaches, teachers should

- Know what each specialist does and what their unique contributions are likely to be. Titles and areas of expertise of typical team members are listed in Figure 11.5. Depending on the situation, there might also be a cultural and language specialist, home–school liaison, or parent coordinator. Some communities have public health nurses who survey, screen, and manage family and community health care or case managers who coordinate a variety of services for individuals and families. Teachers trained in special education may have their own specialties, such as teaching children with hearing loss.
- Remember that classroom teachers, too, are specialists, with knowledge of how children develop and learn both as individuals and in groups.

Figure 11.5   Role Descriptions of Possible Team Members in Specialized Assessment and Services

Team Member	Role
Individual with Disabilities	Self-advocate who may need instruction in how to participate and how to have a strong voice in his or her educational experience.
General Education Teacher	Provides the classroom structure and age-appropriate curriculum and experiences to all students, including those with disabilities. Expertise includes grade- or subject-specific curriculum and assessment, and typical student development. Students may have more than one general education teacher, especially at the middle or high school level.
Special Education Teacher	Coordinates the support for a student with disabilities who is included in general education classrooms. Expertise includes instructional strategies, individualized assessment, adaptations and modifications that individualize general education activities, and life-skills curriculum.
Family Members	Experience the closest relationship with the student and will have the longest commitment to the student's education. Family members can provide valuable information about the student's history, culture and family values, likes and dislikes, and goals and vision for the future. They can provide the most information about the student.
Behavior Specialist	Supports the student in mediating behavioral challenges, including conducting functional behavioral assessment and developing and monitoring positive behavioral support plans.
Reading Specialist	Expertise includes knowledge of theories of reading development and experience in reading and writing instruction.
School Psychologist	Administers and interprets standardized tests to determine eligibility for special education services. Assists school personnel in assessing classroom performance, including behavioral assessment.
Physical Therapist	Expertise includes knowledge of balance, coordination, and strength, Assesses the student and assists the team in developing programs in locomotion, maintaining appropriate body posture, and positioning. Assists with maintenance of adaptive equipment.
Occupational Therapist	Provides information and strategies on improving a student's participation in activities of daily living (e.g., dressing, feeding), manipulation of objects, manual dexterity, and use of writing implements.
Speech/Language Pathologist (and Related Professionals)	Assists teams in assessing and improving an individual's communication abilities, including verbal and nonverbal communication and written and oral language. Other levels of professionals trained in this area include speech therapists and speech clinicians.
Vision Specialist	Works with students who experience low vision or blindness. May provide orientation and mobility instruction, assist peers in using social prompts that help students who are blind, and provide Braille instruction.
Audiology Specialist	Provides information, assessment, and intervention for students who are deaf or hard of hearing. Expertise includes monitoring hearing aides and providing sign language or lip reading instruction, to name a few.

(continued)

Figure 11.5 Continued

Nurse	May provide medical services—dispense medication, assist with suctioning or gastronomy tube feedings, assess physical well-being.
Counselor	May conduct assessment, provide support, serve as a resource for student's behavior or emotional health, and provide direct counseling to the student.
Transition Specialist	Assists in the assessment of transition needs and in the development and implementation of the transition plan, including career development, postsecondary education, supported or independent living, self-advocacy, and natural networks of support.
Social Worker	Can provide a link between the school and parents, collect information about the student or the family, and provide a link to student or family support programs that are governed by local agencies. May also provide support for a student's behavioral issues.
Assistive Technology Specialist	May provide different types of support in areas ranging from the use of assistive writing programs and computerized instruction to computerized communication systems.
External Agency Supports	May include social services, parent support groups, technical assistance projects, or advocacy groups. Involvement of these personnel on the assessment team provides a broader perspective of the student's life beyond the school environment.
Other Individuals from Noneducational Settings	May include people who are important in the student's life but are not typically involved in a student's education: coaches, scout leaders, respite providers, family friends, community businesspeople, and so on.

Teachers know more about setting up, planning, and implementing appropriate activities for a group of children than any other members of the team. Teachers may know the best time of the day for intervention or have insight about classroom activities that can be modified to fit a child's needs or about how to fit special needs into the overall curriculum. With well-done classroom assessment, the teacher has documented, authentic evidence of children's everyday functioning.

- Compile, summarize, and write classroom assessment information to help present and discuss the items under consideration. If necessary, point out how the evidence relates to the concern, because others may not have the classroom perspective that enables them to see the relationship.
- Be open and receptive to suggestions from other disciplines. In meetings, practice active listening. If reports are written, read them with an open mind. Even when you disagree, look for and recognize the perspectives that the other discipline brings. Almost always some aspect will contribute to understanding and helping the child or situation.
- Respect the other discipline or specialty and what it can contribute. Expect that same respect in return. There is no place for "just a teacher" or "just a parent." Teachers and parents have unique information.

- Recognize that you can't know and do everything. Seek out information and help from whatever sources are available.
- Advocate for the child.

Transdisciplinary and collaborative approaches may require some additional skills:

- The teacher may be the leader and coordinator of the team. This role includes getting people together on a regular basis to consult, evaluate, and maintain cohesiveness. Sometimes teachers and parents are the only members who are present consistently. Acting as coordinator is particularly important because some team members may be in the setting only part of the time.
- Know how to ask for advice and suggestions that can be integrated into a particular classroom or situation. Specialists may not always have a sense of a developmentally appropriate classroom. Some specialists are excellent working with one or two children but may need help to transfer their expertise to a classroom of twenty or more children. They may be unaware of classroom activities that can be adapted to meet a child's needs or of the impact of their suggestions on the rest of the classroom. Sometimes teachers have to adapt suggestions.
- Ask for clarification of anything you don't understand, and politely persist until it is clear. Reflective listening will help: "Now, let me see if I can put what you're saying in my own words."
- Be clear and specific about who is going to do what.
- With the consent and understanding of those involved, put assignments in writing. Follow up on your own assignments. Contribute to team efforts, such as compiling required reports and data.
- Support, respect, and, if necessary, coach parents who are team members so they can contribute their extensive knowledge of the child and can benefit from the expertise of the other team members.

Working with Specialists Individually. Teachers also work with specialists individually—sharing concerns, seeking advice, consulting, and working together to plan programs that are integrated and complementary. These relationships are often far more informal. A specialist may be able to help with an appraisal, confirm a concern, or come into the classroom to try out some activities. There is no need to wait until you have a full assessment done and summarized, but do have some documentation so consultation is fruitful. Specialists can help teachers know when "red flags" need to be further examined (see Appendix B).

Specialists help develop and monitor "prereferral strategies" to determine whether children can function in the regular classroom without specialized services.

Working with Community Resources. Many private preschools and child care and child development centers do not have specialists, or even a set process to get specialists for consultation. Teachers at these centers have to know and depend on public and private community resources, such as Child Find or local health agencies. If assessment reveals a special concern, have some possible course of action for parents to take, even if it is no more than saying, "Talk with your pediatrician, and get a recommendation and referral from her." School districts usually have defined processes.

Professional and Personal Development and Learning

Self-reflection and self-assessment are part of classroom assessment, for both teachers and children. Teachers keep logs or journals that record their reflections on events of the day or week, their frustrations, joys, triumphs, and hopes in their professional and personal growth and development (Brandt, 1991; Hebert, 1992, 1998).

Professional Development and Learning

Classroom assessment of children, and the use of that information to modify curriculum, is professionally and personally demanding but equally satisfying and rewarding. Teachers have the opportunity to expand and upgrade their professional role as they systematically assess what children know and can do, their attitudes and dispositions, and their interests and abilities. No standardized test, achievement battery, or diagnostic evaluation can bring to children's development and learning the breadth and depth of knowledge that teachers can. Increased expectations of teachers for assessment is a challenge and an opportunity. It can bring back the centrality of a group of children and adults working together to learn and allow them to discard the idea of education as a prescriptive, lock-step process.

Modifying, creating, augmenting, or simplifying curriculum experiences to meet children's needs and help them learn is enormously satisfying. To have personal knowledge, intuitions, hunches, and insights become a legitimate part of the assessment process humanizes scores, grades, and percentiles—and deepens the satisfaction.

Personal Development and Learning

Learning more about children and their development, uniqueness, and individuality and the ways they respond to and interact with people, objects, events, and activities is emotionally and intellectually satisfying. It is also humbling, because teachers begin to appreciate the complexity and mystery of human life and learning and the distressing problems that confront many young children.

On a more personal level, teachers may have to confront and face themselves to understand why it is so difficult to accept this child as she is, why it is easy to deal with a high-spirited child but difficult to help a passive youngster—or the reverse (Hannon, 2000; Humphrey, 1989; Jersild, 1955). Personal values, beliefs, and convictions come to the fore as teachers decide what is important for children's growth and development, a teacher's role in that process, and how the teacher can fulfill that role. As teachers work to help children develop and learn, they also develop and learn.

Summary

Responsibilities relating to assessment go beyond the classroom—to parents, other professionals, funding and regulatory agencies, and citizen groups. Teachers may be expected to prepare variations on two basic types of reports: narrative progress reports and ratings. Both types should be substantiated by valid and reliable data.

The skills and attitudes that create successful communication with parents involve preparing written progress statements; using simple, easy-to-understand language that is free of jargon; being selective about what is reported; being clear and supportive; answering questions; and being sensitive to the impact of what you are communicating. One of the most effective uses of assessment results is to help the family help the child develop and learn.

Teachers should keep administrators informed in a variety of ways. Schools and centers may require specific information from teachers for official administrative purposes and for reporting to funding and regulatory agencies, governing boards, or citizen groups. Increased emphasis on accountability has increased the responsibilities teachers have for such reporting.

Coordination and collaboration with community resources and with specialists in other disciplines are usually essential to meet assessed needs. The major approaches are multidisciplinary, interdisciplinary, transdisciplinary, and collaborative. Teacher roles and responsibilities in the approaches vary somewhat, but all require that teachers know what each specialist does, remember that teachers are also specialists, compile and present assessment information professionally, be receptive to and respect other disciplines, and recognize that teachers must work collaboratively with other people to fulfill their responsibilities. Additional skills and attitudes are needed to implement transdisciplinary and collaborative approaches, to work with specialists individually, and to work with families and communities.

Early childhood teachers should be alert to indicators that signal the need to gather more information and consult with parents and specialists. A guide to those indicators for children ages 3 to 5 appears in Appendix B. Use state, building, or school district guides for older children.

Finally, increased expectations for assessment conducted by teachers in the classroom present both a challenge and an opportunity for professional and personal growth. Understanding and responding to children brings the opportunity to understand more about ourselves.

For Personal Reflection

1. Reflect on the opportunities and challenges this enlarged professional responsibility for assessment offers you personally. Write a short paragraph describing them, perhaps in your teacher's journal. Share your reflections with others in your study group or class.
2. Evaluate and reflect on your current attitudes and skills in communicating assessment results to parents or specialists by comparing what you know how to do with the suggestions given in the chapter.

For Further Study and Discussion

1. Many teachers dislike report card grading and find it difficult to do. List as many reasons as you can to explain why this is so. Identify actions that teachers can take to make this essential task less difficult.
2. Put yourself in the role of a parent of a preschooler, kindergartner, or second-grader. (Some of you may be those parents.) List the assessment information you would like to have from your child's teacher.

Suggested Readings

Airasian, P. W. (2000). *Classroom assessment: A concise approach* (3rd ed.). New York: McGraw Hill.

Alper, S., Ryndak, D., & Schloss, C. (Eds.). (2001). *Alternate assessment of students with disabilites in inclusive settings.* Boston: Allyn & Bacon.

Burns, R. C. (Ed.). (1993). *Parents and schools: From visitors to partners.* Washington, DC: National Education Association.

Marzano, R. J. (2000). *Transforming classroom grading.* Alexandria, VA: Association for Supervision and Curriculum Development.

Popham, W. J. (2000). *Testing! Testing! What every parent should know about school tests.* Boston: Allyn & Bacon.

Stiggins, R. J. (1998). *Classroom assessment for student success.* Washington, DC: National Education Association.

Stone, S. J. (1995). *Understanding portfolio assessment: A guide for parents.* Reston, VA: Association for Childhood Education International.

Wolery, M., & Wilbers, J. S. (1994). *Including children with special needs in early childhood programs.* Washington, DC: National Association for the Education of Young Children.

APPENDIX A

• •

Assessment and Analysis Guides

The following assessment and analysis guides are designed to help in planning authentic assessments and in understanding and interpreting assessment information. Early childhood educators are moving from thinking of development in terms of ages and stages to the concepts of developmental accomplishments and developmental continua. A **developmental accomplishment** describes the knowledge learned or the skill level achieved or attained. In other words, developmental accomplishments describe what children should be expected to know and be able to do based on current research in child development and educational psychology. A **developmental continuum** is a predictable, but not rigid, sequence of developmental accomplishments. The continuum is not rigid because the accomplishments constitute neither an exhaustive inventory nor a required set of behaviors/indicators that a child must have in order to move on to the next accomplishment. For some areas of development, our knowledge is fairly complete, but that is not the case for all areas. Children do not necessarily go through each accomplishment in sequence. Some may skip accomplishments. Others may behave in ways that reflect two different accomplishments at the same time. Typical ages are given for the first and last accomplishments as a general guide for assessment.

The guides include expectations taken from standards documents in the areas of mathematics and literacy for prekindergarten and kindergarten (Bodrova, Leong, Paynter, & Semenov, 2000; Bodrova & Kendall, in press). These expectations were based on research as well as on position statements, standards, or guidelines developed by the National Council of Teachers of Mathematics, National Association for the Education of Young Children, and the International Reading Association.

Development is a complex process that involves multiple interactions between many different areas of development. Although the guides are organized by area, in reality all of the areas interact with each other. We hope that the lessons of Chapters 2, 7, and 8 will support the appropriate use of these guides and underscore the importance of looking at all areas of development at the same time. With use, the developmental accomplishments and continua will become so familiar that the lines that divide them into separate areas of development will become blurred, and consequently, the way that one area of development affects another will become apparent. It is only then that the complex planning and assessment process that results in true developmentally appropriate practice will occur.

Figure A.1   Assessment and Analysis Guide: Large Muscle Development

Examples of Things to Look For	Developmental Continuum
Walking: Placing one foot in front of the other while maintaining contact with floor. *Watch for:* heel–toe progression; placement of arms as child walks (smoothly in opposition to feet); length of stride; balance. Walking on a straight line is easier than on a curved line; forward is easier than walking backwards; spontaneous is easier than in rhythm to music or a drum beat.	Most children: • Can walk in a heel–toe progression with arms in opposition; up and down steps with one foot leading, then with alternating feet. (3 yrs.) • Can walk backwards; a straight path (1" wide); up and down short stairs with alternating feet; a balance beam (2–3" high) with help. • Can walk on balance beam (2–3" high); up and down ten or more stairs alternating feet with hand rail; on a circle. • Can walk in time to music; across balance beam (2–3" high); up and down ten stairs alternating feet; use roller skates. (5–6 yrs.)
Running: Placing one foot in front of the other with a brief period of no contact with floor. *Watch for:* placement of arms (should move smoothly in opposition to the feet, should not flail around, should not be stiff); balance; fluidity; speed; ability to start and stop with balance; ability to run and turn with balance.	Most children: • Can run (length of stride, balance, and smoothness begin to improve). (2–3 yrs.) • Can run more smoothly (even stride but may lack mature arm movements and form). A few children can turn, stop suddenly, or run around objects easily. • Can run with improved form, speed, and control (stopping, starting, and turning without falling). • Can run in an effective adult manner (arms across midline in rhythmic pattern, elbow bent at a right angle); combine run and jump. • Can run with longer stride; coordinate run with other motor skills (e.g., kicking); increased speed and agility. (6–8 yrs.)
Jumping: One or two foot takeoff, landing on both feet. *Watch for:* takeoff and landing, including placement of the arms on takeoff, landing, and as the jump is being made (arms aid in jump and don't flail around); bending of knees (should not be stiff); balance and fluidity. Jumps increase in distance and height. Jumping down is easier than jumping up onto something.	Most children: • Can jump off a step with both feet; jump in place with minimal crouch, may land on one or both feet (one foot ahead). (2–3 yrs.) • Can jump well in place; jump over a small object leading with one foot. • Can jump well in place; crouch for a high jump of 2"; do standing broad jump of 8–10". A few children can jump over a barrier. • Can jump over barriers; make a vertical jump; do a running broad jump. • Can jump rope in a simple pattern; jump onto a target. • Can do jumping jacks; jump rope in complex patterns; a standing broad jump with deep crouch (arms swing further back behind body and continue until body is fully extended, and synchronized); jump and catch ball. (7–8 yrs.)
Hopping: One foot takeoff and landing on the same foot.	Most children: • Cannot hop; make irregular steps instead of a hop. Some children attempt a hop. (2–3 yrs.)

Figure A.1 Continued

Examples of Things to Look For	Developmental Continuum
Watch for: takeoff and landing; placement of arms (arms swing and aid in takeoff and landing, no flailing); isolation of the hopping side; balance; fluidity (should not be stiff); preference for one foot.	Most children: • Can hop once or twice on preferred leg; execute ten hops in a row on preferred leg. (3–4 yrs.) • Can hop a distance of 5'. • Can hop distance of 16'; use arms in opposition to feet; use either foot. • Can hop onto small squares. • Can hop in an alternate rhythmic pattern (2–2, 2–3, or 3–3 pattern). (7–8 yrs.)
Galloping: Step (walk) leap with same foot leading. **Skipping:** Step (walk) hop in rhythmic alternation. *Watch for:* patterned use of the feet; use of arms (should move smoothly, no flailing); coordination; balance; ability to sustain the pattern.	Most children: • Attempt a gallop. (3 yrs.) • Perform a shuffle step (side step). • Step hop on one foot. Some gallop fairly well with preferred foot. • Gallop fairly well (not proficiently). Some children can skip. • Can skip with ease. (6–7 yrs.)
Kicking: Moving an object by striking it with the foot. *Watch for:* stance; standing on two feet, stepping forward with balance (older children may be able to move forward several steps and kick); movement of kicking leg; balance on contact with ball and follow-through; placement of arms (no flailing); fluidity; coordination of nonkicking side (no extraneous movements). Early kicking with stationary ball, then ball rolling directly to child (can't shift position), then ball rolling and child meets it.	Most children: • Kick with leg stiff, straight leg, and little body movement. (2–3 yrs.) • Kick with lower leg bent on backward lift and straight on forward swing. • Kick with greater backward and forward swing; use arms in opposition to legs; step into ball. • Kick using mature pattern; kick through ball with arms synchronized; kick ball tossed into air with straight leg. • Run and kick in stride. • Kick proficiently and accurately; intercept a ball; adjust kicking to height of ball; can aim ball. (7–8 yrs.)
Throwing: Using hands and arm to propel an object through the air—overhand or underhand. *Watch for:* smooth fluid motion of throwing arm; coordination of nonthrowing arm (no extraneous movements); balance; stance; rotation of body (older children also lean slightly backwards); step forward as object is released; follow-through of throwing arm; whipping motion of the arm on release; arc of throw. Early throwing, no weight transfer. Smaller balls are easier to throw.	Most children: • Face target and use both forearms to push; throw with little or no footwork or body rotation; may lose balance while throwing. (2–3 yrs.) • Throw overhand or underhand with one arm fairly well; use some body rotation; may release ball too early or late. • Throw proficiently for longer distances, with more mature overhand motion (at elbow); may prefer overhand or underhand. • Throw in a mature pattern; step forward; improved accuracy; fluid follow-through. • Throw overhand with whipping motion (lean body back in preparation); underhand with explosive release. (7–8 yrs.)

(continued)

Figure A.1 Continued

Examples of Things to Look For	Developmental Continuum
Catching: Using hands to grasp or capture an object thrown through air. *Watch for:* stance (balanced, can move and catch); placement of the arms (trap against body or grasped with hands); following of object's path with eyes; positioning self under object; adjusting hand position to size of object. At the beginning, catches involve a ball rolling on ground. Large balls are easier to catch. Child may show more mature catching with large balls.	Most children: • Stop rolling object with hands; stand with arms stiff; may close eyes, arch body away; close arms after object hits body. (2–3 yrs.) • Hold arms out straight, stiff with hands facing object; trap against body. Catch bounced ball. • Hold arms flexed at elbows; trap against body. Some children catch with hands. • Try catching with hands; may still trap; follow trajectory of ball better. About half of the children can catch with hands. • Are moderately proficient; flex elbows with hands forward; make contact with hands; may juggle object. • Can catch with hands, little juggling; judge trajectory fairly well; move into position; adjust hand position to size of object. (7 yrs. and older)
Perceptual Motor Abilities: Body, timing, and directional awareness. Ability to imitate by watching and listening to a model. *Watch for:* ability to clap to a steady beat; walk, jump, hop, gallop, or skip to a beat or to music; control of body when moving (no extraneous movements); sense of external space (doesn't walk into things, bump into people when moving); mimic movements of another person; perform a movement after listening to verbal directions.	Most children: • Can identify parts of the body; clap a simple rhythm; still lack spatial and directional awareness. (3–4 yrs.) • Can mimic demonstrated movements presented in a sequence (clapping pattern); use verbal directions to execute a simple movement sequence; walk to the beat of a musical selection. • Most children have trouble memorizing a sequence of movements. (6–7 yrs.)
Physical Fitness: The child's physical state after vigorous exercise and the ability to sustain vigorous exercise. *Watch for:* sustained enthusiastic performance of the movements; the amount of time a child spends in vigorous exercise; child's reaction to being tired (shortness of breath, absence of strength).	Most children: • Can exercise vigorously for 10–15 minutes without needing to stop. (5 yrs.) • Can exercise vigorously for 15–20 minutes. (8 yrs.)

Adapted from: National Association for Sport and Physical Education (2004); Berk, 2006; Corbin, 1980; Council on Physical Education for Children, 2000; Gallahue, 1982; Hastie & Martin, 2006; Hetherington, Parke, Gauvain, & Locke, 2005; Poest, Williams, Witt, & Atwood, 1990; Schirmer, 1974; Sinclair, 1973; Thomas, Lee, & Thomas, 1988; Weeks & Ewer-Jones, 1991, Weikert, 1987; Wickstrom, 1983; Williams, 1991.

Figure A.2   Assessment and Analysis Guide: Small Muscle Development

Examples of Things to Look For	Developmental Continuum
Manipulation/Manipulatives: Ability to manipulate with hand and fingers. *Watch for:* dexterity; flexibility; precision and control; coordination; sensory perceptual integration; how child stacks, moves, and rotates objects; which fingers are used; fluid finger movements (no false starts, no using chest or table to aid in manipulation, one finger or group of fingers not sticking out in an awkward manner); preference for right or left hand (one hand will be more coordinated).	Most children: • Place simple geometric shapes in puzzle; string large beads; turn pages of book; work 4-piece puzzle; use pegboard with large pegs; stack small wooden blocks; do a fingerplay (fingers not independent); roll, squeeze, and pound modeling clay. (2–3 yrs.) • Can string small wooden beads; work a 5-piece puzzle; use pegboard with small pegs; use fingers more independently; make balls and use tools with modeling clay (use cookie cutter). • Can work a 12-piece puzzle; build complex structures with small blocks; braid; use fingers independently in fingerplays; attempt a pinch pot, coil pot, or "sculpture." • Can build complex structures with small interlocking blocks; make a pinch, coil pot, or sculpture. • Can swing a hammer accurately; sew and knit. (7–8 yrs.)
Self-Help Skills: Ability to eat, dress, and take care of self. *Watch for:* grasp of eating utensil; eating without dropping or getting food all over clothes/face; size of buttons, how many fingers used, ability to button/unbutton; zipping/unzipping.	Most children: • Can eat with spoon; hold cup in one hand; put on a coat (unassisted); unbutton clothes. (2–3 yrs.) • Can eat correctly with fork; button and unbutton clothes; zip zippers haltingly; put coat on hanger. • Can button/unbutton clothes; zip zippers; eat with knife and fork; dress/undress; comb and brush hair; tie shoelaces. (5–6 yrs.)
Scissors, Paste, and Glue: Ability to use scissors, paste, and glue. *Watch for:* dexterity; precision and control; coordination; sensory perceptual integration; thumbs-up grasp of scissors; thumbs-up grasp of paper; scissors held straight as cut is made, no twisting or tearing of paper, straight not jagged edges, hand holding paper moves along as other hand cuts; control of amount of paste (no excessive globs); use of fingers or stick to spread paste.	Most children: • Snip paper easily (cuts at edge of paper); scissors and paper held incorrectly; use large globs of paste or glue with little control. (2–3 yrs.) • Make one full cut with scissors (cuts one length of scissors); hand position may be incorrect; make two full cuts (two lengths of scissors); have trouble cutting on straight line; use globs of paste or glue but have more control; use index finger to apply paste. • Cut on a straight line and a corner (90-degree angle) moving paper hand forward; use correct hand position; keep paste and glue in right spot and use reasonable amount. • Can cut on a curve; cut out simple geometric figure; cut interior angles (inside angle less than 90 degrees); cut out obtuse and acute angles; cut out a complex figure from a magazine; use scissors and paste/glue to make designs. (5–6 yrs.)

(continued)

Figure A.2   Continued

Examples of Things to Look For	Developmental Continuum
Use of Writing Instruments: Ability to hold and use pencils, pens, crayons, markers, and paint brushes. *Watch for:* dexterity; precision and control; coordination; sensory perceptual integration; grasp of instrument (whole hand or three-point finger grasp); grasp should be firm (should not be too tight or too loose); position of hand on instrument (should not be too close to the eraser/top of pencil/pen or too close to point/paper); type of marks (stabs at paper, fluid scribbles, or careful formation of lines, such as in letters or a figure with a stopping and starting place); child drawings (human face, stick figures, features placed correctly, detail in features, and addition of scenery, such as houses, animals, trees, grass, and the sky); proportionate size of figures in drawing (house should be bigger than child); repeated features in scribbles (do scribbles look random or like attempts at writing?).	Most children: • Grasp writing implements with whole hand or fist; jab at paper; make scribbles with movement of whole arm; copy vertical and horizontal lines. (2–3 yrs.) • Try a three-point grasp but position on instrument inconsistent; copy a cross and a circle; scribble with spots of intense color; use horizontal and vertical lines, crosses, and circles in pictures. • Use correct hand grasp but position on instrument still inconsistent; copy a square and some letters (from first and last name); draw suns; draw human figures, a head with facial features (placement of eye, nose, mouth may not be correct); draw human figures with stick arms and legs and facial parts in correct place; scribble with repeated features and on a horizontal line (looks like writing); scribble leaving space between "words." • Can form written letters (many inverted or mirror images); color between lines; draw buildings, cars, and boats (proportions incorrect—people are larger than the buildings); trees and flowers; draw with correct proportions; incorporate letters into scribbling; write letters of first name (may not write letters in a line); write letters of last name (may not write letters in a line); draw rectangle, circle, and square. • Hold pencil with fingertips; draw triangles; follow simple mazes; copy most letters (some still inverted); form words with letters (words may run together; words may begin on one line and end on another); write upper- and lowercase letters and numbers 1–10. • Can space words when writing; print accurately and neatly; copy a diamond correctly; begin to use cursive writing. (7–8 yrs).

Adapted from: Ashton-Lilo, 1987; Beaty, 1994; Berk, 2006; Bodrova, Leong, Paynter, & Semenov, 2000; Guerin & Maier, 1983; Levine, 1995; Mowbray & Salisbury, 1975; Papalia, Olds, & Feldman, 2004; Schiamberg, 1988; Schickedanz & Casbergue, 2004; Schickedanz, Schickedanz, Forsyth, & Forsyth, 2001; Schirmer, 1974; Schwartz & Robinson, 1982; Thompson, 1986; Weeks & Ewer-Jones, 1991.

Figure A.3 Assessment and Analysis Guide: Knowledge Base—Basic Concepts of Mathematics, Science, and Social Studies

Examples of Things to Look For	Developmental Continuum
Basic Concepts: *Watch for:* how much a child knows prior to instruction; use of knowledge base when learning new information; quantity and quality of information; use of concept at receptive level (point to, place object, nod in response); concept used at expressive level (tell name of); spontaneous use.	Most children: • Know the concepts big/little, tall/short, long/short, high/low, wide/narrow, thick/thin, deep/shallow, on, next to, in, outside, inside, down, and up. • Likely to make errors on underneath, below, over, and under. • Know full/empty, light/heavy, bottom/top/middle; first, second, third; rectangle, triangle, circle, line. (4–5 yrs.) • Can tell which of two objects is same/longer/shorter, lighter/heavier, full/less full. • Uses spatial terms relative to own body as well as relative to other people or objects.
Color Concepts: *Watch for:* ability to point to a color when asked; state color name when asked; spontaneous use of color concepts and names. Infrequently used color concepts are acquired later than those frequently used.	Most children: • Know red, green, black, white, orange, yellow, blue, pink, brown, purple; most color names. (5 yrs.)
Mathematics Concepts: <u>Number and Operation</u> *Watch for the way a child attempts to:* use number to describe objects in the environment and during play; identify the number of objects in a collection without counting and with counting; identify the number of objects when objects are added or subtracted (small total number); use strategies to solve simple problems.	Many children: • Match objects one to one and count a small collection of 1–4 items. Answer question "How many?". • Know number words one to five (rote counts). • "See" and use a number to describe collections of one to three; can add and subtract with one to three objects. (3 yrs.) • Know number words one to ten (rote counting). • Has one to one correspondence. (3–4 yrs.) • Count ten to twenty objects. Know that smaller numbers are first, larger numbers are later (ordinal principle). • Know that the last number is equal to the total number (cardinal principle), and can count any collection of objects (abstraction principle). Understand that the order of the objects counted does not affect the total number. (4–5 yrs.) • Distinguish more/same/not as much (many) as/less (fewer) than (without counting) for collections with visible differences in amount under twenty. • Know ordinal numbers 1st to 5th. • Know whole objects are made up of parts (fractions). • Know that when two groups of objects have the same number, they are the same. • Count starting on a number other than 1 (e.g., 5, 6, 7, 8, 9). • Know that a larger number is made up of smaller numbers. • Recognize and write numbers one to ten. (5–6 yrs.) • Know number words to twenty.

(continued)

Figure A.3 Continued

Examples of Things to Look For	Developmental Continuum
Mathematics Concepts: <u>Number and Operation</u> *(continued)*	• Know that the pattern of number words over twenty is the same as the pattern of number words one to ten (twenty-one, twenty-two, twenty-three, etc.). • Know the concept of "half." Can divide a whole object or collections of objects into two equal parts. • Know if you add an object, you increase the number in the collection. If you take an object away, you decrease the number in a collection. • Count and produce (create) a collection given the number up to 100. (6–7 yrs.) • "See" and label patterned collection (on dice or dominos) and unpatterned collections of up to six items. (6 yrs.) • Add or subtract using counting-based strategies, such as counting on when numbers under ten. • Can use concrete manipulatives to solve simple word problems. • Show an intuitive grasp of number; formal instruction in mathematics has begun. Consult curriculum guides and NCTM standards for information. (6–7 yrs.)
<u>Geometry and Spatial Sense</u> *Watch to see if a child can:* use shapes to make pictures, name different shapes, name shapes contained in objects, label shapes in the environment (two- and three-dimensional), use geometry vocabulary.	Most children: • Begin to match and name two-dimensional and three-dimensional shapes, first naming the object only. (3–4 yrs.) • Know that "shape" is a constant characteristic unchanged by orientation in space. • Use shapes to create a picture. Can find a shape in a simple picture. Link shape to object (round like a ball, etc.). • Use spatial words like "next to," "behind," "under," etc. • Build "maps" using objects to representing places and things (houses, cars, roads, etc.). • Describe shapes using descriptors for size and location or position ("next to the large triangle"); use spatial words "under," "behind." (4–5 yrs.) • Recognize and name a variety of 2-D and 3-D shapes, such as quadrilaterals, trapezoids, rhombi, hexagons, cubes, and spheres; can identify angle, sides. (5–6 yrs.) • Make pictures by combining shapes. • Draw and can follow simple maps of familiar places, such as of the classroom or playground. • Predict what a 3-D shape would look like if it were flipped or rotated in space. • Use spatial terms relative to the position of other people or objects ("The block is in front of you but behind the chair.").
<u>Measurement</u> *Watch for:* attempts to measure using other objects, hand/fingers, arms, footsteps, use of measurement tools, such a scale, ruler, measuring cups, etc.	Most children: • Recognize and label the attributes of objects using measurement terms (heavy/light, long/short, full/less full, taller/shorter, etc.). (3–4 yrs.) • Compare and sort objects according to their attributes. (Place all the tall blocks in one pile and the short blocks in another.) Can sort by two attributes.

Figure A.3   Continued

Examples of Things to Look For	Developmental Continuum
	• Can place objects in order according to a measurable attribute (size, weight, length, etc.). • Experiment with ways of measuring things (uses different size cups to measure water or different objects to compare length). Comment on differences in measurement between children ("I got 2 cups") and between different types of measures ("2 small cups makes 1 big cup"). • Understand vocabulary associated with differences in measurable attributes (smaller, smallest, smaller than, etc.). • Uses nonstandard and standard measuring tools. • Know time words "before," "after," "yesterday," etc. • Know that time measures the duration or length of an event. • Know the purpose of a clock and calendar is to measure time. • Understand basic ideas about using measuring tools (Place the ruler so the end is even with the end of the object you want to measure.). (5–6 yrs.) • Use number with measurement (2 inches). Understand that number principles apply to measurement (You add an inch, the number is bigger). • Estimate measurement and quantity. • Use time words (second, minute, hour, day, week) to describe the duration of events.
Pattern/algebraic thinking *Watch for:* attempts to create patterns during play with manipulatives or responses to patterns in the environment.	Many children: • Notice and copy simple repeating patterns. (3–4 yrs.) • Represent patterns with different objects. • Can extend a pattern. • Can create growing patterns. (4–5 yrs.) • Notice and discuss patterns in arithmetic. (5–6 yrs.)
Displaying and analyzing data. *Watch for:* attempts to represent counting and sorting in a display or representation in a drawing; attempts to understand graphs and tables.	Many children: • Sort objects, count, and compare groups in terms of size of group or number of objects. • Participate in making a simple graph (places choice in correct column of a participation chart). (3–4 yrs.) • Compare simple graphs. (4–5 yrs.) • Create a simple graph using a symbol, such as tally marks or blocks to stand for the objects or attribute. (5–6 yrs.) For example, places two tally marks on a piece of paper to stand for the two blue blocks in the collection. • Represent the data using numerical summaries, such as creating a bar graph using numbers. (6–7 yrs.) • Can read different types of graphs and tables.

(continued)

Figure A.3   Continued

Examples of Things to Look For	Developmental Continuum
Scientific Concepts: *Watch for:* descriptions of scientific phenomena; use of scientific vocabulary; use observation and experimentation to understand the natural world.	Most children: • Know that objects can be perceived by different senses and that these senses give different information. (3–4 yrs.) • Use simple tools to make observations (magnifying glass, scales, etc.). • Ask questions about observable phenomena. (Why are trees so big?) • Know general properties of physical environment (seasons, weather, rock, mountains, rivers, lakes, oceans, etc.). • Ask questions about inferred phenomena. (Why does a plant need roots?) (5–6 yrs.) • Ask questions about details of observations. (Why are there different kinds of hair on my dog?) • Use everyday language to explain scientific phenomena. • Begin to use scientific words to explain phenomena. • Know that physical properties of things can change (ice melts, etc.). • Conduct simple experiments with adult guidance to understand phenomena. • Know simple scientific concepts are based on the observable world. (6–7 yrs.) • Use simple scientific concepts to explain natural phenomena. • Understand how an investigation or experiment can answer scientific questions. • Can classify objects and things based on inferred attributes and knows some scientific categories (mammals vs. reptiles, objects that sink and objects that float, etc.). • Know that the life cycle for different living things is different.
Social Studies: *Watch for:* interest and understanding about culture, people, places and the environment, groups and institutions, other countries, and civic ideas (good citizenship, diversity, sense of community.	The National Council for Social Studies sets the following expectations for early childhood: Kindergarten: Awareness of self in the social setting. First grade: The individual in school and family life. Second grade: The neighborhood. Third grade: Sharing the earth with others in the community.

Adapted from: Baroody, 1993; Berk, 2006; Bodrova & Kendall, in press; Boehm, 1991; Castaneda, 1987; Clements & Sarama, 2004; Clark & Clark, 1977; Cole, Cole, & Lightfoot, 2004; Copely, 1998, 2000; DeVilliers & DeVilliers, 1978; Dutton & Dutton, 1991; Flavell, 1963; Foreman & Kaden, 1987; Fuson, 2003; Hinitz, 1987; Hoff, 2004; Kamii & Houseman, 2000; Mindes, 2005; National Council for Social Studies [NCSS] Task Force on Early Childhood/Elementary School Social Studies, 1988; NAEYC & NCTM, 2002, 2003; NCSS, 1994; Ormrod, 2002; Paynter, Bodrova, & Doty, 2005; Richardson, 2000; Seefeldt, 2000; Wadsworth, 2003.

Figure A.4   Assessment and Analysis Guide: Cognitive Development—Memory

Examples of Things to Look For	Developmental Continuum
Attention: *Watch for:* ability to point to or identify differences between two pictures; confusion between letters (*b* and *d*); sense used to take in information (looking or listening); signs of attending; ability to block out distractions; ability to attend when asked; different levels of attention (concentrates more on certain tasks or at certain points in a task—is there a pattern?); ability to vary attention based on the material to be learned (focus more on items that are not known or that were missed); response to teacher cues to attend (verbal cues such as "Look up here," "Pay attention," or nonverbal cues such as pointing at something); the cues child notices (confusing "this" and "that" when reading).	Be aware of cultural differences in the way children signal they are paying attention. Most children: • Can concentrate and attend when interested; scan something visually to search, but not systematically; discriminate letters with vertical and horizontal lines (*E* vs. *M*) and right side up versus upside down (*M* vs. *W*). • Have trouble attending when asked (if task is not of inherent interest); recognizing and responding appropriately to the teacher's cues to attend, ignoring distractions (color, movement, loudness); discriminating letters that are mirror images (*d* and *b*, *p* and *q*); shifting attention from one task to another or concentrating more on certain tasks or aspects of a task. (4–6 yrs.) • Can control attention; scan systematically; vary attention (although not as well as 12-year-olds); discriminate between letters; recognize and respond to most teacher cues to attend. Beginning of cognitive self-regulation. Uses self-talk (private speech) to maintain attention. • May need significant teacher help to maintain and focus attention or need coaching on interpreting subtle teacher signals for attention. (6 yrs. and older)
Memory Strategies: *Watch for:* amount of information remembered; number of spontaneous strategies used; response to suggested strategies; description of strategies. Strategies are: *Rehearsal*—repeats information over and over, copies it (older children only). *Organization*—sorts or groups items (rearrange the spelling list so that similar words are together). Organizing objects in semantic categories (using words) rather than associations (what goes with this) is more mature. *Elaboration*—makes connections and relationships between new information and prior knowledge and experience ("I saw a frog just like that one at the zoo"; "That word looks kind of like 'thin' except it has a *k* at the end").	Most children: • Have a memory span of two items, use naming and looking as early strategies. (2–3 yrs.) • Show recognition for fifty-plus items; know scripts of familiar routines; begin to use some rehearsal; memory span of three to four items. • Can use rehearsal strategies; use simple organization; state when task is easy or hard to remember. Beginning of cognitive self-regulation. Is aware of own thinking. • Can use rehearsal strategies; use organization. A few children can use elaboration spontaneously. (7–8 yrs.) *Note:* Training in rehearsal, organization, and elaboration will improve ability to remember, even for 2-year-olds. The use of new strategies requires constant adult coaching (telling child which strategy to use).

Adapted from: Beihler & Snowman, 2004; Berk, 2006; Blair, 2002; Berliner & Rosenshine, 1987; Bjorklund, 2004; Brown, 1991; Clark & Clark, 1977; Cole, Cole, & Lightfoot, 2004; Corno, 1987; Feldman, 2001; Gage & Berliner, 1998; Grabe, 1986; Oates & Grayson, 2004; Ormrod, 2002; Phye & Andre, 1986; Resnick & Resnick, 1992; Slavin, 2005; Sternberg & Williams, 2001; Winne & Marx, 1987; Woolfolk, 2003.

Figure A.5   Assessment and Analysis Guide: Cognitive Development—Thinking

Examples of Things to Look For	Developmental Continuum
Symbolic Thought: Ability to manipulate and use symbols in thinking. *Watch for:* use of language as a tool for thinking; use of an object to stand for something else (doll is a baby); plays different roles; representational drawings (drawing of a specific thing decided on in advance); use of written symbols as a tool for thinking (will make marks to signify a pattern, writes words); use of graphs to symbolize numbers.	Information about the manipulation of roles as a part of symbolic thought is in Figure A.9 under Sociodramatic Play. Most children: • Can use language as a tool for thinking; engage in symbolic play (use object to stand for something else or play different roles). Some children can make representational drawings. (2 yrs.) • Can engage in representational drawing. Some children can use written symbols (write name, some numbers); make and interpret graphs with help from teacher. • Can use written symbols; make and interpret graphs. (6 yrs. and older)
Classification: Ability to sort and group objects. *Watch for:* ability to sort and re-sort spontaneously; with properties given by teacher; by a single property (size, color, shape); by many properties simultaneously; by similarity (all buttons, all blocks); by all–some (all same object but different color); into a series (big, bigger, biggest). Children may state attribute; use of same principle to add new objects; create a simple pattern; create a complex, extended pattern.	Most children: • Are not systematic or consistent in use of attributes to form the group. (2–3 yrs.) • Can classify based on one attribute; place objects in a series by one attribute; make a simple line pattern (ABABAB). • Can classify based on two attributes simultaneously (large blue, small blue, large red, small red); classify subgroups once groups are formed; make a complete line pattern (AABBCCAABBCC or ABCCABCCABCC). • Can classify based on multiple attributes; understand relationship between broader classes and subclasses (objects can belong to several classes at the same time); classify based on two attributes at the same time (2 × 2 matrix). (6–8 yrs.)
Problem Solving: Use of available information, resources, and materials to achieve a goal. *Watch for:* scripts (expected sequences of events developed from past); analysis (identify components, features, processes, arguments, events); comparisons; inferences (draw conclusions, make predictions, pose hypotheses, make educated guesses); evaluation of ideas; identification of the problem. Children may use formulas (math formulas, specific "recipes"); rules of thumb (strategies or estimations that	Children of all ages benefit from teacher guidance and help when solutions do not work. Most children: • Can use scripts to solve everyday problems; generate hypotheses (may be intuitive, not logical); use analysis; make comparisons; evaluate ideas; identify problems; use formulas, rules of thumb, and trial and error spontaneously. (3–6 yrs.) • Make inferences based on logical rules; tell if they need more information; make psychological inferences. • Use formulas, rules of thumb, think-aloud strategies, work backwards strategies; use trial and error; and break large problems into smaller ones. (7–8 yrs.) • With teacher support children 5 years and older can engage in metacognitive skills such as thinking about the

Figure A.5   Continued

Examples of Things to Look For	Developmental Continuum
have worked in the past but don't guarantee a solution); think-aloud strategy (talk problem through aloud); work backwards strategy (start with the end or a possible solution first and work backwards to see if this matches the givens); use trial and error (try one solution and when it fails try another); break problem into a number of smaller problems.	problem-solving process; asking clarifying questions; planning a solution; reflecting on learning, errors, and understandings. Are able to think reflectively about mental processes, showing growing self-regulation of cognitive processes.
Conservation: All conservation tasks involve objects with the same physical attributes (number, mass, weight, length, area, volume) that are rearranged in front of the child to look very different. *Watch for:* response to Piagetian tasks or way child plays with quantity or amount; justification for answer; number conservation (the number of objects does not change when objects are arranged differently—one set in a pile and one set in a row); length (the length does not change even though objects are arranged differently); liquid (the amount of liquid does not change even though the liquid is in containers that look different— one tall and thin and the other short and wide); mass (the amount of clay in two balls does not change even though the balls look different—one is a ball and the other rolled into a snake).	Most children: • Cannot conserve; will state one object or group of objects is _____ (more, longer, bigger). Current research suggests that preoperational children can conserve number with four or fewer objects, but may not be able to justify or explain their answers. (2–5 yrs.) • Can conserve number, length, liquid, and mass; typical justifications are: "You didn't add any or take any away"; "You just moved them and if you moved them back, there would be the same _____"; "It doesn't matter how you arrange them"; "They just look different, but they are the same _____." (6–8 yrs.)

Adapted from: Baumeister & Vons, 2004; Beihler & Snowman, 2004; Berk, 2006; Bukatko & Daehler, 2003; Bjorklund, 2004; Blair, 2002; Bronson, 2000; Charlesworth, 2003; Clark & Clark, 1977; Cole, Cole, & Lightfoot, 2004; DeVries, Zann, Hildebrand, & Edmiaston, 2000; Dutton & Dutton, 1991; Flavell, 1963; Gage & Berliner, 1998; Ginsberg & Opper, 1988; Hetherington, Parke, Gauvain, & Locke, 2005; Hoff, 2004; Kamii & Rosenblum, 1990; Papalia, Olds, & Feldman, 2004; Ormrod, 2002; Phye & Andre, 1986; Schultz, Colarusso, & Strawderman, 1989; Slavin, 2005; Tharp & Gallimore, 1988; Wadsworth, 1978, 2003.

Figure A.6   Assessment and Analysis Guide: Language Development—Oral Language

Examples of Things to Look For	Developmental Continuum
Articulation: Ability to pronounce words and to understand speech sounds. *Watch for:* pronunciation and enunciation; deletion of sounds (*nana* for *banana*); substitution of sounds (*dis* for *this*).	Most children: • May repeat initial consonant vowel in multisyllabic words (*gege* for *cookie*); delete unstressed syllables (*nana* for *banana*); replace fricatives' hissing sounds with stop consonants (*tea* for *sea*, *tay* for *say*); replace liquid sounds (*l* and *r*) with glides (*w* or *j*)—(*wed* for *red*, *yewwo* for *yellow*, *jap* for *lap*); reduce consonant clusters (*pay* for *play*, *tain* for *train*); pronounce vowel sounds and *p* (pin), *b* (big), *m* (mama), *w* (want), *h* (house) correctly. (2–3 yrs.) • Have few mispronunciations; still replace liquid sounds; pronounce *d* (dog), *k* (cat), *g* (gone), *f* (feet), *n* (no), *ng* (swing). • Are 90% intelligible; have mastered most sounds, including *sh* (ship), *s* (sit), *ch* (chip), *v* (very), *r* (run), *l* (lamp). • Are 100% intelligible; can pronounce *z* (zip), *th* (this, thin), *j* (jump), *zh* (sure). (7–8 yrs.)
Vocabulary: Understanding word and sentence meaning. The type of concepts understood are discussed in Figure A.3. *Watch for:* use and understanding of words and sentences; literal versus abstract meanings; use of jokes and humor.	Receptive level/comprehension vocabulary much larger (for example, 3–4 years receptive = 1,500 words, expressive = 600–1,000 words). Most children • Understand possessives, common verbs, adjectives; understand function of many common nouns ("What do you write with?"). (2–3 yrs.) • Follow complex three-step commands; interpret words literally ("She's a cold person," meaning she feels cold). • Understand polite forms (Would you like to sit down?). • Understand indirect speech acts ("It's cold outside," meaning it's cold next to the window); words less literally ("She's a cold person," meaning she does not express affection); jokes based on phonological ambiguity—play on sounds ("What do you call a cow that eats grass? A lawn-moo-er"). • Appreciate jokes based on puns or double meanings of words—lexical ambiguity ("What did the grape say when the elephant stepped on it? It just let out a little 'wine' "); understand the difference between *promise* and *tell, ask* and *tell.* (6–7 yrs.)
Grammar: Ability to use the rules of grammar to produce sentences. *Watch for:* number of words used in an utterance; types of words used (nouns, pronouns, verbs, adjectives, and adverbs); verb tenses used (present, present progressive, simple	Most children: • Use present progressive tense (-ing); prepositions (on, in); plural nouns (dogs); verb "be" with adjective ("He is fun"); prepositions (in, for, from, with, to); noun phrases ("The book of dogs"); articles (a, an, the); regular past tense (walk*ed*); third-person regular present tense (he read*s* it); irregular present tense (has, does); contractions

Figure A.6   Continued

Examples of Things to Look For	Developmental Continuum
past, complex past, future); use of negatives (not, -n't); types of questions asked (simple: "What are you doing?"; tag questions: "This is yours, isn't it?"); coordinating conjunctions such as *and* to join two sentences ("The car was red and it made a lot of noise."); verb phrases ("He wanted to eat dinner."); embedded clauses ("I know he went home."); indirect object–direct object constructions ("Taylor gave me the toy."); passive voice ("The gingerbread man was eaten by the fox."); infinitive phrases ("Marcia is easy to please."); pronoun and referent ("When he liked you, he was nice.").	with "be" (He's tall); overregularizations, such as went*ed*, fell*ded*, foot*es*, men*s*, and mouse*s*. Some children use negations (-n't, not); questions ("What he doing?" "Where she going?"). (2–3½ yrs.) • Can use complex sentences with *and* and *wh* clauses (what, who, why, where, or when) ("I don't know *where* it is."). Most children use question forms with inverted auxiliary verb ("What *are* you doing?"), negations (-n't, not). • Use three- to four-syllable words; more adjectives, adverbs, and conjunctions; four- to six-word sentences. Ask meaning of words. • Use long complex sentences (more than six words); clauses ("The man who lived next door."); pronouns with referent ("After he ate, Bill went home."); passive voice with more than one attribute ("This is taller and thinner."); indirect requests ("Can I interest you in some cake?"); a variety of semantic structures to express the same idea; use grammar consciously and can describe why something is or is not correct (metalinguistic awareness). (5 yrs. and older)
Conversational skills: Ability to engage in effective and appropriate conversations with others. *Watch for:* the number of times child takes turns talking; appropriate turn-taking (doesn't interrupt, distract); sensitivity to listener's needs (clarification of unclear utterances); adjustments in speech with context (peers, teacher, younger children, or when playing different roles); manner of introducing new conversation topics (gradually or abruptly); ability to understand humor, irony, and sarcasm; use of different forms of speech, such as polite forms ("May I please have some?"), indirect forms ("Would you mind if I looked at it?"), and current slang.	Most children: • Can sustain conversations for two turns (respond to previous utterances); change tone of voice when playing "baby"; use language as a tool (i.e., make a request, get attention of others, assert rights). (2–3 yrs.) • Sustain conversations for three to four turns; understand intent of indirect requests for action; revise speech when asked (primarily by pointing); ask others to clarify ambiguous sentences; change speech used when playing stereotypic roles (doctor, mother, father); use some slang; more adept at using language as a tool; use polite forms; monitor conversations and make comments; project beyond present and create images for play. • Carry on complex conversations (six turns or more); change conversation by modifying topic gradually; use slang with peers; use deference when making requests from adults; use subtle cues in speech to adjust to, convey, and maintain social status; adjust speech depending on need of listener (can judge when to add more detail); are sophisticated at using language as a tool. (5 yrs. and older)

Adapted from Adger, Snow, & Christian, 2002; Berk 2006; Blank, Rose, & Berlin, 1978; Cazden 1972, 2001; Charlesworth, 2003; Clark & Clark, 1977; Cole, Cole, & Lightfoot, 2004; DeVilliers & DeVilliers, 1978; Genishi, 1987, 1988, 1992; Gleason, 2004; Hoff, 2004; Linfors, 1987; Locke, 1993; Menyuk, 1988; Messer, 1995; Owens, 2004; Petty, Petty, & Salzer, 1989; Roskos, Tabors, & Lenhart, 2004; Schaefer, Staub, & Smith, 1983; Trawick-Smith, 2005; Tough, 1977; Woolfolk, 2003.

Figure A.7 Assessment and Analysis Guide: Language Development—Literacy Development

Examples of Things to Look For	Developmental Continuum
Book and Print Concepts: Understanding how books and print work. *Watch for:* book held correctly; page turning (without bending or ripping) moving from the front to the back of the book; ability to identify cover and end of the book; ability to point out print in the environment and in books; ability to distinguish print from pictures and an understanding that text is read; ability to point along the line of print; ("reading" left to right and top to bottom, sweep to the next line); growing understanding of what print is.	Most children: • Hold a book right side up. (2–3 yrs.) • Recognize book by its cover. • Turn pages carefully. • Differentiate between print and pictures. • Identify environmental print. (3–4 yrs) • Know that print is oral language written down. • Pretend to read: turn pages, label objects, mimic adults. • Point to the text when asked what one reads. (4–5) • Understand terms "beginning of the book," "end of the book," and "cover of the book." • Can point to the word to read first in a line of text when placement of text is conventional (on left side of the page). • Point to the words following left-to-right directionality, regardless of the length of the sentence. Sweep left to right. • "Read" familiar texts emergently, generally recalling the text. • Track print when "reading" familiar text (own writing, known story, or when being read to). Point to each word with voice-to-print match. (5–6 yrs.) • Know what the author and illustrator do and what a title is. • Will read a word the same way no matter how it is written (different font) or where it is located. • Know the difference between a letter, a word, and a sentence and can point to each on a page of text when asked. • Make the transition between emergent reading to real reading. (first grade)
Phonological Awareness: *Watch for:* phonemic awareness—awareness that the spoken word is made up of sounds; how many sounds are in the word (tap the number of phonemes); identify the phonemes in order (alphabetic principle) and their position in the word (at the beginning, middle, or end of the word); ability to recognize phonemes that are similar; ability to delete and substitute phonemes; ability to rhyme; identify syllables (tap or clap syllables while saying the word); identify words in a sentence (tap out the number of words as they are said).	Most children: • Notice repeating sounds in language. (3–4 yrs.) • Pay attention to beginning sounds and rhyming sounds. • Can count or tap out the sounds in a word. • Can isolate the initial sound of a word. (4–5 yrs.) • Can identify rhymes when given several words or words within a poem. • Can isolate more than the initial sound in a word, can identify the ending sound and then medial sounds. At first these are not in order and later follow the alphabetic principle. (5–6 yrs.) • Can count or tap out the syllables in a word. • Can count or tap the words in a sentence. • Can take away an initial sound or syllable and say the rest of the word. • Can take a word pronounced as separate phonemes or syllables and reconstruct the word. • When given a word, can produce a rhyming word. • Can count the number of syllables in a word. (6–7 yrs) • Can blend or segment the phonemes in most one-syllable words.

Figure A.7 Continued

Examples of Things to Look For	Developmental Continuum
Alphabetic Knowledge, Phonics and Decoding of Text: *Watch to see if the child can:* identify letters in familiar contexts (name, familiar book, environmental print, own writing) and later in less familiar contexts (unfamiliar books); identify uppercase and lowercase letters; identify the sounds that a letter represents (phonics); use letter sounds to attempt to decode words; recognize and use word patterns and other phonics strategies to decode words; recognize familiar words by sight; read increasing number of irregular and multisyllabic words; read books for that grade level.	Most children: • Recognize the letters in own name, names of friends or print symbols. (3–4 yrs.) • Know that letters are a special category of symbols/visual graphics that can be named. Can point to a letter on a page of text. • Identify ten letters of the alphabet, primarily letters in their name. • Confuse some letters (m/n, p/q, d/b) or numbers with letters (the letter *l* often looks like the number *1*). • Identify upper and lowercase letters. • Can give the symbol-to-sound correspondence for some initial consonants (the letter b stands for the sound *b* in "bat"). • Name all uppercase and lowercase letters. (5–6 yrs.) • Know that the sequence of letters in a written word represents the sequence of sounds in a spoken word (alphabetic principle). • Know most symbol-to-sound and sound-to-symbol correspondences. • Recognize some familiar words by sight (a, the, I, my, you, is, etc.). • Recognize word patterns. (6–7 yrs.) • Recognize consonant blends ("ch," "bl", "th") and vowel sounds represented by two-letter patterns ("oo," "ee"). • Accurately decode one-syllable words and nonsense words using print-sound mapping and word patterns. • Monitor own reading and self-correct. • Recognize common irregularly spelled words by sight ("where," "two," etc.). • Have a reading vocabulary of about 300–500 words: sight words and simple, easy-to-decode words. • Accurately decode orthographically regular multisyllable words and nonsense words. (7–8 yrs.) • Accurately read many irregularly spelled words and spelling patterns (diphthongs, etc.). • Use letter–sound correspondence, word patterns, and other structural analyses to decode words. (8–9 yrs.)
Writing: *Watch for:* differentiation between scribbles for drawing and writing; scribbles and letter-like forms; use of pictures to represent thoughts; writing of own name and other words; use of invented spellings (child represents the salient sounds in a word with appropriate sound-to-symbol correspondences); use of word patterns and conventionally spelled words; increasingly more complex writing in response to questions or text.	Most children: • Scribble to represent something (picture or writing). (2–3 yrs.) • Produce some letter-like forms or scribbles with repeated features that look like writing. • "Write" messages as a part of play or to communicate with someone. (4–5 yrs.) • Distinguish writing from drawing. • Write their first name. • May copy familiar words, names of friends, environmental print (name of the center, etc.). • Dictate stories and slow their speech to match writing of person taking dictation. • Write uppercase and lowercase letters. (5–6 yrs.) • Use phonemic awareness and sound-to-symbol correspondence to represent words by writing the initial sound.

(continued)

Figure A.7   Continued

Examples of Things to Look For	Developmental Continuum
Writing *(continued)*	• Use invented spellings (represents more than one sound in a word—usually beginning and ending sounds and then beginning, medial, and ending sounds). • Write first and last name. Write first names of friends. • Can write letters and some words when dictated. • Write some conventionally spelled words, usually familiar words. • Compose simple stories and can answer simple written comprehension questions based on a book that was read. (6–7 yrs.) • Are sensitive to conventional spelling and can use phonics rules to spell. • Use capitalization and punctuation. • Correctly spell words that have been studied and use spelling patterns in writing. (7–8 yrs.) • Can represent all of the sounds in a word when spelling independently. • At times, can use formal language patterns as opposed to oral language patterns in writing. • Can clarify and refine writing with help. • Write in varied genres: narrative stories, expository for informational reports.
Comprehension of Text: *Watch for:* ability to listen to a story and understand it; ability to retell, predict, infer, and summarize accurately; ability to identify the components or structure of the story (beginning, middle, and end); knowledge of story grammar: characters, problem solved, etc.; ability to modify the story line and predict possible consequences of changes.	Most children: • Listen to stories. (2–3 yrs.) • Comment on the characters and pictures in the book. • While listening to a story, connect the information and events to own life: "My brother had a bicycle like that one," or "I want a party, too." (3–4 yrs.) • Show a literal understanding of the story being told. Can answer and ask literal questions about the story. • Can paraphrase the story when asked. • Can retell story in vignettes that may not be in the same order as the action in the story. • Can retell most stories accurately. (5–6 yrs.) • Can dramatize a story that was read or parts of the story. • Can answer questions requiring simple predictions based on the story and inferences about the story.

Figure A.7   Continued

Examples of Things to Look For	Developmental Continuum
	• Can discuss prior knowledge related to nonfiction/expository texts. (6–7 yrs.) • Can discuss "how," "why," and "what-if" questions related to text. Include story structure elements in story retellings, such as the setting, theme, plot episodes, resolution. • Can respond to text with interpretive comments and questions. • Can respond to text with critical comments and questions. • Can discuss similarities in characters and events across stories. • Can connect and compare information across factual, nonfiction texts. • Can identify specific words or wordings that cause comprehension problems. (7–8 yrs.) • Can summarize major points in fiction and nonfiction texts. • Can discuss underlying themes in fictional works. • Can begin to distinguish cause and effect, fact and opinion, main idea and supporting points in text.

Adapted from Adams, 1980; Applebee, 1978; Bertelson, 1986; Bodrova, Leong, Paynter, & Semenov, 2000; Clay, 1991; Daniels, 1992; Dickenson, McCabe, & Clark-Chiarelli, 2004; Gentry, 1982; Goodman, Goodman, & Hood, 1989; Lapp et al., 2004; Lonigan, 2003; McGhee & Richgels, 1990; Morrow, 2004; National Reading Panel, 2000; Neuman, Copple, & Bredekamp, 2000; Owocki, 1999; Paynter, Bodrova, & Doty, 2005; Peterson, 1995; Raines, 1990; Rhodes & Shanklin, 1993; Rodari, 1996; Roskos, Tabors, & Lenhart, 2004; Schickedanz, 1999; Schickedanz & Casbergue, 2004; Snow, Burns, & Griffin, 1998; Snow, Griffin, & Burns, 2005; Sulzby, 1990.

Figure A.8 Assessment and Analysis Guide: Personal–Social Development–Personal Development

Examples of Things to Look For	Developmental Continuum
Self-Concept: Child's description of self. *Watch for:* ability to distinguish between private thoughts and imaginings and public ones; descriptions of self in terms of concrete characteristics; descriptions of self in terms of psychological and emotional disposition.	Most children: • Distinguish between inner self (private thoughts, imaginings accessible only to child) and outer world; describe self in terms of concrete characteristics (name, physical appearance, possessions, typical behaviors—what I can do, or temporary states—how I feel at this moment). (4–7 yrs.) • Describe self in terms of psychological characteristics and traits (honest, trusting), emotional characteristics and traits (happy, get angry easily, moody), increasingly complex combination of characteristics; use social comparisons; attribute stable personality characteristics to self and others. (7 yrs. and older)
Self-Esteem: Evaluation of self-concept. Can be high where child sees self in a positive light, is satisfied with own strengths and accepts own weaknesses. Can be low where child sees self in negative light. *Watch for:* descriptions of self in terms of social acceptance, competence, physical prowess, academic/cognitive competence, and social self-worth; positive or negative evaluations of own characteristics.	Most children: • Evaluate self-esteem in terms of social acceptance ("Do people like me?") and competence ("I can do _____"); tend to rate selves extremely high on all aspects. (4–6 yrs.) • Evaluate self-esteem in terms of cognitive/academic competence (i.e., math, reading), physical prowess (sports), and social self-worth (good person, funny person); display global sense of self-esteem; show a decline in overall self-esteem at this age because unrealistically high assessments are adjusted. After a period of decline, self-esteem rises again. (7–8 yrs.)
Achievement Motivation: Tendency to evaluate one's performance against a standard of excellence. Adaptive motivation style: strive for success; desire to do well; and select challenging, but not impossibly difficult, tasks. *Watch for:* efforts to achieve mastery; selection of challenging, but not impossibly difficult, tasks; mastery efforts in all subjects/areas.	Most children: • Recognize success and failure and begin to attribute causes; tend to choose easy tasks; are "learning optimists"—overestimate their own abilities and underestimate task difficulties; believe they can learn if they try harder; need help setting realistic, reasonable short-term goals. (3–5 yrs.) • More realistically view their abilities and other levels of achievement; compare own performance to that of other children. • Set high levels of aspiration for selves; feel anxiety about failure. • Need help setting realistic, reasonable short-term goals. • Can develop adaptive mastery-oriented styles (attribute success to high ability, failure to lack of effort, like challenges) or can develop patterns of test anxiety.

Figure A.8   Continued

Examples of Things to Look For	Developmental Continuum
Emotional Development: Child's ability to feel, describe, and regulate emotions. Ability to identify emotions in others. *Watch for:* feelings expressed in different situations (pleasant or stressful situations); ability to recognize and label the emotions of self and others with words: "I feel happy." "He looks sad."	Most children: • Can describe basic emotions (happy, sad, scared). (3 yrs.) • Exhibit pride, envy, and guilt. • Can learn through social referencing (reading the emotions of others). • Recognize facial expressions (sad, happy, angry, surprised, and fearful). • Begin to mask or hide emotions; describe cause and consequences of emotions. • Decline in separation distress and other attachment behaviors. • Use multiple cues to evaluate emotions in others; recognize that the cause of feelings can be internal and not visible to another person. • Know that someone may hide feelings. • Can suppress feelings, such as anger. • Know emotions fade with time and can be controlled by thoughts. • Understand mixed emotions (can feel happy and sad at the same time). (8 yrs.)
Self-Regulation—Social & emotional: *Watch for:* signs of emotional self-control; use of language to control emotions; ability to delay gratification; knowledge of and ability to abide by classroom rules; ability to sustain effort in spite of failure; monitoring of success and failure on academic tasks.	Most children: • Are capable of controlling emotions. (3–5 yrs.) • Refrain from forbidden behaviors. • Can internalize the rules of behavior of the classroom. • Use language to control own emotions and emotions of others (says "No!" rather than hitting). • Are capable of sustained social interactions involving negotiation and compromise of own wishes and desires. • Can wait for their turn. Can propose taking turns as a social solution. • Can plan play interactions prior to engaging in them. • Can voice strategies for regulating self (I don't think about it, I count to 10, etc.). (5–8 yrs.) • Are capable of conscious self-control. • Can use strategies that focus on the problem rather than on the emotions. • Reflect on own and other children's motivation for actions. • Have begun developing internalized standards of behavior in many areas (pro-social, achievement, etc.). • Engage in conscious pro-social behaviors.

Adapted from: Baumeister & Vons, 2004; Barnett & Zucker, 1990; Berk, 2006; Blair, 2002; Bodrova & Leong, 2006; Bronson, 2000; Charlesworth, 2003; Cole, Cole, & Lightfoot, 2004; Curry & Johnson, 1990; Damon, 1977; Damon & Eisenberg, 1998; Denham, 1998; Eisenberg & Fabes, 1998; Harter, 2001; Johnson, Christie, & Yawkey, 1987; Ladd, 1990; LeFreniere, 1999; Masten, 1989; Mergendoller & Marchman, 1987; Ormrod, 2002; Rogers & Sawyers, 1988; Samuels, 1977; Slavoey & Sluyter, 1997; Stipek, 2000; Selman, 1989.

Figure A.9 Assessment and Analysis Guide: Personal–Social Development—Social Development

Examples of Things to Look For	Developmental Continuum
Peer Relations: The type of interactions children have with age-mates. *Watch for:* amount of positive interactions (turn-taking, sharing, conversations, initiations, and responses); negative interactions (aggression, rejecting the requests of others); parallel play (play next to but not with another child); solitary play (play alone); associative play (play with other child but theme of play and roles not coordinated); cooperative play (play with others with common theme and planned roles); rough-and-tumble play interactions (physical play that ends in a positive exchange and not aggression); helping behavior (do they ask first, or just jump in and start helping?).	For all ages, group size influences group interaction. Fewer than five is the optimal size for children under 5 years. Five is optimal size for children 5 years and older. Peer acceptance is associated with positive emotional adjustment at all ages. Most children: • Have interactions marked by fairly high rates of positive and negative exchanges; engage in parallel, solitary, and some associative play; begin to balance leading with following others; engage in simple turn-taking. (3–4 yrs.) • Have higher rates of positive than negative interactions; longer verbal exchanges (some turn-taking); reciprocal, coordinated interactions; engage primarily in associative play with some parallel, solitary, and cooperative play; engage in rough-and-tumble play. • Have high levels of positive interaction; engage primarily in cooperative play with some parallel, solitary, and associative play; engage in rough-and-tumble play; have peer interactions governed by social norms such as sharing and helping; are better at sustaining conversations (turn-taking); are more sensitive to others' needs; are concerned about being lonely. (5 yrs and older)
Friendships: Special sustained relationship with one or two other people. *Watch for:* children who seem to play together more often, choose each other, and talk about being friends; length of relationship; momentary (for time children are next to each other) or stable (persists over weeks, months, years); child's understanding of what it means to be a friend. After being asked how to make friends, how does the child respond? Six social processes are related to friendship formation: communicate clearly (ask for clarification of unclear messages); exchange information (ask questions of each other, exchange information and ideas); establish common ground (find something both enjoy or can do); resolve conflicts successfully (compromise, negotiate); show positive reciprocity (respond to other's ideas and requests); disclose information about self (share inner feelings, solicit feelings from others).	Sensitivity and intimacy are features of all friendships but not verbalized by younger children. At all ages, children give more positive reinforcement, have more interactions, and are more emotionally expressive with friends. Children use all six processes of friendship formation by 4 years. Most children: • Have friendships that are momentary and fleeting (whomever child is playing with at that time is a friend); have disagreements over territory and space; solve disagreements by leaving or aggressive behavior. (2–6 yrs.) • Describe friendship as concrete and activity based, affirmed by giving and sharing things (friends do the same thing); have friendships that are not fleeting, but not long-term either; have disagreements when one child will not compromise; solve disagreements by leaving or giving in; tend to have same-sex friends. • Describe friendship as trust and intimacy, sharing of feelings, and providing mutual support (friends share personal problems); have longer-term relationships than earlier; have disagreements over jealousy, breaking trust, or gossiping behind back; have disagreements that do not end the friendship; must acknowledge trust was broken to repair friendship; are more likely to express disagreements with friends than other children. (8 yrs. and older)

240

Figure A.9   Continued

Examples of Things to Look For	Developmental Continuum
Perspective Taking: Ability to take the role or position of another person and take more than one perspective at a time. *Watch for:* situations in which the child describes one or more perspectives ("He wanted the toy. I didn't want to give it to him"); responses showing child can take another's perspective; discussion of perspectives of characters in stories; recognition that others may think or feel differently; anticipation of another's thoughts and feelings; placing self in different roles and evaluating from each perspective.	Most children: • Fail to distinguish between own interpretation and another person's (I like cookies so everyone likes cookies). (3–5 yrs) • Realize that other people have different perspectives, thoughts, and feelings because they are in different situations or have different information. • Are aware that each person has different perspectives; know that what other people think influences their own perspective; can adopt another person's perspective and anticipate her reaction. (6 yrs. and older)
Empathy: Child's ability to feel the same feelings and respond to the feelings of another person. *Watch for:* situations in which child helps another person; situations in which child talks about needs of another; child's response to empathetic statements made by adults or other children; child's response to questions about "why we help other people"; response to stories about empathy.	Modeling and direct teaching all have a positive influence on empathy at all ages. Most children: • Respond empathetically to others based on self-interest or simple empathetic feelings (without adopting other's perspective, but simply feeling for other person); offer help to another person and give it even if it is not wanted. (3–5 yrs.) • Have feelings of empathy based on stereotypic images of good and bad and concern for approval (people will think I am a good person); have empathetic responses imagining what another person is feeling; respond to the intensity of others' feelings; ask if help is needed before acting. (6 yrs. and older)
Social Problem-Solving Skills: Ability to generate and implement a number of possible solutions for social problems. *Watch for:* situations in which children have disagreements and how conflicts are handled; responses to typical classroom problems; number and type of strategies (mainly meet own or consider other's needs); ability to merge with rather than disrupt social interaction.	Most children: • Use some strategies, but these are impulsive and based primarily on own needs. (2–5 yrs.) • Generate more solutions than younger children do; have strategies that take into account the needs of others; generate solutions based on coordination of needs; can interpret social cues better than younger children do; evaluate probable effectiveness of a strategy better than younger children do; enter social group by merging with others (observe what others are doing, copy members of group, make positive comments, enter social group). (6 yrs. and older)

(continued)

Figure A.9   Continued

Examples of Things to Look For	Developmental Continuum
Aggression: *physical*—hitting, pushing, kicking; *verbal*—name calling, teasing, putting down; *instrumental*—fighting over a toy, territory, or attention; *hostile*—designed to injure another person. *Watch for:* type of aggression; a pattern to behavior (with whom and when aggression occurs); reasons for the aggression.	Extreme aggression is a highly stable trait for both boys and girls (likely to be highly aggressive at 10 years, associated with peer rejection, poor achievement levels, school dropouts, and delinquent behavior). Highly aggressive children may misinterpret social cues and read aggressive intent into most social interactions (neutral or friendly). Most children: • Exhibit primarily physical, instrumental aggression; are aggressive with children they are interacting with. Boys instigate and receive more aggression than girls. (2–3 yrs.) • Engage in some verbal and physical aggression; engage in less instrumental aggression. Some engage in hostile aggression. • Engage in less aggressive behavior than younger children; are verbally aggressive (teasing, name calling, taunting); engage in some hostile aggression. (6 yrs. and older)
Functioning in Learning Groups: *Watch for:* general social skills and ability to form cooperative group; stay with the group, volunteer ideas to others; support and acceptance of others' ideas (use praise, no criticism of individuals); give diplomatic reasons for not using ideas; take responsibility for own work; resist dominating group or doing other's tasks; energize group when motivation is low; set/call attention to time limits; summarize ideas (seek accuracy, ask for elaboration, discuss reasoning).	There is no known developmental pattern for this area. However, many of the behaviors are related to advanced levels of perspective taking, empathy, peer relations, and social problem solving described previously. In addition, the child's cognitive level and level of language development also influence the child's ability to learn in cooperative groups. The quality of cooperative learning in preschool will be very different from that found in elementary school. Younger children will require much more coaching in exactly how to state criticisms, for example, because they may not know how to word their opinions in an acceptable manner.
Sociodramatic Play: Acting out everyday and imaginary roles. *Watch for:* number and type of roles; number and type of actions performed; number and manner of use of objects (uses one object to be another—a block becomes an airplane; imaginary play—pretends to sweep with a broom); discussion of play (makes statements, describes actions, tells story, prompts action, proposes pretending); expression of emotions	• Less mature sociodramatic play has a few roles with a few actions and objects; children use statements and descriptions of play when talking about and during play ("I'm washing the dishes"; "This is my house"). • More mature play has more roles (several at the same time, switching back and forth—plays the mother and the baby); actions (intricate, series of actions—goes outside, hunts for berries, comes back, makes dinner); objects (more props are used or "pretended"); complex discussions (tell story—"We live in another time, like the future. They don't use cars"); prompting of actions, and proposals about pretending ("Let's say you're the good guy and you have a best friend, that's me"); changes in

Figure A.9   Continued

Examples of Things to Look For	Developmental Continuum
(enacting forbidden actions, unpleasant scenes, or actions and consequences—hurts people and goes to prison); use of rules in games (plays tag with rules).	emotional tenor (more forbidden, unpleasant situations and action—consequence sequences—"She steals the jewels because she is very bad and then she gets caught by the police"). • Rule-based games and play appear at about 6–11 years.

Adapted from: Arends, 2003; Asher & Renshaw, 1981; Berndt & Ladd, 1989; Barnett & Zuker, 1990; Berk, 2006; Bodrova & Leong, 1998b; Cole, Cole, & Lightfoot, 2004; Damon, 1977; Damon & Eisenberg, 1998; Dunn, 2004; Frost, Wortham, & Reifel, 2001; Hetherington, Parke, Gauvain, & Locke, 2005; Howes, 1980, 1988; Kostelenik, Whiren, Soderman, & Gregory, 2001; Johnson, Christie, & Yawkey, 1987; Johnson, Johnson, Holubec, & Roy, 1984; Ladd, 1990; Masten, 1989; Ruben, Bukowski, & Parker, 1998; Rogers & Sawyers, 1988; Samuels, 1977, Slavin, 2005; Trawick-Smith, 2005.

Developmental Red Flags for Children Ages 3 to 5*

What Are Red Flags?

Red flags are behaviors that should warn you to stop, look, and think. Having done so, you may decide there is nothing to worry about, or that a cluster of behaviors signals a possible problem. These guidelines will help you use red flags more effectively.

- Behavior descriptions are sometimes repeated under different areas of development. It is difficult to categorize children's behavior. Your job is to notice and describe what you see that concerns you. Do not try to decide into which category it fits.
- Look for *patterns* or *clusters* of red flags. One, or a few in isolation, may not be significant.
- Observe a child in a variety of situations in order to watch for the behaviors that concern you.
- Compare the child's behavior to the "norm," which should include children who are 6 months younger or 6 months older as well as the same age.
- Note how the child has grown during the past 3 to 6 months. Be concerned if you believe the child has not progressed.
- *Know normal patterns of growth and development.* What may be a red flag at one age can be a perfectly normal behavior at another.
- Keep in mind that each child's development is affected by personality, temperament, family structure and dynamics, culture, experiences, physical characteristics, and the match of child and family to your program.

Consultation and Referral

None of us knows all there is to know about normal growth and development. Use all of your area resources to help you think about a child.

- Describe in detail what you see that concerns you. Do not try to conclude what it means or to label it. It is much more helpful to parents, consultants, and to the child to have descriptions, not conclusions.

*Adapted from A. S. Kendrick, R. Kaufman, and K. Messenger (Eds.), (1988). *Healthy Young Children: A Manual for Programs,* pp. 123–127. Used with permission of the publisher, the National Association for the Education of Young Children. The list is a joint effort of the Administration for Children, Youth, and Families; U.S. Department of Health and Human Services; Georgetown University Child Development Center; Massachusetts Department of Public Health; and the National Association for the Education of Young Children.

- Talk with the child's parent(s).
- Wait and watch for a while *if* you have observed growth in the past 3 to 6 months. If no growth in the area of concern can be described, then it is time to ask for help.
- Know that if you recommend further evaluation of a problem and your concerns are confirmed, you have helped a child and family begin to solve a problem.

Note: **These categories are intended to guide your observation of children ages 3 to 5 only. For older children, consult state or school district guidelines.**

Major Developmental Areas

Social–Emotional Development, Which Includes

- Relationships
- Focusing
- Anxiety level
- Separations
- Affect (mood)
- Impulse control
- Involvement
- Self-image
- Transitions

Red Flags.   Be alert to a child who, compared with other children the same age or 6 months older or younger, exhibits these behaviors:

- Does not seem to recognize self as a separate person, or does not refer to self as "I"
- Has great difficulty separating from parent or separates too easily
- Is anxious, tense, restless, compulsive, cannot get dirty or messy, has many fears, engages in excessive self-stimulation
- Seems preoccupied with own inner world; conversations do not make sense
- Shows little or no impulse control; hits or bites as first response; cannot follow a classroom routine
- Expresses emotions inappropriately (laughs when sad, denies feelings); facial expressions do not match emotions
- Cannot focus on activities (short attention span, cannot complete anything, flits from toy to toy)
- Relates only to adults; cannot share adult attention, consistently sets up power struggle, or is physically abusive to adults
- Consistently withdraws from people, prefers to be alone; no depth to relationships; does not seek or accept affection or touching
- Treats people as objects; has no empathy for other children; cannot play on another child's terms
- Is consistently aggressive, frequently hurts others deliberately; shows no remorse or is deceitful in hurting others

How to Screen

1. Observe child.
   - Note overall behavior. What does the child do all day? With whom? With what does child play?
   - Note when, where, how frequently, and with whom problem behaviors occur.
   - Describe behavior through clear observations. Do not diagnose.

2. Note family history.
   • Make-up of family: Who cares for the child?
   • Has there been a recent move, death, new sibling, or long or traumatic separation?
   • What support does the family have—extended family, friends?
3. Note developmental history and child's temperament since infancy.
   • Activity level
   • Regularity of child's routine—sleeping, eating
   • Distractibility
   • Intensity of child's responses
   • Persistence/attention span
   • Positive or negative mood
   • Adaptability to changes in routine
   • Level of sensitivity to noise, light, touch

Motor Development—Fine Motor, Gross Motor, and Perceptual—Which Includes

• Quality of movement	• Level of development
• Sensory integration	

Red Flags.   Pay extra attention to children with these behaviors:

• The child who is particularly uncoordinated and who
   Has lots of accidents
   Trips, bumps into things
   Is awkward getting down/up, climbing, jumping, getting around toys and people
   Stands out from the group in structured motor tasks—walking, climbing stairs, jumping, standing on one foot
   Avoids the more physical games
• The child who relies heavily on watching own or other peoples' movements in order to do them and who
   May frequently misjudge distances
   May become particularly uncoordinated or off balance with eyes closed
• The child who, compared to peers, uses much more of her or his body to do the task than the task requires and who
   Dives into the ball (as though to cover the fact that she or he cannot coordinate a response)
   Uses tongue, feet, or other body parts excessively to help in coloring, cutting, tracing, or with other high-concentration tasks
   Produces extremely heavy coloring
   Leans over the table when concentrating on a fine motor project
   When doing wheelbarrows, keeps pulling the knees and feet under the body, or thrusts rump up in the air
• The child with extraneous and involuntary movements, who
   While painting with one hand, holds the other hand in the air or waves
   Does chronic toe walking
   Shows twirling or rocking movements
   Shakes hands or taps fingers
• The child who involuntarily finds touching uncomfortable and who
   Flinches or tenses when touched or hugged
   Avoids activities that require touching or close contact

> May be uncomfortable lying down, particularly on the back
> Reacts as if attacked when unexpectedly bumped
> Blinks, protects self from a ball even when trying to catch it

- The child who compulsively craves being touched or hugged, or the older child who almost involuntarily has to feel things to understand them, who both may
  > Cling to, or lightly brush, the teacher a lot
  > Always sit close to or touch children in a circle
  > Be strongly attracted to sensory experiences such as blankets, soft toys, water, dirt, sand, paste, hands in food

- The child who has a reasonable amount of experience with fine motor tools but whose skill does not improve proportionately, such as
  > An older child who can still only snip with scissors or whose cutting is extremely choppy
  > An older child who still cannot color within the lines on a simple project
  > An older child who frequently switches hands with crayon, scissors, paintbrush
  > An experienced child who tries but still gets paste, paint, sand, water everywhere
  > A child who is very awkward with, or chronically avoids, small manipulative materials

- The child who has exceptional difficulty with new but simple puzzles, coloring, structured art projects, and drawing a person, and who, for example, may
  > Take much longer to do the task, even when trying hard, and produce a final result that is still not as sophisticated compared to those of peers
  > Show a lot of trial-and-error behavior when trying to do a puzzle
  > Mix up top/bottom, left/right, front/back, on simple projects where a model is to be copied
  > Use blocks or small cubes to repeatedly build and crash tower structures and seem fascinated and genuinely delighted with the novelty of the crash (older child)
  > Still does a lot of scribbling (older child)

How to Screen

Note level and quality of development as compared with other children in the group.

Speech and Language Development, Which Includes

- Articulation (pronouncing sounds)
- Dysfluency (excessive stuttering—occasional stuttering may occur in the early years and is normal)
- Voice
- Language (ability to use and understand words)

Red Flags

- Articulation. Watch for the child
  > Whose speech is difficult to understand, compared with peers
  > Who mispronounces sounds

Whose mouth seems abnormal (excessive under- or overbite; swallowing difficulty; poorly lined-up teeth)

Who has difficulty putting words and sounds in proper sequence

Who cannot be encouraged to produce age-appropriate sound

Who has a history of ear infections or middle ear disorders

Note: **Most children develop the following sounds correctly by the ages shown (i.e., don't worry about a 3-year-old who mispronounces *t*).**

2 years—all vowel sounds

3 years—*p, b, m, w, h*

4 years—*t, d, n, k, h, ng*

5 years—*f, j, sh*

6 years—*ch, v, r, l*

7 years—*s, z,* voiceless or voiced *th*

- Dysfluency (stuttering). Note the child who, compared with others of the same age,

    Shows excessive amounts of these behaviors:

        repetitions of sounds, words (m-m-m; I-I-I-I-)

        prolongations of sounds (mmmmmmmmmmmmmm)

        hesitations or long blocks during speech, usually accompanied by tension or struggle behavior

        putting in extra words (um, uh, well)

    Shows two or more of these behaviors while speaking:

        hand clenching

        eye blinking

        swaying of body

        pill rolling with fingers

        no eye contact

        body tension or struggle

        breathing irregularity

        tremors

        pitch rise

        frustration

        avoidance of talking

    Is labeled a stutterer by parents

    Is aware of her or his dysfluencies

- Voice. Note the child whose

    Rate of speech is extremely fast or slow

    Voice is breathy or hoarse

    Voice is very loud or soft

    Voice is very high or low

    Voice sounds very nasal

- Language (ability to use and understand words). Note the child who

    Does not appear to understand when others speak, though hearing is normal

    Is unable to follow one- or two-step directions

    Communicates by pointing, gesturing

    Makes no attempt to communicate with words

    Has small vocabulary for age

    Uses parrotlike speech (imitates what others say)

    Has difficulty putting words together in a sentence

Uses words inaccurately
Demonstrates difficulty with three or more of these skills:
 making a word plural
 changing tenses of verb
 using pronouns
 using negatives
 using possessives
 naming common objects
 telling function of common objects
 using prepositions

Note: **Two-year-olds use mostly nouns, few verbs. Three-year-olds use nouns, verbs, some adverbs, adjectives, prepositions. Four-year-olds use all parts of speech.**

How to Screen

1. Observe child. Note when, where, how frequently, and with whom problem occurs.
2. Check developmental history—both heredity and environment play an important part in speech development.
3. Look at motor development, which is closely associated with speech.
4. Look at social–emotional status, which can affect speech and language.
5. Write down or record speech samples.
6. Check hearing status.
7. Note number of speech sounds or uses of language.

Hearing

Even a mild or temporary hearing loss in a child may interfere with speech, language, or social and academic progress. If more than one of these red flag behaviors is observed, it is likely that a problem exists.

Red Flags

- Speech and language. Look for the child
    Whose speech is not easily understood by people outside the family
    Whose grammar is less accurate than other children of the same age
    Who does not use speech as much as other children of the same age
    Who has an unusual voice (hoarseness, stuffy quality, lack of inflection, or voice that is usually too loud or soft)
- Social behavior (at home and in school). Look for the child who
    Is shy or hesitant in answering questions or joining in conversation
    Misunderstands questions or directions; frequently says "huh?" or "what?" in response to questions
    Appears to ignore speech; hears "only what he wants to"
    Is unusually attentive to speaker's face or unusually inattentive to speaker, or turns one ear to speaker
    Has difficulty with listening activities such as storytime and following directions
    Has short attention span
    Is distractible and restless; tends to shift quickly from one activity to another

Is generally lethargic or disinterested in most day-to-day activities

Is considered a behavior problem—too active or aggressive, or too quiet and withdrawn

- Medical indications. Look for the child who

Has frequent or constant upper respiratory tract infections, congestion that appears related to allergies, or a cold for several weeks or months

Has frequent earaches, ear infections, throat infections, or middle ear problems

Has had draining ears on one or more occasions

Is mouth breather and snorer

Is generally lethargic; has poor color

How to Screen

1. Observe current behavior related to speech and hearing.
2. Consult behavioral and medical history.
3. Consult audiologist or communication disorders specialist.

Vision, Which Includes

- Skills
- Disease
- Acuity (ability to see at a given distance)

Red Flags

- Eyes
  Are watery
  Have discharge
  Lack coordination in directing gaze of both eyes
  Are red
  Are sensitive to light
  Appear to cross or wander, especially when child is tired
- Eyelids
  Have crusts on lids or among lashes
  Are red
  Have recurring sties or swelling
- Behavior and complaints
  Rubs eyes excessively
  Experiences dizziness, headaches, nausea on close work
  Attempts to brush away blur
  Has itchy, burning, scratchy eyes
  Contorts face or body when looking at distant objects, or thrusts head forward; squints or widens eyes
  Blinks eyes excessively; holds book too close or too far; inattentive during visual tasks
  Shuts or covers one eye; tilts head

How to Screen

1. Has child had an eye exam? If not, recommend one.
2. Screen using a screening tool appropriate for young children, such as the Snellen E chart or Broken Wheel cards.

Glossary

Accommodation: A change in assessment procedures that allows a child to participate in the assessment but does *not* alter what the assessment measures or its comparability.

Accountability: Being held responsible for something, such as holding schools, administrators, and teachers responsible for student achievement.

Alignment: Agreement between the expected outcomes of educational experiences (standards, goals), the curriculum, and assessment. Also used to indicate continuity in expectations from one educational level to another.

Alternative Assessment: Almost any kind of assessment approach other than conventional standardized tests, inventories, and instruments.

Amplification: Assisting the emergence of behavior and understanding that are *within* a child's Zone of Proximal Development, rather than accelerating beyond the child's ability to understand and perform.

Assessment: A term used loosely to refer to any type of appraisal of young children. In a narrower sense it refers to information from multiple indicators and sources of evidence, which is then synthesized, integrated, interpreted, and evaluated to make an assessment.

Assessment Instruments, or Assessment Tools: Checklists, inventories, structured observation guides, rating scales, and other systematic means of collecting and recording information about young children.

Assessment Procedures: Methods and techniques used in the assessment process, such as observation, interviews, work sampling, collection and analysis of children's work products, and tests of various kinds.

Authentic, Direct, or Performance Assessment: Type of assessment that uses tasks as close as possible to real-life practical and intellectual challenges. *Performance assessment* refers to the type of pupil response. If motor coordination is to be measured, the child performs an appropriate action. If writing is of concern, the child writes. *Authentic assessment* refers to the situation or context in which the task is performed. In authentic assessment the child completes the desired behavior in a context as close to real life as possible.

Bell Curve: *See* Normal curve.

Benchmark: A point of reference for measurement and evaluation. Used especially in connection with content standards. For example, standards may state that "by the end of second [or fourth, or eighth] grade, children should be able to . . . ."

Classroom Assessment: Assessments developed and used by teachers in their classrooms on a day-to-day basis.

Collaborative Team: A group of people who work together to provide assessment and educational services to children with special needs.

Continuous Assessment: Type of assessment embedded within the daily processes of instruction so that appraisal of children's responses and actions—and subsequent adjustment of curriculum and teaching—is ongoing.

Criterion-Referenced Standardized Tests: A standardized test in which an individual's score is compared to a criterion—a specific level or cut-off score for acceptable performance.

Criterion Referencing: A means of determining where an individual stands in relation to a criterion or performance standard rather than to other individuals. The meaning comes from comparison to an expected standard or criterion.

Curriculum-Embedded Assessment: A process of assessment that is an integral part of the curriculum, in contrast to tests or assessments that are given apart from daily teaching and instruction.

Developmental Accomplishment: A statement that describes the knowledge or skill level achieved or attained.

Developmental Continuum: A predictable but not rigid sequence of developmental accomplishments.

Diagnostic Assessment or Evaluation: An in-depth appraisal of an individual child by a specialist, frequently after a child has been identified by a screening process or a teacher.

Documentation: The process of classroom observation and record keeping over time and across learning modalities to keep track of children's learning.

Dynamic Assessment: Type of assessment in which adults give clues, leads, and hints or ask questions or pose problems to see what the person being assessed can do, both with and without assistance. It builds on conceptions of children's learning based on insights from Vygotsky and cognitive psychologists.

Evaluation: The establishment of specific values by which to judge whatever is being considered.

Formative Evaluation: Type of evaluation that provides necessary information to facilitate children's progress toward identified goals and objectives. It is concerned both with student learning and with the curriculum's responsiveness to children's needs.

"High-Stakes" Assessment: Any assessment that has the potential to influence educational opportunities for children, such as placement in special programs, ability grouping, or retention in grade.

Inclusion: Including children with disabilities or developmental delays in the educational setting where they would have been if they did not have a disability or delay.

Indicator: Evidence that documents children's attainment of a specific level of a benchmark or standard.

Interdisciplinary Assessment: Type of assessment in which specialists from several disciplines work together with school personnel and parents outside the classroom to integrate their separate findings, reports, and perspectives.

Mean: The average score in a distribution.

Measurement: Quantification of some kind.

Median: The middlemost score in a distribution.

Mode: The most common score in a distribution.

Modification: A change in assessment procedures that *does* alter what the assessment measures and the comparability of results.

Multidisciplinary Assessment: Type of assessment in which specialists from several disciplines assess and evaluate a child independently and submit separate reports.

Norm-Referenced Standardized Tests: A standardized test in which a person's score is compared to other people's scores.

Norm Referencing: A means of determining an individual's performance in relation to the performance of others on the same measure. The meaning of the score emerges from comparison with the group of children, who constitute the norm.

Observational Measurement: The process of observing and assessing behavior in ways that yield descriptions and quantitative measures of individuals, groups, and settings.

Portfolio: A purposeful collection of children's work and other indicators of learning, collected over time, that demonstrates to the student and others the student's efforts, progress, or achievement in particular developmental or subject area(s).

Portfolio Assessment: Type of assessment that evaluates the child's performance based on evidence that teachers and children have selected and compiled in a portfolio.

Prereferral strategies: Instructional approaches and activities used in the classroom to help determine a child's response to intervention and whether a child should be referred for an in-depth assessment.

Reflection: A process by which an individual or group thoughtfully considers an experience, idea, work product, or learning. It is a "looking back" and reconstruction that usually involves language and may lead to revision based on the reflection.

Reliability: The extent to which any assessment technique yields results that are accurate and consistent over time.

Rubric: A rule or guide presenting clear criteria by which a complex performance can be judged.

Scaffolding: Providing, then gradually removing, external support for learning.

Scoring Rubric: A fixed scale and a list of characteristics describing performance for each of the points on the scale. Usually one level of the rubric is considered the acceptable level of performance.

Screening: Brief, relatively inexpensive, standardized procedures designed to quickly appraise a large number of children to find out which ones should be referred for further assessment.

Social Context: Everything in the environment that has been directly or indirectly influenced by the culture, including people (parents, teachers, peers) and materials (books, learning materials and supplies, equipment).

Standard Deviation: A statistical term that describes the average deviation of scores from the mean and is one of several ways to measure variation of a distribution.

Standard Error of Measurement (SEM): A psychometric term that describes the average error of measurement contained in any given test score. It forms a confidence interval around an individual's test score.

Standardized Aptitude Tests: Standardized tests that are intended to predict future performance or success in a given area of training or in an occupation.

Standardized Screening and Diagnostic Tests: Standardized tests used to identify or diagnose children with potential learning problems.

Standardized Test: A test with specific characteristics: (1) developed according to APA/AERA guidelines with high levels of reliability and validity; (2) prescribed methods for administration and security; and (3) scoring systems based on comparisons with other people or to a specified criterion.

Standards: Outcome statements that specify what children should know and be able to do at different points in their school learning. Some statements of standards also address attitudes, values, and dispositions toward learning. In child assessment, standards are often used as a way of expressing expectations about intent and outcomes. *Content standards* state what every child should know and be able to do. *Performance standards* state how well a child should demonstrate knowledge and skills. They gauge the degree to which children have met the content standards.

Summative or Summary Evaluation: An evaluation that takes place at the end of a unit, course of study, year, or unit of schooling, and determines the degree of children's attainment of objectives. Results are often used for reporting to others.

Tests: Systematic procedures for observing a person's behavior and describing it with the aid of numerical scales or fixed categories.

Transdisciplinary Assessment: Type of assessment in which appropriate specialists and classroom personnel work together in regular classroom activities to conduct a child assessment.

Validity: The extent to which any assessment technique fulfills the purpose for which it is intended.

Zone of Proximal Development (ZPD): A concept from the Vygotskian theory of child development and learning. The zone encompasses the area of development that is emerging. The lower level of the zone is what a child can do independently. The higher level is what a child can do with maximum assistance.

References

Abbott, C. F., & Gold, S. (1991). Conferring with parents when you're concerned that their child needs special services. *Young Children, 46*(4), 10–14.

Adams, M. J. (1990). *Beginning to read: Thinking and learning about print.* Cambridge, MA: MIT Press.

Adger, C. T., Snow, C. E., & Christian, D. (Eds.). (2002). *What teachers need to know about language.* McHenry, IL: Delta Systems.

Administration for Children, Youth, and Families. (1986). *Easing the transition from preschool to kindergarten: A guide for early childhood teachers and administrators.* Washington, DC: U.S. Department of Health and Human Services.

Airasian, P. W. (2001). *Classroom assessment: Concepts and applications* (4th ed.). Boston: McGraw-Hill.

Almy, M. (1969). *Ways of studying children: A manual for teachers.* New York: Teachers College Press.

Almy, M., & Genishi, C. (1979). *Ways of studying children.* New York: Teachers College Press.

Alper, S. (2001). Alternate assessment of students with disabilities in inclusive settings. In S. Alper, D. L. Ryndak, & C. N. Schloss (Eds.), *Alternate assessment of students with disabilities in inclusive settings.* Boston: Allyn & Bacon.

American Association for the Advancement of Science (AAAS). (1993). *Benchmarks for science literacy.* Washington, DC: Author.

American Educational Research Association. (2000). *AERA position statement concerning high-stakes testing in preK–12 education.* Washington, DC: Author.

American Educational Research Association, American Psychological Association, & National Council on Measurement in Education. (1999). *Standards for educational and psychological testing.* Washington, DC: American Educational Research Association.

American Federation of Teachers, National Council on Measurement in Education, & National Education Association. (1990). *Standards for teacher competence in education assessment of students.* Washington, DC: Author.

Anastasi, A., & Urbina, S. (1997). *Psychological testing* (7th ed.). Upper Saddle River, NJ: Prentice Hall.

Applebee, A. N. (1978). *The child's concept of story.* Chicago, IL: University of Chicago Press.

Arends, R. (2003). *Learning to teach* (6th ed.). New York: Random House.

Armstrong, T. (1995). *The myth of the A.D.D. child: 50 ways to improve your child's behavior and attention span without drugs, labels, or coercion.* New York: Dutton.

Arter, J. A. (1990). *Using portfolios in instruction and assessment.* Portland, OR: Northwest Regional Educational Laboratory.

Arter, J. A., & Paulson, P. (1991). *Composite portfolio work group summaries.* Portland, OR: Northwest Regional Educational Laboratory.

Arter, J. A., & Spandel, V. (1992, Spring). Using portfolios of student work in instruction and assessment. *Educational Measurement: Issues and Practice, 11*(1), 36–44.

Asher, R. S., & Renshaw, P. D. (1981). Children without friends: Social knowledge and social skill training. In S. R. Asher & J. M. Gottman (Eds.), *The development of children's friendships* (pp. 273–296). Cambridge, England: Cambridge University Press.

Ashton-Lilo, J. (1987). *Pencil grasp developmental sequence checklist.* Unpublished manuscript.

Athey, I. (1990). The construct of emergent literacy: Putting it all together. In L. M. Morrow & J. K. Smith (Eds.), *Assessment for instruction in early literacy* (pp. 45–61). Englewood Cliffs, NJ: Prentice Hall.

Au, K. A. (1997). *Literacy instruction in multicultural settings* (2nd ed.). Chicago: Harcourt Brace.

Bagnato, S. J., & Neisworth, J. T. (1991). *Assessment for early intervention.* New York: Guilford Press.

Banks, S. R. (2005). *Classroom assessment: Issues and practices.* Boston: Allyn & Bacon.

Barker, R. G. (1968). *Ecological psychology.* Stanford, CA: Stanford University Press.

Barnett, D. W., & Zucker, K. B. (1990). *The personal and social assessment of children: An analysis of current status and professional practice issues.* Boston: Allyn & Bacon.

Baroody, A. J. (1993). *Problem solving, reasoning, and communication, K–8: Helping children to think mathematically.* New York: Macmillan.

Baumeister, R. F., & Vons, K. D. (2004). *Handbook of self-regulation: Research, theory, and applications.* New York: Guilford Press.

Beaty, J. J. (1994). *Observing development of the young child* (3rd ed.). New York: Macmillan.

Beihler, R. F., & Snowman, J. (2004). *Psychology applied to teaching* (8th ed.). Boston: Houghton Mifflin.

Belmont, J. M. (1989). Cognitive strategies and strategic learning: The socio-instructional approach. In F. D. Horowitz & M. O'Brien (Eds.), Children and their development: Knowledge base, research agenda, and social policy application [Special issue] (pp. 142–148). *American Psychologist, 44*(2).

Bennett, J. (1992). Seeing is believing: Videotaping reading development. In L. Rhodes & N. Shanklin (Eds.), *Literacy assessment in whole language classrooms K–8.* Portsmouth, NH: Heinemann.

Bentzen, W. R. (2000). *Seeing young children: A guide to observing and recording behavior* (4th ed.). Albany, NY: Delmar Publishers.

Berk, L. E. (2006). *Child development* (7th ed.). Boston: Allyn & Bacon.

Berk, L. E., & Winsler, A. (1995). *Scaffolding children's learning: Vygotsky and early childhood education.* Washington, DC: National Association for the Education of Young Children.

Berk, R. A. (1982). *Handbook of methods for detecting test bias.* Baltimore, MD: The Johns Hopkins University Press.

Berliner, D. C. (1987). But do they understand? In V. Richardson-Koehler (Ed.), *Educator's handbook: A research perspective.* New York: Longman.

Berliner, D. C., & Rosenshine, B. V. (Eds.). (1987). *Talks to teachers.* New York: Random House.

Berndt, T. J., & Ladd, G. W. (1989). *Peer relations in child development.* New York: Wiley.

Bertelson, P. (Ed.). (1986). *The onset of literacy: Cognitive processes in reading acquisition.* Cambridge, MA: MIT Press.

Billups, L. R., & Rauth, M. (1987). Teachers and research. In V. Richardson-Koehler (Ed.), *Educators' handbook* (pp. 328–376). New York: Longman.

Bjorklund, D. F. (2004). *Children's thinking: Developmental function and individual differences* (4th ed.). Belmont, CA: Wadsworth/Thompson.

Blair, C. (2002). School readiness: Integrating cognition and emotion in a neurobiological conceptualization of children's functioning at school entry. *American Psychologist, 57*(2), 111–127.

Blank, M., Rose, S. A., & Berlin, L. J. (1978). *The language of learning: The preschool years.* Boston: Allyn & Bacon.

Bloom, B. S., Englehart, M. B., Furst, E. J., Hill, W. H., & Krathwhol, D. R. (1956). *Taxonomy of educational objectives: The classification of educational goals: Handbook 1, cognitive domain.* New York: McKay.

Bodrova, E., & Kendall, J. S. (In press). *A framework for early mathematics and early science instruction.* Aurora, CO: McREL.

Bodrova, E., & Leong, D. J. (1996). *Tools of the mind: The Vygotskian approach to early childhood education.* Englewood Cliffs, NJ: Merrill.

Bodrova, E., & Leong, D, J. (1998a). Adult influences on play: Vygotskian approach. In D. P. Fromberg & D. Bergen (Eds.). *Play from birth to twelve: Contexts, perspectives, and meanings* (pp. 277–282). New York: Garland Press.

Bodrova, E., & Leong, D. J. (1998b). Development of dramatic play in young children and its effects on self-regulation: The Vygotskian approach. *Journal of Early Childhood Teacher Education,19*(2), 38–46.

Bodrova, E., & Leong, D. J. (2001a, March). *Dynamic assessment.* Paper presented at the Early Literacy Institute for Children At Risk: Research-Based Solutions. Sponsored by the Center for the Improvement of Early Reading Achievement (CIERA), Council for Exceptional Children (CEC), International Reading Association (IRA), National Association for the Education of Young Children (NAEYC), and the National Center for Learning Disabilities, Ann Arbor, MI.

Bodrova, E., & Leong, D. J. (2001b). *Tools of the mind: A case study of implementing the Vygotskian approach in American early childhood and primary classrooms.* Geneva, Switzerland: International Bureau of Education, UNESCO, United Nations.

Bodrova, E., & Leong, D. J. (2006). The development of self-regulation in young children: Implications for teacher training. In M. Zaslow & I. Martinez-Beck (Eds.), *Future directions in teacher training.* New York: Brooks Cole.

Bodrova, E., Leong, D. J., Paynter, D. E., & Semenov, D. (2000). *A framework for early literacy instruction: Aligning standards to developmental accomplishments and student behaviors Pre-K to Kindergarten.* Aurora, CO: McREL Mid-continent for Research for Education and Learning.

Boehm, A. E. (1991). Assessment of basic relational concepts. In B. A. Bracken (Ed.), *The psychoeducational assessment of preschool children* (2nd ed., pp. 241–258). Boston: Allyn & Bacon.

Boehm, A., & Weinberg, R. (1997). *The classroom observer: Developing observation skills in early childhood settings* (3rd ed.). New York: Teachers College Press.

Bowman, B. (1992). Reaching potentials of minority children through developmentally and culturally appropriate programs. In S. Bredekamp & T. Rosegrant (Eds.), *Reaching potentials: Appropriate curriculum and assessment for young children* (Vol. 1). Washington, DC: National Association for the Education of Young Children.

Bowman, B., Donovan, M. S., & Burns, M. S. (2001). *Eager to learn: Educating our preschoolers.* Washington, DC: National Academy Press.

Bracey, G. W. (1998). *Put to the test: An educator's and consumer's guide to standardized testing.* Bloomington, IN: Phi Delta Kappa.

Brandt, R. S. (Ed.). (1991). The reflective educator. *Educational Leadership, 48*(6).

Bredekamp, S. (Ed.). (1987). *Developmentally appropriate practice in early childhood programs serving children from birth through age 8.* Washington, DC: National Association for the Education of Young Children.

Bredekamp, S., & Rosegrant, T. (Eds.). (1992). *Reaching potentials: Appropriate curriculum and assessment for young children* (Vol. 1). Washington, DC: National Association for the Education of Young Children.

Bredekamp, S., & Rosegrant, T. (Eds.). (1995). *Reaching potentials: Transforming early childhood curriculum and assessment* (Vol. 2). Washington, DC: National Association for the Education of Young Children.

Bronson, M. B. (2000). *Self-regulation in early childhood: Nature and nurture.* New York: Guilford Press.

Brown, A. L. (1991). Knowing when, where, and how to remember: A problem of metacognition. In R. Glaser (Ed.), *Advances in instructional psychology* (Vol. 1, pp. 77–165). Hillsdale, NJ: Lawrence Erlbaum Associates.

Bukatko, D., & Daehler, M. W. (2003). *Child development: A topical approach* (5th ed.). Boston: Houghton Mifflin.

Burnette, J. (1998). *Reducing the disproportionate representation of minority students in special education.* Reston, VA: ERIC Clearinghouse on Disabilities and Gifted Education. ERIC/OSEP Digest #E566.

Burnette, J. (1999, November). Critical behaviors and strategies for teaching culturally diverse students. (ERIC Number ED435147) ERIC Clearinghouse on Disabilities and Gifted Education. http://ericec.org/digests/e584.html. Retrieved October, 2000.

Burns, M. S., Bodrova, E., Leong, D. J., & Midgette, E. (2001). *Prekindergarten benchmarks for early literacy.* Fairfax, VA: George Mason University.

Caluns, L., Montgomery, K., & Sarlman, D. (1999). Helping children to master the trials and avoid the traps of standardized tests. *Practical Assessment, Research, and Evaluation, 6*(8), 58–69.

Cambourne, B., & Turbill, J. (1990). Assessment in whole-language classrooms: Theory into practice. *The Elementary School Journal, 90,* 337–349.

Campione, J. C., & Brown, A. L. (1985). Linking dynamic assessment with school achievement. In C. S. Lidz (Ed.), *Dynamic assessment: An interactional approach to evaluating learning potential* (pp. 82–195). New York: Guilford Press.

Campione, J. C., Brown, A. L., Reeve, R. A., Ferrara, R. A., & Palinscar, A. S. (1991). Interactive learning and individual understanding: The case of reading and mathematics. In L. T. Landsmann (Ed.), *Culture, schooling, and psychological development* (pp. 136–170). Norwood, NJ: Ablex Publishing.

Capps, R., Passel, J. S., Perez-Lopez, D., Fix, M. E. (2003). *The new neighbors: A user's guide to data on immigrants in U.S. communities.* Annie E. Casey Foundation. Retrieved July 1, 2005 from www.urban.org/url.cfm.D=310844.

Cartwright, C. A., & Cartwright, G. P. (1984). *Developing observation skills* (2nd ed.). New York: McGraw-Hill.

Casey, M. B. (1986). Individual differences in selective attention among prereaders: A key to mirror-image confusion. *Developmental Psychology, 22,* 58–66.

Castaneda, A. M. (1987). Early mathematics education. In C. Seefeldt (Ed.), *The early childhood curriculum: A review of current research* (pp. 165–184). New York: Teachers College Press.

Cazden, C. B. (1972). *Child language and education.* New York: Holt, Rinehart & Winston.

Cazden, C. B. (2006). *Classroom discourse: The language of teaching and learning* (2nd ed.). Portsmouth, NH: Heinemann.

Ceci, S. J. (1991). How does schooling influence general intelligence and its cognitive components? A reassessment of evidence. *Developmental Psychology, 27*(5), 703–722.

Charlesworth, R. (2003). *Understanding child development* (3rd ed.). Albany, NY: Delmar Publishers.

Chicago Public Schools. (2000). *Preparing young elementary students to take standardized tests.* Chicago IL: Author.

Chittenden, E., & Courtney, R. (1989). Assessment of young children's reading: Documentation as an alternative to testing. In D. S. Strickland & L. M. Morrow (Eds.), *Emerging literacy: Young children learn to read and write* (pp. 107–120). Newark, DE: International Reading Association.

Clark, C. M., & Yinger, R. H. (1987). Teacher planning. In D. C. Berliner & B. V. Rosenshine (Eds.), *Talks to teachers* (pp. 342–365). New York: Random House.

Clark, H. H., & Clark, E. V. (1977). *Psychology and language: An introduction to psycholinguistics.* New York: Harcourt Brace Jovanovich.

Clay, M. M. (1991). *Becoming literate: The construction of inner control.* Portsmouth, NH: Heinemann.

Clements, D. H., & Sarama, J. (Eds.). (2004). *Engaging young children in mathematics: Standards for early childhood mathematics.* Mahwah NJ: Lawrence Erlbaum Associates.

Clemmons, J., Laase, L., & Cooper, D. L. (1993). *Portfolios in the classroom: A teacher's sourcebook.* Jefferson City, MO: Scholastic, Inc.

Cohen, D. (1995). What standard for national standards? *Phi Delta Kappan, 76*(10), 751–757.

Cohen, D. H., Stern, V., & Balaban, N. (1997). *Observing and recording the behavior of young children* (4th ed.). New York: Teachers College Press.

Cole, M., Cole, S., & Lightfoot, C. (2004). *The development of children* (5th ed.). New York: WORTH Publishers.

Coleman, J. S. (1991). *Parent involvement in education.* (OERI, Order No. 065-000-00459-3). Washington, DC: U.S. Government Printing Office.

Committee for Economic Development. (1985). *Investing in our children: Business and the public schools.* New York: Author.

Committee for Economic Development. (1991). *The unfinished agenda: A new vision for child development and education.* New York: Author.

Copley, J. V. (Ed.). (1998). *Mathematics in the early years.* Reston, VA: National Council of Teachers of Mathematics and National Association for the Education of Young Children.

Copley, J. V. (2000). *The young child and mathematics.* Washington, DC: National Assocation for the Education of Young Children and National Council of Teachers of Mathematics.

Corbin, C. B. (1980). *A textbook of motor development* (3rd ed.). Dubuque, IA: Wm. C. Brown Publishers.

Corno, L. (1987). Teaching and self-regulated learning. In D. C. Berliner & B. V. Rosenshine (Eds.), *Talks to teachers* (pp. 249–266). New York: Random House.

Council for Exceptional Children. (1998). *IDEA 1997: Let's make it work.* Reston, VA: Author.

Council for Exceptional Children. (2005). *What's new in the new IDEA 2004? Frequently asked questions and answers.* Arlington, VA: Author.

Council of Chief State School Officers. (2005). *The words we use: A glossary of terms for early childhood educators.* Washington, DC: Author. Retrieved June 22, 2005.

Council on Physical Education for Children. (2000). *Appropriate practices for elementary school physical education.* Reston, VA: National Association for Sport and Physical Education.

Cronbach, L. J. (1990). *Essentials of psychological testing* (5th ed.). New York: Harper & Row.

Curry, N. E., & Johnson, C. N. (1990). *Beyond self-esteem: Developing a genuine sense of human value.* Washington, DC: National Association for the Education of Young Children.

Damon, W. (1977). *The social world of the child.* San Francisco: Jossey-Bass.

Damon, W., & Eisenberg, N. (Eds.). (1998). *Handbook of child psychology: Social, emotional and personality development* (5th ed., Vol. 3). New York: John Wiley.

Denham, S. (1998). *Emotional development in young children.* New York: Guilford Press.

Derman-Sparks, L., & A.B.C. Task Force. (1989). *Anti-bias curriculum: Tools for empowering young children.* Washington, DC: National Association for the Education of Young Children.

DeVilliers, J. G., & DeVilliers, P. A. (1978). *Language acquisition.* Cambridge, MA: Harvard University Press.

Devries, R., Zann, B., Hildebrand, R., & Edmiaston, R. (2000). *Developing a constructivist early education curriculum: Practical principles and activities.* New York: Teachers College Press.

Diana v. California State Board of Education et al. No. C-70-37 (N.D.Cal., filed Jan. 7, 1970).

Dickinson, D. K., McCabe, K., & Clark-Chiarelli, N. (2004). Preschool-based prevention of reading disability: Realities vs. possibilities. In C. A. Stone, E. R. Silliman, B. J. Ehren, & K. Apel (Eds.), *Handbook of language and literacy: Development and disorders* (pp. 209–227). New York: Guilford Press.

Dodge, K. A., Pettit, G. S., McClaskey, C. L., & Brown, M. M. (1986). Social competence in children. *Monographs of the Society for Research in Child Development, 51* (2, Serial No. 213).

Dodge, K. A., & Somberg, D. R. (1987). Hostile attributional biases among aggressive boys are exacerbated under conditions of threats to the self. *Child Development, 58,* 213–224.

Dunn, J. (2004). *Children's friendships: The beginning of intimacy.* Malden, MA: Blackwell.

Dutton, W. H., & Dutton, A. (1991). *Mathematics children use and understand: Preschool through third grade.* Mountain View, CA: Mayfield Publishing.

Education for All Handicapped Children Act of 1975. 20 U.S.C. 1401 (P.L. 94-142).

Education of the Handicapped Act Amendments of 1986. 20 U.S.C. 1400 (P.L. 99-457).

Education Week/Special Report. (1995, April 12). *Struggling for standards.*

Eisenberg, N. (1982). The development of reasoning regarding prosocial behavior. In N. Eisenberg (Ed.), *The development of prosocial behavior* (pp. 219–249). New York: Academic Press.

Eisenberg, N., & Fabes, R. A. (1998). Prosocial development. In N. Eisenberg (Ed.), *Handbook of child development: Vol. 3. Social emotional, and personality development* (5th ed., pp. 708–778). New York: Wiley.

Eisner, E. (1991). What really counts in schools. *Educational Leadership, 48*(5), 10–17.

Eisner, E. (1995). Standards for American schools: Help or hindrance? *Phi Delta Kappan, 76*(10), 758–764.

Elkind, D. (1979). *The child and society: Essays in applied child development.* New York: Oxford University Press.

Engel, B. (1990). An approach to assessment in early literacy. In C. Kamii (Ed.), *Achievement testing in the early grades: The games grown-ups play* (pp. 119–134). Washington, DC: National Association for the Education of Young Children.

Epstein, A. S., Schweinhart, L. J., DeBruin-Parecki, A., and Robin, K. B. (2004). Preschool assessment: A guide to developing a balanced approach. *Preschool Policy Matters.* Issue 7/July 2004. National Institute for Early Education Research.

Epstein, J. L. (1987). Parent involvement: What research says to administrators. In E. E. Gotts & R. F. Purnell (Eds.), *Education and urban society: School–family relations* (pp. 119–136). Newbury Park, CA: Sage Publications.

Erdley, C. A., & Nangle, D. W. (Eds.). (2001). *The role of friendship in psychological adjustment: New directions for child and adolescent development.* San Francisco: Jossey-Bass.

ERIC Clearinghouse on Disabilities and Gifted Education. (1994). *Rights and responsibilities of parents of children with disabilities.* Reston, VA: Author.

FairTest. (1990). What's wrong with standardized tests? *Factsheet.* Cambridge, MA: National Center for Fair and Open Testing.

Family Educational Rights and Privacy Act of 1974, 513(b) (1). 20 U.S.C. 1232 (P.L. 93-380).

Feldman, R. S. (2001). *Child development: A topical approach* (2nd ed.). Upper Saddle River, NJ: Prentice Hall.

Feuerstein, R. (1979). *The dynamic assessment of retarded performers: The Learning Potential Assessment Device, theory, instruments, techniques.* Baltimore, MD: University Park Press.

Finn, C. E., Jr. (1991, March 11). National testing, no longer a foreign idea. *Wall Street Journal,* p. 10A.

Flavell, J. H. (1963). *The developmental psychology of Jean Piaget.* New York: Van Nostrand.

Forman, G., & Kaden, M. (1987). Research on science education for young children. In C. Seefeldt (Ed.), *The early childhood curriculum: A review of current research* (pp. 141–164). New York: Teachers College Press.

Frank, C. (1999). *Ethnographic eyes: A teacher's guide to classroom observation.* Portsmouth, NH: Heinemann.

Frede, E. C., Dessewffy, M., Hornbeck, A., & Worth, A. (2000). *Preschool classroom mathematics inventory (PCMI).* Ewing, NJ: College of New Jersey.

Frost, J. L., Wortham, S. C., & Reifel, S. (2001). *Play and child development.* Upper Saddle River, NJ: Prentice Hall.

Fuson, K. C. (2003). Pre-K to grade 2 goals and standards: Achieving 21st century mastery for all. In D. H. Clements & J. Sarama (Eds.), *Engaging young children in mathematics* (pp. 105–147). Mahwah, NJ: Lawrence Erlbaum Associates.

Gage, N. L., & Berliner, D. C. (1998). *Educational psychology* (6th ed.). Boston: Houghton Mifflin.

Gage, N. L., & Berliner, D. C. (1992). *Educational psychology* (5th ed.). Boston: Houghton Mifflin.

Gallahue, D. L. (1982). *Developmental movement exercises for young children.* New York: John Wiley and Sons.

Gallahue, D. L. (1993). Motor development and movement skill acquisition in early childhood education. In B. Spodek (Ed.), *Handbook of research on the education of young children* (pp. 24–41). New York: Macmillan.

Gardner, H. (1985). *Frames of mind: The theory of multiple intelligences.* New York: Basic Books.

Gardner, H. (1991). *The unschooled mind.* New York: Harper & Row.

Genishi, C. (1987). Acquiring oral language and communicative competence. In C. Seefeldt (Ed.), *The early childhood curriculum: A review of current research* (pp. 75–106). New York: Teachers College Press.

Genishi, C. (1988). Children's language: Learning words from experience. *Young Children, 44*(1), 16–23.

Genishi, C. (1992). *Ways of assessing children and curriculum: Stories of early childhood practice.* New York: Teachers College Press.

Gentry, J. R. (1982). An analysis of developmental spelling in GYNS AT WRK. *The Reading Teacher, 36*(2), 192–200.

Geography Education Standards Project. (1994). *Geography for life: National geography standards.* Washington, DC: National Geographic Research & Evaluation.

Gilles, D., & Clark, D. (2001). Collaborative teaming in the assessment process. In S. Alper, D. L. Ryndak, & C. N. Schloss (Eds.), *Alternative assessment of students with disabilities in inclusive settings* (pp. 75–112). Boston: Allyn & Bacon.

Ginsburg, H. P. (1997). *Entering the child's mind: The clinical interview in psychological research and practice.* Cambridge, U.K.: Cambridge University Press.

Ginsburg, H., & Opper, S. (1988). *Piaget's theory of intellectual development* (3rd ed.). Englewood Cliffs, NJ: Prentice Hall.

Glaser, R. (1987). The integration of instruction and testing: Implications from the study of human cognition. In D. C. Berliner & B. V. Rosenshine (Eds.), *Talks to teachers* (pp. 329–343). New York: Random House.

Gleason, J. B. (2004). *The development of language* (6th ed.). Boston: Allyn & Bacon.

Gonzalez-Mena, J. (1997). *Multicultural issues in child care* (2nd ed.). Mountain View, CA: Mayfield Publishing Company.

Goodenow, C. (1992). Strengthening the links between educational psychology and the study of social contexts. *Educational Psychologist, 27*(2), 177–196.

Goodman, K. S., Goodman, Y. M., & Hood, W. J. (Eds.). (1989). *The whole language evaluation book.* Portsmouth, NH: Heinemann.

Goodman, Y. M. (1978). Kid watching: An alternative to testing. *National Elementary School Principal, 57*(4), 41–51.

Goodwin, W. R., & Driscoll, L. A. (1980). *Handbook for measurement and evaluation in early childhood education.* San Francisco: Jossey-Bass.

Goodwin, W. R., & Goodwin, L. D. (1993). Young children and measurement: Standardized and nonstandardized instruments in early childhood education. In B. Spodek (Ed.), *Handbook of research on the education of young children* (pp. 441–463). New York: Macmillan.

Gotts, E. E. (1984). Using academic guidance sheets. In O. McAfee (Ed.), *School–home communications: A resource notebook.* Charleston, WV: Appalachia Educational Laboratory.

Grabe, M. (1986). Attentional processes in education. In G. D. Phye & T. Andre (Eds.), *Cognitive classroom learning: Understanding, thinking, and problem solving.* Orlando, FL: Academic Press.

Gregory, R. J. (2003). *Psychological testing: History, principles, and application.* Boston: Allyn & Bacon.

Guerin, G. R., & Maier, A. S. (1983). *Informal assessment in education.* Palo Alto, CA: Mayfield Publishing.

Gullo, D. F. (2005). *Understanding assessment and evaluation in early childhood education* (2nd ed.). New York: Teachers College Press.

Gumperz, J. J., & Gumperz, J. C. (1981). Ethnic differences in communicative style. In C. A. Ferguson & S. B. Heath (Eds.), *Language in the USA.* Cambridge, England: Cambridge University Press.

Hakuta, K., Butler, Y. G., & Win, D. (2000). *How long does it take English learners to attain proficiency?* (Policy Report No. 200–1). Palo Alto, CA: The University of California Linguistic Minority Research Institute.

Hamilton, R. N., & Shoemaker, M. A. (2000). *AMCI 2000: Assessment matrix for classroom instruction.* Portland, OR: Northwest Regional Educational Laboratory.

Haney, W., & Madaus, G. (1989). Searching for alternatives to standardized tests: Whys, whats, and whithers. *Phi Delta Kappan, 70,* 683–687.

Hanfmann, F., & Kasanin, J. (1937). A method of study of concept formation. *Journal of Psychology, 3,* 521–540.

Hannon, J. H. (2000). Learning to like Matthew. *Young Children, 55*(6), 24–28.

Harms, T., Clifford, R. M., & Cryer, D. (1998). *Early childhood environment rating scale: Revised edition.* New York: Teachers College Press.

Harter, S. (2001). *The construction of the self: A developmental perspective.* New York: Guilford Press.

Hastie, P. A., & Martin, E. (2006). *Teaching elementary physical education: Strategies for the classroom teacher.* San Francisco: Pearson Benjamin Cummings.

Haywood, K., & Gretchell, N. (2001). *Lifespan motor development.* Champaign, IL: Kinetics Publications.

Hebert, E. A. (1992, May). Portfolios invite reflection—from students and staff. *Educational Leadership, 49*(8), 58–61.

Hebert, E. A. (1998). Lessons learned about student portfolios. *Phi Delta Kappan, 79*(8), 583–585.

Helm, J. H., Beneke, S., & Steinheimer, K. (1998). *Teacher materials for documenting young children's work.* New York: Teachers College Press.

Helm, J. H., Beneke, S., & Steinheimer, K. (1998). *Windows on learning.* New York: Teachers College Press.

Helm, J., & Katz, L. (2000). *Young investigators: The project approach in the early years.* New York: Teachers College Press.

Hendrick, J. (1997). *First steps toward teaching the Reggio way.* Upper Saddle River, NJ: Prentice Hall.

Hendrick, J., & Weisman, P. (2005). *The whole child* (8th ed.). Englewood Cliffs, NJ: Merrill.

Herman, J. L., Aschbacher, P. R., & Winters, L. (1992). *A practical guide to alternative assessment.* Alexandria, VA: Association for Supervision and Curriculum Development.

Hetherington, E. M., Parke, R. D., Gauvain, M., & Locke, V. O. (2005). *Child psychology: A contemporary viewpoint* (6th ed.). New York: McGraw-Hill.

Hiebert, E. F., & Calfee, R. C. (1989). Advancing academic literacy through teachers' assessments. *Educational Leadership, 47*(3), 50–54.

High/Scope Educational Research Foundation. (1992; 2003). *Child observation record.* Ypsilanti, MI: Author.

Hills, T. W. (1992). Reaching potentials through appropriate assessment. In S. Bredekamp & T. Rosegrant (Eds.), *Reaching potentials: Appropriate curriculum and assessment for young children* (Vol. 1). Washington, DC: National Association for the Education of Young Children.

Hinitz, B. F. (1987). Social studies in early childhood education. In C. Seefeldt (Ed.), *The early childhood curriculum: A review of current research* (pp. 237–270). New York: Teachers College Press.

Hodgkinson, H. (2003). *Leaving too many children behind: A demographer's view on the neglect of America's youngest children.* Washington, DC: The Institute for Educational Leadership, Inc.

Hoff, E. (2004). *Language development* (3rd ed.). Belmont, CA: Wadsworth Publishing.

Holmes, C. T., & Matthews, K. M. (1984). The effects of nonpromotion on elementary and junior high school pupils: A meta-analysis. *Review of Educational Research, 54,* 225–236.

Honig, A., Wittmer, D. S., & Honig, A. S. (1992). *Prosocial development in children: Caring, helping and cooperating: A bibliographic resource guide.* New York: Garland.

Hopkins, K. D., Stanley, J. C., & Hopkins, B. R. (1990). *Educational and psychological measurement and evaluation* (7th ed.). Englewood Cliffs, NJ: Prentice Hall.

Howes, C. (1980). Play scale as an index of complexity of peer interaction. *Developmental Psychology, 16,* 371–381.

Howes, C. (1988). *Peer interaction of young children.* Chicago: Society for Research in Child Development.

Humphrey, S. (1989). The case of myself. *Young Children, 45*(1), 17–22.

Individuals with Disabilities Education Act Amendments of 1997, P. L. 105–17, 105th Cong., 1st sess.

Individuals with Disabilities Education Improvement Act (IDEA) of 2004. P. L. 108-466. H. R. 1350.

Invernizzi, M., Juel, C., Swank, L., & Meier, J. (2004). *Kindergarten technical reference for the phonological awareness literacy screening test (PALS).* Richmond, VA: University of Virginia, Curry School of Education.

Invernizzi, M., Sullivan, A., Meier, J., & Swank, L. (2004). *Pre-K teacher's manual: PALS phonological awareness literacy screening.* Richmond, VA: University of Virginia Curry School of Education.

Irwin, D. M., & Bushnell, M. M. (1980). *Observational strategies for child study.* New York: Holt, Rinehart & Winston.

Jagger, A. M. (1985). Introduction and overview. In A. M. Jagger & M. T. Smith-Burke (Eds.), *Observing the language learner* (pp. 1–7). Newark, DE: International Reading Association.

Jersild, A. T. (1955). *When teachers face themselves.* New York: Teachers College Press.

Jewett, J. (1992, February). *Effective strategies for school-based early childhood centers.* Portland, OR: Northwest Regional Educational Laboratory.

Johnson, D. W., Johnson, R. T., Holubec, E. J., & Roy, P. (1984). *Circles of learning: Cooperation in the classroom.* Alexandria, VA: Association for Supervision and Curriculum Development.

Johnson, J. E., Christie, J. F., & Yawkey, T. D. (1987). *Play and early childhood development.* Glenview, IL: Scott, Foresman.

Johnston, P. (2003). Assessment conversations. *The Reading Teacher, 57*(1), 90–92.

Joint Committee on Standards for Educational Evaluation. (2003). *The student evaluation standards: How to improve evaluations of students.* Thousand Oaks, CA: Corwin Press.

Jones, E., & Derman-Sparks, L. (1992). Meeting the challenge of diversity. *Young Children, 47*(2), 12–18.

Jones, R. L. (1988). *Psychoeducational assessment of minority group children: A casebook* (2nd ed.). Boston: Allyn & Bacon.

Juarez, T. (1996). Why any grades at all, Father? *Phi Delta Kappan, 77*(5), 374–377.

Kagan, S. L., Moore, E., & Bredekamp, S. (Eds.). (1995). *Reconsidering children's early development and learning: Toward common views and vocabulary.* Washington, DC: National Educational Goals Panel.

Kamii, C. (Ed.). (1990). *Achievement testing in the early grades.* Washington, DC: National Association for the Education of Young Children.

Kamii, C., & Rosenblum, V. (1990). An approach to assessment in mathematics. In C. Kamii (Ed.), *Achievement testing in the early grades: The games grown-ups play* (pp. 146–162). Washington, DC: National Associatoin for the Education of Young Children.

Kamii, C., & Houseman, L. B. (2000). *Young children reinvent arithmetic: Implications of Piaget's theory* (2nd ed.). New York: Teachers College Press.

Kaplan, R., & Sccuzzo, D. (2004). *Psychological testing: Principles, applications, and issues* (6th ed.). New York: Wadsworth.

Katz, L. G., & Chard, S. C. (1989). *Engaging children's minds: The project approach.* Norwood, NJ: Ablex Publishing.

Katz, L. G., Evangelou, D., & Hartman, J. A. (1990). *The case for mixed-age grouping in early education.* Washington, DC: National Association for the Education of Young Children.

Kendall, J. S., & Marzano, R. J. (1997). *Content knowledge: A compendium of standards and benchmarks for K–12 education.* Alexandria, VA: Association for Supervision and Curriculum Development.

Kendall, J. S. (2001). A technical guide for revising or developing standards and benchmarks. Aurora, CO: Mid-Continent Research for Education and Learning.

Kendrick, S. K., Kaufman, R., & Messenger, K. P. (Eds.). (1988). *Healthy young children: A manual for programs.* Washington, DC: National Association for the Education of Young Children.

Keyser, D. J., & Sweetland, R. C. (2006). *Test critiques.* (Vol. I–XI). Austin, TX: Pro-Ed Publishing.

Kingore, B. (1993). *Portfolios: Enriching and assessing all students.* Des Moines, IA: Leadership Publishers, Inc.

Kostelnik, M., Whiren, A., Soderman, A., Stein, L., & Gregory, K. (2001). *Guiding children's social development* (4th ed.). Albany, NY: Thomas Delmar Learning.

Kounin, J. S. (1970). *Discipline and group management in classrooms.* New York: Holt, Rinehart & Winston.

Krechevsky, M. (1991). Project spectrum: An innovative assessment alternative. *Educational Leadership, 48*(5), 45–48.

Kuschner, D. (1989). "Put your name on your painting, but . . . the blocks go back on the shelves." *Young Children, 45*(1), 49–56.

Kusimo, P., Ritter, M., Busick, K., Ferguson, C., Trumbull, E., & Solano-Flores, G. (2000). *Making assessment work for everyone: How to build on student strengths,* San Francisco, CA: WestEd.

Ladd, G. W. (1990). Having friends, keeping friends, making friends, and being liked by peers in the classroom: Predictors of children's early school adjustment? *Child Development, 61,* 1081–1100.

LaParo, K., & Pianta, R. C. (2001). *Classroom assessment scoring system (CLASS).* Charlottesville, VA: Curry School of Education, University of Virginia.

Lapp, D., Block, C. C., Cooper, E. J., Flood, J., Rose, N., & Tinaiero, J. V. (Eds.). (2004). *Teaching all the children: Strategies for developing literacy in an urban setting.* New York: Guilford Press.

Lau v. *Nichols,* 414 U.S. 563 (1974).

Lawson, J. (1986). A study of the frequency of analogical responses to questions in black and white preschool-age children. *Early Childhood Research Quarterly, 1*(4), 379–386.

Lay-Dopyera, M., & Dopyera, J. E. (1987). *Becoming a teacher of young children* (2nd ed.). Lexington, MA: D. C. Heath.

LeFreniere, P. (1999). *Emotional development: A biosocial perspective.* New York, NY: Wadsworth.

Leong, D. J., McAfee, O., & Swedlow, R. (1992). Assessment and planning in early childhood classrooms. *The Journal of Early Childhood Teacher Education, 13*(40), 20–21.

Levine, K. (1995). *Development of prewriting and scissor skills: A visual analysis.* Boston: Communication Skill Builders.

Lewis, A. (1991). America 2000: What kind of a nation? *Phi Delta Kappan, 72*(10), 734–735.

Lewis, A. (1995). An overview of the standards movement. *Phi Delta Kappan, 76*(10), 745–750.

Lidz, C. S. (1991). *Practitioner's guide to dynamic assessment.* New York: Guilford Press.

Lidz, C. S. (2003). *Early childhood assessment.* Hoboken, NJ: John Wiley & Sons.

Linder, T. W. (1993). *Transdisciplinary play-based assessment: A functional approach to working with young children.* Baltimore: Paul H. Brooks.

Lindfors, J. W. (1987). *Children's language and learning* (2nd ed.). Englewood Cliffs, NJ: Prentice Hall.

Locke, J. L. (1993). *The child's path to spoken language.* Cambridge, MA: Harvard University Press.

Lonigan, C. J. (2003). Development and promotion of emergent literacy skills in preschool children at-risk of reading difficulties. In B. Foorman (Ed.), *Preventing and remediating reading difficulties: Bringing science to scale* (pp. 23–50). Timonium, MD: New York Press.

Love, J. M. (1991, November 9). *Transition activities in American schools.* Paper presented at the National Association for the Education of Young Children Conference, Denver, CO.

Love, J. M., & Yelton, B. (1989). Smoothing the road from preschool to kindergarten. *Principal, 68*(5), 26–27.

Lynch, E. W., & Hanson, M. J. (2004). Family diversity, assessment, and cultural competence. In M. McLean, M. Wolery, & D. B. Bailey (Eds.), *Assessing infants and preschoolers with pecial needs.* Upper Saddle River, NJ: Merrill Prentice-Hall.

Maeroff, G. I. (1991). Assessing alternative assessment. *Phi Delta Kappan, 73,* 272–281.

Manning, M. L., & Lucking, R. (1990). Ability grouping: Realities and alternatives. *Childhood Education, 66*(7), 254–256.

Marzano, R. J. (2000). *Transforming classroom grading.* Alexandria, VA: Association for Supervision and Curriculum Development.

Marzano, R. J., Pickering, D., & McTighe, J. (1993). *Assessing student outcomes: Performance assessment using the dimensions of learning model.* Alexandria, VA: Association for Supervision and Curriculum Development.

Mason J. M., & Stewart, J. J. (1990). Emergent literacy assessment for instructional use in kindergarten. In L. M. Morrow & J. K. Smith (Eds.), *Assessment for instruction in early literacy* (pp. 155–175). Englewood Cliffs, NJ: Prentice Hall.

Masten, A. S. (1989). Resilience in development: Implications of the study of successful adaptation for developmental psychopathology. In D. Cicchetti (Ed.), *The emergence of a discipline: Rochester symposium on developmental psychopathology* (Vol. 1, pp. 261–294). Hillsdale, NJ: Lawrence Erlbaum Associates.

Mayer, R. E. (1992). Cognition and instruction: Their historic meeting within educational psychology. *Journal of Educational Psychology, 84*(4), 405–412.

Mid-Continent Research for Education and Learning. (2004). *Online standards and benchmark database* (4th ed.). Aurora, CO. Author. Available online at www.mcrel.org.

McAfee, O. (1985). Circle time: Getting past "two little pumpkins." *Young Children, 40*(6), 24–29.

McAfee, O., Leong, D. J., & Bodrova, E. (2004). *Basics of assessment: A primer for early childhood educators.* Washington, DC: NAEYC.

McGhee, L. M., & Richgels, D. J. (1990). *Literacy's beginnings.* Boston: Allyn & Bacon.

Meisels, S. J. (1997). Using work sampling in authentic assessment. *Educational Leadership, 54*(4), 60–65.

Meisels, S. J. (2000). On the side of the child. *Young Children, 55*(6), 16–19.

Meisels, S. J., Jablon, J. R., Marsden, D. B., Dichtelmiller, M. L., Dorfman, A. B., & Steele, D. M. (1994). *The work sampling system: An overview* (3rd ed.). Ann Arbor, MI: Rebus Planning Associates, Inc.

Meisels, S. J., & Steele, D. (1991). The early childhood portfolio collection process. *Center for Human Growth and Development.* Ann Arbor, MI: University of Michigan.

Meisels, S. J., Steele, D. M., & Quinn-Leering, K. (1993). Testing, tracking, and retaining young children: An analysis of research and social policy. In B. Spodek (Ed.), *Handbook of research on the education of young children* (pp. 279–292). New York: Macmillan.

Mendelson, A., & Atlas, R. (1973). Early childhood assessment: Paper and pencil for whom? *Childhood Education, 49,* 357–361.

Menyuk, P. (1988). *Language development: Knowledge and use.* Boston: Scott, Foresman.

Mercer, J. (1972). *Labeling the mentally retarded.* Berkeley, CA: University of California Press.

Mergendoller, J. R., & Marchman, V. A. (1987). Friends and associates. In V. Richardson-Koehler (Ed.), *Educators' handbook: A research perspective* (pp. 279–328). New York: Longman.

Messer, D. J. (1995). *The development of communication from social interaction to language.* New York: John Wiley and Sons.

Meyer, C. A. (1992, May). What's the difference between authentic and performance assessment? *Educational Leadership, 49*(8), 39–40.

Mindes, G. (2005). Social studies in today's early childhood curriculum. *Young Children, 60*(5), 12–19.

Moats, L. C., Good, R. H., & Kaminski, R. A. (2003). *DIBELS: Dynamic indicators of basic early literacy skills* (6th ed.). Longmont, CO: Sopris West.

Morine-Dershimer, G. (1990, November 12). Paper presented at the meeting of the National Association of Early Childhood Teacher Educators, Washington, DC.

Morrow, L. M. (1990). Assessing children's understanding of story through their construction and reconstruction of narrative. In L. M. Morrow & J. K. Smith (Eds.), *Assessment for instruction in early literacy* (pp. 110–134). Englewood Cliffs, NJ: Prentice Hall.

Morrow, L. M. (2004). *Literacy development in the early years* (5th ed.). Boston: Pearson.

Morrow, L. M., & Smith, J. K. (Eds.). (1990). *Assessment for instruction in early literacy.* Englewood Cliffs, NJ: Prentice Hall.

Mowbray, J. K., & Salisbury, H. H. (1975). *Diagnosing individual needs for early childhood education.* Columbus, OH: Merrill.

Murphy, S., & Smith, M. A. (1990, Spring). Talking about portfolios. *The quarterly of the national writing project and the center for the study of writing.* Berkeley, CA: University of California.

National Association of Early Childhood Specialists in State Departments of Education (NAECS/SDE). (2000). *Still unacceptable trends in kindergarten entry and placement: 2000 revision and update.* Washington, DC: Author.

NAECS/SDE Minnesota State Summary for 2002–2003. Paper presented at NAECS/SDE Conference, November 2003, Chicago, IL.

National Association for the Education of Young Children (NAEYC). (1988). Position statement on standardized testing of young children 3 through 8 years of age. *Young Children, 43*(3), 42–47.

NAEYC. (2001). *NAEYC standards for early childhood professional preparation: Initial licensure programs.* Washington, DC: Author.

NAEYC. (2005). *Screening and assessment of young English-language learners: Supplement to the NAEYC position statement on early childhood curriculum, assessment, and program evaluation.* Washington. DC: Author.

NAEYC & NAECS/SDE. (2003). *Early childhood curriculum, assessment, and program evaluation.* Washington, DC: Author.

NAEYC & National Council of Teachers of Mathematics (NCTM). (2002). *Early childhood mathematics: Promoting good beginnings.* Washington, DC: Author.

NAEYC & NCTM. (2003). Learning paths and teaching strategies in early mathematics. *Young Children, 58*(1), 41–43.

National Association for Sport and Physical Education (NASPE). (2004). *Active starts: A statement of physical activity guidelines for children birth to five.* Reston, VA: Author.

National Association of State Boards of Education (NASBE). (1988). *Right from the start: The report of the NASBE task force on early childhood education.* Alexandria, VA: Author.

National Council for Social Studies (NCSS). (1994). *Curriculum standards for social studies: Expectations for excellence.* Silver Springs, MD: Author.

National Council of Teachers of Mathematics. (1989). *Curriculum and evaluation standards for school mathematics.* Reston, VA: Author.

National Council of Teachers of Mathematics. (2000). *Principles and standards for school mathematics.* Reston, VA: Author.

National Education Association. (1993). *Student portfolios.* West Haven, CT: Author.

National Governors' Association. (1990). *America in transition: Report of the Task Force on Children.* Washington, DC: Author.

National Reading Panel. (2000). *Teaching children to read: An evidence-based assessment of the scientific literature on reading and its implications for reading instruction.* Bethesda, MD: National Reading Panel.

NCSS Task Force on Early Childhood/Elementary School Social Studies. (1988). *Social studies for early childhood and elementary school children preparing for the 21st century.* Silver Spring, MD: Author.

Neuman, S. B., Copple, C., & Bredekamp, S. (2000). *Learning to read and write: Developmentally appropriate practices for young children.* Washington, DC: National Association for the Education of Young Children.

New, D. A. (1991). Teaching in the fourth world. *Phi Delta Kappan, 73*(5), 396–398.

New Jersey Department of Education. (2004). Preschool learning and teaching expectations: Standards of quality. Retrieved February 2, 2006 from www.state.nj.us.njded/ece/expectations.

Newman, D., Griffin, P., & Cole, M. (1989). *The construction zone: Working for cognitive change in school.* Cambridge: Cambridge University Press.

Nicholson, S., & Shipstead, S. G. (1998). *Through the looking glass: Observations in the early childhood classsroom* (2nd ed.). Upper Saddle River, NJ: Prentice Hall.

No Child Left Behind Act. (2002). P.L. 107-110. H.R.1

Northwest Regional Educational Laboratory. (1991, June). New rules, roles, relationships explored. *Northwest Report,* 1–2.

Northwest Regional Educational Laboratory. (1994). *Portfolio resources bibliography.* Portland, OR: Author.

Oakes, J. (1991). *Can tracking research influence school practice?* Paper presented at the meetings of the American Educational Research Association, Chicago, IL.

Oates, J., & Grayson, A. (Eds.). (2004). *Cognitive and language development in children.* Cambridge, England: Blackwell.

Ormrod, J. E. (2002). *Educational psychology* (4th ed.). Upper Saddle River, NJ: Merrill/ Prentice Hall.

Owens, R. L. (2004). *Language development: An introduction.* New York: Macmillan.

Owocki, G. (1999). *Literacy through play.* Portsmouth, NH: Heinemann.

Papalia, D. E., Olds, S. W., & Feldman, R. D. (2004). *A child's world: Infancy through adolescence* (8th ed.). New York: McGraw-Hill.

Parten, M. B. (1933). Social participation among preschool children. *Journal of Abnormal and Social Psychology, 27,* 243–269.

Patterson, K., & Wright, A. (1990). Speech, language, or hearing impaired children: At risk academically. *Childhood Education, 64*(2), 91–95.

Paulson, F., Paulson, P., & Meyer, C. (1991). What makes a portfolio a portfolio? *Educational Leadership, 48,* 60–63.

Paynter, D., Bodrova, E., & Doty, J. K. (2005). *For the love of words: Vocabulary instruction that works.* San Francisco: Jossey-Bass.

Pepler, D. J., & Rubin, K. H. (1991). *The development and treatment of childhood aggression.* Hillsdale, NJ: Erlbaum.

Perrone, V. (1991). *On standardized testing: A position paper of the Association for Childhood Education International.* Wheaton, MD: Association for Childhood Education International.

Peterson, M. (1995). Research analysis of primary children's writing. ERIC Document ED-382-986.

Petty, W. T., Petty, D. C., & Salzer, R. T. (1989). *Experience in language* (5th ed.). Boston: Allyn & Bacon.

Phillips, S. U. (1983). *The invisible culture: Communication in classroom and community on the Warm Springs Indian Reservation.* White Plains, NY: Longman.

Phinney, J. S. (1982). Observing children: Ideas for teachers. *Young Children, 37,* 14–17.

Phye, G. D., & Andre, T. (Eds.). (1986). *Cognitive classroom learning: Understanding, thinking, and problem solving.* Orlando, FL: Academic Press.

Poest, C. A., Williams, J. R., Witt, D. D., & Atwood, M. E. (1990). Challenge me to move: Large muscle development in young children. *Young Children 45*(5), 4–10.

Popham, W. J. (2000). *Testing! Testing!: What every parent should know about school tests.* Boston: Allyn & Bacon.

Popham, W. J. (2005). *Classroom assessment: What teachers need to know* (4th ed.). Boston: Allyn & Bacon.

Powell, D. (1989). *Families and early childhood programs.* Washington, DC: National Association for the Education of Young Children.

Raines, S. C. (1990). Representational competence: (Re)presenting experience through words, actions, and images. *Childhood Education, 66,* 139–144.

Raver, C. C. (2002). Emotions matter: Making the case for the role of young children's emotional development for early school readiness. *Social Policy Report.* A Publication of the Society for Research in Child Development. (Vol. XVI, 3).

Ravitch, D. (1995). *National standards in American education.* Washington, DC: Brookings Institution.

Resnick, L. B., & Resnick, D. L. (1992). Assessing the thinking curriculum: New tools for educational reform. In B. R. Gifford & M. C. O'Connor (Eds.), *Future assessments: Changing views of aptitude, achievement, and instruction* (pp. 737–750). Boston: Kluwer.

Rhodes, L., & Shanklin, N. (1992). *Literacy assessment in whole language classrooms K–8.* Portsmouth, NH: Heinemann.

Rhodes, L., & Shanklin, N. (1993). *Windows into literacy: Assessing learners K–8.* Portsmouth, NH: Heinemann.

Richardson, K. (2000). *Mathematics standards for prekindergarten through grade 2* (No. EDO-PS-00-11). Champaign, IL: ERIC Clearinghouse on Elementary and Early Childhood Education.

Rodari, G. (1996). *The grammar of fantasy: An introduction to the art of inventing stories* (J. Zipes, Trans.). New York: Teachers & Writers Collaborative.

Rogers, C. S., & Sawyers, J. K. (1988). *Play in the lives of children.* Washington, DC: National Association for the Education of Young Children.

Rogoff, B. (1990). *Apprenticeship in thinking: Cognitive development in social context.* New York: Oxford University Press.

Rogoff, B., & Gardner, W. (1984). Adult guidance of cognitive development. In B. Rogoff & J. Lave (Eds.), *Everyday cognition: Its development in social context* (pp. 95–116). Cambridge, MA: Harvard University Press.

Roskos, K. A., Tabors, P. O., & Lenhart, L. A. (2004). *Oral language and early literacy in preschool: Talking, reading and writing.* Newark, DE: International Reading Association.

Rowe, D. W. (1993). *Preschoolers as authors: Literacy learning in the social world of the classroom.* Creskill, NJ: Hampton Press.

Rubin, K. H., Bukowski, W., & Parker, J. G. (1998). Peer interactions, relationships, and groups. In W. Damon & N. Eisenberg (Eds.), *Handbook of child psychology* (5th ed., Vol. 3, pp. 619–700). New York: John Wiley.

Sakharov, L. S. (1990). Methods for investigating concepts. *Soviet Psychology, 28*(4), 35–66.

Salvoey, P., & Sluyter, D. (Eds.). (1997). *Emotional development and emotional intelligence: Educational implications.* New York: Basic Books.

Samuels, S. C. (1977). *Enhancing self-concept in early childhood.* New York: Human Sciences Press.

Sandoval, J., & Irvin, M. G. (1990). Legal and ethical issues in assessment of children. In C. R. Reynolds & R. W. Kamphaus (Eds.), *Handbook of psychological and educational assessment of children: Intelligence and achievement* (pp. 239–252). New York: Guilford Press.

Santrock, J. (2003). *Child development* (10th ed.). New York: McGraw-Hill.

Sattler, J. M. (2001). *Assessment of children* (5th ed.). San Diego, CA: Jerome M. Sattler.

Schaefer, R. E., Staub, C., & Smith, K. (1983). *Language functions and school success.* Glenview, IL: Scott Foresman.

Schiamberg, L. B. (1988). *Child and adolescent development.* New York: Macmillan.

Schickedanz, J. A. (1999). *Much more than the ABC's.* Washington, DC: National Association for the Education of Young Children.

Schickedanz, J. A., & Casbergue, R. M. (2004). *Writing in preschool.* Newark, DE: International Reading Association.

Schickedanz, J. A., Schickedanz, D. I., Forsyth, P. D., & Forsyth, G. A. (2001). *Understanding children* (4th ed.). Boston: Allyn & Bacon.

Schirmer, G. J. (1974). *Performance objectives for preschool children.* New York: Adapt Press.

Schultz, K. A., Colarusso, R. P., & Strawderman, V. W. (1989). *Mathematics for every young child.* Columbus, OH: Merrill.

Schwartz, S. L., & Robinson, H. F. (1982). *Designing curriculum for early childhood.* Boston: Allyn & Bacon.

Seefeldt, C. (2000). *Social studies for the preschool–primary child* (6th ed.). Columbus, OH: Merrill.

Selman, R. L. (1981). The child as a friendship philosopher. In S. R. Asher & J. M. Gottman (Eds.), *The development of children's friendships* (pp. 242–272). Cambridge, England: Cambridge University Press.

Shaklee, B. D., Barbour, N. E., Ambrose, R., & Hansford, S. J. (1997). *Designing and using portfolios.* Boston: Allyn & Bacon.

Shepard, L. A. (1982). Definition of bias. In R. A. Berk (Ed.), *Handbook of methods for detecting test bias* (pp. 9–30). Baltimore: The Johns Hopkins University Press.

Shepard, L. A. (1989). Why we need better assessments. *Educational Leadership, 46*(7), 4–9.

Shepard, L. A. (1991a). Psychometricians' beliefs about learning. *Educational Researcher, 20*(7), 2–16.

Shepard, L. A. (1991b). Will national tests improve student learning? *Phi Delta Kappan, 73,* 232–238.

Shepard, L. A. (2000). The role of assessment in a learning culture. *Educational Researcher, 29*(7), 4–14.

Shepard, L. A., & C. L. Bliem. (1993). *Parent opinions about standardized tests, teacher's information, and performance assessments: A case study of the effects of alternative assessment in instruction, student learning, and accountability practices.* Los Angeles, CA: National Center for Research on Evaluation, Standards, and Student Testing. (ERIC Document Reproduction Service No. ED 378227).

Shepard, L. A., & Graue, M. E. (1993). The morass of school readiness screening: Research on test use and test validity. In B. Spodek (Ed.), *Handbook of research on the education of young children* (pp. 293–305). New York: Macmillan.

Shepard, L. A., & Smith, M. A. (1986). Synthesis of research on school readiness and retention. *Educational Leadership 44*(3), 76–86.

Shepard, L. A., Kagan, S. L., & Wurtz, E. (Eds.). (1998). *Principles and recommendations for early childhood assessments.* Washington, DC: National Educational Goals Panel.

Shonkoff, J. P., & Phillips, D. (Eds). (2000). *From neurons to neighborhoods: The science of early childhood development.* Washington, DC: National Academy Press.

Shore, R., Bodrova, E., & Leong, D. Child outcome standards in pre-K programs: What are standards; What is needed to make them work? *Preschool Policy Matters.* (Issue 5/March 2004). Available online at www.nieer.org.

Sinclair, C. B. (1973). *Movement of the young child: Ages two to six.* Columbus, OH: Merrill.

Slavin, R. E. (1987). Ability grouping and student achievement in elementary schools: A best-evidence synthesis. *Review of Educational Research, 57,* 293–336.

Slavin, R. E. (2005). *Educational Psychology* (9th ed.). Boston: Allyn & Bacon.

Smilanski, S., & Shefatya, L. (1990). *Facilitating play: A medium for promoting cognitive, socio-emotional, and academic development in young children.* Gaithersburg, MD: Psychosocial and Educational Publications.

Smith, J. K. (1990). Measurement issues in early literacy development. In L. M. Morrow & J. K. Smith (Eds.), *Assessment for instruction in early literacy* (pp. 62–74). Englewood Cliffs, NJ: Prentice Hall.

Smith, M. L., & Shepard, L. A. (1988). Kindergarten readiness and retention: A qualitative study of teachers' beliefs and practices. *American Educational Research Journal, 25,* 307–333.

Smith, M. W., Dickinson, D. K., Sangeorge, A., & Anastasopoulous, L. (2002). *ELLCO toolkit.* Baltimore: Brookes Publishing.

Smith, S., Davidson, S., Weisenfeld, G., & Katasaros, S. (2001). *Supports for early literacy assessment (SELA)*. New York: New York University.

Snow, C. E., Burns, M. S., & Griffin, P. (Eds.). (1998). *Preventing reading difficulties in young children*. National Research Council. Washington, DC: National Academy Press.

Snow, C. E., Griffin, P., & Burns, M. S. (Eds.). (2005). *Knowledge to support the teaching of reading: Preparing teachers for a changing world*. San Francisco: Jossey Bass.

Spies, R. A., & Plake, B. S. (Eds.) (2005). *The sixteenth mental measurements yearbook*. Lincoln, NE: The Buros Institute of Mental Measurement.

Staff. (1989, January/February). Unpopular children. *The Harvard Education Letter*. 5(1), 1–3.

Steinberg, L., & Belsky, J. (1991). *Infancy, childhood, and adolescence: Development in context*. New York: McGraw-Hill.

Stenmark, J. K. (1991). *Mathematics assessment: Myths, models, good questions, and practical suggestions*. Reston, VA: National Council of Teachers of Mathematics.

Sternberg, R., & Williams, W. (2001). *Educational psychology*. Boston: Allyn & Bacon.

Stiggins, R. J. (1995). Assessment literacy for the 21st century. *Phi Delta Kappan*, 77(3), 238–245.

Stiggins, R. J. (1997). *Student-centered assessment*. New York: Merrill.

Stiggins, R. J. (1998). *Classroom assessment for student success*. Washington, DC: National Education Association.

Stiggins, R. J., & Conklin, N. J. (1992). *In teachers' hands: Investigating the practices of classroom assessment*. Albany, NY: State University of New York Press.

Stipek, D. (2002). *Motivation to learn: Integrating theory and practice*. Boston: Allyn & Bacon.

Stone, S. J. (1995). *Understanding portfolio assessment: A guide for parents*. Reston, VA: Association for Childhood Education International.

Sulzby, E. (1990). Assessment of writing and children's language while writing. In L. M. Morrow & J. K. Smith (Eds.), *Assessment for instruction in early literacy* (pp. 83–109). Englewood Cliffs, NJ: Prentice Hall.

Suro, R. (1992, December 15). Poll finds Hispanic desire to assimilate: National Hispanic Political Survey. *New York Times*, p. 1.

Tabors, P. O. (2002). Language and literacy for all children. *Head Start Bulletin* (74).

Taylor, R. L. (2000). *Assessment of exceptional students: Educational and psychological procedures*. Boston: Allyn & Bacon.

Taylor, R. T., Willits, P., & Lieberman, N. (1990). Identification of preschool children with mild handicaps: The importance of cooperative effort. *Childhood Education*, 67, 26–31.

Tharp, R. G., & Gallimore, R. (1988). *Rousing minds to life: Teaching, learning, and schooling in social context*. New York: Cambridge University Press.

Thomas, J. R., Lee, A. M., & Thomas, K. T. (1988). *Physical education for children: Concepts into practice*. Champaign, IL: Human Kinetics Books.

Thompson, C. (1986). *Scissors cutting program*. Unpublished manuscript. University of Kansas, Dept. of Human Development and Family Life.

Tough, J. (1977). *The development of meaning*. London: Allen & Unwin.

Trawick-Smith, J. (1988). Play leadership and following behavior of young children. *Young Children, 54*, 51–59.

Trawick-Smith, J. (2005). *Early childhood development: A multi-cultural perspective* (4th ed.). Upper Saddle River, NJ: Prentice Hall.

Tuma, J. M., & Elbert, J. C. (1990). Critical issues and current practice in personality assessment of children. In C. R. Reynolds & R. W. Kamphaus (Eds.), *Handbook of psychological and educational assessment of children: Intelligence and achievement* (pp. 239–252). New York: Guilford Press.

Tyler, R. W., & Wolf, R. M. (1974). *Crucial issues in testing.* Berkeley, CA: McCutcheon.

Valencia, S. (1989). *Assessing reading and writing: Building a more complete picture.* Seattle, WA: University of Washington Press.

Valencia, S. (1990). A portfolio approach to classroom reading assessment: The whys, whats, and hows. *The Reading Teacher, 43*(4), 338–340.

Valencia, S. W., Hiebert, E. F., & Afflerbach, P. P. (Eds.). (1994). *Authentic reading assessment: Practices and possibilities.* Newark, DE: International Reading Association.

Valencia, S. W., & Place, N. A. (1994). Literacy portfolios for teaching, learning, and accountability: The Bellevue Literacy Assessment Project. In S. W. Valencia, E. F. Hiebert, & P. P. Afflerbach (Eds.), *Authentic reading assessment: Practices and possibilities* (pp. 134–156). Newark, DE: International Reading Association.

Villegas, A. M. (1991). *Culturally responsive pedagogy for the 1990's and beyond* (Report). Princeton, NJ: Educational Testing Service.

Vygotsky, L. S. (1962). *Thought and language.* Cambridge, MA: MIT Press.

Vygotsky, L. S. (1978). *Mind and society: The development of higher mental processes.* Cambridge, MA: Harvard University Press. [Original works published 1930, 1933, 1935]

Wadsworth, B. J. (2003). *Piaget's theory of cognitive and affective development* (5th ed.). Boston: Allyn & Bacon.

Webb, N. (1983). Predicting learning from student interaction: Defining the interaction variables. *Educational Psychologist, 18,* 33–41.

Weeks, Z. R., & Ewer-Jones, B. (1991). Assessment of perceptual motor and fine motor functioning. In B. A. Bracken (Ed.), *The psychoeducational assessment of preschool children* (2nd ed., pp. 259–283). Boston: Allyn & Bacon.

Weikert, P. S. (1987). *Round the circle: Key experiences in movement for children ages 3 to 5.* Ypsilanti, MI: High/Scope Press.

West, B. (1992). Children are caught between home school, and culture and school. In B. Neugebauer (Ed.), *Alike and different: Exploring our humanity with young children* (pp. 127–139). Washington, DC: National Association for the Education of Young Children.

White House. (2002). *Good start, grow smart: The Bush administration's early childhood initiative.* Washington, DC: Author. Available online at www.whitehouse.gov/infocus/earlychildhood/earlychildhood.pdf.

Whitehurst, G., & Lonigan, C. (2001). *Get ready to read!* Columbus, OH: Pearson Early Learning.

Wickstrom, R. L. (1983). *Fundamental motor patterns* (3rd ed.). Philadelphia: Lea and Febiger.

Williams, H. G. (1991). Assessment of gross motor functioning. In B. A. Bracken (Ed.), *The psychoeducational assessment of preschool children* (2nd ed., pp. 284–216). Boston: Allyn & Bacon.

Winne, P. H., & Marx, R. W. (1987). The best tool teachers have—their students' thinking. In D. C. Berliner & B. V. Rosenshine (Eds.), *Talks to teachers* (pp. 267–306). New York: Random House.

Wittmer, D. S., & Honig, A. S. (1994). Encouraging positive social development in young children. *Young Children, 49*(5), 4–12.

Wittrock, M. C. (Ed.). (1986). *Handbook of research on teaching* (3rd ed., pp. 255–296). New York: Macmillan.

Wolery, M., & Dyk, L. (1984). Arena assessment: Description and preliminary social validity data. *Journal of the Association for Persons with Severe Handicaps, 9,* 231–235.

Wolery, M. P., Strain, P. S., and Bailey, D. B. (1992). Reaching potentials of children with special needs. In S. Bredekamp & T. Rosegrant (Eds.), *Reaching potentials: Appropriate curriculum and assessment for young children.* (Vol. 1, pp. 92–111). Washington, DC: National Association for the Education of Young Children.

Wolery, M., & Wilbers, J. M. (Eds.). (1994). *Including children with special needs in early childhood programs.* Washington, DC: National Association for the Education of Young Children.

Wolf, D. P. (1989). Portfolio assessment: Sampling student work. *Educational Leadership, 46*(7), 35–39.

Woolfolk, A. (2003). *Educational psychology* (9th ed.). Boston: Allyn & Bacon.

Wortham, S. C. (1995). *The integrated classroom: Assessment–curriculum link in early childhood education.* New York: Macmillan.

Wortham, S. C. (2005). *Assessment in early childhood education* (4th ed.). Upper Saddle River, NJ: Pearson Education, Inc.

Wortham, S. C., Barbour, A., & Desjean-Perrotta, B. (1998). *Portfolio assessment: A handbook for preschool and elementary educators.* Olney, MD: Association for Childhood Education International.

Zaporozhets, A. V., & Elkonin, D. B. (1971). *The psychology of preschool children.* Cambridge, MA: MIT Press.

Zill, N., Collins, M., West, J., & Hausken, E. G. (1995). Approaching kindergarten: A look at preschoolers in the United States. *Young Children, 51*(1), 35–38.

Name Index

Subject Index